PENGUIN BOOKS
THE MUGHAL WORLD

Abraham Eraly is the author of two critically acclaimed books on Indian history, *The Last Spring: The Lives and Times of the Great Mughals* (1997) and *Gem in the Lotus: The Seeding of Indian Civilisation* (2000). His other books include *Night of the Dark Trees: A Novel* and *Tales Once Told: Legends of Kerala*, both published in 2006.

Born in Kerala, and educated there and in Chennai, Eraly has taught Indian history in colleges in India and the United States, and was the editor of a current affairs magazine for some years. He now lives in Chennai, and is working on a study of classical Indian civilization. He can be contacted at abraham_eraly@yahoo.co.in

BY ABRAHAM ERALY

The Mughal World

Life in India's Last Golden Age

ABRAHAM ERALY

PENGUIN BOOKS

PENGUIN BOOKS
Published by the Penguin Group
Penguin Books India Pvt. Ltd, 11 Community Centre, Panchsheel Park, New Delhi 110 017, India
Penguin Group (USA) Inc., 375 Hudson Street, New York, New York 10014, USA
Penguin Group (Canada), 90 Eglinton Avenue East, Suite 700, Toronto, M4P 2Y3 (a division of Pearson Penguin Canada Inc.)
Penguin Books Ltd, 80 Strand, London WC2R 0RL, England
Penguin Ireland, 25 St Stephen's Green, Dublin 2, Ireland (a division of Penguin Books Ltd)
Penguin Group (Australia), 250 Camberwell Road, Camberwell, Victoria 3124, Australia (a division of Pearson Australia Group Pty Ltd)
Penguin Group (NZ), 67 Apollo Drive, Rosedale, North Shore 0632, New Zealand (a division of Pearson New Zealand Ltd)
Penguin Group (South Africa) (Pty) Ltd, 24 Sturdee Avenue, Rosebank, Johannesburg 2196, South Africa

Penguin Books Ltd, Registered Offices: 80 Strand, London WC2R 0RL, England

First published by Penguin Books India 2007
Published in Viking as part of *The Last Spring: The Lives and Times of the Great Mughals* by Penguin Books India 1997

Copyright © Abraham Eraly 2007

All rights reserved

10 9 8 7 6 5 4 3 2 1

For sale in the Indian Subcontinent and Singapore only

ISBN-13: 9-780-14310-262-5   ISBN-10: 0-14310-262-1

Typeset in Sabon by Mantra Virtual Services, New Delhi
Printed at Gopsons Papers Ltd, Noida

If there be a paradise on earth,
It's this, it's this, it's this!
—Mughal inscription on the durbar hall in the Delhi fort

∾

In the palaces of these lords dwells all the wealth there is, wealth
which glitters indeed, but is . . . wrung from the sweat of the
poor . . . resting on no firm foundation . . . [though] resplendent
in the eyes of the world.
—Francis Pelsaert, a Dutch trader in Mughal India

Contents

Chapter Seven: Pearls and Pebbles

Prologue

The Mughal Saga

AT MIDDAY ON Friday, 14 February 1556, a time and date that was considered astrologically auspicious, in the obscure little town of Kalanaur on the Ravi river in Punjab, an illiterate and unruly youth of fourteen, Jalaluddin Muhammad Akbar, was enthroned as the Mughal emperor on a hastily built, rough masonry platform. Thus began, in a lowly and bleak setting, the reign of the greatest ruler of India after Asoka, the celebrated Buddhist emperor of the third century BCE.

The grand destiny of Akbar was not evident at the time of his accession. Quite the contrary: the future looked very grim for the nascent empire and its boy-king, for the Mughals had yet only a tenuous toehold in India, and in Akbar there was no sign at all of any greatness. But the scene changed entirely in the next couple of decades. Not only did Akbar build an extensive and powerful empire, but he also, more importantly, inaugurated the second golden age of India, after the decline of its classical civilization a thousand years earlier. He and his immediate successors so decisively stamped their personality on India that the Mughal Empire became, in public perception, synonymous with India. And it remained so for quite a long time, even after the empire had entirely disappeared, and the emperor had became a humble pensionary of the British.

THE SAGA OF this fabulously talented dynasty* began seventy-three years earlier, when another boy-king, Zahiruddin Muhammad (Babur), Akbar's grandfather, just twelve years old then, ascended the throne of the tiny Mughal principality of Fergana in faraway Central Asia. Fergana was a lovely land of lush valleys and gurgling streams, and Babur loved it dearly. But the boy-king, who had the blood of Timur (on the paternal side) and Chingiz Khan (on the maternal side) coursing in his veins, was a dreamer of great dreams, and Fergana was too small to sate his ambition. So, though a mere boy, he set out, soon after his accession, to invade the neighbouring kingdom of Samarkand, dreaming of empire and glory.

The fledgling had taken wing too soon. Not only did he fail to hold Samarkand, but soon lost Fergana as well, and for many years he had to wander about in the mountains of Central Asia, a king without a kingdom,

---

* This story is told in *Emperors of the Peacock Throne*.

even without a home, seeking a safe anchor somewhere, but not finding any. 'It came very hard on me,' wrote Babur in his engaging memoirs. 'I could not help crying a good deal.' But he never lost hope, and fortune favoured him eventually, bestowing on him the secure throne of Kabul.

Babur was now king again. And in Kabul his eyes turned eastwards, where, beyond the mountains, lay the vast, fertile Indo-Gangetic Plain, renowned for its wealth, which was then ruled by the Afghan dynasty of Lodis. In November 1525, Babur descended from the snow-capped mountains, crossed the Indus, and swept into Hindustan. This was a perilous enterprise, for he had only a small army of just 12,000 men, while opposing him was the mammoth Lodi army of some 100,000 men and a formidable contingent of 1000 elephants. But in a five-hour battle fought at Panipat, about eighty kilometres north of Delhi, he entirely routed the enemy. Babur, forty-three, was at last an emperor.

His life was fulfilled. Four years later Babur died, and was succeeded by his son Humayun. A lovable and easy-going bon vivant, Humayun was devoted more to the pleasures of life than to the pursuit of power, and did not have the grit and ruthlessness needed to prevail in the turbulent political environment of India. The Mughal's adversaries, though routed in several battles by Babur, were not destroyed, and they hovered on the periphery of the empire, regrouping, watching, waiting. In 1540, the resurgent Afghans struck, seized the imperial throne and drove Humayun out of India.

For three years Humayun wandered about in the western borderland of India with a small band of followers, hoping for a turn of fortune. That did not happen. So he finally crossed the Indus and, scurrying through the domains of his hostile brothers in Afghanistan, took refuge with the shah of Persia. The shah welcomed Humayun as an honoured royal guest, and Humayun basked in the opulent Persian hospitality for a year, 'feasting and carousing,' as his personal attendant Jauhar described it. But he had to vindicate his honour, win back his empire. So he set out again, though rather reluctantly. Humayun was now accompanied by a contingent of troops provided by the shah, and with their help he seized Afghanistan from his brothers and, after consolidating his power there over several years, finally headed for India, to recover his lost empire.

Humayun had with him only a tiny army of around 5000 at this time. That was enough, though. Sher Shah, Humayun's great Afghan adversary, had died a few years earlier, and North India was in political disarray. In July 1555, Humayun stormed back into Delhi, fifteen years after he was driven out of it by Sher Shah. But he died soon afterwards in a tragic accident, tumbling down the stairs of his astronomical observatory, where, obsessed with astrology, he had gone to study what the stars boded.

SO THE DAUNTING task of consolidating the Mughal Empire fell to young Akbar. Akbar, however, was not yet ready to assume that responsibility, and for the time being he left governance entirely to his guardian, Biram Khan, a suave Persian noble of exceptional ability. For four years Biram Khan ruled as the de facto emperor while Akbar remained 'behind the veil'. But despite his seeming disinterest in government, Akbar was all the while observing, learning, quietly preparing himself for the role that destiny had assigned to him.

By 1560, he was ready. That year Akbar dismissed Biram Khan from his service, and shortly thereafter, in what seemed like a ravenous earth-hunger, launched a rapid series of conquests which enlarged the Mughal kingdom in India into a vast subcontinental empire. Entirely fearless, and blessed with phenomenal physical prowess and stamina, he invariably led his army from the front, impetuously plunging in where the fight was the fiercest.

Exuberant physicality characterized Akbar in his youth. As he grew older, however, his life became more and more austere, and he revealed himself to be a man of wide cultural interests and insatiable intellectual curiosity. Though as a child he had stubbornly refused to learn to read and write despite the persistent efforts of his erudite father, and would remain formally illiterate all his life, he now had his officers read regularly to him from the books in the vast royal library, and in time he became quite a savant.

Akbar was eclectic in his tastes, liberal in his outlook, and entirely open-minded, without any prejudice of race, religion or culture. In 1564, when he was twenty-two, he took the bold step of abolishing jizya, the poll tax that Muslim states mandatorily imposed on non-Muslims, thus ending a major discrimination against Hindus in his empire. Later, he invited to his court leaders of diverse religions—Hindus, Muslims, Buddhists, Jains and Parsis—and often held night-long discussions with them. There was also a small group of Jesuit missionaries in his court, and he paid careful attention to their expositions as well, once even attending service in their chapel.

But what Akbar sought was knowledge, not faith. 'He is a man who makes justice the guide of the path of inquiry, and takes from every sect what is consonant with reason,' he held. And it was the practical aspect of knowledge that interested Akbar. 'Although knowledge in itself is regarded as the summit of perfection, yet unless displayed in action, it bears not the impress of worth,' he contended.

In 1582, when he was forty, Akbar took the revolutionary step—most unusual for a monarch—of founding a syncretic religious fraternity of his own called Din Ilahi (Divine Faith). 'For an empire ruled by one head, it is a bad thing to have its people divided among themselves and at variance with one another,' Akbar said, explaining his reason for founding the fraternity. 'We ought, therefore, to bring them all into one, but in such fashion that they should be both one and all; with the great advantage of not losing what is good in any one religion while gaining whatever is better in another. In this way, honour would be rendered to God, peace would be given to the people, and security to the empire.'

Din Ilahi was more an elite socio-political brotherhood than a religious sect in the conventional sense. Its orientation was more towards rationalism than towards faith. It had no pantheon, no theology, no transcendental concerns. Its sole objective was to guide its followers to lead sensible, responsible lives as human beings and citizens. Religious tolerance was its bedrock. 'No one,' Akbar declared, 'should be interfered with on account of his religion. Anyone should be allowed to go over to any religion he pleases.'

Unfortunately, Din Ilahi did not survive Akbar. It could not—like its creator, it was way ahead of its time. When Akbar died, the medieval culture of the age entombed Din Ilahi as well. But, on the whole, Akbar had a singularly fortunate career, and nearly everything in his life worked out perfectly for him—everything, except his own sons. Growing up in the awesome shadow of the great emperor, the personalities of the princes became stunted and warped. Two of them drank themselves to death in their youth, and his only surviving son, Jahangir, also became an alcoholic and opium addict.

Akbar in his last years was hardly the emperor—or the man—the world had known. Fortune no longer waited on his pleasure. Aggravations and misfortunes broke his once indomitable spirit. His health collapsed and in October 1605, at the age of sixty-three, he died, after a reign of forty-nine years.

AKBAR'S VERY LAST act on his deathbed was to invest Jahangir, aged thirty-two, with the regalia. Jahangir had broken out in rebellion towards the close of Akbar's reign, but no one held that against him. The fight of son against father, and of brother against brother, over the throne was the norm among the Mughals—Babur, Humayun, Akbar, Shah Jahan and Aurangzeb had all fought fratricidal wars, and most of the emperors had to face rebellions by their sons as well. Such clashes were a rite of passage for Mughal princes, which enabled the fittest of them to survive and rule.

In character and temperament, Jahangir was like his grandfather Humayun—a debonair, gregarious, fun-loving epicure. And just as Humayun had had a serious interest in astronomy and astrology, Jahangir took a serious interest in nature studies, and was a connoisseur of art. He also prided himself on being a poet and wrote his own candid memoirs. He was very much his father's son, too, being open-minded and liberal in his cultural and religious attitudes. Unlike Akbar, however, he had no deep interest in religion, and was generally scornful of all faiths. 'Jhehangier Shah . . . is an atheist,' stated Sir Thomas Roe, the first British royal ambassador to India. According to Roe, Jahangir once told the Jesuits in his court: 'If yee cast the Crucifix and Picture of Christ into fire before me, if it burne not, I will become a Christian.'

In comparison to Akbar, Jahangir pales into insignificance—but only in comparison to Akbar. He was a man of diverse talents and, despite a certain playfulness, quite conscientious in the discharge of his royal duties. But he was a physical wreck during most of his reign, due to his long addiction to wine and opium, and his life would have probably ended in disgrace but for his good fortune in having by his side the imperiously beautiful and enormously talented Nur Jahan, his chief queen. As the reins of power began to slip from his enfeebled hands, she stood beside him and gave him strength. She, noted the Mughal courtier Inayat Khan, 'gradually acquired such unbounded influence on His Majesty's mind that she seized the reins of government and took on herself the supreme civil and financial administration of the realm, ruling with absolute authority till the conclusion of the reign.'

On the whole Nur Jahan's role in government was positive. There were two major rebellions towards the close of Jahangir's reign—by the prince Shah Jahan and by the royal commander Mahabat Khan—but both were effectively and decisively suppressed under the leadership of Nur Jahan. And when Jahangir died after a reign of twenty-two years, the great empress had the grace and wisdom to retire quietly from public life and spend the last eighteen years of her life in contented obscurity in the provincial town of Lahore.

JAHANGIR WAS SUCCEEDED by Shah Jahan, aged thirty-five, and with him the Mughal golden age reached its culmination. Shah Jahan was the quintessential Great Mughal, who by the splendour of his dress and ornaments, and his lordly bearing and conduct, personified the opulence and grandeur of the empire. In him the Mughal rumbustiousness was at last tamed under the influence of Persian courtly formalism. Though courteous and soft-spoken, his bearing in public was always stiffly dignified. 'I never saw so settled a countenance, nor any man keepe so constant a gravity, never smiling, or in face showing any respect or difference of men, but mingled with extreme pride and contempt of all,' observed Roe.

Shah Jahan, unlike his ancestors, particularly unlike his father and grandfather, was a rigidly orthodox Muslim, and with him began the attempt to convert the Mughal Empire into a theocratic Muslim state, in a deliberate reversal of the established Mughal policy. Though all his predecessors, except Akbar, had occasionally persecuted Hindus and demolished temples, they had done so in random and impulsive acts. Now it was state policy. Furthermore, while Akbar and Jahangir had allowed anyone to adopt any religion, Shah Jahan prohibited Muslims from changing their religion. He also directed that Hindus should dress differently from Muslims—while Muslims tied the tunic on the right-hand side, Hindus were required to tie it on the left.

A major influence on the formulation of Shah Jahan's policies was his queen, Mumtaz Mahal. She was a niece of Nur Jahan, and, like her aunt, she played a crucial role in government, but discreetly, from behind the throne. Mumtaz, wrote the Mughal chronicler Aminai Qazvini, was the emperor's 'intimate companion, colleague, close confidante in distress and comfort, joy and grief.' Shah Jahan was totally devoted and faithful to her, and though he had other wives, he begot children only by her. And she was marvellously fecund—she bore him fourteen children in the nineteen years they lived together, but tragically died at the age of thirty-four while delivering her last child. Shah Jahan was devastated by the tragedy, and it was to commemorate his love for her that he built the Taj Mahal, often considered to be the most beautiful building in the world.

Shah Jahan had a keen interest in music and dance—he used to sing at the private gatherings of his intimate nobles—but his main artistic interest was in architecture, which found expression in a number of magnificent buildings he erected. He took enormous pride in them, as reflected in the couplet he got inscribed on the hall of public audience in his Delhi palace:

If there be a paradise on earth,
It's this, it's this, it's this!

That indeed was how the contemporary world saw the Mughal court. Shah Jahan was the richest and most exalted monarch in the world in his time, and he lived in the greatest possible magnificence. But his last years were pathetic. Trouble erupted in the summer of 1657 when Shah Jahan fell seriously ill. This sent shivers of anxiety through his four sons stationed in the different provinces of the empire, for each knew that if the emperor died, his own life would be in peril, as the successor would liquidate him as a potential contender for the throne. The only way a prince could save his life was by securing the throne for himself. It was the throne or death for each of them.

Soon the princes were on the march with their armies, headed for the imperial capital. Once these moves had been initiated there was no turning back for them, even though Shah Jahan recovered, and the immediate threat to their lives and fortunes passed. A prolonged and traumatic war of succession ensued, out of which the emperor's third son, Aurangzeb, emerged victorious, eliminating all his brothers and usurping the throne. And he, saturnine and remorseless, kept Shah Jahan confined in the Agra fort for eight years, till the end of his life.

AURANGZEB WAS AN unlikely Mughal hero. He did not have the dynamism, charisma and verve that characterized his ancestors, but was a dour, joyless drudge. This, however, was a persona that he deliberately cultivated. He had in his early youth loved music, enjoyed hunting, and was susceptible to feminine charms, but he burnt out all those vulnerabilities with his searing, inexorable will, so as to focus his whole life and his entire being on the business of winning the throne and ruling. Utterly implacable and cold-blooded in his pursuit of power, his life was a triumph of mind over body and of will over nature.

Aurangzeb believed that he had a divine dispensation to rule, not for his own enjoyment of power, but for the restoration of the true kingdom of Islam in India. Characteristically, when his sister Jahanara pleaded with him to spare the life of his brother Dara, he said: 'Dara is an infidel and a friend of Hindus. He must be extirpated for the sake of the true faith and the peace of the realm.' He had no feeling for his father either, and in all the years he kept him confined in the Agra fort, he never once visited him, not even during his final illness, and did not attend his funeral. He had no weakness of sentiment or love.

Yet he was a man of great humility, soft-spoken, mild-mannered and of equable temper. He was particularly kindly in his treatment of the lowly. Once, when a eunuch stumbled against him and knocked him down, and himself collapsed in fright, Aurangzeb spoke to him kindly: 'Wherefore fearest thou a created being, one like thyself . . . Rise and be not afraid.' He led an ascetic life, was very simple in dress, wore hardly any jewels, and met his personal expenses by making caps. Contemporary Muslims regarded him as a saint.

Under Aurangzeb, the very nature of the Mughal Empire changed. Shah Jahan had tentatively begun the conversion of the secular empire into a theocratic Muslim state; this process was now completed by Aurangzeb. He reimposed jizya, 115 years after Akbar abolished it, and imposed various disabilities on non-Muslims as required by orthodox Islamic tradition. However, in all this he acted strictly within the law, doing what was permitted and obligatory for a Muslim ruler but nothing beyond that, and he did on occasion pull up his officers who, in their theocratic fervour, unlawfully persecuted Hindus.

One phase of Aurangzeb's life ended in 1681 when, after reigning from north India for twenty-three years, at the age of sixty-three he crossed into the peninsula, to begin the final ascent to the summit of the Mughal Empire. He would spend the next twenty-six years there in ceaseless wars, conquering new territories, subduing rebels, capturing forts. At the end of this titanic effort, a vast sweep of land from Kabul across virtually the entire Indian subcontinent lay under his sway. There were no more lands to conquer, no more forts to take or armies to defeat. Aurangzeb had become the master of the largest empire that India has ever known.

Mughal imperial destiny had been fulfilled, it seemed. Yet, just when Aurangzeb appeared absolutely triumphant, everything was in fact utterly lost. At the moment of his supreme triumph, Aurangzeb found to his horror that the very ground on which he stood was crumbling.

The Marathas were his nemesis. Aurangzeb thought that he had pounded them into the earth; and indeed he had, but they rose again out of the soil everywhere to confound him. When the weary old emperor began his slow trek northwards to Delhi, his mission 'accomplished', the Marathas hounded him, incessantly snapping at his heels. Meanwhile, seeing the emperor's helplessness, panic began to spread through the empire, and the immense, multitiered Mughal administrative edifice began to crack and crumble. Rebels and bandits roamed the land freely and, as Aurangzeb's end neared, his sons, even his grandsons, squared off to fight for the succession.

Aurangzeb trudged on. But on the way, while camping at Ahmadnagar in central Maharashtra, he fell ill with a high fever. And on 3 March 1707, a Friday, in the early morning while he was saying his prayers, Aurangzeb, eighty-nine years old and emperor for forty-nine years, slid into death.

'*Az ma-st hamah fasad-i-baqi*,' Aurangzeb had once said: After me, chaos!

And that was how it would be.

Chapter One

THE LAND
AND THE PEOPLE

The Land

THE OVERWHELMING REALITY of India for the Mughals when they first arrived was the broiling sun. 'Three things oppressed us in Hindustan,' writes Babur, 'its heat, its violent winds, its dust.' Sometimes, says Badauni, it got 'so extremely hot . . . that the very brain boiled in the cranium.' Moans Bernier: 'I have been reduced by the intenseness of the heat to the last extremity . . . My parched and withered body has become a mere sieve, the quart of water which I swallow at a draught, passing at the same moment through every one of my pores, even by the ends of my fingers. I am sure that today I have drunk more than ten pints . . . My body is entirely covered with small red blisters, which prick like needles . . . I feel as if I should myself expire before night. All my hopes are in four or five limes still remaining for lemonade, and in a little dry curd which I am about to drink diluted with water and with sugar.'

The summer heat was made worse by dust storms. 'It gets up in great strength every year in the heats . . . when the rains are near,' writes Babur; 'so strong and carrying so much dust and earth that you cannot see one another. People call this wind *andhi*, the darkener of the sky.' Says Pelsaert, 'In April, May and June the heat is intolerable, and men can scarcely breathe. More than that, hot winds blow continuously, as stifling as if they came straight from the furnace of hell. The air is filled with the dust raised by violent whirlwinds from the sandy soil, making day like the darkest night that human eyes have seen or that can be grasped by the imagination.'

The monsoon brought some relief. 'The climate during the rains is very pleasant,' concedes Babur, but adds that it had its own miseries. 'During the rainy season you cannot shoot, even with the bow of our country . . . the coats of mail, books, clothes, and furniture, all feel the bad effects of moisture.' Says Ovington: 'The whole Hemisphere then is most sullenly Dark, and the Sky overcast with the thickest weighty clouds, so that the Earth seems rather inclosed within a huge ocean of Water, than only a few watery Clouds, whose black and lowering Aspect is so very melancholy, that it gives the fairest representation imaginable of the terrors of a second universal Deluge. Sometimes in Three or Four Hours time, such showers fall from these full Clouds, that the Currents run along the Streets, swelled to that height, that they are scarce fordable on Horseback. After this Excess in July the Showers gradually decrease, the Horizon clears up like the first dawning of the Day, 'till at length the heavens are all over Bright, and the benighted Sun displays his vigour and banish'd Rays again.'

The most pleasant season in India were the winter months from November to February, but Pelsaert grumbles about it too, for in winter the poor burned cow-dung outside their houses to keep warm: 'The smoke from these fires all over the city is so great that the eyes run, and the throat seems to choke.' And, says Linschoten, 'winter endeth with thunder and lightning', heralding not the blessed rains, but the dreaded dust-storms. Manucci would not even acknowledge the season of winter in India. 'As for winter,' he says, 'they do not know in India what that means;' there was only 'the less hot season'.

The heat was not just physical discomfort; it sapped energy, desiccated the spirit. 'The excessive heat makes a man powerless, takes away his desire for food, and limits him to water-drinking, which weakens or debilitates his body,' says Pelsaert. Physician Bernier however noted some advantages in the Indian climate. 'Few persons in these hot climates feel a strong desire for wine, and I have no doubt that the happy ignorance which prevails of many distempers is fairly ascribable to the general habits of sobriety among the people, and to the profuse perspiration to which they are perpetually subject. The gout, the stone, complaints in kidney, catarrhs and quartan agues are nearly unknown; and persons who arrive in the country afflicted with any of these disorders, as was the case with me, soon experience complete cure. Even the venereal disease, common as it is in Hindustan, is not of the virulent character, or attended with such injurious consequences, as in other parts of the world. But although there is a greater enjoyment of health, yet there is less vigour among the people than in our colder climates; and the feebleness and languor both of body and mind, consequent upon excessive heat, may be considered a species of unremitting malady, which attacks all persons indiscriminately.'

If men did not thrive in the tropical climate, vermin did. 'The aboundance of flyes in those parts doe ... much annoy us; for in the heate of the day their numberlesse number is such as that we can be quiet in no place for them,' writes Terry. 'They are ready to cover our meate as soone as it is placed on the table; and therefore wee have men that stand on purpose with napkins to fright them away as wee are eating. In the night likewise we are much disquieted with musquatoes, like our gnats, but somewhat lesse. And in their great cities there are such aboundance of bigge hungrie rats that they often bite a man as he lyeth on his bed.'

HEAT APART, THE most remarkable fact about India for the Mughals was the sheer crush of people. The vast concourses of people he saw in India astounded Babur. 'As far as Bengal, as far indeed as the shore of the great ocean, the peoples are without break . . . The population of Hindustan is unlimited,' he writes. Says Jahangir about Agra: 'The mass of people is so great that moving about in the lanes and bazaars is difficult.'

Moreland estimates that the total population of India in 1600 was about 100 million, while Kingsley Davis gives a figure of 125 million, and Irfan Habib of 142 million. The annual rate of growth of the population in Mughal India was low, probably only about 0.14 per cent. A surprisingly large number of Mughal Indians lived in urban centres, about fifteen per cent according to Irfan Habib, which was higher than the percentage of the urban population in contemporary Europe, and higher even than that of India in the nineteenth century. The great cities of India had a population of between a quarter-million and a half-million, according to Moreland.

These figures are rough appraisals, and the possible margin of error is wide. We do, however, have a fair estimate of the number of villages and towns in the Mughal empire. According to Nizamuddin Ahmad, an officer of Akbar, the Mughal empire in his time had 120 large cities and 3200 townships (qasbas), each controlling between 100 and 1000 villages; according to another source, Aurangzeb's empire (excluding Bijapur and Golconda) had over 400,000 villages. Not all these villages were inhabited, a village being, in the Mughal parlance, merely 'a specific area of land', whether populated or not.

Villages, even towns, were ever in flux in medieval India, appearing and disappearing with bewildering rapidity. 'In Hindustan hamlets and villages, towns indeed, are depopulated and set up in a moment,' Babur notes. 'If the people of a large town, one inhabited for a few years even, flee from it, they do it in such a way that no sign or trace of them remain in a day or a day and half. On the other hand, if they fix their eyes on a place to settle, they need not dig water courses or construct dams, because their crops are all rain-grown, and as the population of Hindustan is unlimited, it swarms in. They make a tank or dig a well; they need not build houses or set up walls—khas-grass abounds, wood is unlimited, huts are made, and straightaway there is a village or a town!'

What was true of villages and towns was in a sense true of great cities too. Cities did not of course disappear overnight, but they sometimes became derelict almost overnight, a worse plight. India was dotted with forlorn ruins, monuments of a people who did not care for the past and had no thought of the future. Typical was the fate of the great city of Fatehpur Sikri that Akbar built at the height of his power. William Finch, who arrived in India in 1608, just three years after Akbar's death, found Fatehpur already a ghost city. 'It is all ruinate,' writes Finch, 'lying like a waste desart, and very dangerous to passe through in the night, the buildings lying waste without inhabitants; much of the ground beeing now converted to gardens, and much sowed with nill and other graine, that a man standing there would little thinke he were in the middest of citie.'

The sight of crumbled monuments and desolate cities, with their unmistakable odour of the decay of civilization, saddened even the casual visitor. 'Nothing is permanent, yea, even the noble buildings—gardens, tombs, or palaces—which, in and near every city, one cannot contemplate without pity or distress because of their ruined state,' laments Pelsaert. 'For in this they are to be despised above all the laziest nations of the world, because they build them with so many hundreds of thousands, and yet keep them in repair only so long as the owner is alive and has the means. Once the builder is dead, no one will care for the buildings; the son will neglect his father's work, the mother her son's, brothers and friends will take no care for each other's buildings; everyone tries, as far as possible, to erect a new building of his own, and establish his own reputation alongside that of his ancestors . . . If all these buildings and erections were attended to and repaired for a century, the lands of every city, and even village, would be adorned with monuments; but as a matter of fact the roads leading to the cities are strewn with fallen columns of stone.'

The monuments that survived best were those that were preserved by nature itself, not by man, and among them were the great cave temples of Ellora, a well-known site even in Mughal times. Aurangzeb used to picnic there with his family. And so did many Mughal nobles. Says Mustaid Khan, a courtier of Aurangzeb: '[There] is a place named Ellora where in ages long past, sappers possessed of magical skill excavated in the defiles of the mountain spacious houses for a length of one *kos* (3.2 kilometres).

On all their ceilings and walls many kinds of images with lifelike forms have been carved . . . In all seasons, and particularly in the monsoons, when this hill and the plain below resemble a garden in the luxuriance of its vegetation and the abundance of its water, people come to see the place. A waterfall a hundred yards in width tumbles down from the hill. It is a marvellous place for strolling, charming to the eye.' The monuments themselves were however in a state of 'desolation in spite of its strong foundations', notes the Khan.

THE MUGHAL CITIES are the true memorials of Mughal culture, at once thriving and decrepit, magnificent and squalid. 'There is no city or town which, if it be not already ruined and deserted, does not bear the evident marks of approaching decay,' says Bernier. The neglect of their own monuments by the Mughals is surprising, for they, unlike Hindus and the Turko-Afghans, had great dynastic pride, a fine sense of history, and were moreover fastidious about their environment, being connoisseurs of beautiful things and the good life. Yet Jahangir had let Fatehpur Sikri run to seed, and Shah Jahan had no qualms about demolishing Akbar's palace complex in Agra. Moreover, they were indifferent to town planning, even to the layout of the imperial citadels, so that although many of the individual structures in the Agra and Delhi forts are magnificent, the buildings do not harmonize well with each other.

Beyond the citadel, the cities were a chaotic jumble of wretched hovels and stately mansions, royal avenues and mean, twisting lanes, parodying the transience and the awful inequity of Mughal society. In urban planning it has been downhill in India since the Mauryan age, possibly even from the time of the Indus Valley Civilization. 'They (Mughal cities) appear very pleasant from afar; for they are adorned with many towers and high buildings, in a very beautiful manner,' says Monserrate. 'But when one enters them, one finds that the narrowness, aimless crookedness, and ill planning of the streets deprive these cities of all beauty.' Says Pelsaert: 'The city (Agra) is exceedingly large, but decayed, open, and unwalled. The streets and houses are built without any regular plan.'

Promiscuous, random clusters of mud and thatch slums disfigured the face of Mughal cities like festering scabs. Even in the mansions of amirs, 'externally there [was] nothing to delight the eye,' says Monserrate, for though they had gardens, ponds and fountains within, they were hidden behind high walls, to provide privacy for women. 'If a traveller has seen one of these cities, he has seen them all,' concludes Monserrate.

'Most towns in Hindustan are made up of earth, mud, and other wretched materials,' says Bernier. He saw Agra and Delhi not as cities proper, but as cantonments, deriving their 'chief support' from the presence of the army. 'The population,' he says, 'is reduced to the necessity of following the Mogul whenever he undertakes a journey of long continuance.' Thevenot, a Frenchman in India in the mid-seventeenth century, reports that more than eighty per cent of the estimated 400,000 population of Delhi was transient with the imperial court, so that when the emperor moved out of Delhi, its population shrank to some 65,000. The influx of troops or pilgrims could also dramatically, though temporarily, alter the population of towns. 'These cities resemble any place other than Paris; they might more fitly be compared to a camp, if the lodgings and accommodations were not a little superior to those found in the tents of armies,' comments Bernier.

A pleasing feature of Mughal cities and towns was the abundance of trees in them. 'Both in their villages and cities are usually many faire trees among their houses, which are a great defence against the vilence of the sunne,' says Terry. 'They commonly stand so thicke that, if a man behold a citie or towne from some conspicuous place, it will seeme a wood rather than a citie.' Says Careri, an Italian traveller in India towards the close of the seventeenth century: 'They live in low Houses, with Trees about them, so that their Cities at a distance look like Woods.'

AGRA AND DELHI, and for a short while Fatehpur Sikri, were the primary Mughal capitals, and they were great metropolises. 'Agra and Fatepore are two very great cities, either of them much greater than London and very populous,' says Ralph Fitch, an English merchant who was in Fatehpur in 1584. 'Betweene Agra and Fatepore are 12 miles (12 kos actually: 37 kilometres), and all the way is a market of victuals and other things, as full as though a man were still in a towne, and so many people as if a man were in a market.' William Finch says of Agra: 'It is spacious, large, populous beyond measure, that you can hardly passe in the streets . . .'

Agra, the Lodi capital (founded in 1505 by Sikandar, the father of Ibrahim) was taken over by Babur as his capital after the battle of Panipat, but the city really came into its own only with Akbar, who demolished the Lodi fort and erected a great new citadel in its place, which took some 15 years to build and cost about 3.5 million rupees. But even before the fort complex was completed, Akbar shifted to Fatehpur, where he lived for fourteen years, and then moved on to Lahore for the next fourteen years, returning to Agra only towards the close of his reign.

Jahangir loathed Agra. 'The air of Agra is warm and dry,' he writes; 'physicians say that it depresses the spirit and induces weakness. It is unsuited to most temperaments, except to the phlegmatic and melancholy, which are safe from its bad effects.' Only elephants and buffaloes could thrive in Agra, Jahangir believed, and he avoided living there as much as possible. Shah Jahan lived the longest in Agra, and he extensively rebuilt the citadel there, tearing down most of Akbar's sandstone buildings to erect his own marble-and-gilt palaces. Later, his vanity still not sated, he moved to Delhi to build a new capital there, Shahjahanabad, where he lived for nine years, before moving back to Agra. It was only with Aurangzeb that Delhi became the prime Mughal capital.

Agra was dominated by its citadel, an immense complex of 2.4 kilometre circumference, built on a low swell of land on the western bank of the Yamuna. 'It lyeth in the manner of a half-moon, bellying landward,' observes William Finch. The royal apartments were on the riverside ramparts, overlooking a sandy maidan, where parades and elephant fights were held. 'Internally . . . the fort is built over like a city with streets and shops, and has very little resemblance to a fortress,' says Pelsaert, 'but from the outside anyone would regard it as impregnable.' Its walls, about nine metres thick at the base, rose to a height of about 21.5 metres, and were girded (except on the riverside) by a deep, broad moat filled with water drawn from the Yamuna.

Next to the moat, on the western side, was a large garden, and beyond it the great royal square, where the main roads of Agra converged. The royal square, which doubled as a bazaar, was the hub of the city, and it was here that the great amirs on guard duty at the citadel pitched their tents.

The two principal streets of Agra ran straight from the royal square as far as the eye could see, flanked by shopping arcades. The arcades, flat-roofed and single-storied, housed 'open shops, where, during the day, artisans work, bankers sit for the dispatch of their business, and merchants exhibit their wares,' reports Bernier. 'Within the arch is a small door, opening into a warehouse, in which these wares are deposited for the night. The houses of the merchants are built over these warehouses, at the back of the arcades: they look handsome enough from the street, and appear tolerably commodious within; they are airy, at a distance from the dust, and communicate with the terrace-roofs over the shops, on which the inhabitants sleep at night.' These were the residences of middle-class merchants. 'The rich merchants,' Bernier notes, 'have their dwellings elsewhere, to which they retire after the hours of business.' Princes and nobles usually lived in mansions outside the city.

Apart from the two main streets, Agra had five secondary streets, 'not so long nor so straight as the two principal ones, but resembling them in every other respect', and from these streets branched innumerable haphazard lanes, 'built at different periods by individuals who paid no regard to symmetry,' says Bernier. 'Amidst these streets are dispersed the habitations of Mansebdars, or petty Omrahs, officers of justice, rich merchants, and others; many of which have a tolerable appearance . . . Intermixed with these different houses is an immense number of small ones, built of mud and thatched with straw, in which lodge the common troopers, and all that vast multitude of servants and camp-followers who follow the court and the army.'

Agra was not as extensive as Delhi, and was in fact even smaller than Lahore—it was 'in everie respect much inferior to Lahore,' says Coryat. Agra, says Bernier, 'wants the uniform and wide streets that so eminently distinguish Delhi. Agra has more the appearance of a country town . . . The prospect it presents is rural, varied, and agreeable; for the grandees having always made it a point to plant trees in the gardens and courts for the sake of shade, the mansions of Omrahs, Rajas, and others are all interspersed with luxuriant and green foliage . . . Such a landscape yields peculiar pleasure in a hot and parched country, where the eye seeks in verdure for refreshment and repose.'

As befitting the imperial capital, Agra was also an international mart. 'All the necessities and conveniences of human life can be obtained here, if desired,' says Monserrate. 'This is even true of the articles that have to be imported from distant corners of Europe. There are great numbers of artisans, iron-workers and goldsmiths. Gems and pearls abound in large number. Gold and silver are plentiful, as also are horses from Persia and Tartary. Indeed, the city is flooded with vast quantities of every type of commodity.'

THE DECLINE OF Agra began when Shah Jahan shifted the capital to Delhi, one of the oldest city sites in India. Six (or fourteen, according to some) cities preceded Shahjahanabad, and here the British too would build their capital, New Delhi, the eighth city. All these many Delhis lie in a triangular area of about seventy square miles (about 18,138 hectares) called the Delhi Triangle, bounded on the west and the south by the stark Aravalli Range and on the north by the Yamuna River. The city straddles the eastern end of the corridor between the Himalayas and the Great Indian Desert, and is well placed strategically to defend the heartland of Hindustan lying to the east.

Legend places the fabled *Mahabharata* city of Indraprastha in the environs of Delhi, near Purana Qila. 'Delhi,' says Abul Fazl, 'is one of the greatest cities of antiquity. It was first called Indrapat.' The name Delhi is believed to be derived from Raja Dhilu of the first century BC, but more than a thousand years would pass before Delhi would gain any historical prominence. There is no mention of Indraprastha or Delhi in any of the ancient accounts of India; not even Fa Hsien or Hsuan Tsang refers to it, though in Ptolemy there is a mention of a town called Daidal, which some believe could be Delhi. At the close of the twelfth century, Delhi was the capital of Prithiviraj, a Rajput monarch, and it was from him that the Turks wrested the city and made it their capital, the first of the identifiable historical cities of Delhi.

Early in the fourteenth century, Alauddin Khilji built the second city of Delhi; a couple of decades later, Ghiyasuddin Tughluq built the third city; his son Muhammad built the fourth, and Firuz, the next ruler, built the fifth. Then for about a century there was a lull, till Humayun, inspired by a visit to Gwalior, began to build Din Panah, the sixth Delhi. On Humayun's expulsion from India, Din Panah was taken over and rebuilt by Sher Shah. In the mid-seventeenth century, Shah Jahan built the seventh city just north of Din Panah, and two and a half centuries later, the British, shifting their capital from Calcutta, built the eighth city.

Looming over Shah Jahan's Delhi was the Qila Mubarak, Auspicious Fort, which would later be known as the Red Fort. The medieval traveller, arriving in Delhi from Agra, would enter the citadel through its southern gate, which Bernier found rather plain, except for two large stone elephants, with the statues of Jaimal and Patta, the Mewar heroes, on them. The gate, says Bernier, opened into 'a long and spacious street, divided in the midst by a canal of running water. The street has a long divan, or raised way, on both sides ... five or six feet high and four broad. Bordering the divan are closed arcades, which run the whole way ... It is upon this long divan that all the collectors of market-dues and other petty officers exercise their functions without being incommoded by the horses and people that pass in the street below. The Mansabdars or inferior Omrahs mount guard on this raised way during the night.' The other principal gate of the fort, the Lahore Gate, also opened into an arcaded street, but was flanked by shops instead of offices. 'Properly speaking, this street is a bazaar, rendered very convenient in the summer and the rainy season by the long and high arched roof with which it is covered,' observes Bernier. 'Air and light are admitted by several large round apertures in the roof.'

Besides these main streets, there were several small streets in the citadel, leading to the 'many divans and tents in different parts of the fortress, which serve as offices for public business', to the workshops of artisans, and to the 'splendid' garden alcoves where the amirs mounted guard, notes Bernier. As in Agra, the royal apartments were on the eastern ramparts of the fort, overlooking the Yamuna. Water for the city was tapped from the Yamuna 116 kilometres up-river, at Kizirabad, and brought in by a canal called Nahr-i Bihisht, Stream of Paradise.

Delhi was an overcrowded city, teeming with men and cattle. 'There is no house, by whomsoever inhabited, which does not swarm with women and children . . . the streets are crowded with people,' says Bernier, most of them 'poor, ragged, and miserable beings'. Both Delhi and Agra had extensive suburbs, and beyond them were the camps of the great amirs, which often grew into satellite townships, like Jaisinghpur and Jaswantpur outside Shahjahanabad.

Like all medieval cities, Delhi and Agra were fire traps. 'Most part of the city (Agra) is straw houses, which once or twice a year is burnt to the ground,' says John Jourdain, an early-seventeenth-century English trader in India. In Delhi 'more than sixty thousand roofs were consumed this last year by three fires, during the prevalence of certain impetuous winds which blow generally in summer,' notes Bernier. Even royal residences sometimes got burnt down, as happened to Akbar's palace in Lahore. In Delhi once, when a fire broke out 'on a day when there was a high wind blowing . . . in the twinkling of an eye it spread to the buildings constituting the private residence of Prince Shah Shuja,' reports Inayat Khan. The prince personally rescued many of his women, but some seventy-five of them perished in the fire, 'and the buildings containing the Prince's jewels, property and wardrobe, together with all the adjoining offices, were reduced to a heap of ashes.'

AGRA, DELHI AND Fatehpur were Mughal capitals only in a formal sense, for the imperial capital was in effect wherever the emperor was encamped for some length of time, as the entire governmental machinery moved with him, with all the essential records and treasures. In this sense, Lahore was the western capital of the empire, and Aurangabad, the southern capital. 'Lahor is one of the greatest cities of the East,' says Finch. 'This city is second to none, either in Asia or in Europe, with regard to size, population and wealth,' writes Monserrate. 'It is crowded with merchants, who forgather there from all over Asia . . . There is no art or craft useful to human life which is not practised there. The population is so large that men jostle each other in the streets.' This was the scene in Akbar's time. Three generations later, Bernier found the city in ruins: 'There are still five or six considerable streets, two or three of which exceed a league in length; but not a few of the houses in there are tumbling to the ground.'

Another prosperous city in Mughal India was Ahmadabad in Gujarat, a great trading centre. The city was, says Withington, 'very near as bigge as London.' Jahangir heartily detested Ahmadabad. 'I am amazed to think what pleasure or goodness the founder of this city could have seen in a spot so devoid of the favour [of God] as to build a city on it,' he writes. 'Its air is poisonous, and its soil has little water, and is of sand and dust . . . Its water is very bad and unpalatable, and the river, which is by the side of the city, is always dry except in the rainy season. Its wells are mostly salty and bitter, and the tanks in the neighbourhood of the city have become like buttermilk from washermen's soap . . . Outside the city, in place of green and grass and flower, all is an open plain full of thorn-brakes.'

Surat, also in Gujarat, was the most prosperous port in the Mughal empire, which yielded, according to Thevenot, an annual revenue of 1.2 million rupees to the imperial treasury, before Shivaji's raids scared trade away and ruined the city. Even if the actual revenue was only half of this, as Moreland estimates, Surat was a rich city. But it was a typical traders' town, and was, for all its wealth, grubby and mean-looking, with narrow, crooked streets and mud-and-bamboo tenements, though along the river-front there were a few grand mansions and warehouses of the local merchant princes and the establishments of the English, Dutch, Turkish and Armenian traders. 'The private Houses are built with Mud mixt with Cows Dung, and small Brush-wood broke; there are not above a dozen good ones belonging to French, English, Dutch and Mahometan Merchants,' says Careri.

'The Streets [of Surat] are some too narrow, but in many places of convenient breadth; and in an Evening, especially near the Bazar, or Market-place, are more populous than any part of London and so much throng'd, that 'tis not very easie to pass through the multitude of Bannians and other Merchants that expose their Goods,' says Ovington. The city had a large floating population—'the seasons render it unequal,' notes Thevenot: 'There are a great many all the Year round; but in the time of the Monsson, that is to say, in the time when Ships can go and come to (the Indies without danger . . . the Town is so full of People, that Lodgings can hardly be had, and the three Suburbs are full.' A puzzling sight for travellers in Surat were the hospitals for cows, horses, insects, flies and so on maintained by pious Jains.

Outside the Mughal empire, the most prosperous city in India in early Mughal times was probably Bijapur, of which Asad Beg, Akbar's courtier, has left a vivid account. Bijapur would, in a few short decades of Mughal-imposed wars, lose its prosperity and joyous spirit, so that by the time Tavernier got there in the mid-seventeenth century, the city had become a shabby provincial town. 'Visapour is a great scambling city, wherein there is nothing remarkable, neither as to public edifices, nor as to trade,' writes Tavernier. 'The King's palace is a vast one but ill built.'

Hyderabad, another great Deccani city, had a somewhat different reputation. Founded in 1591 by Muhammad Qutb Shah for his favourite wife Bhagmati, a Hindu, the city was originally called Bhagnagar, but was later renamed Hyderabad, after Bhagmati's Muslim name, Haider Begum. 'That woman,' scoffs Khafi Khan, 'established many brothels and drinking shops in that place, and the rulers [of Golconda] had always been addicted to pleasure and to all sorts of debauchery . . . so the city got an evil name for licentiousness.'

BEYOND THE SCATTERED cities and towns, India in Mughal times was largely a wilderness, with clusters of villages here and there. The countryside was sparsely populated. Forests encased even the imperial cities of Delhi and Agra, and wild animals—and wild men—roamed their environs. 'The whole kingdome is as it were a forest,' says Terry, from his knowledge of the Malwa-Gujarat region. But others, travelling in other parts of the empire, had other views. Says Pelsaert: 'Trees are plentiful round the city, but very scarce in the open country; even four or five trees usually mark the site of a village.'

There was not much cross-country traffic in Mughal India. Even along the regular trade, military or pilgrim routes, the quality of roads varied, and often there were no roads at all. Mughal India could, however, boast of one of the finest roads in the medieval world, the renowned Agra-Lahore highway. Thomas Coryat, the peripatetic British eccentric travelling around the world on foot, who had seen the best and the worst roads of Asia and Europe, says of the highway in the time of Jahangir: 'The most incomparable shew of that kind that ever my eies survaied.'

Terry, who had not seen the road, describes it by hearsay as 'one of the rarest and most beneficial works in the whole world.' Tavernier, in India during the reign of Shah Jahan, also found the highway admirable, though he noticed the signs of neglect too. 'From Lahor to Delhy, and from Delhy to Agra, is a continual walk set on both sides with fair trees, an object most pleasing to the sight,' he writes; 'but in some places the trees are decayed, and there is no care taken to plant others in their stead.'

This was an old highway, probably the same as the arterial road that in Maurya times had stretched from Patna to the north-west frontier. Under the Mughals, work to restore the highway—it was the Mughal lifeline to Kabul—was begun by Babur himself, who ordered, as he states in his memoirs, that 'at every 9th *kuroh* (about 29 kilometres) a tower was to be erected [on the highway, where] . . . 6 post-horses were to be kept fastened; and arrangement was to be made for the payment of post-master and grooms, and for horse corn.'

Nothing is known about the state of the highway under Humayun, but Sher Shah during his short reign did much to improve it. 'On both sides of the highway Sher Shah planted fruit-bearing trees, such as also gave much shade, that in the hot wind travellers might go along under the trees; and if they should stop by the way, might rest and take repose,' reports Abbas Khan. The next major improvement came under Jahangir, who states in his memoirs that he planted avenue trees from Bengal to the Indus, and 'ordered that from Agra to Lahore they should put up a pillar at every *kos*, to be sign of a *kos*, and every three kos make a well, so that wayfarers might travel in ease and contentment.' Bernier confirms this, noting that there were, on important roads, 'small pyramids or turrets [called *kos-minars*], erected from kos to *kos*, for the purpose of pointing out the different roads. Wells are also frequently met with, affording drink to travellers, and serving to water the young trees.'

Except for the Agra-Lahore highway there were few good roads in Mughal India, and most of the overland travel was over rough tracks, which often disappeared altogether in forests and ravines. 'Here are no beaten roads or mending of high wayes,' complained the English traders of Surat in a letter to London in 1666, 'but the first carts that travail must cut them anew with their wheeles, that make it very tedious and troublesome travelling in the first of the year.' Peter Mundy travelling from Allahabad to Varanasi in August 1632 found the highway 'very badd . . . for the aboundance of water, bad way and uneven ground'. During the monsoon, rains wrought havoc even on the best of roads, turning them, as Sleeman noted in 1835, into watercourses. In south India there were hardly any roads, notes Tavernier. 'From Golconda southwards ... carts were practically unknown, and pack-animals or porters were the only means of transport by land,' writes Moreland.

THE ABSENCE OF roads was an impediment to the growth of trade and the integration of the empire, but it did not matter much to the common people, who travelled, if at all they travelled outside their habitat, on foot. For the affluent, the commonest mode of transport was the ox-cart—not the creaky, wobbly carts of goods transport drawn by emaciated oxen, but luxury carriages drawn by well-groomed white oxen—majestic animals 'almost six Foot high', according to Thevenot—the symbol of status and wealth in Mughal India, fit even for the emperor to ride in. Sir Thomas Roe once saw Jahangir and Nur Jahan returning from an evening joy-ride in an ox-cart, with the emperor himself as the carter. 'They have white Oxen there, which are extraordinarily dear, and I saw two of them which the Dutch had, that cost them two hundred Crowns a piece,' says Thevenot; 'they were really lovely, strong and good, and their chariot that was drawn by them, made a great shew.'

'Carriages and manner of travelling in India,' says Tavernier, 'is more commodious than anything that has been invented for use in France or Italy.' Confirms Ralph Fitch: 'They have many fine cartes, and many of them carved and gilded with gold, with two wheeles, which be drawen with two litle buls about the bignesse of our great dogs in England, and they will runne with any horse, and carie two or three men in one of these cartes; they are covered with silke or very fine cloth, and be used here as our coches be in England.' The cart bulls, says Mandelslo, 'express'd as much mettle as we could have expected from the best Horses in Germany.' Says Tavernier, 'They will travel upon the trot twelve or fifteen leagues a day for sixty days together.' After half a day's journey, they were fed two or three balls of wheat kneaded with butter and 'black sugar'. Carts were dismantled for taking across rivers or while crossing difficult terrain.

Carriage oxen of good breed were expensive—Tavernier once paid 600 rupees for a cart with two oxen, but considered it well worth it. Travellers could also hire carts, at the rate of one rupee a day 'more or less', says Tavernier, but they usually had problems with the casual ways of carters, who, says Peter Mundy, 'doe and demand what they list, goe, come, sett out and Remaine when and where they please.' A cart would normally seat four, or sleep two. Horse-drawn carriages were also known, but were rare; Monserrate once saw Akbar riding in a two-horse chariot, sitting cross-legged on a seat covered with scarlet rugs. Jahangir sometimes favoured a European style coach-and-four (the replica of a carriage presented to him by Roe), though usually the emperor and the grandees travelled in palanquins or in howdahs mounted on elephants.

The palanquin was a covered divan carried on poles by men, in which the traveller lounged on cushions—'a sort of little couch six or seven foot long, and three broad, with balusters round about it,' notes Tavernier. 'A kind of cane, called bamboue, which they bend like an arch, sustains the covering of the palanquin, which is either of satin or cloth of gold; and when the sun shines upon one side, a slave that goes that side, takes care to pull down the covering.' Another slave carries 'at the end of a long stick a kind of target of osier, covered over with gentile stuff, to preserve the person that is in the palanquin from the heat of the sun.' Palanquins would normally cover about twenty to thirty miles a day, and travelling in them 'is as easie and pleasant as that of our Chairs in the Streets of London, but far surpasseth them in point of State and quick dispatches of a Journey,' says Ovington. Palanquin bearers were professionals, not ordinary coolies, and were nimble enough to hold the couch steady while travelling over rough tracts. They were paid at the same rate as the traveller's armed escorts—'not above four rupees a month,' says Tavernier, though if the journey was over sixty days, the pay would be over five rupees.

Those who could not afford carts or palanquins, rode buffaloes or oxen—or horses, ponies, mules, donkeys or camels. Most people simply walked, usually travelling at night, to avoid the heat of the sun.

A major impediment to overland travel in India was the near total absence of bridges over major rivers. The only substantial bridge in the Mughal empire was the Bridge of Ten Arches at Jaunpur constructed early in Akbar's reign, and it is probably this bridge that Finch describes as 'a stone bridge of eleven arches, over a branch of the Gemini [Yamuna].' Pontoon bridges were maintained at major riverside cities when the state of the river permitted it, and small streams sometimes had bridges over them. Armies crossed rivers at fords or on temporary boat-bridges, usually taking several days to cross and suffering many casualties in accidents. Ferries plied at river crossings, but the poor often swam across on inflated goat skins tied to their stomachs, pushing their children ahead of them in clay pots. Manrique says he had to cross streams 'on big earthen pots', lying on his 'stomach on the jar, covering its mouth, and so cross by paddling with hands and feet'. Navigable rivers were few in India, and river transport was largely confined to the Indus and the Ganga-Yamuna system, which were used for military as well as commercial transport.

Only in Bengal were boats used extensively for 'travelling . . . especially in the rains', says Abul Fazl.

Travel across the countryside was hazardous, though the experiences of travellers varied greatly. Terry, for instance, says that Indians 'in general are very civil, and we never had any affronts or ill usage from them, if we did not first provoke them,' and Thevenot believed that 'there was not so great danger upon the Roads, as some would have us believe.' On the whole, travel in Mughal India seems to have been no more—and no less—perilous than in medieval Europe. Highwaymen infested the roads in India, as they did in Europe. 'A man can travell no way for out-lawes,' says Hawkins. Says Tavernier: 'Whether it be in a coach or a palanquin, he that will travel honourably in the Indies, must take along with him twenty or thirty armed men, with bows and arrows some, others with muskets.' The escort was partly for show—'sometimes for more magnificence they carry a banner'—but mainly for security. River travel was equally risky; Tavernier, for instance, was warned that if sailors discovered that he carried money, they were likely to capsize the boat and retrieve the money later.

People usually travelled in groups and under guard, sometimes in caravans of two or three hundred carts. When attacked, the caravan would form a circle, says Withington, 'bringinge our cammells round about us in a ringe and makinge them sitt downe . . . and soe were within them as in a forte, plyinge our bows and arrows.' According to Withington, thieves could sometimes be bought off. Bandits had their own code of conduct, and usually avoided harming men of religion— Thevenot was once told to take a minstrel with him for protection on the road, and Badauni was once freed by robbers when he told them that he was just returning from the hermitage of a saint. Similarly, highwaymen seldom molested women. But then, there were women bandits too on the road, and they showed no mercy to men—Thevenot says that these women would entice the unwary traveller with some sad tale or other, get on the horse behind him, garrotte him, and flee with his goods.

The danger on the road was not from brigands alone. Travellers, especially traders, were oppressed by local authorities with all sorts of illegal exactions. 'When you are delivered from the peril [of highwaymen], you fall into the hands of . . . [customs officers] or publicans,' says Manucci. 'These take what they please unjustly and by force, and if they know that anyone has money on him, they rob him, cut his throat, and bury him.' Prominent persons usually carried *dastaks* (passports), which cleared their passage through the hands of local officials.

A GREAT CONVENIENCE for the traveller in Mughal India were the caravanserais in towns and along the highways, usually at the end of each day's journey. Building serais as a charitable act was a custom among Hindus and Muslims, and some of the best serais in India—such as the massive Begum Ki Serai of Jahanara in Delhi—were built by private charity. 'For their workes of charitie many rich men build Sarraas, or make wells or tankes neere to high-wayes,' says Terry. But most of the serais were built and maintained by the state and served an administrative purpose as well, as junctions of the royal communication and intelligence grid. Soldiers were not allowed to billet in serais, and the periods of stay for different categories of travellers were regulated, to prevent people from turning serais into residences, though foreign traders were permitted to stay for longer periods by paying a monthly rent.

Serais were essentially fortified enclosures where the traveller could camp in safety, but the nature of the structure and the conveniences available in it varied from place to place. British ambassador Norris found the serais in the Deccan deplorable. 'A square of about 100 yards & on each side of the square are doores like a College wch leades to a little apartment wch ye first comer may take as he pleases,' writes Norris. 'They are very dirty & nasty, fit for nobody but carters & camel drivers. About ye midle of ye square stands a little mosck.' Finch, on the other hand, found the serai at Chapraghata 'a goodly castle than an inne to lodge strangers; the lodgings very faire of stone, with lockes and keyes, able to lodge a thousand men.'

Usually serais were built around a central courtyard, with arcaded chambers all round, but sometimes they were, as Tavernier states, merely enclosures of walls or hedges, within which fifty or sixty thatched huts were arranged. Serais provided only bare accommodation; travellers had to bring their own bedding and in most places had to cook their own food too, though sometimes cooks were available. 'Passengers my have roome freely, but must bring with him his Bedding, his Cooke, and other necessaries wherein to dresse his meate,' says Terry. Some serais were reserved for particular communities. If accommodation was not available in a serai, travellers could hire tents.

Sher Shah is reputed to have built some 1700 serais, 'and in every serai he built separate lodgings, both for Hindus and Musulmans, and at the gate of every serai he had placed pots full of water, that any one might drink,' says Abbas Khan, 'and in every serai he settled Brhamans for the entertainment of Hindus, to provide hot and cold water, and beds and food, and grain for their horses; and it was a rule in these serais, that

whoever entered them received provision suitable to his rank, and food
and litter for his cattle, from Government. Villages were established all
round the serais. In the middle of every serai was a well and a masjid of
burnt brick; and he placed an imam and a muezzin in every masjid,
together with a custodian and several watchmen; and all these were
maintained from the land near the serai.'

The serai gates were closed at sundown, says Manucci, and the official
in charge would call out 'that everyone must look after his belongings,
picket his horses . . . , above all that he must look out for dogs, for the
dogs of Hindustan are very cunning and great thieves.' In the morning,
before the gates were opened, travellers were asked to check their
belongings, and if anything was found missing, gates were opened only
after it was found.

In Rajasthan serais were few, and in the Deccan, mosques and temples
were the common resting places of travellers. 'The townes and villages
are built of Mudd, soe that there is not a house for a man to rest in,' says
Roe of his experience while travelling from Surat to Burhanpur. Villagers
were usually hospitable towards travellers, says Withington, who once
found refuge in a village after he was robbed on the road. Where there
were no resting places, people camped in the open, often under trees.
Sometimes particular trees attained a reputation of their own as resting
places, like the famous banyan tree near the town of Hardoi in Uttar
Pradesh, which had so vast a spread that in 1856 two regiments of soldiers
are reported to have encamped under the shade of its branches.

The People

THE MUGHAL CONQUEST of India did not involve any major changes in the racial, linguistic or religious make-up of the subcontinent. There were in fact very few Mughals in Mughal India. Babur had brought with him into India about 10,000 of his own people, but a number of them had returned to Kabul after the battle of Khanua, and even those who remained were later driven out by Sher Shah. The reconquest of India by Humayun involved even fewer Mughals, a mere 5000 cavalrymen. However, under Akbar and his immediate successors, when the Mughal empire became renowned as the largest, richest and most dynamic Muslim kingdom in the world—the land of opportunity for Muslims everywhere—there was a steady migration of Muslims from Central Asia and Persia into India. These migrants occupied the top echelons in the Mughal government, but their total number was at no time large, a drop in the vast ocean of Indian population. Even this dribble of migration virtually stopped during the reign of Aurangzeb, as the Mughal empire lost its vitality, and Muslim culture everywhere went into decline.

There was some population movement within India in Mughal times, as groups migrated to avoid famine or oppression or war, but these were insignificant compared to the great shufflings of people that had taken place in the early medieval India. By and large, the racial, religious and linguistic mix of India, and the geographical rooting of its peoples and their socio-cultural contours, had firmed up by the time the Mughals arrived.

What the people had congealed into, however, was not a nation, or even a family of nations. Though the Mughals had imposed on the subcontinent such political unity as had never before existed, and had given it a uniformity of administrative system, court culture, coinage and official language, there was no sense that the subjects of. the empire were one people. Nor was there any concept of citizenship, either in the Mughal empire or in any other Indian state—it was land, not people, that made up the state, and frontiers, indefinite and ever shifting, were always porous. There was an Indian empire; there was no Indian nation.

The people of one part of the subcontinent hardly knew those of the other parts, and had little in common with them. They spoke different languages, worshipped different gods, had different social systems. Only in the thin top crust of society, among brahmins and the Persianized Muslim aristocracy, were there pan-Indian linkages. Even among them there was no real sense of belonging together.

Paradoxically, there was no regional cohesiveness either, not even among the Rajputs and the Marathas. Tribally fragmented, or divided into castes and sects, even the people who spoke the same language, lived in the same area and belonged to the same broad religious group, developed no sense of shared history or common identity. The only sharp distinctions were those of caste and tribe. All other identities were amorphous, all other barriers permeable. This absence of sharp we/they distinctions between the regional peoples of India, or between Indians and foreigners, in part accounts for the docile acceptance of conquerors by Indians. Foreign rule was seldom perceived as foreign rule.

Even the name India is not Indian. The word is derived from the Persian mispronunciation of Sindhu (Indus River) as Hindu, which the Greeks turned into Indus, and used the term India to refer to the region around and beyond the Indus. It was only in the sixteenth century, at the beginning of the Mughal rule, that the term India was for the first time used in the subcontinental sense, initially by the Spaniards or the Portuguese. Its usage was confined to Europeans. Indians themselves never used the term India in pre-modern times to describe their country, nor did the Mughals. The alternate term, found in Mughal chronicles, was Hindustan, but this meant only the Indo-Gangetic plain; the Deccan was not part of it, nor the north-west or the north-east, nor Kashmir. The term Bharat is not mentioned in any Mughal work.

Babur recognized India as a distinct geological and bio-cultural entity—'It is quite a different world . . . ,' he writes. 'Its hills and rivers, its forests and plains, its animals and plants, its inhabitants and their languages, its winds and rains, are all of a different nature . . . You have no sooner passed the river Sind [Indus] than the country, the trees, the stones, the wandering tribes, the manners and customs of the people, are all entirely of Hindustan.' But the distinctiveness of India that Babur saw existed only in the eyes of the outsider, and was no more meaningful than the designation of all Europeans as Feringhees by Indians, or of all fair-complexioned Muslims as Mughals by Europeans.

'They were called Moguls, that is, white of complexion . . . the natives being all brown or olive colour,' says Tavernier. According to Bernier, 'to be considered a Mogol, it is enough if a foreigner have a white face and profess Mahometanism.' Some Europeans even thought that the term Mughal meant simply a circumcised man; Terry thus believed that the Great Mughal meant 'the Chiefe of the Circumcision'.

The term Mughal is an Arabic and Persian corruption of Mongol. The Mughals were Mongols. But they generally preferred to call themselves Chaghatai Turks—Chaghatai, because their ancestral homeland was north of the river Amu Darya (Oxus), which was the domain of Chaghatai Khan, the second son of Chingiz Khan; Turks, because they had become Turks in language and culture due to their long residence in Turkish countries. In Indian history, the term Mughal is specific to the dynasty founded by Babur, but is also applied loosely to their immigrant officers and men.

THE MUGHAL COSMOS revolved around the emperor. Everyone else was either his servant or his subject. Broadly speaking, his servants made up the leisure class, and his subjects the productive class. The leisure class was the ruling class, and had its own work (administrative, military or religious) but not many members of the class were economically productive, or even supportive of production—by and large they merely appropriated what others produced. This polarization was further accentuated by the fact that the productive class was overwhelmingly Hindu, while the leisure class was predominantly Muslim. Muslims as a community belonged to the ruling class, by community right; others, such as the Rajputs and other local chieftains, were merely admitted to the class as a matter of administrative, political or military expediency.

The ruling class was not a homogeneous class. Apart from racial, religious and social differences, there were great economic disparities among the members of the class, and the majority of them lived a life not very different from that of the common productive class. Within Muslim society there were, in addition to class divisions based on wealth and position, divisions based on race and profession, although Muslims did not have the social and ritual taboos that vacuum-sealed the Hindu castes. Different Muslim classes and occupational groups even had different graveyards in cemeteries. And Persians formed a very superior class by themselves.

If Mughal India, or indeed the whole eastern Muslim world, had a natural aristocracy, they were Persians. Everyone looked up to Persians, and Persians looked down on everyone. Their language was the Mughal court language, their culture the Mughal court culture, and it was from the Shah of Persia that the Mughal emperor sought peer recognition. Apart from their assumed superior culture, the fair skin of Persians also helped to establish their superior status—a bias for fair complexion was part of the Indian psyche, and in Mughal India, in popular perception, all fair-skinned Muslim immigrants were viewed as Mughals, and therefore as masters. 'The children of the third and fourth generation,' writes Bernier, 'who have the brown complexion, and the languid manner of this country of their nativity, are held in much less respect than new comers.'

Persians often sneered at Mughals and Indians as semi-barbarians; they snickered at the Indian efforts to speak and write Persian, and ridiculed the Indian imitations of Persian courtly manners as vulgar, very much in the same way in which the British would later privately mock Anglicized Indians. Persians, says Bernier, often indulged in much 'satirical merriment' about Indians; Manucci says that Persians often called Indians 'slaves' or 'blacks'.

The topmost positions in the Mughal empire were invariably held by Persians. It was not, however, merely their racial origin or superior culture that won Persians their privileged place, but rather their high talent, hard work, and devotion. 'No other nation is better than the Persians for acting as clerks,' Aurangzeb maintained. 'In war, too . . . none of this nation has turned his face away from the field, and their firm feet have never been shaken. Moreover, they have not once been guilty of disobedience or treachery to their master. But, as they insist on being treated with great honour, it is very difficult to get on together with them. You have anyhow to conciliate them and should employ subterfuges.' The traits of Persians, Aurangzeb believed, were derived from their astrological status. 'As the Sun is the guardian planet of the Persians, the intellectual keenness of those men in quickness of perception and foresight is four times as great as that of the Indians, whose tutelary planet is Saturn,' he stated. 'Their only defect is that by reason of its conjunction with Venus, they have grown ease-loving, whereas men governed by Saturn are accustomed to toil.'

In contrast to Persians, Afghans, whom the Mughals overthrew from power in Hindustan, were generally seen, in the jaundiced eyes of the victor, as a crude and vulgar people, without manners, gluttons and drunkards. 'These Afghans remain very rustic and tactless!' says Babur. Afghans were a tough, unruly people, 'an intractable race,' as Bernier puts it. 'Even the menials and carriers of water belonging to that nation are high-spirited and warlike.'

The sharpest division among Muslims in India at this time was the north-south division. The northern Muslims were predominantly Sunnis, while in the south they were mainly Shiahs. In the north, India-born Muslims and Hindu converts were held in low esteem, and were denied any major role in government. In contrast, in the south, native Muslims held high positions, along with Afghans, Ethiopians and a few Persians. The preferred language of Muslims in the north was Persian; in the south, it was Dakhini (Deccani Urdu). Further, as Muslims constituted only a small percentage of the population in the south, a far greater number of Hindus were employed in high positions in the southern Muslim kingdoms than in the Mughal empire.

HOWEVER, WHETHER IN the south or the north, a Muslim, whatever be his race and sect, automatically belonged to the ruling class in Mughal times. It was a matter of wonder to contemporary as well as later European writers that a small number of Muslims should have been able so effortlessly to dispossess Hindus of power and rule over them for so many centuries, treating them as second-class citizens, and subjecting them to severe political, social and economic disabilities. 'It seems a wonderful thing, that such a prodigious multitude of men should be cowed by a handful, and bow so easily under the yoke of the Mahometan princes,' says Tavernier.

Hindus and Muslims were in every respect antipodal communities. Yet, by and large, they coexisted in peace if not in harmony. Though there were innumerable revolts against Muslim rulers in India, nearly all of them were by Muslim nobles, hardly any by Hindu chieftains. There were occasional communal flare-ups over such issues as cow-slaughter, Holi revelry and Diwali fireworks, and sometimes Hindus retaliated against temple demolitions—remarks Sher Shah: '[Hindus] have thrown down masjids and buildings of believers and placed idol-shrines in them'— but there were no major communal conflicts in Mughal India. Foreign travellers, who would normally have reported such matters, are entirely silent on them.

How do we account for this strange amicability? One reason could be that Muslim rulers were not as harsh to Hindus as is commonly assumed. Contemporary Muslim writers of course exultingly tell gory tales, of the oppression of Hindus by Muslim rulers, but there is little doubt that they were panegyrically exaggerating the religious fervour of their patrons in the conventional hyperbolic style of the times.

Infidel-bashing was more a matter of literary overkill than of physical excess. Typical was the comment of Badauni on the death of a Hindu officer: 'He went to his natural abode—Hell, where he got into hot water.' And on the death of Todar Mal and Bhagwan Das, he wrote that they 'hastened to the abode of hell and torment, and in the lowest pit became the food of serpents and scorpions—may God scorch them both!' Such affectations had become so common a routine that even the Hindu chroniclers of the age writing in Persian, like Ishwardas Nagar, adopted it, invoking damnation on Hindus in the manner of the Muslim chroniclers—they, as H. M. Elliot points out in his classic mid-nineteenth century compilation of the chronicles of Muslim rule, routinely referred to fellow Hindus as infidels, and stated that when Hindus were killed 'their souls were dispatched to hell', and that when Muslims were killed they drank 'the cup of martyrdom'.

It was not that there was no discrimination. Though the actual conditions of life for Hindus under Muslim rule was not as rough as the chronicles of the age would have us believe, there is no doubt that they lived under severe restrictions. For a short while, under Akbar, their inferior status virtually disappeared, but even then not entirely, and at no time would a Muslim of even the lowest status have considered giving a daughter in marriage to a Hindu of even the highest status. It was a major crime for a Hindu to keep a Muslim woman as wife or concubine. Even the easy-going Jahangir was incensed when he learned that a Muslim community in the Bhimbhar district of Kashmir was giving daughters to Hindus, and he forbade the practice on penalty of death. In the same spirit, Jahangir cut off the tongue of a son of Raja Bikramjit, imprisoned him and ordered that he should eat only with dog-keepers and outcasts—for the crime of keeping a Muslim concubine, and for killing her mother and father to keep it a secret.

The degree of discrimination that Hindus had to suffer varied from ruler to ruler and from province to province, depending on the ethos of the region and the temper of its governor. A ludicrous case was that of the Mughal governor of Lahore, Husain Khan, who once committed what he considered to be a most awful faux pas, in greeting a Hindu with civility, mistaking him to be a Muslim, because he was dressed in the Muslim style. On realizing his mistake, the Khan was so thoroughly ashamed of himself that, to avoid similar blunders in future, he ordered that Hindus thereafter 'should sew a patch of stuff of *a* different colour on their garments near the bottom of the sleeve,' says Badauni. He further ordered that Hindus, 'in accordance with the requirements of the Holy Law, should not ride on saddles, but should sit on a pack-saddle.'

Such fiats were as much the expressions of ruling class arrogance as of religious prejudice. In fact, the Hindu–Muslim relationship was primarily a relationship between masters and subjects, not just between two competing communities. This largely accounts for Muslim haughtiness and Hindu subservience. Hindus suffered disabilities not merely because of their religion, but also because they were a subject people, and they deferred to Muslims because they (Muslims) were the masters. The 300-odd years of Muslim rule that preceded the Mughal regime had ingrained in Hindus a subject mentality.

Hindus were moreover long habituated to discriminations within Hindu society itself, because of caste and sectarian divisions, and the taboos and tyrannies associated with them. To most Hindus, ill-treatment by Muslims would have seemed like any other caste or sectarian outrage, maybe more virulent than anything within Hindu society, but not fundamentally different. Besides, for the common people, who were brutally exploited by their own rulers, the establishment of Muslim rule meant merely the substitution of one predator by another, which did not significantly alter the quality of their lives.

Passivity was in any case a Hindu cultural trait. Their lot was their karma, Hindus believed, and by and large they fatalistically accepted their subject status, as if it were their natural, immutable condition of life, and they tried to make do within that environment, taking all excesses and humiliations in their sluggish stride. Through all the political and social upheavals in medieval India, and some radical movements within Hinduism itself, the Hindu social order endured, its structure and indwelling spirit the same. It accommodated all things new or deviant in its capacious fold by applying the principle of tolerance by exclusion. Hindu society yielded to change like a plant bending to the wind, but did not itself change. This was its means of survival. The 'peaceable and submissive Deportment [of Hindus] wins mightily upon the Moors and takes off much of that scornful Antipathy which they harbour against them,' says Ovington.

There was in any case little chance of a Hindu/Muslim divide in Mughal India, because Hinduism, unlike Islam, was not a monolithic religion, but a conglomeration of divergent sects and castes. 'The idolaters,' says Tavernier, 'have no union among themselves, and . . . superstitions have introduced so strange a diversity of opinions and customs that they never agree with one another.' Writes Manucci: 'The inhabitants of these places differ in their customs, as well as in their mode of life, the ceremonial at their temples, and the doctrines of their religion.' Despite the traditional brahminical endeavour to incorporate local and tribal deities into the Hindu pantheon, and the devotional bhakti movement tending to efface regional differences, Hindu gods in Mughal India remained mostly localized. The gods worshipped by one Hindu community were not worshipped by other Hindu communities.

Divergence in the occupations of Muslims and Hindus also helped to deflect communal tensions. Muslims were mostly in government service or in some sinecure or other; a small number of them were traders and craftsmen, but they generally avoided agriculture, which they considered a demeaning occupation, while trade and agriculture, especially agriculture, were the primary occupations of Hindus. 'First, they are the leading merchants and jewellers, and they are most able and expert in their business,' says Pelsaert about the occupations of urban Hindus. 'Next, they are workmen, for practically all work is done by Hindus, the Moslems practising scarcely any crafts but dyeing and weaving . . . Thirdly, they are clerks and brokers: all the business of the lords' palaces and of the Moslem merchants is done by Hindus—book-keeping, buying, and selling. They are particularly clever brokers, and are consequently generally employed as such throughout all these countries, except for the sale of horses, oxen, camels, elephants, or any living creatures, which they will not handle as the Moslems do.'

Communal peace was also facilitated by the fact that Hindus in general did not come into everyday contact with Muslims, for Muslims in India were largely an urban people, while most Hindus lived in villages. In the urban centres where the two communities mingled, peace generally prevailed because the Hindu urban elite belonged either to the political or the trading class, and both these classes had a vested interest in avoiding strife, though for different reasons—the political class, especially the Rajputs, had made a cosy career for themselves by serving the Mughals; as for the trading class, they kept as low a profile as possible, to make themselves and their wealth invisible to the rapacious rulers. The urban Hindu adroitly adopted Mughal culture to blend with the new rulers, dressing like them, living in homes like theirs, and speaking their language.

It was all politics (or business) as usual. On the few occasions when the Hindu political elite clashed with Muslim rulers, the primary issue involved was power, not religion. The Maratha, Rajput and Sikh rebellions, though they had some communal aspects to them, were essentially political conflicts. Thus we see Maratha captains, on occasion Shivaji himself, serving in Muslim armies, and we see Muslim captains in the Maratha army; there were Muslim chiefs in the army of Rana Pratap Singh opposing Akbar, and there were Rajput chiefs, including the Rana's brother, in Akbar's army menacing the Rana; Vijayanagar had Muslim divisions in its army fighting against the Deccan Sultanates, who in turn had Hindu divisions in their armies; the Sultans sometimes sought the help of Vijayanagar against each other, while Vijayanagar factions often invited Bijapur to intervene in their internal squabbles; Ranga Rayal, the last of the Vijayanagar rulers, once even offered to become a Muslim along with his family in return for Mughal help against his enemies; the list could go on.

Only very rarely do we hear of Hindu chieftains seeking to protect Hindus. Akbar's general Man Singh is said to have once forbidden the Mughal army under his command from plundering in Rajasthan, but normally Rajput chieftains offered no opposition even to temple demolitions by the Mughals. As for Muslim rulers, temple demolitions were a part of their victory rite rather than a specifically religious act. Though Muslim rulers often termed their wars against Hindu kings as jihad, this was done more as a matter of convention than as a deliberate policy: their objective was political rather than religious.

MUSLIM RULERS, EVEN the Turko-Afghans were, on the whole, careful not to push Hindus beyond endurance. By the time the Turks invaded India, the religious fervour of Islam had largely dissipated—the motive of their conquest was essentially political, not religious—and this had a moderating influence on Muslim theocracy in India. As for the Mughals, except in Aurangzeb and to some extent in Shah Jahan, the religious impulse was virtually non-existent in them, and they sought to conciliate Hindus to their rule through such measures as the abolition of jizya and the prohibition of cow slaughter. 'Oxen and cows are not slaughtered, as they have to work while they are young, doing everything that is done by horses in Holland; and besides, their slaughter is strictly forbidden by the King on pain of death, though buffaloes may be freely killed,' says Pelsaert of what he observed in Jahangir's India. 'The King maintains this rule to please the Hindu rajas and banias, who regard the cow as one of the most veritable gods or sacred things.'

The Mughals also took care to give the Hindu political elite an important role in the governance of the empire. The number of Hindus in Mughal service was however small relative to their population, and only a handful of them occupied top government positions even in the best of times, and no Hindu was ever elevated to the post of the Vizier, the highest office in the Mughal empire. Hindus were mostly in subordinate positions.

Hindus generally had a greater political role in small Muslim kingdoms than in the Mughal empire—the Vizier of Sultan Abdul Muzaffar Shah of Malwa early in the sixteenth century, for instance, was a Rajput, Basant Rai; later, another Rajput, Medini Rai, became the de facto ruler of the kingdom under Sultan Mahmud, and Rajputs occupied all the important positions in the government. In Bijapur during the reign of Muhammad Adil Shah, the government was 'delivered . . . over to a mischievous, turbulent brahmin, named Murari Pundit,' says Lahori; and in Golconda, Madanna, another brahmin, ruled supreme for several years in the name of the sultan. A few Hindus of the lower castes also rose to high positions in Muslim states—they in fact had far greater career opportunities in Muslim states than in caste-bound Hindu kingdoms, as the dramatic rise of Hemu under Adil Shah of Bihar demonstrated. The Hindu–Muslim barrier was a soft barrier, which could be easily pierced by men of ability.

Surprisingly, there were hardly any brahmins, the traditional Hindu ministerial class, among the top officers of the Mughal empire, Raja Birbal, Akbar's companion, and Raghunath, Aurangzeb's revenue minister, being the only distinguished exceptions. Though the Mughals preferred Hindus as revenue administrators—at one time Hindus headed the revenue departments in eight of the twelve Mughal provinces—the top positions were held by Khattris and Kayasthas and an occasional Rajput, not by brahmins.

The most prominent Hindu community in the Mughal service were the Rajputs, and they were held in high esteem by the emperors. 'Rajas,' writes Bernier, 'bear an equal rank with the foreign and Mahometan Omrahs.' Still, the Rajputs could not aspire to the high administrative positions held by Persians, and were mostly in military service. Says Pelsaert, 'In wartime the race is much esteemed, and is feared by other classes of soldiers, but during peace they get the cold shoulder, because in palaces or camps they make less show or display than the Moguls or Hindustanis.' Even under Akbar, Rajput soldiers were paid less than Muslim soldiers.

The Rajputs were a heterogeneous people. Though some of them in bold flights of fancy traced their origin to Vedic Aryans or epic heroes, most of them were descendants of early medieval immigrants, while some were of the Dravidian and aboriginal stock. What distinguished them was not race but martial culture. 'They are a bold and courageous people, determined and loyal,' lauds Pelsaert. 'Rasbooches . . . knowe as well howe to dye as anye men in the world, in regard to theire desperatenesse,' says Withington. 'Those (Rajputs) excepted,' remarks Terry, 'all the rest in the countrey are in generall pusilanimous, and had rather quarrell than fight.' Rajput chiefs, says Manucci, 'carry on such a disastrous warfare against each other that it is rare to see one of them die of disease.'

Like many other medieval people, the Rajputs were given to banditry, and, though they had a certain reputation for chivalry, they were by no means the white knights that British romantics like James Tod imagined them to be. 'Rashbootes, a number of which live by spoyle; who in troopes surprize poore passengers, cruelly butchering those they get under their power,' says Terry. Confirms Careri: 'The Rashootis are very great Thieves.' The odium of this charge is somewhat mitigated by the fact that the term Rajput was at one time a synonym for brigand, and the Rajputs, like the Marathas in later times, often had unfairly to bear the blame for the crimes of others.

Whatever their faults, the Rajputs had a relatively high sense of personal honour, and they were usually steadfast in loyalty and relentless in battle. These were not, however, absolute virtues, but relative to the political and military culture of the age. The Rajputs were not a people apart. Even the best of them sometimes opportunistically switched loyalties—as Jai Singh did when he abandoned Dara for Aurangzeb—and many valued life and career over honour. Jaswant Singh, for instance, often changed sides and betrayed trust. His valour too was suspect. According to Khafi Khan, after the battle of Dharmat 'Raja Jaswant's chief wife . . . strongly condemned her husband's conduct, and refused to sleep with him.' The raja, in her view, should have died in the battlefield, rather than return home defeated.

Honour was everything to the Rajput. It was his strength. And also his weakness. 'One of the fundamental rules of their caste is never to give way, but either to die or conquer,' says Manucci. Unfortunately, most of the time the Rajputs died rather than conquered. Their fierce obstinacy, though awesome, was not always an advantage, for to retreat tactically was as important in battle as to fight heroically. They were so fearless in battle as to seem almost senseless. Aurangzeb had, therefore, only disdain for what he termed 'the crass stupidity of the Hindustanis, who would part with their heads but not leave their positions [in battle]'.

The Rajputs were voluptuaries of death. Cultural habituation was a major factor in their daredevilry, but so was poppy chemistry. Living in a state of perpetual war, the Rajput had become a familiar of carnage.

Death meant little to him, his own or that of others. And this trait was augmented, perhaps crucially, by the Rajput practice of going into the battlefield heavily drugged with opium. 'They are slow to retreat in a fight, and are obstinate in attack, because the quantity of opium they eat excites them, and causes them to care little for their lives,' says Pelsaert.

The most awesome Rajput rite of honour was jauhar, in which, when faced with certain defeat, a fate worse than death for them, they sacrificed their women and children—normally in fire, but if time was short, by sword and dagger—and then, frenzied with opium, shed all their clothes, and offered themselves to be ritually slaughtered by their own captains, or charged naked on the enemy, to kill and be killed, in a carnal embrace of death beyond defeat and victory.

The fearsome rite was probably a primitive tribal custom brought into India by migrants, but the term jauhar seems to have been derived from *jauhara*, the Prakrit version of the Sanskrit term *jatu-griha*, meaning a lac-house, like the inflammable house in which the Kauravas tried to burn the Pandavas alive in the Hindu epic *Mahabharata*. The Mughals beheld *jauhar* for the first time at Chanderi. Records Babur: 'In a short time the Pagan, in a state of complete nudity, rushed out to attack us, put numbers of my people to flight . . . Two or three hundred of them slew each other in the following manner: One person took his stand with a sword in his hand, while the others, one by one, crowded in and stretched out their necks eager to die.'

Jauhar was not an individual decision, but a community choice. Women and children had to be killed to save them from dishonour at the hands of the enemy, and perhaps also for the warriors thus to sever all earthly attachments, so they could face death without anxiety. 'It is the custom of Indian rajas under such circumstances to collect wood, cotton, grass, ghee, and such like into one place, and to bring the women and burn them, willing or unwilling,' notes Abul Fazl. 'This they call jauhar . . . Whoever out of feebleness of soul was backward [to sacrifice herself] was, in accordance with their custom, put to death.' In most cases Rajput women needed no inducement to perform jauhar. 'Women, especially Rajput women, have often a higher sense of honour than men,' says Khafi Khan; 'and for this reason will rather bear the torture of fire than suffer disgrace.'

THE RAJPUTS, FOR all their valour and romantic history, had no political future in India. Their time in the sun had in fact been over long before the

Mughal conquest of India. The Mughal connection potentiated them temporarily by opening up for them a theatre of operation far wider than they could have otherwise had, but they became too enmeshed with the Mughals to survive the fall of the empire.

The Rajputs were eager collaborators of the Mughals, and not even the theocratic rigour of Aurangzeb turned them away. It was only when Aurangzeb began to abrogate their political privileges that they turned hostile. This willing subservience of the rajas was a major reason for the remarkable dynastic stability of the Mughals. Says Bernier: 'Fifteen or sixteen of these Rajas are rich and formidable . . . [and if some of them] chose to enter into an offensive league, they would prove dangerous opponents to the Mogol.' Manucci believed that 'if they (the Rajputs) were only of one mind they would be able to thrust out every other tribe and race.'

Internecine squabbles among the Rajputs precluded any possibility of a Rajput league against the Mughals. Even if the Rajput clans had united, it is doubtful whether they could have fought off the Mughals—a desert people, they were poor in resources, and their mode of warfare, which relied on individual valour rather than on discipline and training, was archaic and ineffective. The Rajput domains were tiny in comparison to the Mughal empire all their kingdoms together made up only a small portion of the vast land mass of the Mughal empire; the great Rajput states of Chitor, Jodhpur and Bikaner were just districts in the Mughal province of Ajmer, and Jaipur a taluq subdivision of a district.

As the political role of the Rajputs atrophied, that of the Marathas swelled, and they would emerge from the shambles of Shivaji's little kingdom to sweep across the subcontinent. In another respect, the future also belonged to brahmins, who, despite their numerous sectarian and lineage divisions, were the only distinctive all-India community. They were a baffling people to Europeans, an embodiment of the mystery of the mysterious East. Terry, reflecting the common prejudice of the Christian clergy, says that brahmins were 'so sottish and inconstant in their grounds that they scarce know what they hold.' Manucci sarcastically notes that brahmins, 'according to their view, are the noblest family of all mankind, and the one most venerated, not merely as superiors, but as gods.' Their ingenuity, however, could not be denied. Writes Pelsaert, 'Some of the brahmans are very ingenious, good astronomers, familiar with the course of stars.'

With the near total eclipse of Hindu kingdoms in medieval India, brahmins had lost their secure traditional role as royal advisors, and though here and there they did rise above the tide—there was even a dreaded brahmin bandit by the name of Chintu Chimma in Bijapur—the community was in general on the decline in Mughal India. It was only with the establishment of the Maratha kingdom that brahmins finally began to rehabilitate themselves, achieving a position of political prominence, which they would further expand and consolidate under the British, by both serving and battling the new empire.

In trade, the dominant community in Mughal times were Baniyas. They concentrated almost exclusively on making money, and were viewed with resentful respect by Europeans who also had their eyes glued to money. Rivalling Baniyas in commercial acumen were Parsees, a tiny community with a great future. They were ancient Zoroastrian fire-worshippers who had fled from religious persecution in Iran, to settle in Gujarat in the tenth century. From Gujarat they gradually spread southward towards Bombay, living quietly and obscurely as farmers and weavers. 'Their profession is, for the generality, all kinds of husbandry,' says Terry. Peter Mundy found them cultivating palm-trees. 'Their habitations are for the most part along the Sea-Coast,' writes Mandelslo, 'and they live very peaceably, sustaining themselves by the advantage they make out of the Tobacco they plant, and the Terry (toddy) they get out of the Palms of these parts, and whereof they make Arak, in regard they are permitted to drink Wine. They intermeddle also with Merchandise, and the exchange of Money and keep Shops, and are of all Trades, except those of Farriers, Blacksmiths and Locksmiths; in regard it is an unpardonable sin among them to put out the fire.' 'In their Callings they are very Industrious and diligent, and careful to train up their Children to Arts and Labour,' says Ovington.

In 1578, the community suddenly and dramatically emerged into Mughal history, when Akbar invited their leader, Dastur Mahyarji Rana, to explain Zoroastrianism to him. In the seventeenth century, Parsees established an energizing and immensely profitable association with European traders, especially the English. The chief broker of the English factory at Surat in 1660, for instance, was a Parsee, Rustom Manek, and it was to a Parsee, Kharshedji Pochaji, that the English entrusted, in 1664, the construction of their fort in Bombay. Thus began the community's ascent to prosperity and national prominence.

There are in Mughal accounts a few other sketches, brief and random, of several other Indian communities. Kashmiris, especially Kashmiri women, fascinated Bernier; he considered them as beautiful as the women of Europe and spent a good amount of his time (and money) in the engaging hobby of girl-watching in Kashmir. As for the men of Kashmir, they were, says Bernier, 'celebrated for wit, and considered much more intelligent and ingenious than the Indians.'

At the other end of the subcontinent from Kashmir were the 'Malabaris', the people of Kerala, whom Linschoten at the close of the sixteenth century considered as 'verie arrogant and proud, of colour altogether blacke, yet verie smooth both of haire and skinne, which commonly they anoynt with Oyle, to make it shine . . . Of Face, Bodie and Limbes, they are altogether like men of Europe, without any difference, but onley in colour. The men are commonly verie hairie, and rough upon the brest, and on their bodies.' Ralph Fitch found them bizarre, with 'horrible great eares, with many rings set with pearles and stones in them.'

BEYOND THE PALE of medieval Indian society were the untouchables. 'To give some conception of the infamy attached by the Hindus to these blacks, I will say that there are no words to express the vileness of the esteem in which they are held,' says Manucci. The outcastes passively accepted their lot, observes Ovington, and 'go thro' with their Drudgery without noise and concern.' In Kerala, outcastes were not allowed to get closer than about twenty metres to a high-caste Hindu, says Thevenot; a Nair could kill an untouchable if his breath fell on him. As for the forest tribes, they were regarded as no different from wild beasts. During the royal hunt, says William Finch, 'the beasts taken, if mans meat, are sold and the money given to the poore; if men, they remain the Kings slaves, which he yearely sends to Cabull to barter for horses and dogs; these beeing poore, miserable, theevish people that live in woods and desarts, little differing from beasts.' The Marathas, it is said, 'trapped and slew them (jungle tribes) in numbers as pests and outcasts.'

Slavery was also common in Mughal India, as in other parts of the medieval world. Enslaving the conquered people had the sanction of tradition among both Hindus and Muslims, and slaves were as numerous in the Hindu kingdom of Vijayanagar as in any Muslim state. Slaves abounded in Goa too, where, according to Linschoten, they 'were sold daily in the market like beasts.' During times of famine, children were often sold into slavery or hawked in the streets. A Persian envoy once bought a large number of slaves in India, for they were, says Bernier, 'extremely cheap' on account of the famine. The normal price of a slave in India was fifteen or twenty rupees, though at times it rose to as much as fifty rupees; a slave girl in Goa cost forty to sixty rupees. Insolvent debtors and tax defaulters were also enslaved; sometimes their wives and children were taken in payment of debts. Agricultural bondage was also common.

To be a slave was not, however, odious in the Muslim world. Many slaves rose to high positions in government, and some even rose to be sultans in Delhi before the Mughals. In the Deccan they—like Malik Amber, the de facto ruler of Ahmadnagar, who was originally a slave—continued to play a major role in politics in Mughal times. Slaves from Ethiopia (Habshis) were especially valued in the Deccan as eunuchs and bodyguards, and it was they who manned the local navies.

Akbar disfavoured slavery and 'forbid the restriction of personal liberty and the selling of slaves', says Abul Fazl. Elsewhere he amplifies: 'It had been the custom of the royal troops, in their victorious campaigns in India, to sell forcibly and keep in slavery the wives, children, and dependents of the natives. But His Majesty, actuated by his religious, prudent, and kindly feelings, now issued an order that no soldier of the Royal Army should act in this manner.'

Still, slavery persisted in India. In the mid-nineteenth century, the British, who had by then become the dominant power in India, formally abolished slavery, and the practice then gradually died out. There was no agitation against its abolition. Slavery has always been mild in India.

BY THE CLOSE of the seventeenth century, there were a fair number of Europeans all over India, in trading and political centres. The Portuguese were the first to arrive, in 1498, when Vasco da Gama landed in Calicut on the Kerala coast, seeking, as he put it, 'Christians and spices', and went on to rule the Indian seas in the name of Mammon and Christ. A century later, the Dutch arrived on the scene, and then came the English, the French and the Danes, while Portuguese power declined. As traders, Europeans were generally welcomed by Indian rulers, for the curiosities they brought from Europe—ranging from works of art to wine and pet dogs—as well as for the profit from their trade, and occasionally for military supplies like cannons and horses. Indian Muslim rulers also looked to them for protection of the overseas pilgrim traffic to Mecca.

Akbar was the first emperor to admit Europeans to the Mughal court, Jesuit priests whom he summoned from Goa to instruct him in Christianity and European culture. By the mid-seventeenth century, European professionals in various fields, especially artillerymen, were employed in growing numbers by Indian rulers. European gunners were a pampered class, who, says Manucci, 'only took aim; as for all the rest—the fatigue of raising, lowering, loading, and firing—this was the business of . . . labourers kept for the purpose.' Some of them were paid as much as 200 rupees a month, about fifteen times more than what was paid to Indian artillerymen. When Aurangzeb cut the European artillerymen to size by reducing their pay, and in addition required them to load the guns, several of them, including Manucci, left the imperial service.

Europeans in India were a motley lot—traders, professionals like physicians and jewellers, royal ambassadors, missionaries, adventurers, romantics, as well as cheats, vagabonds and desperadoes. The first English settler in India was probably Fr. T. Stevens, an Oxford-educated Jesuit missionary who landed in Goa in 1579, lived there for forty years, mastered the Marathi language, compiled its grammar and wrote in it an epic poem of 11,000 strophes titled Krishta Purana on the life and teachings of Christ. The letters of Stevens to his father in England, which were later published, are believed to have contributed to the growing British interest in India, roused already by legends of Portuguese adventures.

European physicians were favoured by the Mughal aristocracy, for most of them, like Bernier, were highly qualified, though some, like Manucci, the gunner-turned-physician, were shameless quacks. Such was the faith of Indians in the healing powers of Europeans that even quacks thrived sensationally. Once a surgeon accompanying Norris was called to attend to a man dead for several hours, which drew from the acerbic ambassador the comment that Indians were so ignorant that they believed the English could 'almost raise ye deade'.

A number of wild European adventurers, the dregs of European society, also began to descend on India around this time. 'They are of many nations, mostly thieves and criminals,' says Manucci. 'The Christians who served in the artillery of the Moguls retained of Christianity nothing but the mere name . . . were devoid of the fear of God, had ten or twelve wives, were constantly drunk, had no occupation but gambling and were eager to cheat whomsoever they could.' European pirates roamed the Indian seas, infamous desperadoes like William Kidd and Henry Bridgman (alias Evory), who terrorized the Indian seas at the turn of the seventeenth century. The most villainous of the lot were the Portuguese and half-caste pirates operating in the Bay of Bengal—'They were unworthy not merely of the names of Christians, but of men,' says Manucci.

Many Europeans in India adopted the Indian lifestyle, but many others, especially those from the upper classes, did not; they had no empathy for Mughal culture, and looked down on India with the pride of a resurgent

Europe. But then, Indians had no great regard for Europeans either. While Europeans saw themselves as major players in India, the Mughals regarded them as minor curiosities. Thus while Sir Thomas Roe, the British ambassador, and Captain Hawkins, the presumed ambassador, claimed intimacy with Jahangir, and their journals are full of lore about their relationships with the emperor, there is not even a passing word about either of them in the 745-page long (in English translation) memoirs of Jahangir, though the visits of Persian ambassadors are described in detail, and even the missions from petty Central Asian potentates are noted. European powers did not amount to much in Mughal estimation.

Chapter Two

THE RIGHT ROYAL LIFESTYLE

The Emperor at Work

THE MUGHAL EMPIRE at its height covered some 4.5 million square kilometres, a vast and varied land with countless people and untold wealth. And all that was the property of one man, the emperor, for him to do as he pleased.

The formal justification for the exercise of absolute power by the emperor was that he worked for the good of the people. 'It is my duty not to think of my own happiness except so far as it is inseparably connected with the happiness of the people,' claimed Aurangzeb. But since the good of the people was in the emperor's eyes indistinguishable from the good of the empire, and the empire indistinguishable from the emperor, in practice it was only the interests of the emperor that prevailed—in the happiness of the king was the happiness of the people!

But the happiness of the king was not in the easily sated pleasures of the common human pursuit, but in power and glory, to be won by the sword, preserved by the sword, by ceaseless exertion. The only benefit that a ruler could look forward to in life, Aurangzeb maintained, was 'the gaining of fame'. All the Mughal emperors, except Humayun, were extremely hard-working, even the hedonistic Jahangir during most of his reign. 'I . . . have looked on ease of body as something unlawful for me,' says Jahangir. The price of ease was the throne, perhaps even the head.

The emperor worked tirelessly, but the distinction between his work and play was ambiguous. Were Akbar's wakeful nights of philosophical inquiry work or play? And what about his polo games, which Abul Fazl maintains were a means for the emperor to assess the character and spirit of imperial officers? Hunting, the favourite sport of the Mughals, was quite often a warm-up for battle. And wasn't the emperor's patronage of the arts and crafts as much a public service as a private indulgence? The same could be said of his patronage of religion. His sex life too was of public concern, for to beget heirs was a crucial obligation of the king. Akbar, claims Abul Fazl, did not spend any time at all 'idly or uselessly'. This in a sense was true. The emperor's work was not external to him.

His life was his work. The Mughal emperor, of course, lived in extravagant luxury—'In the Mogul kingdom the nobles, and above all the king, live with such ostentation that the most sumptuous European courts cannot compare in richness and magnificence with the lustre beheld in the Indian court,' says Manucci—but this too was a requirement of his office, not a matter of personal gratification. The crown was not worn for comfort.

The pomp and magnificence of the emperor's lifestyle was an essential display of the grandeur of the empire, an expression of the mystique of power that distanced the emperor from his subjects and inspired awe and devotion in them. In the same spirit, various regalia, even particular sports, were reserved exclusively for the emperor, or for him to confer as privileges on others—the use of the crimson tent, the beating of the kettle-drum, the prerogative to hunt the lion, to order elephant fights, and so on. Jahangir extended the exclusivity to royal apparel. 'Having adopted for myself certain special clothes and cloth-stuffs,' says Jahangir, 'I gave an order that no one should wear the same but he on whom I might bestow them.'

The royal mystique insulated the emperor. But the mystique was only a shroud. Beneath it was a hard core of endeavour and achievement. Not surprisingly, the emperor's life, in contrast to the absolute and arbitrary power that he enjoyed, was marked by discipline rather than wilfulness. His daily routine, for instance, was organized into so rigid a schedule that, notes Roe, it was 'as regular as a clock that striks at sett howers'. A water-clock kept the time at the court. 'Everything that goes on in the palace is regulated by this clock,' says Monserrate.

The emperor's routine was of course what he decided himself, and he could alter it to suit his convenience or mood. Thus Akbar, who usually held the public durbar soon after the first watch of the day, around 9 a.m., sometimes held it, says Abul Fazl, 'towards the close of day, or at night'. Some days, instead of attending to his regularly scheduled work, the emperor went out in the afternoons to hunt or for a boat ride on the Yamuna. But these were exceptions. Normally the emperor strictly followed his routine, whether he was in the capital or in camp, except when he was actually on the march or in the midst of a war. Even when sick he tried to keep to the schedule at least in a token manner, for it was his routine, like an engine turning gears, that activated the administration of the empire—if the emperor ceased to work, or if he worked haphazardly, it would throw the entire imperial administration out of gear. In his unvarying routine was the assurance of his subjects that everything was all right with the emperor and therefore with the empire.

Akbar, according to the detailed account of his daily routine given by Abul Fazl, spent two hours in devotions; about an hour and twenty minutes on his toilet and dressing; about four and half hours in durbar; 'offices of decency' and meals occupied less than one hour; about an hour and forty-five minutes were spent 'with elephants, horses, camels and mules and the like', checking their maintenance and grooming; he spent about six hours in the harem, looking into the 'affairs of his secluded wives, and of the other chaste ladies who make petitions to him'; and he slept for about seven and a half hours.

The main elements of the emperor's daily routine were the darshan (in which he presented himself to public view at dawn), the public durbar, the private durbar, the cabinet meeting, and a session in the harem to do confidential work and to deal with palace affairs. He also had to observe the various mandatory Islamic prayers and rites. How much time the emperor spent on these different activities, and how they were fitted into his daily schedule depended on his personal inclination, and varied from ruler to ruler. Aurangzeb, for instance, spent more time in prayers and the reading of the Koran than his predecessors; he also woke up later than most others (at around 5 a.m., instead of the usual 4 a.m.) and retired to the harem for the night earlier (at around 8 p.m., instead of 8.30 p.m., as Shah Jahan did); on the other hand, his lunch-and-siesta break was shorter, about two hours, instead of, for example, Shah Jahan's four hours.

Apart from the emperor's daily schedule, there was also a weekly schedule, in which his different functions (such as the administration of justice, looking into matters of religion and so on) were assigned to different days. Humayun had initially made these allocations on an astrological basis, but his successors altered them according to their disposition. The only fixed rule was that there would be no court on Fridays, the day of the Muslim sabbath; Aurangzeb made Thursday into a half working day. Wednesdays were usually reserved for judicial matters.

THE EMPEROR'S DAY began well before sunrise, usually at around 4 a.m., when he woke up to the sound of music played by 'musicians of all nations', says Abul Fazl. Humayun in his hard times had a simpler arrangement. 'It was the custom of his Majesty always to keep a Cock in the Ewry,' recalls Jauhar, 'for the purpose of awaking the servants early in the morning: it was a beautiful white bird, and the King used frequently to feed it with raisins.'

After his ablutions, the emperor dressed and (in the case of Shah Jahan in Agra) walked to the private chapel attached to the palace, the Pearl Mosque, to read the Koran, say his morning prayers, and spend a little time in quiet meditation. Then he returned to his rooms and, as the sun rose over the horizon, appeared, bathed in the glancing first light of the day, at the *jharokha-i-darshan*, an ornate bay-window (or balcony) on the eastern wall of the palace overlooking the Yamuna, to acknowledge the greetings of the men gathered in the maidan there. The darshan was an old Hindu custom, adopted by Humayun but given its sunrise timing by Akbar. The practice, being un-Islamic, was abolished by Aurangzeb, but it served an important practical purpose in reassuring the public that the emperor was alive and well. If the emperor did not appear at the jharokha even for a day, it made the people restive, spawned wild rumours, and sometimes set off riots. For this reason, says Jahangir, 'even in the time of weakness I have gone every day to the jharokha, though in great pain and sorrow, according to my fixed custom.'

The emperor usually spent about three-quarters of an hour at the jharokha, inspecting newly captured elephants, reviewing the contingents of mansabdars, watching elephant fights, cavalry parades and other spectacles, and also attending to the supplications of the common people, who could attach their petitions to a string let down from the fort. Sometimes people gathered outside the jharokha for protest demonstrations, as in 1641, when a mass of starving people in Lahore pleaded with Shah Jahan for famine relief, and in 1679, when Hindus protested against the imposition of jizya by Aurangzeb. Jahangir usually went right back to bed for a nap after a brief darshan at sunrise, to appear again at the jharokha at noon, to watch elephant fights and parades. Akbar himself, says Abul Fazl, was in the habit of returning to his private apartments in the morning to 'repose a little'.

After the darshan, the next public function of the emperor was the durbar held in the Diwan-i-am, the hall of public audience. The time of the durbar varied. Akbar usually held it at around 9 a.m., while Jahangir preferred an afternoon session; Shah Jahan held it at 7.40 a.m., and Aurangzeb at 9.15 a.m. Sometimes there was also a second session later in the day. 'The King presenteth himselfe thrice every daie without faile to his nobles,' says Coryat about Jahangir's routine; 'at the rising of the sunne, which he adoreth by the elevation of his hands; at noone; and at five of the clocke in the evening.'

Akbar and Jahangir held the public durbar in a courtyard of the Agra palace, where courtiers and supplicants gathered under awnings, but Shah Jahan erected there a magnificent, forty-pillared Diwan-i-am, roughly sixty-one by twenty metres, built of red sandstone and painted a lustrous white. The hall was open on three sides, and had on its closed eastern side, abutting the palace, the throne alcove, a recessed balcony placed at a height higher than a man could reach, built of pure white marble and decorated with inlays of semi-precious stones.

On special occasions, like the emperor's birthday and the anniversary of his coronation, the durbar hall was virtually turned into a jewelled casket. 'The pillars of the hall were hung with brocades of gold ground, and flowered satin canopies were raised over the whole expanse of the extensive apartment fastened with red silken cords, from which were suspended large tassels of silk and gold,' writes Bernier about a celebratory scene in the Delhi citadel early in the reign of Aurangzeb. 'The floor was covered entirely with carpets of the richest silk, of immense length and breadth. A tent . . . was pitched outside, larger than the hall, to which it was joined by the top. It spread over half the court, and was completely enclosed by a great balustrade, covered with plates of silver.' The arcaded galleries of the Diwan i am courtyard were given over to amirs, as a privilege, to decorate, which they did at great expense and in a competitive spirit.

During the durbar, the emperor's personal attendants and royal standard bearers stood immediately below the throne balcony, carrying the imperial ensign (described by Careri as 'a Gold Ball between two Gilt Hands, hanging by a chain') and the imperial standard (a yak's tail) as well as several flags and totems: a fish, a dragon, a lion, hands, scales 'and several more . . . to which the Indians attach a certain mystic meaning,' says Bernier. Eunuchs with fly-whisks and fans attended on the emperor, and he was guarded by a squad of armed sergeants under a sheriff. The very bearing of these attendants defined the ambience of the durbar; they, notes Bernier, stood there 'with undivided attention and profound humility to perform the different services allotted to each.'

High decorum was maintained in the durbar, with the courtiers standing in their precisely allotted places, group by group and rank by rank. The top amirs, rajas and ambassadors stood closest to the royal balcony, in an area marked off by a low silver railing; the next rank stood behind them, within a red lacquered wood railing, and beyond them the servants of amirs and foot soldiers, 'all standing, their eyes bent downward, and their hands crossed . . . [in a] posture of profound reverence,' says Bernier. 'The remainder of the spacious room, and indeed the whole courtyard, is filled with persons of all ranks, high and low, rich and poor; because it is in this extensive hall that the King gives audience indiscriminately to all his subjects.' Entrance into the various sections of the hall was controlled by mace-bearing sentries and sergeants-at-arms in colourful uniforms. There was music in the background, says Tavernier, 'so sweet and soft, that it never takes off the mind from the seriousness of business at that time managed.'

A mid-seventeenth-century Mughal painting of Shah Jahan's durbar shows an elegant assemblage of amirs, a handsome, aristocratic lot, colourfully dressed, with well-groomed beards or moustaches, all looking alert and cheerful. There were usually several foreign ambassadors among the courtiers, for, as Bernier says, 'the Great Mogol is in the habit of detaining all ambassadors as long as can reasonably be done, from an idea that it is becoming his grandeur and power, to receive the homage of foreigners, and to number them among the attendants of his court.' The throne, a broad divan, was gilded and studded with gems, and the emperor sat cross-legged on it, leaning against bolsters. His sons stood to one side of the throne, on the balcony.

On either side of the throne balcony were windows with marble grills, from which the ladies of the palace could watch the durbar in privacy, and there were similar arrangements for them when the emperor held durbar in camp. Once, when Roe was attending Jahangir's durbar at his Ajmer camp, he could sense the presence of the begums behind a screen of reeds at one of the windows overlooking the assembly area. 'At one side in a window were his two Principal Wives, whose curiositie made them breake little holes in a grate of Reed that hung before it, to gaze on mee. I saw first their fingers, and after laying their faces close nowe one eye, nowe another; sometyme I could discerne the full proportion,' writes Roe. 'They were indifferently white, black hayre smoothed up; but if I had no other light, their diamonds and pearles had sufficed to show them. When I looked up they retyred, and were so merry that I supposed they laughed at mee.'

THE EMPEROR ENTERED the throne balcony through the door at its back, to a flourish of kettledrums. 'When His Majesty seats himself on the throne,' says Abul Fazl, 'all that are present perform the kornish, and then remain standing at their places, according to their rank, with their arms crossed, partaking in the light of his imperial countenance, of the elixir of life, and enjoying everlasting happiness in standing ready for any service.'

Sir Thomas Roe, seeing Jahangir in durbar, thought the scene was stagy and that the emperor looked like a costumed king in a London play. The theatricality was deliberate, and it was matched by a highly formal court etiquette, both of which served to demonstrate and enhance the emperor's pre-eminence and glory.

'The silence preserved [in the Mughal court] was astonishing, and the order devoid of confusion,' notes Manucci, who notes that officials with gold and silver batons in hand took care 'that throughout the court nothing was done which could displease the king.' 'No person,' says Tavernier, 'is to leave the durbar or move from his place as long as the emperor is there, without special permission.' Court etiquette and protocol were prescribed in minute detail and strictly enforced: how to stand before the emperor, how to sit, how to salute him, how to receive orders or favours— or punishment—and so on. There was even a dress code. 'Blue may not be worne in his (the emperor's) presence,' says Terry, for that was the colour of mourning, 'nor the name of death sounded in his ears; but such casually is mollified by termes to this purpose: Such an one hath made himselfe a sacrifice at Your Majesties feet.'

Decorum in dress was expected of courtiers, and violators were liable to be humiliated or punished. Says Aurangzeb in a letter: 'Today Marhamat Khan came into my presence, having put on a rich dress. The skirt of his robe was so long that his feet were not visible. I ordered Muharam Khan to curtail two inches of the skirt of that foolish Khan . . . The skirt must be of the same length that has been fixed by the court custom . . . A man should put on a simple and durable dress.'

The correct manner of standing before the emperor on being called by him was with arms crossed, the fingertips of the left hand touching the right elbow and those of the right hand touching the left elbow, signifying that the officer was ready to receive and obey the orders of the emperor. An acceptable alternative was to stand with the fingers of each hand tucked under the upper arm of the opposite side and the lower arms resting horizontally on the cummerbund. The officer usually stood at attention, with his feet close together, but sometimes the right foot was crossed over the left, with only its toes touching the ground. Shoes were left outside the durbar hall.

No one, except sometimes the crown prince, was allowed to sit before the emperor in the public durbar, though amirs were usually invited to sit at private and informal gatherings. This was the custom from the time of Babur, who notes in his memoirs his resentment over an Afghan amir asking to be allowed to sit in the durbar. The practice became more rigorous under Akbar. 'From Akbar's days . . . Mogul kings accord seats to no one,' says Manucci, 'and do not take a letter direct from the hand of any man. Letters are delivered to the Vizier, and he reads them to the king.' The only recorded deviation from the rule requiring everyone to stand before the emperor in durbar was the favour that Akbar showed to an elder relative, Sulaiman Mirza, the fugitive king of Badakshan, who was invited by the emperor to sit beside him on the throne.

The traditional mode of saluting the emperor was the kornish, in which the courtier placed the palm of his right hand on his forehead and bowed his head, indicating, as Badauni puts it, that the saluter had 'placed his head into the hand of humility'. Humayun introduced a variation of the kornish, called taslim, which consisted of 'placing the back of the right hand on the ground, and then raising it gently till the person stands erect, when he puts the palm of his hand upon the crown of his head, which pleasing manner of saluting signifies that he is ready to give himself as an offering,' says Abul Fazl. 'Upon taking leave, or presentation, or upon receiving a mansab, a jagir or a dress of honour or an elephant or a horse, the rule is to make three taslims, but only one on all other occasions, when salaries are paid or presents made.'

Humayun also introduced in the Mughal court the custom of prostration before the emperor, called sijda. 'When he arrived at Agra,' writes Badauni, 'he imposed upon the populace a new self-invented form of salutation, and wished them to kiss the ground (before him).' This was a variation of a common Hindu practice— Badauni was wrong in attributing the innovation to Humayun—which was first adopted in the Muslim court in Delhi by Balban in the mid-thirteenth century. Unlike the full prostration practised by Hindus, sijda involved only kneeling down and bending over to touch the ground with the forehead. In Akbar's reign, courtiers looked 'upon a prostration before His Majesty as a prostration performed before God,' writes Abul Fazl, 'for royalty is an emblem of the power of God, and a light-shedding ray from this Sun of the Absolute.'

This worshipful attitude of the courtiers, and the fact that sijda resembled a posture of Islamic prayer, upset orthodox Muslims and made 'dark-minded men' misconstrue it as man-worship, says Abul Fazl. Akbar, therefore, forbade anyone from performing the sijda in the open court, but his personal attendants and disciples were permitted to do so 'in the private assembly . . . when they receive the order of seating themselves.' Jahangir had no such inhibition about sijda, and the practice was common during his reign. Religious leaders and holy men were excused from all obsequious salutations, though many performed them in private, to cadge royal favour, and maybe sometimes out of genuine reverence.

Courtesies as at the court were required of amirs even when they received royal presents or firmans at their provincial posts, as if the emperor himself were present there. Manucci reports that even dependent rulers, like 'the kings of Bijapur and Golconda, and the Rana, when the Mogul king sent them *sarapas* (head-to-foot ceremonial dresses), were under obligation to come out one league from their capital and be invested with the robes, after making obeisance three times, as usual in Hindustan, with their face turned in the direction of the court and letters [bearing the royal orders] placed on the top of their head.'

SPECIAL CEREMONIES WERE prescribed for the reception of a great noble returning to the court after an absence of some years. From the gate of the palace complex he would be escorted in by the 'Vizir and Lieutenant-Generall and Knight Martiall,' notes Hawkins. 'Then he is brought to the gate of the outermost rayles ... where he standeth in the view of the King, in the middest betweene these two nobles. Then he toucheth the ground with his hand and also ... his head, very gravely, and doth thus three times. This done, he kneeleth downe touching the ground with his forehead; which being once done, he is carried forward towards the King, and in the midway he is made to doe this reverence againe. Then he commeth to the doore of the red rayles, doing the like reverence ...; and having thus done, he commeth within the red rayles and doth it once more upon the carpets. Then the King commandeth him to come up the stakes or ladder of seven steppes ... where the King most lovingly embraceth him before all the people, whereby they shall take notice that he is in the King's favour.' If however the amir had been summoned to court out of royal displeasure, he was required to remain in his house till he was called to trial.

Court ceremonies were raised to an even higher level of pageantry during the visits of foreign dignitaries. Thus when Sulaiman Mirza arrived in Fatehpur Sikri to seek refuge, Akbar along with his amirs advanced some sixteen kilometres to receive him. 'And on that day 5000 elephants, some with housings of European velvet, and some with Turkish cloth of gold, and some with chains of gold and silver, and, with black and white fringes hung on their heads and necks, were drawn up in line on both sides: also Arabian and Persian horses with golden saddles of like splendour,' says Badauni. 'And between each pair of elephants they placed a car of cheetahs with golden collars, and coverings of velvet and fine linen, and an oxen car with fillets of embroidered gold.' Nizamuddin Ahmad adds that 'when all the arrangements were made, the Emperor went out with great pomp and splendour. Upon approaching, the Mirza hastened to dismount, and ran forward to His Majesty; but the emperor, observing the venerable age of the Mirza, alighted from his horse, and would not allow the Mirza to go through the usual observances and ceremonies. He fondly embraced him; then he mounted and made the Mirza ride on his right hand . . . and on reaching the palace he seated him by his side on the throne.' Persian ambassadors were also usually accorded similar receptions, though on a lesser scale, and without the emperor himself going out to receive them, or allowing them to sit in the durbar.

Foreign ambassadors, especially those from alien cultures, like Europeans, were usually permitted to salute the emperor in the manner of their own country. Thus British ambassadors Sir Thomas Roe (in the reign of Jahangir) and William Norris (in the reign of Aurangzeb) were allowed to greet the emperor in the English fashion. Sometimes, however, efforts were made to pressurize ambassadors from Muslim kingdoms to conform to the Mughal style of salutation, as Aurangzeb is said to have insisted of the Persian ambassador in 1661. Ambassadors usually negotiated protocol matters—including the gifts to be offered to the emperor—with Mughal officials before presenting themselves at the court.

During royal celebrations, such as the emperor's lunar and solar birthdays or the anniversary of his accession, it was customary for amirs to offer presents to the emperor, usually in proportion to their income and status—to give less would be a grave breach of courtesy, to give more was a means of winning royal favour. 'Some of them, indeed, take that opportunity of presenting gifts of extraordinary magnificence, sometimes for the sake of an ostentatious display, sometimes to divert the King from instituting an inquiry into the exactions committed in their official situations or governments, and sometimes to gain the favour of the King, and by that means obtain an increase in salary,' says Bernier. 'Some present fine pearls, diamonds, emeralds, or rubies; others again give a quantity of gold coins.'

By a regulation of Akbar, even the poor when approaching the emperor had to offer him something, whatever trifle it might be, as a homage, to establish the subject/sovereign relationship. And when the emperor went out riding, it was customary for nobles living on the way to stand outside their residences and offer him presents—once Roe, having nothing on hand to offer when Jahangir passed by, presented him with a map.

The emperor himself spent vast sums of money on gifts, to show favour or compassion. Abul Fazl records that Akbar kept a crore dams (250,000 rupees) always ready in the palace for giving away as gifts, 'every thousand of which . . . [was] kept in bags.' Casual rewards were ordinarily thrown unceremoniously into a chute tied from the throne balcony to the floor. Thus when Coryat delivered an oration in Persian in praise of Jahangir, 'He (the emperor) threw downe from a windowe through which he looked out, into a sheete tied up by the foure corners, and hanging very neer the ground, a hundred peeces of silver, each worth two shillings sterling, which countervailed ten pounds of our English money,' writes Coryat. Any trifling matter that pleased the emperor merited a reward. Jahangir once gifted a horse to a man who brought him his favourite fish; another time he conferred 'land, a horse, cash and clothing' on a man who pointed out that the name Jahangir had the same numerical value as Allah Akbar.

The custom of the emperor presenting to favoured courtiers a portrait of himself on a pendant was introduced by Akbar, and was common in the reign of Jahangir. 'All the great men . . . weare the kings Image (which none may doe but to whom it is given) . . . a meddall of gould as bigg as sixpence, with a little chayne of 4 inches to fasten it to their head, which at their own Chardge some sett with stones or garnishe with pendant Pearles,' says Roe, who had himself received the medal from Jahangir. This was an exceptional honour. Usually, to show favour, the emperor presented a *sarapa,* and in special cases a dress he himself had worn. Roe was thus honoured by Jahangir once. 'A cloth of gould Cloake of his owne, once or Twice worne . . . hee caused to bee put on my back,' says Roe. '. . . it is here reputed the highest of fauor to give a garment worne by the prince, or, being New, once layed upon his shoulder.'

The assembly at the Diwan-i-am was, as a modern writer puts it, 'the king-in-court transacting State business in public'. It was at the Diwan-i-am that the emperor received foreign ambassadors, accepted the submission of local rulers, dealt with captured rebels, announced major appointments and promotions, conferred royal gifts and charitable grants, and settled financial matters. It was here too that royal justice was administered. The public had access to the emperor in durbar and could submit petitions to him, though they usually needed some amir to draw the emperor's attention to their case.

The first item of business in the durbar was usually the reading and confirming of the previous day's orders. Then the extracts of dispatches from the provinces were read out to the emperor. These were often rambling accounts, vital information and trivia jumbled together. For instance, the news-writer of Junnar once reported, along with various official matters, that 'a son was born to a zemindar, having two branches or horns of the length of a finger on his head. The child died after two days. A woman delivered a daughter with a black head and face and red and white nose; the child lived.' Diplomatic exchanges too were read in the open court.

For all its high ceremonial, the durbar was also something of a variety show, in which, apart from weighty official matters, private disputes and even love tangles were at times brought before the emperor for decision. After the administrative work in the durbar was over, there were, says Bernier, parades of animals and demonstrations of skill by youthful officers in such feats as slashing through a dead sheep 'without entrails and neatly bound up'. In case the tempo of work in the durbar grew slack, there were always wrestlers and tumblers on hand to enliven the dull interludes. Sometimes freaks were brought into the durbar for the emperor's amusement. Once, reports Abul Fazl, a man was brought before Akbar 'who had no shape of ears and no orifice, yet . . . heard perfectly what was said to him'—the emperor sanctioned him a daily allowance. Now and then children were brought to the emperor for naming.

AFTER THE PUBLIC durbar, which usually lasted a couple of hours, depending on the volume of work, the emperor went into the Diwan-i-khas, the hall of private audience, to meet with his top officials—the executive heads of the empire—and foreign ambassadors. Only a select few had the privilege of crossing the Lai Purdah (crimson curtain) to enter the Diwan-i-khas, and even amirs had to renew their passes 'every moone', according to William Finch. Under Jahangir, courtiers entering this hall were sniffed by guards for alcohol—not because Jahangir disapproved of drinking, but because there was serious work ahead, and probably also because alcohol-fouled breath offended the emperor.

At the Diwan-i-khas, the meeting was more informal and the work often more serious than at the public durbar. Sometimes there were even heated exchanges there, as when Roe complained to Jahangir about the treatment he was receiving from Asaf Khan and Shah Jahan. Courtiers were allowed to sit during the private durbar, but while the emperor sat cross-legged on the throne, they had to sit in the *duzanu* style, by first kneeling down upright and then lowering themselves gently on their heels, their extended hands resting on their knees. This was how men sat in polite society, and it was considered presumptuous for anyone to sit cross-legged like the emperor, even outside the court.

Confidential matters were transacted at the Diwan-i-khas, with the emperor often personally writing out the orders, to show favour to an official or to indicate the seriousness of the matter at hand. Firmans were drafted here, revised, and a final draft prepared, and then sent into the harem to affix the royal seal. It was during this session that Shah Jahan examined architectural plans, a matter of considerable importance to him; if there was time, he also inspected the works of artists and artisans. The meeting at the Diwan-i-khas usually lasted a couple of hours.

It was the practice of Shah Jahan to move from the Diwan-i-khas to the Shah-burj (Royal Tower) for a meeting of what might be called his inner cabinet, consisting of the topmost few officials and the princes. This cabinet room had previously been called Ghusl-khana (Bathroom) from Sher Shah's custom of meeting with his top officials there when he dried his hair after the bath. This session, which began just before noon, lasted less than an hour, and then Shah Jahan retired into the harem for lunch and an hour-long siesta. Waking, he dealt with matters of harem administration, including providing for indigent supplicants who had sought the intercession of the begums.

Around 3 p.m., Shah Jahan performed his *asar* prayer, then returned to the Diwan-i-am to transact the remaining public business and to review the palace guards. After this he, along with his top amirs, moved once again to the Diwan-i-khas—now lit up 'with fragrant candles set in jewelled candelabra'—for the sunset prayer and a couple of hours of work. Around 8 p.m. Shah Jahan held another meeting at the Shah-burj, if there was work. Sometimes, when the administrative work was over, the meeting transformed itself into a soiree, with musicians coming in to perform before the emperor, and occasionally Shah Jahan himself joining in the singing. Shah Jahan never drank at these sessions—in fact, he very seldom drank wine—but Jahangir took to his cups after the day's work was over, sometimes during the working session itself, which affected the transaction of business, according to Roe.

At about 8.30 p.m. Shah Jahan went into the harem for the night. But there was still work for him, for it was then, according to Manucci, that he examined the reports of the secret news-writers of the empire, who sent in their reports once a week. 'These news-letters are commonly read in the king's presence by women of the *mahal* at about nine o'clock in the evening, so that by this means he knows what is going on in his kingdom,' says Manucci. 'There are, in addition, spies, who are obliged to send in reports weekly about other important business, chiefly what the princes are doing, and this duty they perform through written statements.'

After the long day's work was done, Shah Jahan relaxed for a while, listening to harem musicians. Then he retired to bed and drifted to sleep, lulled by pleasant-voiced readers sitting behind a screen and reading to him his favourite books—books on travel, biographies of saints and prophets, and histories; Shah Jahan was particularly fond of Babur's memoirs and the biography of Timur. 'During sleep he is guarded by women slaves, very brave, and highly skilled in the management of the bow and other arms,' says Manucci.

A record of everything that was said and done by the emperor, whether in public or in private, however trivial the matter might be, was maintained by his secretaries. 'Whatever he doth, either without or within, drunken or sober, he hath writers who by turnes set downe everything in writing which he doth,' says Hawkins, 'so that there is nothing passeth in his lifetime which is not noted, no, not so much as his going to the necessary, and how often he lieth with his women, and with whom.'

A Movable City

THE MUGHAL IMPERIAL capital was a movable city. Virtually the whole royal establishment, household as well as official, shifted to camp with the emperor, with staff, records and treasury. His harem moved with him, and so did his artists and artisans, musicians and dancers, even his menagerie and his library. The entire court and the central armed forces moved with him, along with all those dependent on the court and the army, with countless women and servants, camp-followers several times as numerous as the army, artisans and traders and hangers-on with their women and children and all their belongings, and an immense number and variety of animals and carts. The bazaar people, says Bernier, 'when they travel take with them, like our gypsies, the whole of their families, goods, and chattels.'

The royal establishment and the army were the primary means of livelihood of the people of the capital, so they necessarily had to shift with the emperor. So immense was the swarm of people travelling with the emperor that they seemed to Terry like 'a walking republic'. It took the multitude as much as twelve hours to cross a point, despite it being spread out on a broad front, says Terry. According to Bernier, the Mughal camp had about 100,000 horsemen and 200,000 animals comprising horses, mules, elephants and camels. In addition, there were several thousand animals, mostly oxen, belonging the traders. Bernier was told that the royal camp accommodated in all some three or four hundred thousand persons. 'The multitude is prodigious and almost incredible,' says Bernier.

The emperor and the high nobles travelled with two complete sets of tents. 'The king uses two pavilions,' says Monserrate, 'identical in size and appearance, which are employed for alternate marches, one being carried on ahead, while he occupies the other,' so that when he arrived at the new campsite everything would be in perfect readiness for him. According to Abul Fazl, 100 elephants, 500 camels, 400 carts, and 100 bearers were required to transport each set of Akbar's personal camping equipment and paraphernalia. Even puritanical Aurangzeb required about sixty elephants, 200 camels, 100 mules and 100 porters. An elephant-drawn cart with several bathrooms was part of Akbar's travel equipment, but Humayun during his wanderings in Rajasthan once had to make do with 'two hurdles' fixed up as royal privy, says Jauhar.

Akbar's advance camping equipment was escorted by a military contingent and was tended by '500 pioneers, 100 water carriers, 50 carpenters, tent-makers and torch-bearers, 30 workers in leather, and 150 sweepers,' according to Abul Fazl. The bulky gear was packed on elephants, smaller tents on camels, luggage and kitchen utensils on mules. Lighter and more valuable articles (such as the porcelain for the emperor's table) were carried by porters. In the hill country, such as Kashmir, porters instead of carts and pack-animals carried the equipment, and, according to Bernier, the emperor alone needed 'no fewer than six thousand' porters in the reign of Aurangzeb.

When the emperor moved camp, the first to move out was the royal kitchen. 'It is the custom of the court,' says Manucci, 'when the king is to march the next day, at ten o'clock of the night the royal kitchen should start. It consists of fifty camels, and fifty well-fed cows to give milk. Also there are sent dainties in charge of cooks (from each one of whom the preparation of only one dish is required) . . . sealed up in bags of Malacca velvet . . .'

The general movement began very early next morning. 'At three o'clock in the morning the march began,' reports Manucci about what he saw in Aurangzeb's camp. 'First went the heavy artillery, which always marches in front, and is drawn up as an avenue through which to enter the next camp. With it went a handsome boat upon a large cart to ferry the royal person across any river when necessary. Then followed the baggage. In this way, when the morning broke, the camp was free, leaving only the cavalry and infantry, each in its appropriate position. With the rest, in addition to the other transport, went two hundred camels, loaded with silver rupees, and each camel carrying four hundred and eighty pounds' weight of silver; one hundred camels loaded with gold coins, each carrying the same weight; and one hundred and fifty camels loaded with nets used in hunting tigers . . . The royal office of record also was there . . . and this required eighty camels, thirty elephants, and twenty carts, loaded with the registers and papers of account of the empire. In addition to these there were fifty camels carrying water, each camel bearing two full metal vessels for the royal use.'

'Attending on the king are eight mules carrying small tents, which are used on the march when the king desired to rest, or to eat a little something, or for any particular necessity,' continues Manucci. 'Along with them are two mules carrying clothes, and one mule loaded with essences of various odoriferous flowers . . . Again, there marched close to the baggage one thousand labourers, with axes, mattocks, spades and pick-axes to clear any difficult passage. Their commanders ride on horseback carrying in their hands their badges of office, which are either an axe or a mattock in silver. On arriving at the place appointed for the royal halt, they put up the tents and place in position the heavy artillery. When the light artillery comes up, it is placed around the royal tents.'

AT DAYBREAK, THE emperor emerged from his tent to the flourish of the royal band and the hail of the assembled amirs, whose salutation *Padshah sala'mat*! (Hail the King!), says Roe, was so loud 'as would have out cryed cannons'. Says Manucci: 'When the king comes out of his tent to begin a march, the princes, nobles, and generals throng round to pay him court . . . They accompany the king to the end of the camp in which they had halted for the day, then each departs to his proper place in his own division.'

The emperor dressed grandly for the road, for when he travelled he was not just journeying from one place to another, but ceremonially parading through the empire. 'On his head he wore a rich turbant with a plume of herne tops, not many but long; on one syde hung a ruby unsett, as bigg as a walnutt; on the other syde a diamond as great; in the middle an emralld like a hart, much bigger,' says Roe about Jahangir setting out from Ajmer for Mandu. 'His shash was wreathed about with a chayne of great pearle, rubyes, and diamonds drild. About his neck hee carried a chaine of most excellent pearle, three double (so great I never saw); at his elbowes, armletts sett with diamonds; and on his wrists three rowes of several sorts. His hand bare, but almost on every finger a ring; his gloves, which were English, stuck under his girdle; his coate of cloth of gould without sleeves upon a fine semian as thin as lawne; on his feete a payre of embrodered buskings with pearle, the toes sharp and tuning up.' He wore a sword and buckler 'sett all over with great diamonds and rubyes, the belts of gould suteable . . .'

On this occasion Jahangir travelled in a coach and four, an exact replica of an English coach presented to him by Roe, except for coverings which were of 'gold velvet' from Persia. 'I marched in sound health from Ajmer in a European carriage drawn by four horses,' Jahangir writes in his memoirs, 'and I ordered several nobles to make up carriages similar to it, and to attend upon me with them.' The choice of the carriage was not whimsical. 'It is customary in India,' writes Jahangir, 'when a king, prince, or noble undertakes an expedition towards the east, to ride on an elephant with long tusks; when towards the west, to ride a horse of one colour; when towards the north, to go in a litter or palki (palanquin); when towards the south, to go in a carriage drawn by bullocks.' Jahangir substituted horses for oxen.

The emperor's coach horses were 'trapped and harnessed in gold velvets', and were attended to by an English coachman, 'who was clothed as rich as any player and more gaudy,' notes Roe. Before Jahangir entered the carriage, an attendant brought 'a mighty carp', and another brought 'a dish of white stuff like starch', into which the emperor dipped his finger, then touched the fish with the finger and marked his forehead with the 'white stuff', says Roe.

Jahangir's use of a horse-drawn carriage was unusual, for the ox, not the horse, was the common draft animal in India. 'Coaches for the kinge's owne use, whereof 2 only are drawne by 2 horses' and 'the rest by Oxen some of Extraordinarie greatnes, and some again as little, chosen of purpose,' says Roe. Normally the emperor travelled in a howdah, which Bernier describes as 'an oval chair with a canopy on pillars, also superbly decorated with colours and gold'. Riding the elephant, says Bernier, 'is by far the most striking and splendid style of travelling, as nothing can surpass the richness and magnificence of the harness and trappings.' If the emperor wanted to sleep on the way, he travelled in an elephant-mounted cabin called *mekdambar*, which, says Bernier, was like 'a small house, or square wooden tower, gilt and painted'—this was Jahangir's preferred mode of travel, to be gently rocked to sleep by the swaying gait of the elephant. Sometimes the emperor rode a horse, especially if inclined for hunting and if the weather was fine.

Aurangzeb's favourite mode of travel in his old age was the field throne presented to him by the Dutch, 'a species of magnificent tabernacle, with painted and gilt pillars and glass windows, that are kept shut when the weather is bad,' reports Bernier. 'The four poles of this litter are covered either with scarlet or brocade, and decorated with deep fringes of silk and gold. At the end of each pole are stationed two strong and handsomely dressed men, who are relieved by other men constantly in attendance.' Alternately, the emperor used a palanquin.

When the emperor travelled in a palanquin, footmen continually sprinkled water on the road in front of him to prevent dust from rising, and no rider was allowed to get closer than one furlong to the emperor, only those on foot being allowed near. By whatever mode the emperor travelled, unsightly things on his way—corpses of men or beasts—which might be displeasing to the royal eye were covered with white cloth. Jahangir was particular about such matters, and once ordered that 'hereafter at the time when I come out of the palace they should keep away defective people, such as the blind and those whose noses and ears had been cut off, the leprous and the maimed, and all kinds of sick people, and not permit them to be seen.'

Sometimes, as when travelling between Delhi and Agra or proceeding towards Bengal, the emperor journeyed by the river, in a fleet of huge barges carrying even his elephants. 'The spectacle was an astonishing one,' says Abul Fazl. 'The numerous boats of various kinds, the hoisting of sky-high masts, the tumult of the waves of the river, the force of the wind, the rush of the clouds and the rain, the roar of thunder, the flashing of the lightning, produced a strange appearance . . .'

All the tours of the emperor, even the seeming pleasure trips, served some political purpose. Manucci says that the officials of the localities through which the emperor passed were required to be at hand at all times in order to explain 'at once' if the emperor asked anything about the place through which he passed. Men with a measuring rope travelled with the emperor, to log the distances covered; an officer with an hour-glass kept track of the time.

The emperor invariably combined sport with business on his tours, hunting along the way even when he travelled by river. 'From the day that His Majesty set out on this expedition he left the boat every day and enjoyed himself hunting deer with cheetahs,' says Abul Fazl about one of Akbar's river expeditions. Unless there was an emergency, the emperor travelled at a leisurely pace. Says Terry: 'He [the emperor] removed ten or twelve miles a day, more or less, according to the convenience of water.' Jahangir notes that the journey from Lahore to Agra, a distance of just 600 kilometres, once took him two months and two days, 'with forty-nine marches and twenty-one halts. No day of either of marching or halting, on land or water, passed without sport.'

On the march, as at the court, precise etiquette governed the conduct of the amirs. 'When he seats himself in his Palanquin, then do they walk in a lowly Posture on Foot after him; shewing in all things a submissive Deference to his Greatness, and profound Respect to his eminently August Majesty,' says Ovington. 'And till he gives the Word, no Man dares mount before him.' Normally, it was only when the emperor travelled on an elephant that the nobles rode on horses, keeping the same physical and psychological distance between them and the emperor as at the court, although they did not, unlike at the court, array themselves by rank while on the march, but travelled bunched together 'promiscuously in a body, without much method or regularity,' says Bernier.

'Within the frontiers of the empire, the army does not advance in the order of battle, except for a few who are appointed on guard that day,' says Monserrate. 'These guards, together with royal attenders and cavalry, follow the King at the distance of about a stone's throw, in a crescent shaped formation. When the King halts, they await him in two bodies stretching in an unbroken line for two hundred paces on each side of the entrance of the royal head-quarters. On the one flank are the elephants, which are carefully protected by armour from being injured by missiles. On the other flank are the mounted archers, the pike-men and light-armed troops, for the Mongols have no heavy cavalry. As the king passes by, each man in the ranks salutes him. On the march he is followed first by the cavalry and then by the elephants. In front go drummers and trumpeters, mounted on elephants. All are silent except one, who sounds his drum at short intervals, perhaps at every tenth pace, with a slow and dignified rhythm. Mounted scouts go ahead, and drive off everyone they meet.'

The royal harem travelled by itself in a separate group, staying about three-fourths of a kilometre behind the emperor. The begums travelled in covered litters (carried on the shoulders of bearers, or suspended between two camels or small elephants) or in cabins mounted on elephants. 'These lovely and distinguished females, seated in *mekdambars* are thus elevated above the earth, like so many superior beings borne along through the middle region of the air,' says Bernier. 'The queens ride on female elephants, hidden from view in gaily decorated howdahs,' reports Monserrate. 'Great care is taken to drive away to a great distance all who are found in line of the queen's march.'

'You can conceive no exhibition more grand and imposing than when Rauchenara-Begum, mounted on a stupendous Pegu elephant, and seated in a *mekdambar*, blazing with gold and azure, is followed by five or six other elephants with *mekdambars* nearly as resplendent as her own, and filled with ladies attached to her household,' continues Bernier. 'Close to the Princess are the chief eunuchs, richly adorned and finely mounted, each with a wand of office in his hand; and surrounding her elephant, a troop of female servants, Tartars and Kachmerys, fantastically attired and riding handsome pad-horses. Besides these attendants are several eunuchs on horseback, accompanied by a multitude of *pagys*, or lackeys on foot, with large canes, who advance a great way before the princess, both to the right and to the left, for the purpose of clearing the road and driving before them every intruder.'

THE IMPERIAL CAMP, according to Roe (who found so little else to admire in India), was 'one of the wonders of my little experience . . . the circuit being little lesse then twenty English miles . . . the streets orderly, the tents joyned; there are all sorts of shops . . . which as it lies together, may equall almost any Towne in Europe for greatnesse.' Writes Hawkins: the royal camp 'may bee as much as the compasse of London and more.' The camp, says Manucci, 'looks like a great city travelling from place to place.' It had, says Terry, the appearance of 'a most spacious and glorious city . . . very beautiful to behold from some hill.'

The Mughal camp was far better planned than most Mughal cities, with zones precisely allotted for different services and grades of residences, its layout unvarying from place to place, according to a plan originally conceived by Akbar. 'His Majesty,' 'says Abul Fazl, 'has invented an admirable method of encamping his troops, which is a source of much comfort to them.' All the tents in the camp, says Terry, were 'reared up in such a due and constant order, that when we remove from place to place, we can go as directly to those movable dwellings as if we continued still in fixed and standing habitations, taking our directions from several streets and bazaars . . . every one pitched upon every remove alike, upon such or such side of the king's tents, as if they had not been at all removed.'

The site for the imperial camp was chosen with care by the Mir Manzil, the Grand Quarter-master, who, along with his engineers, went one day ahead of the emperor to select and prepare the site. Pioneers then cleared and levelled the place, raising square platforms of earth on which they pitched the tents. 'I had seene it finished, and set up in foure hours,' says Roe. The various locations in the camp were identified by flags mounted on high masts.

Sometimes however, notwithstanding all precautions, there was some confusion, says Bernier, 'particularly on the arrival of the army at the place of encampment in the morning, when every one is actively employed in finding and establishing his own quarters.' Dust obscured the marks placed by officials, and the lesser mansabdars, who had no advance tents, often jostled each other while staking out their campsites. In the evening the entire camp was darkened by the smoke of cooking fires, so people sometimes lost their way.

At the centre of the camp was the royal enclosure, walled in with a palisade of wood, over two metres high, covered with scarlet cloth. The residential area of the compound was enclosed in a second set of high screens, 'some lined with Maslipatam chintz, painted over with flowers of a hundred different kinds, and others with figured satin, decorated with deep silken fringes,' notes Bernier. Light cannons were placed all around the royal enclosure, and a 330-metre-wide space was left open at its back and two sides, into which no one but guards was allowed to enter. The gate of the enclosure, says Bernier, was 'spacious and magnificent', and was flanked by fifty or sixty small field pieces, 'which fire a salute when the King enters his tent, by which the army is apprised of his arrival.' There were two handsome tents on either side of the gate, where a small number of select horses were kept, saddled and caparisoned, ready for any emergency.

The royal enclosure duplicated in tents all the facilities of the palace. The largest tent in the enclosure, and the first to be erected at the campsite, was the durbar tent. 'The outside [of this tent] is covered with a strong and coarse red cloth, ornamented with large and variegated stripes,' reports Bernier; 'but the inside is lined with beautiful hand-painted chintz, manufactured for the purpose at Maslipatam, the ornamentation of which is set off by rich figured satin of various colours, embroideries of silk, silver, and gold, with deep and elegant fringes. Cotton mats, three or four inches in thickness, are spread over the whole floor, and these again covered with a splendid carpet, on which are placed large square brocade cushions to lean upon. The tents are supported by painted and gilt pillars.'

Careri, who saw Aurangzeb's durbar tent in the Deccan, elaborates: 'Under this Tent was a square place, rais'd four Spans above the Ground, enclos'd with silver Banister, two Spans high, and cover'd with fine Carpets. Six Spans further in the middle was another place rais'd a Span higher, at the Angles whereof there were 4 Poles, cover'd with silver reaching to the top of the Tent. Here stood the Throne, which was also square, of gilt Wood, three Spans above the rest; to get up to it there was a little silver Footstool. On it were three Pillows of Brocade, two to serve on the sides, and one at the back.'

'There is something very striking and magnificent in these royal quarters,' says Bernier. 'This vast assemblage of red tents, placed in the centre of a numerous army, produces a brilliant effect when seen from neighbouring eminence; especially if the country be open, and offer no obstruction to usual and regular distribution of the troops.'

Around the royal enclosure were the tents of the great amirs, which were also enclosed in screens to protect the privacy of women, each tent at its allotted place, all facing the royal tents. The tents of the amirs were mostly white, occasionally green or multi-coloured, but never red, which was the royal colour. They were, says Roe, 'in excellent forms ... all encompassed as orderly as any house', compared to which his own tent was shabby, a 'poor house'. Beyond the tents of the amirs were those of their officers and troopers.

Well-organized bazaars supplied all the necessities of the camp. 'There are wanting neither bazaars, nor shops, nor markers, nor sports, nor pastimes, nor gold, nor silver; in short, all that could be looked for in a flourishing city is to be found in this camp,' says Manucci. Confirms Monserrate: 'These bazaars seem to belong to some wealthy city instead of to a camp.' 'There were 250 Bazars or Markets, every Omrah, or General having one to serve his Men,' says Careri.

In that vast camp, orders were conveyed to the army through a 'public crier'. At night, a lofty light called Akasdiah, Light of the Heavens, was lit in front of the durbar tent, to guide people to the camp. The light, an innovation of Akbar, was mounted on a mast about twelve metres high and supported by sixteen ropes. In the evenings, when the amirs had to attend the emperor's private durbar, the lanes of the camp were lit up for them, and it was, says Bernier, 'a grand and imposing spectacle in a dark night to behold, when standing at some distance, long rows of torches lighting these nobles, through extended lanes of tents.' The camp was guarded at night by watchmen posted every 500 paces, who lighted their beat with fires, and every now and then cried out, *Khabar*! Beware! Contingents of soldiers also went around the camp, blowing trumpets. 'Notwithstanding all these measures, robberies are often committed,' says Bernier.

Standards at the Mughal camp fell sharply during the second half of Aurangzeb's reign, and Norris, who visited the emperor in the Deccan, writes that the Mughal camp was 'meaner & poorer then can be expressed or would be believed. Nothing to be seen but confusion & disorder in their encampmt, & the nastinesse & stench of ye place very offensive.'

The Emperor at Play

IN THE MUGHAL scheme of things, there was little distinction between the public and private life of the emperor. Affairs of the royal household were affairs of the state. The harem played a prominent role in the administration of the empire, and was organized as a government department. The emperor often consulted the begums on state matters, and it was in the harem that he reviewed the confidential reports of his intelligence officers. The royal seal too was kept in the harem.

The imperial household had a staff of several thousands, and was organized by Akbar, as a part of his general administrative reform, into various departments—such as stables, wardrobe, tents, kitchen and so on—headed by high and trusted officials, who functioned under the general supervision of the Vizier. The palace staff were all state officials and held military ranks, even the kitchen menial, who had the rank of a foot soldier, and drew a salary of 100 to 400 dams (2.5 to 4 rupees) a month.

Typical of the complex organization and procedures of the palace establishment was the royal kitchen. The kitchen department was headed by Mir Bakawal, Master of the Kitchen, an officer of the rank of the commander of 600—in Akbar's reign, a physician, Hakim Humam, held the post—under the direct control of the Vizier. Says Abul Fazl, 'His Majesty has entrusted to the latter (the Vizier) the affairs of the state, but especially this important department.' Mir Bakawal had under him an army of cooks, tasters and attendants. There was, says Manucci, even a special officer in charge of betel. 'Bad characters, idle talkers, unknown persons are never employed; no one is entertained without a personal security, nor is personal acquaintance sufficient,' says Abul Fazl.

The royal kitchen had its own budget and accountants. 'In the beginning of the year, the Sub-treasurers make out an annual estimate, and receive the amount ... and every month a correct statement of the daily expenditure is drawn up ...,' records Abul Fazl. 'The Mir Bakawal and the writer determine the price of every eatable ... and they sign the day-book, the estimates, the receipts for transfer, the list of wages of the servants, etc., and watch every transaction.'

'Every day one thousand rupees are disbursed for the expenses of the king's kitchen, and the officials are required to furnish therefrom all that is necessary,' reports Manucci. 'They have to lay before the prince a fixed number of ragouts and different dishes in vessels of China porcelain placed on gold stands. As a great favour the king sends of these, or of what is left over, to the queens and princesses and the captains of the guard.' Provisions for the royal kitchen were collected from various parts of the empire without regard to cost—fruits from Kabul, ducks and waterfowl and certain vegetables from Kashmir, water from the Ganga. 'The sheep, goats, berberies (Barbary goats), fowls, ducks, etc., are fattened by the cooks; fowls are never kept less than a month,' notes Abul Fazl. Akbar's kitchen consumed 100,650 *maunds* (about 3800 metric tons) of firewood a year, and six hundred carts were required to fetch the fuel.

The royal household expenses were prodigious. Even under Akbar, a frugal manager of finances, the imperial household expenses towards the end of his reign, according to the calculation of Shireen Moosvi, came to about 187.4 million dams (about 4.7 million rupees) a year, under the following categories: harem, 35 million; kitchen, 13.65 million; wardrobe, 17.73 million; books and paintings, 6.75 million; ornaments and gems, 44.32 million; hunting animals, 13 million; cash allowances and alms, 12.5 million; and so on. Pelsaert reports that an inventory taken on Akbar's death showed the value of cloth in the imperial stores as 16 million rupees; of gold pots, dishes, cutlery, figurines, silver utensils, chandeliers, bedsteads etc. as 14.3 million rupees; of books as 6.5 million rupees. Says Hawkins about Jahangir's household expenses: 'His daily expenses for his owne person, that is to say, for feeding of his cattell of all sorts, and amongst them some few elephants royall, and all other expenses particularly, as apparell, victuals, and other petty expenses for his house, amounts to fiftie thousand rupias a day. The expenses daily for his women by the day is thirtie thousand rupias.' This is an exaggerated figure, but palace expenses did rise dramatically under Jahangir, and continued to rise under his successors.

EVEN DRINKING WATER was a major item of expense in the royal household, for Mughal emperors were fastidious about water, and normally drank only water from the Ganga, which had to be brought from a considerable distance. According to Abul Fazl, 'both at home and on travels he (Akbar) drinks Ganga water [brought in sealed jars from the river] . . . For the cooking of food, rain water or water taken from the

Yamuna and Chenab is used, mixed with a little Ganga water.' This practice was continued by Akbar's successors. Says Ovington about Aurangzeb: 'His Drink is the Water of the River Ganges.' A special department, Abdar Khana, was in charge of water supply to the royal household; experienced water-tasters were a regular unit of the royal entourage and they accompanied the emperor even on hunting expeditions.

In the early part of Akbar's reign water used to be cooled with saltpetre, by a process described in detail by Abul Fazl. Later ice was commonly used. 'Since the thirteenth year of the Divine Era, when the imperial standards were erected in the Punjab, snow and ice have come into use. Ice is brought by land and water, by post carriages or bearers, from the district of Panhan, in the northern mountain, about forty-five *kos* (145 kms) from Lahore. The dealers derive a considerable profit, two to three *seers* of ice being sold per rupee,' records Abul Fazl. 'All ranks use ice in summer; the nobles use it throughout the whole year.'

Great precaution was taken to ensure the purity of the dishes served to the emperor. 'The victuals are served up in dishes of gold and silver, stone and earthenware . . . During the time of cooking, and when the victuals are taken out, an awning is spread, and lookers-on kept away,' records Abul Fazl. 'The cooks tuck up their sleeves, and the hems of their garments, and hold their hands before their mouths and noses when food is taken out; the cook and Bakawal taste it, after which it is tasted by the Mir Bakawal, and then put into the dishes. The gold and silver dishes are tied up in red cloths, and those of copper and China in white ones. The Mir Bakawal attaches his seal, and writes out on a sheet of paper a list of vessels and dishes which he sends inside with the seal of the Mir Bakawal, that none of the dishes may be changed. The dishes are carried by the Bakawals, the cooks, and other servants, and mace-bearers precede and follow, to prevent people from approaching them. The servants of the pantry send at the same time, in bags containing the seal of the Bakawal, various kinds of bread, saucers of curds piled up, and small stands containing plates of pickles, fresh ginger, limes, and various greens. The servants of the palace again taste the food, spread the table cloth on the ground, and arrange the dishes; and when after some time his majesty commences to dine, the table servants sit opposite him in attendance; first, the share of the dervishes is put apart, when his Majesty commences with milk or curds.' The Mir Bakawal was always in attendance.

A great variety of food was prepared every day for the emperor to choose from, and some dishes were always kept half ready, so they could be served quickly should the emperor call for them. 'He hath meate ready at all houres, and calls for it at pleasure,' writes Terry. 'They feede not freely on full dishes of beefe and mutton [as we], but much on rice boyled with pieces of flesh or dressed many other wayes. They have not many roast or baked meats, but stew most of their flesh.' 'Cooks from all countries prepare a great variety of dishes of all kinds of grains, greens, meats; also oily, sweet, and spicy dishes,' says Abul Fazl. 'Every day such dishes are prepared as the nobles can scarcely command at their feasts . . . Cooked victuals may be arranged under three heads, first, such in which no meat is used, called now-a-days *sufiyana*; secondly, such in which meat and rice, etc., are used; thirdly, meats with spices.'

Except at banquets, the emperor always ate alone in the privacy of his harem. 'Hee alwayes eates in private among his women,' says Terry. No outsider could have ever seen the emperor dining, but Sebastien Manrique, an Augustinian friar, once managed, so he claims, to watch Shah Jahan at dinner, by getting a eunuch to smuggle him through obscure passages to a high gallery over the hall in which Asaf Khan, Shah Jahan's father-in-law, was entertaining the emperor in Lahore. He says he watched the banquet for four hours.

On this occasion, apart from the emperor, the only guests at the banquet were Dara and Jahanara, and they were attended by Asaf Khan, his ladies and his eunuchs. The emperor ate sitting cross-legged on a floor covered with carpets. ('All their bravery is upon their floors,' says Terry.) The carpets were protected by sheets made of leather stitched together, which in turn was covered with white calico cloth. Shah Jahan washed before sitting down to eat. Two lovely harem girls knelt on either side of the emperor to serve him the gold and silver dishes handed to them by eunuchs, while musicians sang the praise of the emperor, says Manrique.

It was customary for the emperor to set aside some food for the poor before he himself ate. 'One day, when His Majesty was taking his dinner, it occurred to his mind that probably the eyes of some hungry one had fallen upon the food; how, therefore, could he eat it while the hungry were debarred from it?' says Nizamuddin Ahmad about Akbar's practice. 'He therefore gave orders that every day some hungry persons should be fed with some of the food prepared for himself, and that afterwards he should be served.' After dinner, the emperor prostrated himself in prayer.

Public banquets, when the emperor feasted with his amirs, were common among the Mughals, such as the grand open air reception that Babur held in Agra in the winter of 1528. Babur on that occasion sat in a newly erected octagonal pavilion covered with *khas* (a scented grass), with the amirs and ambassadors flanking him on both sides, each seated according to his rank. The banquet began with the guests offering presents to the emperor. 'While the gifts were being brought and before food, fierce camels and fierce elephants were set to fight on an island opposite, so too a few rams; thereafter wrestlers grappled,' says Babur. After the main courses were served, it was Babur's turn to offer presents to guests. And finally, 'after food had been sent out, Hindustani players were ordered to come and show their tricks ... Many dancing girls came also and danced.'

THE EMPERORS DRESSED regally, for that was a requirement of their office. Even Akbar, who preferred simplicity in dress, maintained a wardrobe so large that it had to be classified and catalogued. 'The garments stored in the imperial wardrobe,' says Abul Fazl, 'are arranged according to the days, months, and years of their entries, and according to their colour, price and weight.' A thousand complete sets of clothes were made for Akbar every six months, most of which he gave away as presents. All the Mughal emperors, including Aurangzeb, but especially Jahangir and Shah Jahan, were loaded with jewels. Says Terry: 'For the Mughals, though his clothing be not so rich and costly, yet I believe that there is never a monarch in the whole world that is daily adorned with so many jewels as he himself.' According to William Hawkins, Jahangir had his personal jewellery organized in such a way that he could wear a different set each day—'that which he weareth this day, till his time be come about to weare it againe he weareth not the same.'

The royal sartorial style grew florid under Jahangir and Shah Jahan, whose costumes were often so richly encrusted with gold and gems that they were like jewels. Typical was the ceremonial dress that Shah Jahan once presented to Dara, which Inayat Khan describes as 'a handsome *khilat* with a gold-embroidered vest, studded with valuable diamonds round the collar; on both sleeves, and the skirts, pearls had been sewn, and it was worth 50,000 rupees; also a *sarband* composed of a single ruby of the purest water, and two magnificent pearls, of the value of a lakh and 70,000 rupees.'

According to Abul Fazl, Akbar's garments—probably each style, not each dress—had names. His jewels and weapons were also given names, classified and catalogued. 'All the weapons for the use of His Majesty have names, and a proper rank is assigned to them,' says Abul Fazl. Akbar's practice was continued by his successors. The sabers of Aurangzeb bore such names as Lightning, Conqueror of the Universe (Alamgir, his favourite), and, of course, Kafir Kush (Infidel-slayer).

The imperial palace was fittingly the grandest mansion in the empire, the most richly decorated. Opulence was the keynote of the Mughal decorative style, and elegance was sometimes sacrificed for richness—at least, so it seemed to Roe, who says of Jahangir's palace decor: 'Rich but of so divers pieces, and so unsuitable, that it was rather patched than glorious, as it seemed to strive to shewe all, like a Lady with her Plate, set on a Cupboord her imbroydered Slippers.'

An army of servants attended on the emperor, in the palace as well as in the camp. They were divided into seven groups, one for each day of the week, each group under the command of a grandee, who would, says Abul Fazl, 'superintend everything during that period, and arrange the diversity of affairs.' The royal household also employed a large number of artists and artisans, singers and dancers, poets, writers and philosophers. It was customary for Kenchens (Kanchanas), a troupe of professional dancing girls, to appear at the court on Wednesdays, to sing and dance and pay homage to the emperor, and sometimes they were admitted into the harem to entertain the emperor and the begums. The palace had an extensive library, its own calligraphy and book-making departments, ateliers, picture galleries and craft units.

The Mughal emperors, though remorselessly savage in the pursuit of power, were also erudite, highly cultured men, patrons or practitioners of the arts, and a part of their charm was that they could turn with ease and pleasure from the slaughter of the battlefield to the seductions of the arts. As connoisseurs of the good life, they also delighted in carnal pleasures.

But they were not debauchees. They had of course several wives— four permanent wives by *nikah* marriage and (in the case of Akbar) several more by temporary *mutah* marriages—and they kept numerous concubines, but none of the Mughal emperors, except Akbar in his youth and Shah Jahan in his middle age, appears to have been sexually hyperactive, if we are to judge them by the small number of children born to them. The Mughal emperors in fact seem almost abstemious when compared to Sultan Ghiyasuddin of Malwa, of whom Jahangir writes, 'They say he had collected 15,000 women in his harem. He had a whole city of them . . . Wherever he heard of a virgin possessed of beauty, he would not desist until he possessed her.'

The use of opium, marijuana and other psychotropic preparations was common among the elite in medieval India, and wine drinking, though prohibited by Islam, was viewed as a venial indulgence. Babur, Humayun and Jahangir were heavy drinkers, Akbar less so, but Shah Jahan, whose weakness was for aphrodisiacs, was temperate, and Aurangzeb, who rigorously abided by the law, abstemious. Akbar's brother and two of his sons drank themselves to death. The common Mughal attitude towards wine was defined by Jahangir by quoting Hafiz:

> *Cupbearer! brighten my cup with*
> *the light of wine;*
> *Sing, minstrel, for the world has ordered*
> *itself as I desire.*

THE ROYAL HOUSEHOLD had an insatiable appetite for luxury goods, and there were a number of shops in the citadel itself to cater to its needs. If the emperor needed anything from the outside, the bazaar went to him. Writes Jahangir: 'Up to this time the custom has been for the people of the bazaar and the artificers of the city in every place to bring their shops according to order into the courtyard of the palace, and bring jewels and jewelled things and various kinds of cloth and other goods such as are sold in the bazaar. It occurred to me that if a bazaar were prepared in the night-time, and a number of lamps were arranged in front of the shops, it would look well. Undoubtedly it came off well and was unusual. Going round all the shops, whatever jewels and jewelled things pleased me I bought.'

The most unusual bazaar held in the citadel was the Meena Bazaar, a fancy fair exclusively for women, with the emperor the only male attending. This bazaar was not for trade, but for the frolic of the begums—and, according to Coryat and Manucci, for the emperor to pick paramours. The other celebratory occasions in the palace were the emperor's birthday—birthdays, in fact, for Akbar had begun the custom of observing both the lunar and solar birthdays—the anniversary of his accession, and the new year celebrations. The Nauruz festival, the Persian New Year's Day, was a high point in the Mughal social calendar, when the begums of the great amirs moved into the palace to celebrate the festival with the royal family, and the emperor conferred honours on his nobles.

The custom of celebrating Nauruz on a grand scale was begun by Akbar. Says Badauni: 'And the Emperor commanded both the private and the public audience chamber be decorated with all sorts of precious materials. And they prepared costly articles of various colours, and European curtains, and they made most incomparable paintings, and erected lofty pavilions. And they decorated the bazaar at Agra and at Fatehpur in a similar manner, and kept high festival for eighteen days. And the Emperor sent for all sorts of troops of singers and musicians, both Hindu and Persian, and dancers, both men and women, by thousands of thousands: and each day he went into the pavilion of one of the renowned Amirs and honoured him with his society, and received from him a considerable present, and other proofs of hospitality.' 'Games were held and pageants conducted each day,' says Monserrate. 'The King . . . gave instructions that all classes of the citizens should be bidden to show their joy either by leaping, singing, or dancing. He welcomed all who came to see the festival with largess, free supply of wine, and free banquets.' Roe, who was present at a Nauruz festival during the reign of Jahangir, writes: 'I sawe what was to be seene, presents, elephants, horses, and many whoores.'

On such celebratory occasions, the emperor was weighed against a variety of materials, which were then set aside for charity. The weighing of the emperor and the distribution of the items against which he was weighed (or their value) for charity was a Hindu royal custom—*tuladana*—which Humayun, ever receptive to fanciful ideas, adopted, but it was Akbar who made it an integral part of the royal birthday ceremonies. Weighing was also held during illness and other misfortunes, as a propitiatory rite. 'On the 28th an eclipse took place,' writes Jahangir, 'in order to do away with the unluckiness of which I weighed myself against gold and silver' and other things and had the amounts distributed among the needy. Similarly, Shah Jahan had Jahanara weighed when she recovered from her burn injuries. It was Akbar's custom, says Jahangir, to have the princes weighed on their solar birthdays.

Roe once watched Jahangir being weighed on his birthday. 'The scales, being hung in large trestles, and a crosse beame plated on with gold thinne: the scales of massive gold, the borders set with small stones, Rubies and Turkey, the chaines of gold large and massive, but strengthencd with silk Cords,' writes Roe. 'Here attended the Nobilitie all sitting about on Carpets untill the King came . . . Suddenly he entered into the scales, sate like a woman on his legs, and there was put in against him many bagges to fit his weight which were changed six times.'

The emperor was weighed against such diverse items as silver, gold, jewels and precious stones, cloth of gold, silk, stuffs, linen, spices, and all sorts of goods, and lastly against foodstuff, all in bags. 'It being in bagges might be Pibles,' says Roe cynically. After the weighing, Jahangir ascended the throne and scattered 'Nuts, Almonds, Fruits, Spices of all sort made in thin silver,' continues Roe, 'and the great men scrabbled prostrate upon their bellies' to gather them. 'If it's found that he has increased in bulk, above what he weighed the preceding Year, this adds excess of Mirth and Joy to the solemnity,' says Ovington; 'but if he prove lighter in the Scales, this diminishes their Triumphs, and damps their cheerful Entertainments.' Bernier reports that one year when Aurangzeb was weighed, 'all the courtiers expressed much joy when it was found that Aurang-zebe weighed two pounds more than the year preceding.'

Sometimes courtiers and others were weighed for the emperor to reward them. Once Jahangir had astrologer Jotik Ray, who had made consistently accurate predictions, weighed against coins—his weight came to 6,500 rupees. 'This was given to him as a reward,' writes Jahangir. Both Jahangir and Shah Jahan had their favourite musicians weighed against rupees and gold; Shah Jahan also had the physician who healed Jahanara's burn wounds weighed against gold.

BABUR AND HIS successors were vigorous outdoorsmen, and hunting was for them the greatest sporting thrill, though Aurangzeb in his middle age abjured it as a waste of time. Even royal ladies loved to hunt. Nurjahan, for instance, was an excellent shikaree. India had plenty of hunting grounds in Mughal times. Palam, the airport of modern Delhi, was Shah Jahan's game preserve, where once 'he devoted four days to the pleasant pastime of hunting and shooting,' bagging as many as forty black bucks in one day, records Inayat Khan.

Certain animals, as well as certain hunting grounds, were reserved exclusively for the sport of the emperor. 'His hunting-ground is . . . taboo. If anyone enters it, he becomes a slave,' says Abul Fazl. Confirms Bernier: Royal hunting grounds were 'guarded with the utmost vigilance; and excepting partridges, quails, and hares, which the natives catch with nets, no person, be he who he may, is permitted to disturb the game, which is consequently very abundant.' Elephants could be hunted only with royal permission. Lion was the exclusive prey of the emperor and the princes.

Great care was taken to ensure the success of the emperor's lion hunt, for a lion kill was considered a good omen, its escape unlucky. The care taken in fact was such that at times the hunt was like a ritual killing. On locating a lion for the emperor, gamekeepers would attach it firmly to the spot by regularly tying an ass there for it to feed on. It could also be (as Bernier had heard, but denied by officers) that the ass provided for the lion on the day before the hunt was loaded with opium, to make the lion torpid and prevent it from wandering away. To further impound the lion, on the day of the hunt, beaters encircled the area around its lair with high nets.

The emperor arrived for the hunt mounted on an elephant, accompanied by the Grand Master of the Hunt and several amirs, all mounted on elephants, along with soldiers on horseback and gamekeepers on foot armed with half-pikes. Despite all these precautions, sometimes the lion attacked the hunters, or escaped by leaping over the encircling net, and had to be pursued and hunted down. A successful lion hunt was celebrated with high ceremony—the carcass of the lion was brought to the emperor sitting on the throne surrounded by amirs, where it was measured, and the details of the *kill*, including the name of the gun used, entered in the records for the royal archives, as Akbar had specified.

Some of the royal hunts were prodigious affairs, planned like a military operation, involving thousands of people. Typical was the battue hunt that Akbar organized near Lahore in 1567, in which some 50,000 beaters were engaged for a month to drive the game. Falcons, cheetahs tame as cats, tame bucks (with a noose on their horns to ensnare wild bucks) were all used in hunting. Often hunting was a warm-up for battle: Akbar invariably began his military campaigns with a hunt.

Part of the thrill of the hunt was in its latent danger. Jahangir was once nearly killed during a tiger hunt—when the tiger attacked, he stumbled and fell, and his terror-stricken attenders scattered. 'In fact, I am sure that two or three of them placed their feet on my chest and passed over me,' says Jahangir. He was saved only by the bravery of a Rajput, Anup Rai, who grappled with the tiger; Occasionally the Mughal emperor, especially Humayun and Jahangir, took to fishing as a sport. Once, on the way to Kabul, Jahangir netted some fish in a lake, and 'strung pearls in their noses and let them go again in the water.'

Aside from hunting, the favourite Mughal royal sport was polo, which was introduced into India by the Turko-Afghans—Qutbuddin Aibak, the first of the Delhi sultans, in fact died in a polo accident. The game was popular in Central Asia. Says Babur about one of his father's amirs: 'He was brave, a good archer, played polo well and leapt well at leap-frog.' Akbar was an avid, almost fanatical polo enthusiast, though, of course, Abul Fazl inevitably saw in it a deeper purpose than just fun. 'Superficial observers regard the game as a mere amusement, and consider it mere play; but men of more exalted views see in it a means of learning promptitude and decision,' he says. 'Strong men learn, in playing the game, the art of riding; and the animals learn to perform feats of agility and to obey reins. It tests the value of a man and strengthens bonds of friendship. Hence His Majesty is very fond of this game. Externally the game adds to the splendour of the Court; but viewed from a higher point, reveals concealed talents.' Akbar was so keen on polo that he even played it at night, with smouldering balls of *palas* wood, and he made it almost a duty for courtiers to prove themselves in the game.

The Mughals played a variety of indoor games also, mainly chess, cards—'I found the Prince earnest at Cards,' says Roe about Shah Jahan—dice and draughts. Sometimes the emperor amused himself, as Akbar did, by using slave girls in place of coins to play draughts on the chequered palace courtyard. Pigeon-flying was a favourite pastime of Akbar and Jahangir, but the sport died out in later times. Music and dance, magic shows, circuses, theatrical performances, fairs and pilgrimages were other diversions of the royal family.

THE MUGHALS WERE, as keen hunters paradoxically are, also great animal lovers. The imperial mews were like a zoo, and had a great variety of animals: deer, dogs, buffaloes, tame lions, hunting cheetahs, rhinoceroses, hawks, pigeons and singing birds, as well as elephants, horses, camels, mules and oxen. Akbar had as many as a 1000 cheetahs and 12,000 deer. He also kept a kennel of dogs, in violation of Islamic injunctions. Jahangir too had a large kennel, including a few dogs imported from Europe, and he had silver tongs made for him to feed them. His favourites were two mastiffs that Roe presented to him; they were pampered and carried about in coaches or palanquins, each looked after by four attendants. Even Aurangzeb was a dog lover, and kept Uzbeg hounds dressed in red coats, says Bernier.

A singular pastime of the emperor, and one that was exclusive to him, was arranging elephant fights; not even the princes were allowed to do this without royal permission. In Delhi and Agra, the arena for elephant fights was the maidan between the fort and the river. A pair of carefully matched elephants, each mounted by two mahouts—the second one to take the place at the neck if the first fell—were chosen, and set to fight against each other across a mud wall three or four feet wide and five or six feet high. The fight began with the elephants rushing on each other and butting, and it ended when the mud wall was demolished and one elephant chased away the other, or they got into a clinch, in which case they were separated by setting off fireworks. Akbar permitted amirs to bet on elephant fights, with the stake limited to five dams. The best fighting elephants, says Bernier, came from Ceylon.

It was a dangerous sport, not only for the mahouts, who often got killed, but also for bystanders, who were sometimes trampled by elephants or by men fleeing from the onrushing beasts. There was danger even for the emperor and the princes—Aurangzeb, as prince, was attacked by an elephant during a fight. The emperor, if he happened to watch the fight from the ground instead of from the fort, was protected by 'soldiers who carry sharp hooks fixed on long handles and bombs filled with powdered sulphur', to frighten away the elephants, notes Monserrate.

The mahouts had no protection other than their skill. 'When the king makes them (elephants) fight, the wives of the drivers remove their ornaments, smash their bracelets, and put on mourning, just as if they were widows,' writes Manucci. 'If their husbands come back alive they give a great feast, just as if newly married, for in these encounters and combats the drivers put their lives in great jeopardy.' The mahouts were however well rewarded, and if they died during a fight, their widows continued to receive their pay, and their children were taken into the imperial service.

Fights of goats, stags, antelopes, dogs, bulls, camels, tigers, deer, cheetahs, boars, leopards, bulls and cocks were also patronized by the Mughals. Akbar had several wrestlers and boxers in his pay, and often ordered well-matched pairs to fight before him for a purse. His pleasure though was not in blood, but in skill. Abul Fazl reports that once when a wrestler, Haibat Tahamtan 'abandoned the rules of wrestling and in a demon-like fashion applied his strength, and tore off the fingers of his antagonist', Akbar in fury hit the offender, knocking him down unconscious.

Jahangir, according to Hawkins, was fond of gladiatorial contests between men and animals, and had once pitted a Pathan against a lion, and when he was killed, sent in ten more. 'The King,' writes Hawkins, 'continued three moneths in the vaine, when he was in his humors, for whose pleasure sake many men lost their lives and many were greviously wounded.' The emperor's intention, it seems, was to tame the lion and familiarize it with the company of men, for Hawkins says that some fifteen lions were thus 'made tame and played one with another before the King, frisking between mens legs and no man hurt in a long time.'

The Indian summer was a tougher beast for the Mughals to tame. Babur gritted his teeth and endured it, Humayun escaped it in the fumes of opium, but Akbar found a refuge from it in Kashmir, where he built a lake city in the valley as a summer sanctuary, which his successors came to regard as a 'terrestrial paradise'. Jahangir was even more vulnerable to the seduction of Kashmir; he visited it as often as he could, and laid out there the great Shalimar garden.

Initially, when Akbar first began vacationing in Kashmir, 'most men were averse to his going on account of the difficulty of the journey,' says Abul Fazl, but later the amirs came to consider it a high privilege to be allowed to accompany the emperor. The honour was conferred only on a select few. Aurangzeb took with him only a small group, and had a high officer take up position at a pass to control entry, in order not to create scarcity in Kashmir. The officer, records Bernier, 'reckons every person one by one, and effectively prevents the ingress of that multitude of Mansebdars and other cavaliers who are eager to inhale the pure and refreshing air of Kachemire.'

SUCH THEN WAS the life of the Mughal emperor. Much about him was on a supra-human scale, but he was also endearingly human, and occasionally he had to suffer awful indignities. Akbar was mocked for trying to play god, Jahangir for being henpecked. Shah Jahan's mistresses were victims of merciless ribbing by the bazaar people. An arrow was once shot at Akbar; there was a coup against Jahangir; and in 1653, one Jasrup Mirathia tried to climb on to the throne balcony of Shah Jahan to attack him.

The worst victim of outrages was Aurangzeb, maybe because of the provocation of his mask of smug piety. Once, when he was on the way to the Jama Masjid for the Friday prayer, a fakir threw a potful of human excrement on him, 'which defiled his throne and his body,' says Manucci. Aurangzeb bore this affront with stoic dignity, and let the fakir, who was arrested, go free. Another time a complainant threw a stick at Aurangzeb as he was mounting his horse in the courtyard of the Diwan-i-am—the man was handed over to the Kotwal. Later in the same year, while Aurangzeb was mounting his horse at the Jama Masjid, 'a wretch came forward with an uplifted sword,' says Mustaid Khan. 'The mace-bearers wanted to slay him, but the Emperor forbade it, settled on him a daily allowance of half a rupee and sent him as prisoner to Ranthambhor.' In a similar incident a couple of months later, 'a mad pauper unsheathed a sword in the Jama Mosque and ran towards the Emperor. The bodyguards captured him.' Another time a Sikh threw a brick at Aurangzeb, to avenge the persecution of Guru Govind Singh.

Aurangzeb was also a victim of the jibes of Niamat Khan, a satirical poet of Delhi, whom he tried to bribe into silence by increasing his stipend, but failing, suffered the taunts patiently thereafter. Even his concubines mocked Aurangzeb. Careri, no doubt reporting a bazaar gossip, says that once 'the Eunuch coming in the Morning to tell him the Bath was ready, as is us'd by the Mahometans after they have had to do with Women; the Woman who had been disappointed [by his continence] cry'd out, there was no need for bath, because the King had not broke Wind; to signify, he had been at Prayers, which if interrupted by Wind, the Mahometans are to Bath.'

Chapter Three

LIVING AND
PARTLY LIVING

Lordly Fireflies

'THIS IS YOUR share of the kingdom of Hind, which has fallen into my hands,' Sher Shah used to tell the Afghan fakirs who sought his charity, granting them annuities. 'Come every year to receive it.' The Mughals were even more proprietorial about their Indian empire, generously sharing the riches of India with their amirs. Under Shah Jahan, the average annual income of the top 655 members of the ruling class was over 200,000 rupees, the equivalent of about fourteen million rupees in the currency of the mid-1990s, and the highest paid of them, Prince Dara, received twenty million rupees, the equivalent of 1.4 billion rupees in modern currency. Though the amirs had to meet certain military obligations from their pay—and they often cheated on that—they were usually left with huge surpluses as their personal incomes.

Under Akbar, a noble of the highest rank (commander of 5000, first class) drew a monthly salary of 30,000 rupees but spent no more than 10,600 rupees on the regiment he had to maintain, according to Moreland's estimate. The amir thus had a minimum net monthly personal income of more than 18,000 rupees—the equivalent of about 1.26 million rupees in modern currency. Under later rulers, the remunerations of amirs were even higher, and the controls over them less rigorous. Satish Chandra, a modern authority on Mughal India, notes: 'The Mughal nobles received salaries which were probably the highest in the world at that time.' Furthermore, the amirs, taking advantage of the laxity of the Mughal government, obtained large sums by way of presents and bribes and (if stationed in the provinces) from all kinds of quasi-legal and illegal exactions. It was a proud boast of the Mughal chronicler that even a Mughal amir of the third grade in Shah Jahan's court had an income greater than that of the king of Balkh.

Yet, for all their immense wealth and power, the Mughal amirs were an insecure lot, for they, unlike the lords of Europe, were not hereditary landed aristocrats, but were merely officials, who held office entirely at the will and pleasure of the emperor. With the exception of a handful of Hindu rajas in possession of their ancestral dominions, the amirs had no base of power or wealth of their own. They owned no extensive estates, but merely received jagirs from the emperor in lieu of pay—they did not own their jagirs, for it was not the land that was assigned to them, but only its revenue. Furthermore, the assignments were temporary, and the emperor periodically shuffled the jagirs among the amirs to prevent any one from taking root in the land. 'The royal grants,' notes Bernier, 'consist only of pensions, either in land or money, which the king gives, augments, retrenches or takes away at pleasure.' Even in the case of the rajas, succession had to be approved by the emperor, and their positions in the Mughal official hierarchy (which were invariably far more remunerative than their inheritances) depended on royal favour, not on their titles.

No amir could bequeath his official title, rank or jagir to his heir, for these were coterminous with his office. Generally speaking, the Mughal amirs could not even save on their incomes and leave legacies for their children, for whatever they left behind—if they left anything at all behind, which was rare—was normally confiscated by the emperor on some pretext or other. Even when sons were allowed to inherit the wealth of their parents, it was usually conferred on them by the emperor at his will, as a favour. Though a successful amir often managed to secure for his sons lucrative official positions, and sometimes a son succeeded his father to office, such assignments were never automatic, and could not be claimed as a right. 'The custome of this Mogoll Emperor,' says Hawkins, 'is take possession of his noblemens treasure when they dye, and to bestow on their children what he pleaseth; but commonly he dealeth well with them, possessing them with their fathers land, dividing it amongst them; and unto the eldest sonne he hath a very great respect, who in time receiveth the full title of his father.'

The only true hereditary office in the empire was that of the emperor. 'The courtiers are often not even descendants of Omrahs,' notes Bernier, 'because, the King being heir of all their possessions, no family can long maintain its distinction, but after the Omrah's death, is soon extinguished, and the sons, or at least the grandsons, reduced generally, we might almost say, to beggary, and compelled to enlist as mere troopers in the cavalry of some Omrah. The king, however, usually bestows a small pension on the widow, and often on the family; and if the Omrah's life be sufficiently prolonged, he may obtain the advancement of his children by royal favour, particularly if their persons be well formed, and their complexions sufficiently fair to enable them to pass for genuine Mogols. But this advancement through special favour proceeds slowly, for it is almost invariable custom to pass gradually from small salaries, and inconsiderable offices, to situations of greater trust and emolument.' Each generation, notes Moreland, 'had practically to start afresh'.

The pervasive insecurity of the Mughal ruling class turned even the most powerful amirs into unblushing flatterers of the royal ego. Says Roe, 'If the king once take offence, the Father will not speake for the Sonne.' Even vassal chiefs 'when . . . in the royal presence . . . feign to be timid and afraid of His majesty,' says Manucci. Cautions Badauni, a victim of wayward royal patronage:

> *Put not thy foot into any office, lest thou*
> *Become the butt of placing and displacing.*

Hypocrisy was the plume on the turban of the Mughal amir. At the imperial court, writes Bernier, 'base and disgusting adulation . . . is invariably witnessed . . . Whenever a word escapes the lips of the King, if at all to the purpose, how trifling soever may be its import, it is immediately caught by the surrounding throng; and the chief Omrahs, extending their arms towards heaven, as if to receive some benediction, exclaim, *Karamat! Karamat!* Wonderful! Wonderful!' The attitude of the courtier was, as the Persian saying goes,

> *If king at noon says it's night,*
> *Exclaim: Behold! the moon, the stars!*

Such words and gestures were not meant to fool the emperor, but only to please him. Babur detested hypocrisy and considered it degrading to accept 'the lies and flattery of rogues and sycophants'. But his successors, though they were 'quite aware of the falseness of such words', were 'pleased nevertheless to hear them, and swallow them at their superficial valuations,' says Manucci.

Sycophancy was a part of the Persian court culture that the Mughals adopted, but in India it over-ripened and putrefied. 'The vice of flattery pervades all ranks,' says Bernier. 'When a Mogul, for instance, has occasion for my services [as a physician], he comes to tell me by way of preamble, and as matter of course, that I am the . . . Aristotle, the Hippocrates, and the Avicenna of the age. At first I endeavoured to prevent this fulsome mode of address . . . but finding that my modesty only increased their praise, I determined to accustom my ears to their flattery as I had done to their music.'

Sometimes, for all their caution, the amirs offended the emperor or the princes and had to suffer abject humiliation at their hands. Tavernier records that once, during the siege of Daulatabad, Prince Shah Jahan 'became so enraged [at something that Azam Khan, one of his generals, said] that, sending at once for one of his *paposhes* or slippers, which they leave at the door, had him given five or six strokes with it on the bonnet, which among the Indians is the highest indignity that can be put upon a man, after which he no more appears in the Prince's presence.' According to Bernier, Dara had once similarly beaten Khalilullah, one of the highest officers of the empire, with a shoe.

Not everyone suffered such disgrace in humility. Rebellions by offended or thwarted officers were common throughout Mughal history. Sometimes amirs even defied the emperor openly in durbar—and surprisingly the emperors were often tolerant of such affronts, sensibly preferring to win over the plucky officers than to turn them into enemies. Once, when Shah Jahan harshly berated an officer for failure of duty and peremptorily dismissed him from service, the officer boldly sat down before the emperor, saying that since he was no longer a vassal or servant of the emperor he could do so—and Shah Jahan, instead of taking offence, laughed off that impudence and restored him to office. Similarly, when one of Aurangzeb's generals, upset over the ill-treatment of his father by the emperor, returned to court from the battlefield without permission, and laid his sword on the floor before the emperor as a token of resigning his commission, Aurangzeb took care to pacify and conciliate him.

Occasionally the nobles ticked off the emperor. When Aurangzeb appointed the relatively young Asad Khan, who had just turned fifty, as Vizier, Mahabat Khan, the governor of Afghanistan, taunted the emperor: 'Your Majesty has appointed that suckling Asad Khan as Grand Vizier . . . an unmanly fellow.' On another occasion, Mahabat Khan, resenting Aurangzeb's excessive reliance on the advice of his Chief Kazi, Abdul Wahab, caustically told the emperor, when they were discussing the strategy to be adopted against Shivaji, that 'it is unnecessary to send any army against him. A proclamation by the Chief Kazi would do the work!'

Such shows of independence were however rare. Most amirs bent with the wind. But while they bowed and scraped before the emperor, they expected nothing less for themselves from their own subordinates. 'Now the great men of the world look to the establishment of their position, and like everyone to court and flatter them,' says Abul Fazl. The Mughal grandees were touchy about status, and it was fatal to make fun of them, as Khwaja Jalaluddin Bujuq, a royal slave and acerbic wit, found out to his grief. 'He had the fault of levity and of making jokes,' says Abul Fazl, 'which perhaps is the worst offence in the eyes of the great . . . so that there was no one who did not carry in his side a wound from the thornbrake of his jesting.' Eventually, Munim Khan, the governor of Kabul, cured him of his mocking tongue by executing him on a trumped-up charge. Niamat Khan, a satirical poet of Delhi, had better luck—Aurangzeb refused to yield to the pressure from amirs to punish him.

THE REWARDS FOR humble, unquestioning service to the emperor were very great, and the Mughal amirs sported extravagantly lavish lifestyles— but this too was as the emperor desired, for the grandeur of the amirs reflected the grandeur of the emperor, and was a means to awe subjects and adversaries. 'It is impossible to believe how dissolute & luxurious ye lives of these greate men are,' exclaims Norris. They lived in great mansions, surrounded by an army of servants, several wives, concubines, singing and dancing girls, and, if they had such inclinations, a few pretty boys too; they dressed in the finest clothes, mostly embroidered with gold and silver threads, and wore rare jewels; they ate the choicest food that could be procured, from whatever far country—fruits from Kabul, ice from Kashmir, wine from Europe; they travelled in gilded, bejewelled palanquins, rode on caparisoned elephants or horses. Their pet dogs were often imported from Europe. One noble had 500 torch-bearers in his service, another had 'a daily service of a thousand rich dishes'. Not surprisingly, as Tapan Raychaudhuri notes, 'in Indian languages, adjectives derived from the word "Mughal" connote the ultimate in luxury and display.'

Impulse ruled the amir. Grandiose gestures were his style. He cavalierly gave away vast sums to reward singers and dancers, and also offered (this out of necessity) fabulous presents to the officers above him and to the emperor. Asaf Khan once gave Jahangir presents worth over one million rupees; similarly, when Mir Jumla entered the Mughal service, the presents he offered Shah Jahan amounted to 1.5 million rupees. The amirs spent recklessly on such family celebrations as childbirths, the shaving of an infant's hair, circumcisions, marriages, and so on, as well as on monumental buildings like tombs and caravanserais. They also gambled.

A major item of expenditure for the amir was the maintenance of his stables, for a horse of good breed cost as much as a thousand rupees, and a good elephant several times as much, though lesser breeds of horses and elephants could be had for a fraction of the cost. Says Moreland:

'With the possible exception of jewellery, more money was spent on the stables than in any other branch of a courtier's household.' According to Manucci, one courtier spent 250,000 rupees a year on his animals.

The amirs could well afford such expenses, but their peculiar thrill was to live dangerously beyond their means. Peer group pressure, and the fact that they could not keep their savings in their families, made them live in thoughtless extravagance. For them, as Moreland puts it, 'money saved was money wasted, unless it could be concealed from the knowledge of the world', and passed secretly to their children.

Such secret savings were rare. 'It might be supposed that wife, or children, or friends, could conceal during his [the lord's] lifetime enough for the family to live on, but this would be very difficult,' says Pelsaert. 'As a rule all the possessions of the lords, and their transactions, are not secret, but perfectly well-known, for each has his diwan, through whose hands everything passes; he has many subordinates . . . and each of them has some definite charge, for which he must account. [When the lord dies], all these subordinates are arrested, and compelled to show from their books and papers where all the cash or property is deposited, and how their master's income has been disposed of; and if there is any suspicion about their disclosures, they are tortured until they reveal the truth.'

Invariably the amirs were broke. 'Notwithstanding these large incomes, I was acquainted with very few wealthy Omrahs,' says Bernier; 'on the contrary, most of them are in embarrassed circumstances, and deeply in debt . . . [because of] the costly presents made to the king at certain annual festivals, and by their large establishment of wives, servants, camels and horses.' Often they had to borrow money from moneylenders, sometimes also from the imperial treasury. Such was the improvidence of the amirs that Akbar found it expedient to introduce a system of advancing them money from the treasury, on interest. Sums up Badauni: 'The Khan is bankrupt, and the slave is wealthy.'

The Amir at Home

THE MUGHAL AMIR did not mind dying poor as long as he could live rich. Living extravagantly and dying bankrupt was for him the natural order of things.

'They maintain the splendour of the court, and are never seen out-of-doors but in the most superb apparel,' says Bernier. 'These Omras generally make a very handsome Figure,' writes Thevenot; 'when they go through the Town, an Elephant or two goes before them, on which three Men carrying Banners are mounted; fifty or sixty Troopers well clothed, and riding on Persian or Tartarian Horses, with Bows and Arrows, Swords by their sides and Bucklers on their backs, follow them at some distance; and after these come other Men on Horse-back, sounding Trumpets, and playing on Fifes. After them comes the Omra on Horse-back, with thirty or forty Footmen about him, some making way, others carrying Lances, and some with fine Napkins driving away the Flies. One of them holds an Umbrello over his Master's head, another carries the Tobacco-Pipe, and others Pots full of water in hanging Cases of Canes. The Palanquin carried by four Men comes next with two other Porters for change; and all this pomp is brought up by a Camel or two, with men beating of Timbals on their backs. When the Omra pleases, he takes his Palanquin, and then Horse is led by him . . . the Lord is to be seen lying in it, holding Flowers in his hand, smoking Tobacco, or else chewing Betle and Areca, shewing by that soft effeminate Posture a most supine dissoluteness . . . there is not a Cavalier but hath his Umbrello bearer, his two Flie-drivers, and his Cup-bearer.' Servants, adds Bernier, also 'brush off the dust with tails of peacocks . . . carry the picquedent (*pikdan*) or spittoon . . . and sometimes account-books, and other papers.'

The amirs lived in palatial mansions, some of which, like Asaf Khan's Lahore palace (which cost two million rupees and took ten years to build) rivalled royal residences. The buildings were designed to suit the Indian climate. 'In these hot countries a house is considered beautiful if it be capacious, and if the situation be airy and exposed on all sides to wind, especially the northern breezes,' says Bernier. 'A good house has its courtyards, gardens, trees, basins of water, small *jets d'eau* in the hall or at the entrance, and handsome subterranean apartments which are furnished with large fans, and on account of their coolness are fit places for repose from noon until four or five o'clock, when the air becomes suffocatingly warm. Instead of these cellars many persons prefer kas-kanays (*khas-khanas*), that is, small and neat houses made of straw or odoriferous roots (*khas-khas*) placed commonly in the middle of a parterre, so near to a reservoir of water that the servants may easily moisten the outside by means of water brought in skins.'

'In these places they have pleasant fountaynes to bathe in and other delights by sundrie conveyances of water, whose silent murmure helps to lay their sense with bonds of sleepe in the hot seasons of the day,' says Terry about the mansions of amirs. The floors of mansions were usually raised to about the height of a man, for the smooth flow of the breeze, and there were terraces for the family to sleep out at night in summer. 'For more than six successive months, everybody lies in the open air without covering,' says Bernier, 'the common people in the streets, the merchants and persons of condition sometimes in their courts or gardens, and sometimes on their terraces, which are first carefully watered.' They would move from the terrace to an adjacent hall in case it rained, or a dust storm arose, or if they wished to avoid the morning chill or guard against 'those light but penetrating dews which frequently cause a numbness in the limbs and induce a species of paralysis.' People usually slept on the floor or on charpais, light cots woven with silk or cotton strings; the bedding of persons of means were quilts and pillows of silk, with covers of cotton or linen.

The residences of mansabdars of lower ranks, unlike those of amirs, were humble, but still quite comfortable. 'Very few are built entirely of brick or stone, and several are made only of clay and straw, yet they are airy and pleasant, most of them having courts and gardens, being commodious inside . . . ,' notes Bemier. 'The thatched roof is supported by a layer of long, handsome and strong canes, and the clay walls are covered with a fine white lime.'

The walls of Mughal mansions were bare, except for numerous niches—'cut in a variety of shapes, tasteful and well proportioned'—holding porcelain vases and flower-pots; 'the ceiling is gilt and painted, but without pictures of man or beast, such representation being forbidden by the religion of the country,' remarks Bernier. 'There are no hangings on the walls of his houses, by reason of the heate, the walls are either painted or else beautified with purer white lime than what we call Spanish,' writes Terry.

The white plaster of the walls, says Pelsaert, 'is very noteworthy, and far superior to anything in our country. They use unslaked lime, which is mixed with milk, gum, and sugar into a thin paste. When the walls have been plastered with lime, they apply this paste, rubbing it with well-designed trowels until it is smooth; then they polish it steadily with agates, perhaps for a whole day, until it is dry and hard, and shines like alabaster, or can even be used as a looking-glass.'

Furniture was minimal in Mughal homes. There were hardly any tables, chairs and cupboards even in the homes of nobles, but chests were common, and also presumably, as in later times, *takhats*, low wooden platforms on legs, on which mattresses were spread for seating. Stools of rush grass and cane were used in gardens and courtyards. Bedsteads and chests and other valued pieces were lavishly ornamented with gold or silver. 'The floores,' says Terry, 'paved with stone or else made with lime and sand, like our plaster of Paris, are spred with rich carpets.' People lounged on carpets or mattresses, against thick, soft bolsters, while attendants with hand fans cooled the air. The ambience of the Mughal mansion was one of languorous sensuality. 'Their *mahals*,' says Pelsaert in puritanical disapprobation, 'are adorned internally with lascivious sensuality, wanton and reckless festivity, superfluous pomp, inflated pride, and ornamental daintiness.'

The traditional mode of lighting in Indian homes was messy, and it disgusted Babur when he first saw it. 'In the place of candle and torch they have a great dirty gang they call lamp-men (*diwati*), who in the left hand hold a smallish wooden tripod to one corner of which a thing like the top of a candlestick is fixed, having a wick in it about as thick as the thumb,' notes Babur. 'In the right hand they hold a gourd, through a slit in which, oil is let trickle in a thin thread when the wick needs it. Great people keep a hundred or two of these lamp-men. This is the Hindustan substitute for lamps and candlesticks! If their rulers and begs have work at night needing candles, these dirty lamp-men bring lamps, go close up and there stand.' The Mughals popularized the use of candles and candelabra in India, but the older manner of lighting seems to have persisted, and amirs retained a large number of lamp-men in their service. The common mode of lighting in the Mughal camp, according to Bernier, was with 'a piece of iron hafted in a stick' wrapped with linen rags steeped in oil, which was replenished by boys carrying narrow-necked vessels of iron or brass.

The mansions of amirs teemed with servants—lamp-men, guards, cooks, eunuchs, palanquin bearers, tent-pitchers and so on. Each of the amir's several wives had her own body of servants, anywhere from ten to a hundred, depending on her status. Even each of his animals had its own allotted servants: an elephant had four attendants, a horse two or three. 'Servants are exceedingly numerous in this country, for everyone, be he mounted soldier, merchant or king's official, keeps as many as his position and circumstances permit,' says Pelsaert. 'Outside the house, they serve for display, running continually before their master's horse; inside they do the work of the house, each knowing his own duties.' Even when the army was on the march, every man in the army, down to the lowest foot-soldier, had an average of two or three servants travelling with him, and amirs travelled with vast retinues. 'I rank only with a two-horse cavalier, and yet I cannot possibly contrive with less than three men,' grouses Bernier.

A large number of servants were needed because the quality of service was dismal. 'In them is no goodness,' complains Manucci about the common run of servants in Mughal India. 'They are full of malice, generally thieves, false, traitors, deniers, slothful, loquacious, incapable of secrecy, devoid of love and fidelity, for ever complaining of their masters. Treat them tenderly as your children, and they behave the worse; and to get any work done you must act against them harshly, and make them do their duty by force.' Servants, says Pelsaert, would take a commission in every transaction; even 'if they buy only a pice-worth of food, they will have their share or *dasturi*.' Says Ovington, 'And every Roupie which the Servant lays out in buying . . . Goods, he peremptorily demands back for his own use a Couple of Pice from the Seller.'

THE AMIR'S RESIDENCE was also his office, where, when not in attendance on the emperor, he held court at the Diwan-khana, the drawing room of the mansion. No outsider was allowed to go beyond the Diwan-khana. Here the floor was covered with four-inch thick cotton mattresses, spread over with a fine white cloth in summer and a silk carpet in winter. The seat of the amir was at the head of the hall, and alongside it was a special place for honoured guests, a mattress with quilted covering embroidered with silk, gold and silver threads, and large bolsters to lean on. Several other bolsters were scattered around the hall for guests.

The hall, reports Pelsaert, 'is spread with handsome carpets, and kept very clean and neat. Here the lord takes his seat in the morning to attend to his business, whatever it is and here all his subordinates come to salaam him. This is a very humble salute, in which the body is bent forward, and the right hand is placed on the head; but persons of equal rank or position merely bend the body. If strangers desire admittance, their names are first announced, and they are then introduced. After saluting, they take seats appropriate to their position in a row on each side of their host, and that so humbly that they seem unlike themselves . . . and no one will move from his place, though they should sit the whole day. There is a certain gravity in their mode of speaking; they make no loud noise, and do not shout or use gestures. If they talk secrets, which they do not wish to be heard by everybody, they hold a handkerchief, or their girdle, before their mouths, so that neither speaker shall be touched by the other's breath. Everyone leaves as soon as he has obtained an answer to his request, but friends and acquaintances, and persons of position remain until the lord retires into the house, or unless the audience is prolonged until meal-time, though there are no fixed hours for meals.'

The Mughal grandees were a suave and urbane lot, even-tempered, civil even to the lowly. Jafar Khan, Aurangzeb's Vizier, 'was so civil and courteous that he addressed everybody as "sir", and he was incapable of displaying anger,' says Manucci. 'He was very polished, and his purity might be called fetish. He declined to listen to coarse language in any shape.' Once when an architect presented him with the plan of a mansion he was building, 'after asking for various sections of the plan, he ended by inquiring about a certain place, where were depicted the privy retreats. The architect said it was the necessary place, whereupon he held his nostril with his right hand, and puckering up his face, made a sign with his left to take the plan away, as if it smelt merely through having this painting on it.'

Provincial amirs, like Mir Jumla, the Vizier of Golconda, generally lacked such over-refined manners. Tavernier, the French jewel merchant, who had met the amir at his camp in Gandikota in Golconda, reports: 'On the 15th, at seven o'clock in the morning, we went to the Nawab, and immediately we were announced he invited us to enter his tent, where he was seated with two of his secretaries before him . . . the Nawab had the intervals between his toes full of letters, and he also held many between the fingers of his left hand. He drew them sometimes from his feet, sometimes from his hand, and sent replies through his two secretaries, writing some also himself. After the secretaries had finished the letters, he made them read them; and he then took them and affixed his seal himself, giving some to foot messengers, others to horsemen . . .'

'While we were with the Nawab he was informed that four prisoners . . . had arrived,' continues Tavernier. 'He remained more than half an hour without replying, writing continually and making his secretaries write, but at length he suddenly ordered the criminals to be brought in; and after having questioned them, and made them confess with their own mouths the crimes of which they were accused, he remained nearly an hour without saying anything, continuing to write and to make his secretaries write. Then there entered into his tent many officers of the army who came to pay their respects with great humility, and to whose salute he replied only by an inclination of the head.' When he was finished with the letters, Mir Jumla ordered the four prisoners to be executed—the heads of two to be cut off, one to have his hands and feet cut off, and the fourth to be disembowelled—and then sat down to his dinner, at which he was joined by his officers and Tavernier.

The Mughals considered Mir Jumla's manners as coarse, and Prince Dara often made fun of him. But what was refinement to one was crudity to another, the appreciation of good manners being culturally subjective. Thus Roe considered the customs and manners of Indians 'either ordinary, or mingled with much barbarisme', while the Mughals in turn considered Europeans filthy and gross. Uzbegs and Afghans were especially considered crude by European visitors.

The only subject of conversation of Uzbegs, according to Manucci, was food. 'As a salute to their repletion, they emit loud eructations, just like the bellowing of bulls,' says Manucci. As for Afghans, they were considered unmannerly enough to spit on the carpet on which they sat. Says Manucci: 'They come to court . . . well-clad and well-armed, caracoling on fine horses richly caparisoned, posing as persons of some consideration, and followed by several servants borrowed or hired for the day. On reaching their house they divest themselves of all this finery, and, tying a scanty cloth round their loins and wrapping a rag round their head, they take their seat on a mat, and live on kichadi or badly cooked cow's flesh of low quality, which is very abundant and cheap.'

IN THE PRIVACY of the home, scanty clothes, usually just a knee-length loin-cloth, were probably the norm in Mughal India, as in later times, because of the warm climate. Writes Bernier: 'Suppose one just returned on horseback, half dead with heat and dust, and drenched, as usual, in perspiration . . . [you] swallow quickly a draught of fresh water, or lemonade . . . undress, wash face, hands and feet, and then immediately drop upon a sofa in some shady place, where one or two servants fan you with their pankhas or fans.'

Nobody stirred outdoors in the afternoon, if they could help it. 'In the heate of the day they keepe [to] their houses,' says Terry; 'where the men of better fashion, lying on couches or sitting on their carpets, have servants stand about them who, beating the ayre with broade fannes of stiffe leather or the like, make winde to coole them. And taking thus their ease, they often call their barbers, who tenderly gripe and smite their armes and other parts of their bodies, instead of exercise, to stirre the bloud. It is a pleasing wantonnesse, and much used in those hot climes.'

'Gorgeous apparell is prohibited by the sunnes heate,' continues Terry; 'the King himselfe being commonly vested with a garment . . . of pure calico lawne.' Still, the amirs spent a small fortune on their wardrobes. A cotton piece (enough to make a complete dress) cost Rs 150; woollen Rs 250; silk Rs 300; brocade anywhere between Rs 700 and Rs 1500. The amirs and their begums made numerous sets of dresses, and many, in imitation of the royal family, made a complete new wardrobe every year. Says Bernier: 'I continually meet with persons neat and elegant in their dress, finely formed, well mounted, and properly attended.'

In matters of grooming, dress and ornament, the high fashion was set by the emperor. If the emperor wore no beard, as Akbar and Jahangir did not, that then was the style preferred by the amirs, and if he bored his ears and wore earrings, as Jahangir did, so did many amirs. Mughal amirs spent vast amounts of money on ornaments, for men as well as women, though Muslims generally wore far fewer jewels than Hindus. 'Continual purchases [were] made of precious stones' by the amirs, writes Manucci. 'From this cause the goldsmiths are almost continuously busy with the making of ornaments.'

Throughout India, except among the Kashmiris in the far north and the Tamils and Malayalees in the far south, among men of means irrespective of community, especially among those connected with the government, the sartorial style was the same, with only some slight regional and communal variations. The basic Mughal dress, of Turko-Persian origin, was unisexual. It consisted of breeches, a tunic (qaba) and a turban, to which various apparels were added depending on the weather and the ceremoniousness of the occasion. The breeches came down to the ankle, and were either a tight-fitting churidar or a loose-fitting shalwar. The rich wore silk breeches, 'striped with different colours, which are so long that they must be pleated upon the Leg, much in the same manner as formerly Silk-stockings were worn in France,' says Thevenot.

Over the breeches was worn the qaba, an elegant calf-length tunic that was tight-fitting around the torso, but pleated and loose from waist down, made of cotton or fine wool, depending on the weather. Thevenot describes it as 'a kind of gown with a long Jerkin fastened to it, open before and pleated from top to bottom, to hinder it from being too clutterly. It hath a collar two fingers breadth high, of the same Stuff with the rest. They button not that Vest as we do our Coats, but they fold it cross ways over the Stomach, first from the right to the left, and then from the left to the right. They tie it with ribbons of the same Stuff, which are two Fingers broad and a Foot long; and there are seven or eight of them from the upper part down to the Haunches, of which they only tie the first and last, and let the rest hang negligently as being more graceful.' The qaba was commodious, and, being open from top to bottom, 'more easily put on and off; besides that, when one is alone, he may open them and take the fresh Air'. Hindus tied the qaba on the left, while Muslims and Europeans tied it on the right.

Mughal paintings show the nobility wearing qaba of bright colours, or of bold stripes and floral patterns, but according to Thevenot white was preferred in the court of Aurangzeb in his old age. 'Some wear them of Painted cloth,' says Thevenot, 'but that is not the Gentlest manner of Apparel, and when the Rich do not wear White they use Silk, and choose the broadest Stuff they can find, which commonly is streaked with several colours.' A cummerbund girded the waist. 'They use only one Girdle . . . and it is not very dear either, being only of White-cloth,' says Thevenot, 'and it is rare to see the Indians make use of the lovely Girdles of Persia, unless they be wealthy persons of Quality.'

In winter, says Thevenot, the amirs wore a vest called cadeby—'they are Cloth of Gold, or other Rich Stuff, and are lined with Sables which cost very dear'—or an overcoat called dagla. Turbans were worn by men throughout India; alternately, some wore Tartar caps. Common people usually wore turbans of white cloth, but the rich used very fine cloth threaded with gold. 'The Rich have them of so fine a Cloth, that five and twenty or Thirty Ells of it which are put into a Turban, will not weigh four Ounces,' notes Thevenot.

'As for Stockings the Indians are at no charge, for they use neither Stockings nor Socks, but put their Shoes on their naked Feet,' continues Thevenot. Made of leather or velvet, the sandals were without heels, their toes pointed and curved. The sandals worn by the amirs and begums were embroidered with gold and studded with gems, and were as expensive as jewels. The amirs, being men of leisure, usually wore their sandals with the back portion folded down, says Thevenot, so they 'go with their Shoes slipshod', but the Baniyas kept the back part up: 'being men of business they would walk with freedom, which is very hard to be done, when the Foot is not on all sides begirt with the Shoe.' Men removed their sandals when they entered a house and, according to Manucci, when speaking 'to a person of quality, for it is a great piece of bad manners in this country to speak to such a person with your shoes on and your head uncovered. The monks, called sannyasis, are excepted, also ascetics, called tavagi, and Brahmans.'

Upper-class men were heavily perfumed. 'All persons in India being extremely choice about, and fond of, scents and flowers, they disburse a great deal for essences of many kinds, for rosewater, and for scented oils distilled from different flowers,' says Manucci. 'Besides all that expense, there is the betel, which is always in their mouths.' The amirs also used perfumed pottery, which came from Patna. Sometimes even their horses were perfumed. 'Everybody in India knows how dear and scarce essence of roses is . . . Yet neither scarcity nor high cost deterred this general (Jafar Khan) from having his horses rubbed with this liquid as a matter of course,' reports Manucci.

THE AMIRS WERE equally unsparing on food. They gladly paid as much as two and a half rupees for a melon from Badakshan, a rupee per pound of ice, and so on. Cooks from many parts of the world were employed to stimulate the jaded taste-buds of the amirs; according to Manrique, even European pastries, cakes and other sweets were served in their households. The table of Abul Fazl, scholar and gourmet, was justly celebrated in his time: he was served a hundred dishes at every meal. The sybarites of eighteenth-century Lucknow are said to have held that 'the most important activity in human life is eating', and this seems to have been the attitude of many Mughal amirs too. Characteristically, though the Mughals did not pay much attention to the adornment of the dining place, their food itself was always richly adorned, stained in different pigments, garnished with silver foil, some items made to look like gems, fruits cut in the shape of flowers, and so on. Tableware of gold, silver and fine china was common. 'They use more gold and silver in serving food than we do,' says Pelsaert.

Typical of Mughal culinary extravagance was the dinner that Asaf Khan hosted for Roe and Terry. The banquet, writes Terry, was held 'in a very spacious and a very beautiful tent . . . kept full of a very pleasant perfume . . . The floor of the tent was covered all over with very rich and large carpets, which were covered again, in the places where our dinner stood, with other good carpets made of stitcht leather . . . ; and these were covered again with pure white and fine calico cloths; and all these covered with very many dishes of silver; but for the greater part of those silver dishes, they are not larger than our largest trencher plates, the brims of all of them gilt.'

There were just the three of them for the dinner: Asaf Khan, Roe and Terry. 'We sat in that large room as it were in a triangle; the Ambassador on Asaph Chan's right, a good distance from him; and myself below; all of us on the ground, as they there all do when they eat, with our faces looking each to the other, and every one of us had his separate mess. The Ambassador had more dishes by ten, and I less by ten, than our entertainer had; yet for my part I had fifty dishes. They were all set before us at once, and little paths left betwixt them, that our entertainer's servants . . . might come and reach them to us one after another, and so they did; so that I tasted of all set before me, and of most did but taste, though all of them tasted very well.

'Now for the provision itself; for our larger dishes, they were filled with rice, dressed . . . and this rice was presented to us, some of it white, in its own proper colour, some of it made yellow with saffron, some of it was made green, and some of it put into a purple colour . . . it all tasted very well. And with rice thus ordered, several of our dishes were furnished; and very many more of them with flesh of several kinds, and with hens and other sorts of fowl cut in pieces . . .

'To these we had many jellies and culices (savoury meat jellies); rice ground to flour, then boiled, and after sweetened with sugar-candy and rose-water, to be eaten cold. The flour of rice, mingled with sweet almonds, made as small as they could, and with some of the most fleshy parts of hens stewed with it, and after, the flesh so beaten into pieces, that it could not be discerned, all made sweet with rose-water and sugar-candy, and scented with Ambergrease (ambergris) . . . Many other dishes we had, made up in cakes, of several forms, of the finest wheat flour, mingled with almonds and sugar-candy, whereof some were scented, and some not. To these potatoes excellently well dressed; and to them divers sallads of the curious fruits of that country, some preserved in sugar, and others raw; and to these many roots candied, almonds blanched, raisons of the sun (sun dried grapes), prunellas (dried plums) and I know not what, of all enough to make up the number of dishes before named.' Bread was round, white and light, of excellent wheat.

'At this entertainment we sat long, and much longer than we could with ease cross-legged; but all considered, our feast in that place was better than Apicius, that famous Epicure of Rome . . . could have made with all provisions had from the earth, air, and sea,' concludes Terry. His only complaint was that to drink they were served only water, but that, he admits 'in those hot climates . . . is very sweet, and allays thirst better than any other liquor can, and therefore better pleaseth, and agreeth better with every man that comes and lives there, than any other drink.'

Vast quantities of the most expensive fruits were consumed by the Mughal nobility, and shops in Delhi, says Bernier, were well-stocked with nuts and dried fruits from Persia, Balkh, Bukhara and Samarkand, 'such as almonds, pistachios, and walnuts, raisins, prunes, and apricots; and in winter with excellent fresh grapes, black and white, brought from the same countries, wrapped in cotton; pears and apples of three or four sorts, and those admirable melons which last the whole winter. These fruits are, however, very dear; a single melon selling for a crown and a half. But nothing is considered so great a treat: it forms the chief expense of the Omrahs, and I have frequently known my Agah spend twenty crowns on fruit for his breakfast.' In summer, local melons were plentiful, but they were not as good as those from Central Asia. For two months in summer, mangoes were plentiful and cheap, the best coming from Bengal, Golconda and Goa. 'I do not know of any sweetmeat more agreeable,' says Bernier.

'There are many confectioner's shops in the town (Delhi), but the sweetmeats are badly made, and full of dust and flies,' continues Bernier. 'Bakers are numerous, but the ovens are unlike our own, and very defective. The bread, therefore, is neither well made nor properly baked . . . In its composition they are not sparing of fresh butter, milk, and eggs; but though it be raised, it has a burnt taste . . . In the bazaars there are shops where meat is sold roasted and dressed in a variety of ways. But there is no trusting to their dishes, composed, for aught I know, of the flesh of camels, horses, or perhaps oxen which have died of disease. Indeed no food can be considered wholesome which is not dressed at home.' Beef was often palmed off as lamb; capons were not available, though fowls were plentiful and 'tolerably good and cheap'; pigeons, partridges, ducks and hares were sold alive, but good fish was difficult to come by. And water in Delhi was foul, says Bernier, 'the impurities of which exceed my power of description as it is accessible to all persons and animals and the receptacle of every kind of filth.'

What Bernier missed most in India was 'wine, that essential part of every entertainment', the Muslim prohibition of alcohol being rigorously enforced by Aurangzeb. Occasionally imported wine could be bought, but it was so expensive that 'the taste is destroyed by the cost'. Arrack, the country liquor, though also prohibited, was more easily available, but was 'harsh and burning . . . and the use of it to the least excess occasions nervous and incurable disorders,' warns Bernier. 'A wise man will here accustom himself to the pure and fine water, and to the excellent lemonade, which costs little and may be drunk without injury. To say the truth, few persons in these hot climates feel a strong desire for wine.'

'THERE ARE NO fixed hours for meals' in India, says Pelsaert. 'Before eating they first wash their hands; then the tablecloth is brought and spread on the floor . . . The . . . head servant sits in the middle, and serves each guest according to his rank, the senior first. In eating, they use little in the way of spoons or knives except their five fingers, which they besmear up to the knuckles soldier-fashion for napkins are not used, and it is very bad manners to lick the fingers. Each guest confines himself to the portion served before him; no food is touched with the left hand; and little or nothing is drunk while eating, whether water or wine, until they have said their prayer and washed their hands.'

The table manners of Hindu kings and nobility were somewhat different from those of the Muslim amirs. 'Princes and kings eat in the following manner: They are seated on the ground on a piece of fine cloth,' says Manucci. 'Then the house or the room in which they are to eat is rubbed over with a solution of cow-dung. As the palaces of kings have floors made of a cement which looks like fine marble, there they do nothing more than throw down some cow-dung mixed in water, and then wipe the floor with a piece of cloth. The floor then looks like a looking-glass. Without all this ceremonial of cleansing with the dung of this animal . . . no person of quality sits down to eat. These preparations finished, they bring a great platter of enamelled gold, which is placed on the ground in front of the diners, but without allowing it to touch the cloth on which they are seated. After this some small gold dishes are placed around, and the food is brought from the kitchen in bowls or vessels of silver, fashioned in the shape of cooking-pots. First of all, from these bowls they place rice cooked without salt or other condiment in the large dish, and on this they put some stew. If the whole cannot be contained in the large dish, they put the remainder in the small dishes round about it.

'Then the raja takes whatever pleases him, throwing it with his hand into a plate of rice, where he mixes it and rolls it into balls, which he throws into his mouth with the right hand. The left hand is not allowed to touch any food. All is swallowed without mastication. This fashion they consider very cleanly, and there is no better way of satisfying oneself; and they say that Europeans eat rice like pigs. Then, before finishing the meal, they send as much as they think sufficient to their wives. For in this country these never eat with their husbands, even though those waiting on the king be eunuchs, children, or women.'

These were ancient Indian practices, and were followed by all orthodox Hindus, not just by the rajas. Taboos ruled the world of the Hindu, and that of the Muslim too, though less so.

The Amir at Play

ISLAM ORDAINED ABSTINENCE from alcohol, so the Mughal emperors, including unorthodox Akbar, dutifully issued prohibition decrees. According to the Hanifi school of jurists, a man guilty of wine drinking had to be punished with eighty whip lashes, as against 100 for fornication, but none except Aurangzeb was particularly serious about enforcing prohibition, especially as dry intoxicants like hemp and opium were permitted. The emperors themselves, with the exception of Shah Jahan and Aurangzeb, were heavy drinkers, and Babur, Humayun and Jahangir delighted in drinking in the company of their amirs. Akbar was indulgent. Once, during the feast of Nauruz, when some of his religious amirs became drunk, Akbar wryly quoted Hafiz:

> In the era of the fault-forgiving king
> The Kazi drained flagons,
>   the Mufti quaffed cups.

Jahangir went further and encouraged drinking during Nauruz. 'I gave orders that whoever might wish for intoxicating drinks and exhilarating drugs should not be debarred from using them,' he writes. Akbar made toddy an approved drink, and other forms of alcohol lawful as a medicine. And it was this medicinal value of alcohol that Jahangir emphasized when he pressed wine on Shah Jahan, quoting Avicenna:

> A raging enemy, but a prudent friend is wine;
> Antidote in moderation, but poison in excess,
> In much there's no little injury,
> And much profit in little.

Such benign tolerance of venial sins was not uncommon in Islam. The sensible attitude, as recommended by Barani, a fourteenth-century orthodox Indian Muslim historian, was that 'if in secret and privately, habitual sinners indulge in their practices, severe investigations about their activities should not usually be made . . . what is secret and hidden should not be revealed and published.'

It is therefore no surprise that, though the open sale of alcohol was prohibited in the Mughal empire, drinking was fashionable and common among Mughal amirs, and they often took exotic concoctions, mixing wine, hemp and opium. Jahangir writes that Pisharu Khan, one of his nobles, 'was never for a moment without the intoxication of wine'. The drink habit was so widespread that, according to Manucci, even Aurangzeb's Chief Kazi drank secretly. British ambassador Norris records that Mughal amirs were 'greate Lovers of English spirits', and that the presents he sent to Asad Khan, Aurangzeb's Vizier, included 'some of all sorts of ye choicest glasse ware', and especially 'ye strong waters' for which 'their mouths waterd att'. Once, when he sent an amir two cases of spirits secretly, the Kazi, coming to hear of it, asked for some for himself, says Norris.

Jafar Khan, Asad Khan's predecessor as Vizier, also 'used to drink his drop of liquor' and, as Manucci tells the story, when Aurangzeb upbraided him for that, 'replied that he was an old man, without strength in his hands or firmness in his feet, had little sight in his eyes, and was very poor. By drinking wine he got sight for seeing, power for wielding the pen in the service of His Majesty, felt strength in his feet to run to court when His Majesty called, and seemed in imagination to become rich . . . Aurangzeb laughed at this speech.' Even Mughal elephants were guzzlers. Asad Beg reports that an elephant which the Sultan of Bijapur presented to Akbar had to be given 'two *mans* of wine daily'.

Despite such wide prevalence of drinking, public drunkenness was rare among the upper classes, as courtly breeding among amirs and social taboos among orthodox Hindus moderated behaviour. 'None of the people there are at any time seen drunk (though they might find liquor enough to do it) but the very offal and dregs of that people, and these rarely or very seldom,' says Terry. 'Such meate or drinke as their law allowes they use onely to satisfie nature, not appetite; hating gluttonies, and esteeming drunknesse (as indeed it is) a second madnesse, and therefore have but one word in the language (*musth*) for a drunkard and a mad-man.' Common people had no such inhibitions, and the few who drank among them did so without restraint. 'I have noticed that these people of India, generally those of low extraction, are not fitted for the drinking of wine, and when they drink they become like animals, both in body and in intellect,' says Manucci. 'If they have drunk only a little, you can tell it by their hesitating speech.'

Though the Mughal emperors generally condoned drinking in private, they forbade anyone from attending the court while drunk, for that was taken as a sign of a lack of seriousness or even as a show of disrespect. Akbar endeavoured to regulate drinking by bringing the sale of alcohol under state control, and requiring buyers to register themselves with authorities. And when a noble once attended the court in a drunken state, Akbar had him led around tied to a horse's tail. Jahangir had breath sniffers at the entrance to the Diwan-i-khas, to turn out those who smelled of alcohol. Aurangzeb imposed strict prohibition, inflicting severe punishment on the vendors of liquor, and ordering all Europeans, except physicians and surgeons, to live in an area near the artillery park at one league's distance from the city, where they were allowed to prepare and drink spirits, but not to sell them. Still the amirs continued to drink, but secretly, says Manucci.

In the Deccan, the sultans were on the whole far laxer in enforcing Islamic proscriptions. Toddy was freely available in Hyderabad, says Tavernier, and every day some five or six thousand horses brought it into the city from the suburbs, each horse carrying two earthen jars on each side. In Surat, toddy was drunk 'plentifully' by Europeans and Indians, says Ovington. 'A Quart of it may be got for a Pice or two, and is so strong that it turns the Brain as soon as English Beer . . .' Terry was also a toddy enthusiast, and speaks of it 'as pleasing to the taste as any white wine, if drunke betimes in the morning'. In Hyderabad, alongside the toddy shops were brothels.

COFFEE HAD BECOME a popular drink among upper-class Indians by the early seventeenth century, but the position of tea is uncertain. The earliest reference to tea in India is the journal of Mandelslo, a German traveller in India in 1638. 'At our ordinary meetings every day we took only The which is commonly used all over the Indies, not only among those of the country, but also among the Dutch and English, who take it as a drug that cleanses the Stomach and digest the superfluous humours, by a temperate heat particular thereto,' notes Mandelslo of his experience in Gujarat. Ovington, who was in Surat in 1689, writes: 'The Bannians are not restrained for liberal Draughts of Tea and Coffee, to revive their wasted Spirits, any part of the Day . . . Tea . . . is a common Drink with all the Inhabitants of India, as well Europeans as Natives; and by the Dutch is used as such a standing Entertainment, that the Tea-pot's seldom off the Fire, or unimploy'd . . . Tea, with some hot Spice intermixt and boiled in the Water, has the Repute of prevailing against the Headache, Gravel, and Griping in the Guts, and 'tis generally drunk in India, either with Sugar-Candy, or, by the more curious, with small Conserv'd Lemons.'

There are no other references to tea in India at this time, and it seems likely that Ovington, a tea enthusiast, and Mandelslo were blindly generalizing from what they saw in Surat. There is no evidence that tea was cultivated in India in the seventeenth century, though wild tea plants were discovered in the hills of Assam in the 1830s. Tea planting in India would begin only in the mid-nineteenth century. It is, however, likely that some tea was off-loaded in India from the consignments going from China to Europe, where tea was introduced in the seventeenth century by the Dutch. It could even be that some tea had been coming into India before that too, because tea had been in use in China for at least a couple of thousand years, and India and China had close trade contacts from ancient times. Still, the use of tea in India in the seventeenth century was most probably confined to European settlements and port towns; being an imported item, it could not have been in any case in common use.

Coffee too was imported, and it was a luxury beverage in Mughal India. 'As for India, it (coffee) is but little used there,' says Tavernier. Coffee (said to have been first discovered in Kaffa in Ethiopia) was extensively cultivated in Arabia at this time, and it was from there that it was imported into India. It is also possible that some coffee was grown in India in Mughal times. Legend has it that coffee was introduced into India in the fourteenth century by a Sufi, Baba Budan, who had come across it during his travels in the Middle East, and that it was first cultivated in Karnataka, where coffee plantations thrive even today in the Baba Budan Hills. Says Terry, 'They use a liquor more healthful than pleasant, they call it Cohha (coffee, from Arabic kahwa): a blacke seed boyled in water, which doth little alter the taste of the water. Notwithstanding, it is very good to helpe digestion, to quicken the spirits, and to dense the bloud.'

Similar medicinal properties were claimed for paan too, a chew of areca-nut, lime paste, spices and (from the seventeenth century on) tobacco, folded in betel-leaf. 'It bytts in the mouth, avoydes rume, cooles the head, strengthens the teeth . . .' says Roe; 'it makes one unused to it giddy, and makes a man's spittle redd, and in tyme coullers the teeth which is esteemed a beawty.' Adds Terry: 'It hath many rare qualities, for it preserves the teeth, comforts the braine, strengthens the stomacke, and cures and prevents a tainted breath.' Warns Fryer: 'If swallowed, it inebriates as much as Tobacco.'

Chewing paan was a universal habit in India. Says Careri, 'Their greatest delight is to chew Betle all Day.' When Manucci first landed in India, he was, he writes, 'much surprised to see that almost everybody was spitting something red as blood. I imagined it must be due to some complaint of the country, or that their teeth had become broken.' According to Tavernier, women chewed paan even when they mounted the sati pyre.

The custom of offering paan to guests was a civility in polite society in India. It was good manners to offer paan to the visitor at the time of his leaving, and to call for paan to be served was a courteous way of indicating the termination of a meeting. Similarly, when a servant of any consequence was dismissed from service, it was customary to give him paan, as a gesture of goodwill—thus when the Sultan of Malwa dismissed the Rajputs in his service, he had 40,000 paans prepared and sent to them.

Tobacco—and the hookah, the ubiquitous symbol of princely India in later times—was unknown in the Mughal court until the seventeenth century. Tobacco was introduced into the Deccan from South America by the Portuguese, in the second half of the sixteenth century. Courtier-historian Asad Beg chanced upon it during a mission to the Deccan towards the close of Akbar's reign, and when he returned to Agra he carried with him a bag of 'fine tobacco, such that if one leaf be lit the whole will continue burning'. At the court, he presented some of the tobacco to the emperor in a betel bag 'of very superior workmanship', along with a 'jewel work' hookah, 'all arranged elegantly on a silver tray'.

Akbar was curious, and asked Asad to prepare a smoke. When the pipe was ready and Akbar took it to smoke, the emperor's 'physician approached and forbade his doing so,' says Asad Beg. 'But His Majesty was graciously pleased to say he must smoke a little to gratify me, and taking the mouth piece into his sacred mouth, drew two or three breaths. The physician was in great trouble, and would not let him do more.' Akbar then summoned his druggist to explain the qualities of tobacco, but all he could say was that 'there was no mention of it in his books, but that it was a new invention . . . and the European doctors had written much in its praise.' A lively debate followed, in which Asad Beg strongly pleaded that tobacco should not be rejected out of hand simply because it was new, but should be examined and then judged. Akbar agreed and passed the pipe to others to smoke, and the habit caught on. As Asad Beg puts it, 'As I had brought a large supply of tobacco and pipes, I sent some to several of the nobles, while others sent to ask for some; indeed, all, without exception, wanted some, and the practice was introduced. After that the merchants began to sell it, so the custom of smoking spread rapidly. His Majesty, however, did not adopt it.'

Jahangir disliked tobacco; in fact, he banned smoking, as did his Persian contemporary, Shah Abbas. 'In consequence of the disturbance that tobacco brings about in most temperaments and constitutions, I had ordered that no one should smoke it,' says Jahangir. The orthodox ulema also issued fatwas against it, as smoking tobacco was an innovation not sanctioned by Islamic tradition. These prohibitions however had little effect, and in the course of time the tobacco habit became so widespread that the duty on it turned out to be a major source of income for the empire, yielding 'a vast revenue' in the reign of Aurangzeb, says Mustaid Khan.

The hookah, probably invented by Persians, was turned into a jewelled status symbol by the Mughal amir, who had hookah attendants, *hookahburdars*, keeping pace with him even when he travelled in a palanquin or on horseback, so he could smoke at a trot. And tobacco itself was enriched in flavour by mixing it with dried fruits and infusing it with various fragrant essences and allowing the mixture to mature in earthen jars buried in the ground for a few weeks.

THE AMIRS LIVED steeped in sensuality, and maintained huge harems. Even when camping away from home, they kept small temporary harems of local concubines. The royal elephants too were polygamous. 'The King allowes every one of his great elephants foure females, which in their language they call wives,' says Terry. Aurangzeb's Vizier Asad Khan in his prime was a notorious philanderer, who kept a large troupe of handmaids and singing-girls, on whom he spent a good part of his vast income. According to Asad Beg 'debauchery and gambling' were endemic among the Mughal nobles in Burhanpur and elsewhere. Amirs often pestered physicians and quacks for potions to improve their sexual vigour, says Manucci. Several of the drugs and stimulants used in Mughal times derived their popularity, in part at least, from their supposed aphrodisiac potency. Advises Mullah Ayyub, scholar and poet:

Eat O Sir, an atom of opium,
That it may help thee in not giving way
soon in copulation.

Some of the Mughal amirs were vigorously bisexual, and kept a number of comely pages in their train. Pederasty, which was considered 'pure love', was in vogue among Mughal aristocrats in Central Asia, and catamites were often transformed into luminous mystic idols in Sufi literature. As a medieval poet had it,

> Harken to this advice of Saifi
> That it may suffice thee all thy life:
> On good poetry and a handsome boy,
> Pin thy faith . . .

The homosexual culture did not however thrive in India, though now and then there were major scandals, leading, in one instance reported by Tavernier in the reign of Shah Jahan, to the murder of the governor of Burhanpur by one of his pages, 'a young boy that was very beautiful', whom the governor tried to seduce. The most sensational homosexual scandal in Mughal India was the one involving Khan Zaman (Ali Quli Khan, the hero of the second battle of Panipat) and Shahim Beg, a gentleman soldier of Akbar, who, according to Badauni, was 'pre-eminent for beauty of disposition and appearance, the beau ideal of the age . . . So the Khan Zaman, following the manners of Transoxiana, manifested wonderful affection for Shahim Beg, and called him "my king", and gave himself entirely to humouring him, and many times waited on him like an ordinary servant . . .' At the same time, Khan Zaman was also deeply in love with Aram Jan, a talented courtesan, who, in the wounding phrase of Abul Fazl, 'was the embraced of thousands'. The triangular bisexual dalliance outraged even jaded Mughal society, and its complex ramifications led to the death of Shahim Beg in a drunken brawl—which, says Abul Fazl, made Khan Zaman so disconsolate that he presently flew into the hands of 'a boy . . . named Qabul Khan who knew how to dance'.

A few other quaint instances of homosexual romance are also mentioned in Mughal chronicles. Thus it is said of Sarmad, a seventeenth-century Persian Jew turned Sufi living in India, that he once fell desperately in love with a Hindu boy, Abhai Chand, 'and casting off his clothes, sat down at the door of his beloved'. Strangely, this did not outrage the boy's father; rather, when he became convinced of the purity of Sarmad's love, he handed the boy over to Sarmad.

LESS EXACTING THAN such games of passion were the many indoor and outdoor games that the amirs played. In Akbar's reign we find them picnicking at the lakeside gardens in Fatehpur Sikri, 'some . . . playing at checkers, some at chess, and many . . . occupied with cards', as Abul Fazl reports. Chess was a Mughal addiction, and two-sided as well as four-sided chess were played. 'All the great men are fond of amusing themselves with chess-playing,' says Manucci, 'by which, as they say, they learn to govern, place and displace, give and take, with discretion, to the glory and gain of their projects.' After meals, it was a courtesy for the host to invite his guest to a game of chess. 'Dinner ended, they played at Chesse,' says Roe about a feast given by a Mughal noble.

It is not known when card games were introduced into India, but the Mughal pack, and the games, differed greatly from what they are in modern times. The amirs were avid about the game from the beginning—Babur in his memoirs mentions that he sent a pack to one of his provincial governors—and gradually it became so engrossing a pastime that they sometimes neglected even emergency calls to duty in order to play on. The governor of Daman, says Manucci, once refused to act when Arabs, who had landed in ships, attacked the town, because he was 'intent on his game of cards'. Jai Singh, Aurangzeb's great general, was also a cards enthusiast, and Manucci used to play with him at night during the Mughal campaign against Shivaji. The other aristocratic pastimes were hunting, holding animal fights, playing polo—and gambling, which had religious sanction for Hindus, and was considered auspicious on the night of Diwali. 'The Gentiles being great lovers of Play at Dice, there is much Gaming, during the five Festival days . . . a vast deal of Money lost . . . and many People ruined,' says Thevenot.

For family entertainment, the amirs had in their employ a number of musicians, dancers and other medieval showbiz professionals like mountebanks, jugglers, acrobats, snake-charmers, and producers of fireworks. Variety was provided by itinerant magicians, who were so skilled in creating illusions that they could, apart from performing the usual rope tricks, seemingly raise any fruit tree that was desired and have it bear fruit in an hour, and perform other such miracles. Pets were another diversion, and many amirs, in imitation of the royal custom, kept pet dogs and even swine, says Badauni, and took to fondling and kissing dogs and eating with them. 'A considerable Value is set upon any of our European Dogs, either Spanials, Greyhounds, or Mastiffs,' says Ovington. Pigeon flying was in the beginning a favourite sport of the Mughals, but as an aristocratic pastime it gradually died out.

As men of leisure and wealth, Mughal amirs were patrons of culture and learning, and several of them—Biram Khan, Todar Mal and Abdur-

Rahim, for instance—were acclaimed writers. The amirs were also great builders, and spent money extravagantly on mansions, caravanserais, mosques and temples. And sometimes, though they enjoyed the best of life, the good times palled on them, and some of them took to asceticism.

WHATEVER THE AMIR did, the decision would have been made on the advice of astrologers, who were omnipresent in Mughal society and were major initiators of action in every sphere of Mughal life. The higher the person, the graver the issues, the greater the role of astrologers. Royal astrologers were highly paid professionals. From the rationalist Akbar to the cynical and saturnine Aurangzeb, the Mughal emperors were all firm believers in astrology, and so were the Mughal amirs. 'The King puts so much confidence that hee will not undertake a journey, nor yet doe any thing of the least consequence, unless his wizards tell him 'tis a good and prosperous houre,' says Terry about Jahangir. Writes Aurangzeb: 'The passages of my horoscope—composed by Fazil Khan Ala-ul-mulk, [giving the incidents] from the day of my birth till after my death—have all been verified by actual experience.'

Most of the astrologers were shameless frauds. A royal astrologer once confidently told Dara that he would succeed Shah Jahan, but when Manucci asked him how he could make such a bold prediction, 'the astrologer laughed long and heartily at my question, and said to me that if the said prince should come to be king, he would accord to him the greatest credit; if not, the prince would be sufficiently busied in saving his own life, and not likely to have time to seek that of an astrologer.'

European travellers, often no mean enthusiasts of astrology themselves, found the Indian obsession with the stars droll. 'The majority of Asiatics are so infatuated in favour of being guided by the signs of the heaven, that, according to their phraseology, no circumstance can happen below, which is not written above,' writes Bernier. 'In every enterprise they consult their astrologers. When two armies have completed every preparation for battle, no consideration can induce the generals to commence the engagement until the Sahet (*saiet*) be performed; that is, until the propitious moment for attack is ascertained. In like manner no commanding officer is nominated, no marriage takes place, and no journey is undertaken, without consulting Monsieur the Astrologer. Their advice is considered absolutely necessary even on the most trifling occasions, whether the proposed purchase of a slave, or the first wearing of new clothes . . . The astrologer is necessarily made acquainted with every transaction public and private, with every project common and extraordinary.'

'They (astrologers) tell a poor person his fortune for a payssa . . .; and after examining the hand and face of the applicant, turning over the leaves of the large book, and pretending to make certain calculations, these impostors decide upon the Sahet or propitious moment of commencing the business he may have in hand,' says Bernier. 'Silly women, wrapping themselves in a white cloth from head to foot, flock to the astrologers, whisper to them all the transactions of their lives, and disclose every secret with no more reserve than is practised by a scrupulous penitent in the presence of her confessor.' Indeed, it could be said that astrologers served about the same useful social function as confessional priests or modern psychiatrists, and probably did no greater harm.

'The ignorant and infatuated people really believe that the stars have an influence which the astrologers can control . . . ,' continues Bernier. 'The most ridiculous of these pretenders to divination was a half-caste Portuguese, a fugitive from Goa. This fellow sat on his carpet as gravely as the rest, and had many customers notwithstanding he could neither read nor write. His only instrument was an old mariner's compass, and his books of astrology a couple of old Romish prayer-books in the Portuguese language, the pictures of which he pointed out as the signs of the European zodiac. *A tal Bestia, tal Astrologuo* (For such brutes, such an astrologer), he unblushingly observed.'

AT THE FRINGE of the Mughal high society lived a growing number of Europeans in India. Mostly transients, their backgrounds and status, their lifestyles and the way they related to India, all varied considerably. If they were royal ambassadors or representatives of European trading companies they generally lived according to the customs of their own countries, but if they were in the service of an Indian prince they usually adopted Indian ways, and some of them became Muslims to promote their careers. Roe and Norris, British ambassadors, rigidly adhered to British ways, but William Hawkins who preceded them, despite his claim to be the British ambassador, accepted appointment as a Mughal mansabdar and adopted the Mughal lifestyle. He was called English Khan by Jahangir. Hawkins, says Jourdain, 'in his howse . . . used altogether the custome of the Moores or Mahometans, both in his meate and drinke and other customes . . .' In the European enclaves like Goa it was the European mode of life that prevailed.

The common run of Europeans in India were crass mercenaries, for whom the passage to India was a means to escape from the rigours and privations of life in Europe into a rich, wild and debauched life. The better class of Europeans, on the other hand, had worthier reasons to love (or hate) India. Such a man was Bernier. His critique of India, though savaged by Indian nationalists and ideologues of the twentieth century, still remains startlingly fresh, and in many respects valid. What interested Bemier were the broad social concerns of good government and economic progress, in both of which he found Mughal India wanting. But there were other Europeans in India who hearkened to a different drummer, for whom social progress and material well-being were not everything, and several of them yielded to the seduction of the slow, sensuous rhythm of life in India. Bernard, a fabulously successful French physician in Jahangir's court, for instance, made India his home, earned a fortune, but merrily gave it all away. Even Manucci, cannoneer and quack physician, despite his brutal indictment of India, lived here for sixty-one uninterrupted years, till his death.

Mughal amirs regarded Europeans as socially and culturally inferior, and, according to Roe, they considered it 'a kind of uncleanenesse to mingle with us ... They ate not willingly with us.' Confirms Terry: 'Mahometans in generall thinke us Christians so uncleane they will not eate with us, nor yet of any thing dressed in our vessels.' Christians were considered men of little worth, and one Mughal officer, says Manucci, maintained that 'for a Mahomedan who killed a Christian, it was sufficient punishment to make a slight cut on the end of the little finger until he had lost three drops of blood and make him pay ten *patacas*.'

Taboo-ridden Hindus would of course have nothing to do with Europeans. 'As they hold the Farangis to be vile and abominable,' says Manucci, 'they have persuaded themselves that that people have no polite manners, that they are ignorant, wanting in ordered life, and very dirty. For these things they would sooner die unaided than drink a cup of water from the hand of a Farangi; nor would they eat anything that he has prepared. They believe such an act to be an irremediable disgrace, and a sin for which there is no remission ... They state openly that a man of low birth is as despicable as is a Farangi ... This contempt is even greater than that of persons of quality in France for night-soil workers and scavengers.' Echoing what Albiruni had said about Indians 600 years earlier, Manucci remarks, 'The first error of these Hindus is to believe that they are the only people in the world who have any polite manners; and the same is the case with cleanliness and orderliness in business. They think all other nations, and above all Europeans, are barbarous, despicable, filthy, and devoid of order.'

For the common people of India, Europeans were objects of endless curiosity and amusement. From the time the Jesuits first arrived in Fatehpur Sikri in the reign of Akbar, to the Norris embassy in the reign of Aurangzeb, Europeans always attracted swarms of people around them—people even went to watch the mass performed at the camp of Norris on Sundays, as if it were a pageant.

Life at the Bottom

THERE WAS A seeming unreality about the world of the Mughal amir, like a shimmering oasis in the middle of a vast desert. The oasis was not of course a mirage. It was real enough.

But the greater reality was of the desert. The barren life of the common people. Half-naked and illiterate, barely scraping out a living, the average Indian in Mughal times had advanced little from the conditions of life of his ancestors of a thousand or more years before his time. He lived in a dingy, one-room hovel, its floor of beaten earth plastered with cow-dung, with walls of mud and a thatched roof barely high enough for a man to stand in the middle, and one lone, low opening for a door. There were no windows. If he had any cattle, he shared the hut with them. The huts of the commoners were, says Terry, 'miserably poor, little and base'. Adds Roe: 'Your swyne lye better than any man.'

'Their dwellings and Houses are verie little and low,' writes Linschoten, 'covered with Straw, without windowes, and verie low and narrow doores, so that a man must almost creape upon his knees to goe in.' Confirms Manucci: 'Excluding the temples . . . and the palaces of a few kings, princes, et cetera, which are built of brick and mortar . . . all other houses are constructed of earth and pieces of wood bound together with ropes, without much regard to appearances. These wooden posts serve as supporting pillars, and the roof is thatch. In this way they build a house without using a single nail. The floors of the houses are not stone-paved, nor covered with the sort of cement they make in this country of lime, eggs, and other ingredients mixed together. The floors are of pounded earth only, spread over with a wash of cow's dung.'

The poor slept on the bare mud floor. 'A stone or a piece of wood serves as bolster. This that would be looked on in Europe as a severe penance is in this country the ordinary habit,' says Manucci. Only the middle class, the thin upper crust of the vast underclass, had a marginally better quality of life, but even in their homes, notes Careri, 'they use no Quilts because of the Heat, but lay on Blankets and Sheets on the Bed, made of Cords without Boards.' 'There are no tables or chairs; everybody sits on the ground,' says Manucci. Says Linschoten, 'Their Household stuffe is Mats of straw, both to sit and lie upon; their Tables, Table-clothes, and Napkins, are made of the great Indian Fig-leaves; they serve them not onley for Tables, sheets, and other Linnen, but also for Dishes . . . They likewise joyne them together in such sort that they can put both Butter, Oyle, and such liquid stuffes therein, and also whatever commeth to hand.' The household utensils were mostly of earthenware. There were hardly any copper, brass or bronze vessels in the average Indian home, though Linschoten mentions that people around Goa 'drink out of a copper can with a spout, which is all the metal they have in their houses'.

THE POOR THROUGHOUT India went virtually naked. 'Peasants and people of low standing go about naked,' notes Babur. 'They tie on a thing called *lunguta*, a decency-clout which hangs two spans below the navel. From the tie of this pendant decency-clout, another clout is passed between the thighs and made fast behind. Women also tie on a cloth, one half of which goes round the waist, the other is thrown over the head.' Half a century later, in 1579, Thomas Stevens, a Jesuit in Goa, wrote to his father in England: 'They that be not of reputation, or at least the most part, goe naked, saving an apron a span long, and as much in bredth before them, and a lace two fingres broad before them, girded about with a string and no more; and thus they thinke them as well as we with all our trimming.'

At the close of the seventeenth century, Manucci found commoners in India dressed in about the same manner as Babur had described. Little had changed in nearly two centuries. 'As for the soldiers, labourers, and other ordinary people, they have no more than a cloth bound round their head, and a little string round their middle, attached to which is a morsel of cloth, a span wide and a cubit in length, about the size of our ordinary napkins,' writes Manucci. 'With this cloth they cover the parts of the body that natural modesty requires to be concealed. Lastly, they have another cloth, somewhat of the same size, bound round the body, which servers in the day-time as a garment and at night as a bed, their mattress being identical with the damp earth . . . There are some so badly provided that they content themselves with the piece of cloth . . . as used to cover the private parts. In this equipment they hold themselves fully dressed and fit to talk to anyone, wherever it might be.'

Writes Bernier about the urban scene in Mughal India in the mid-seventeenth century: 'In Delhi, for two or three who wear decent apparel, there may always be reckoned seven or eight poor, ragged, and miserable beings, attracted to the capital by the army.' In Golconda, says Fitch, 'the men and the women do go with a cloth bound about their middles without any other apparel.' In Vijayanagar 'men of condition wear a short shirt, and on their head a cloth of gold and silk in the Moorish fashion, but nothing on the feet,' says Varthema. 'The common people go quite naked, with the exception of a piece of cloth about their middle.' So it was in nearly every region of India.

This mode of dress suited the generally hot Indian climate, but poverty and social environment, not climate, was the main reason for the scanty dress. People dressed as well as their circumstances permitted. The great pundits of Varanasi are described as wearing silk dhotis and scarves. In the cold regions of India, and in the cold season elsewhere, people of course wore heavier clothing; in Kashmir both men and women wore a long woollen tunic.

What the commoner saved on clothes, he spent on ornaments. 'All the troops, from the Omrah to the man in the ranks, will wear gilt ornaments; nor will a private soldier refuse them to his wife and children, though the whole family should die of hunger,' says Bernier. Most Hindu men wore their hair long, usually tied into a roll on the side of the head—'The Indians wear their Hair for Ornament, contrary to the Mahometans [especially Shiahs] who shave their Heads,' says Thevenot—and nearly all wore moustaches. Most Muslims wore beards.

As in dress, the food of commoners was minimal and dreary. 'For their monotonous daily food, they have nothing but a little khichri, made of green pulse mixed with rice, which is cooked with water over a little fire until the moisture has evaporated, and eaten hot with butter in the evening,' writes Pelsaert; 'in the day time they munch a little parched pulse or other grain, which they say suffices for their lean stomachs.' In rural India, the big meal of the day was usually eaten at midday. 'They Feed on a little Rice swimming in the dish,' says Careri about the common people of Goa. Except brahmins, most Hindus were non-vegetarians, but few could afford meat. At best the common people had 'a portion of dry and salted fish' along with rice, says Manucci, 'for goats, sheep, chicken . . . are only for the nobility, and if other men eat of these, it is solely at their festivals and at marriages . . .'

Beef was cheap, but no caste Hindu would eat it, says Manucci, 'for to do so is a very low thing, a defilement, and sinful beyond all imagination,' the cow being a sacred animal. Even among Muslims, beef was considered a low food, and Terry says that very little beef was available in the Gujarat-Malwa region, presumably because of the prohibition of cow slaughter by Akbar and Jahangir. Peacock was considered sacred, shellfish impure. Pork was taboo to Muslims, but not to Rajputs who, says Pelsaert, 'eat all kinds of meat except beef and drink wine.' In the Tamil country, says Muhammad Sharif Hanafi, who visited the region in the early seventeenth century, 'all the people . . . are idolaters, and eat all the wild animals of the forest.'

Common people in Mughal India subsisted on rice, millets and pulses. Wheat was too expensive for them, and even in the wheat-growing regions of Hindustan 'the meaner sort of people' could not afford it, says Terry. Ghee and edible oils were cheap, but salt and sugar were expensive. Most people used jaggery instead of sugar. Chillies were not commonly used in Mughal cookery—they had just been introduced from South America by the Portuguese, who also brought maize, potatoes, pineapple and several other fruits and vegetables—nor was the common Indian food spicy and hot, for pepper was grown only along the Western Ghats and most of the spices had to be imported from South-east Asia and were expensive. Opium and ganja (a preparation of cannabis) were freely available, and so was toddy. 'The drinke of this countrey is good water, or wine of the Palme tree, or of a fruit called Cocos,' notes Stevens. Arrack was the common spirituous liquor.

There were few taboos about food among the common people—they ate whatever they could get—but among the upper classes and castes there were many restrictions about what they could eat, how they should eat, and with whom they could eat. 'They will rather die . . . than eate or drinke any thing their law prohibits,' says Terry. Among Hindus, the higher the ritual status of a community, the fewer the people its members would eat with, and brahmins, at the top of the ritual hierarchy, would eat with no one else at all, nor would they eat food cooked by anyone else. Yet, curiously, the brahmin would cook for other communities, and, though he would not clear the leaves on which others had eaten, he would even pour water to wash the hands of those who had eaten. This, observes Manucci, appeared to be 'a moral contradiction, for if it dishonours them to be served by others, how can they be servants to others?' Similar but less rigorous taboos prevailed among Muslims too—they would not normally eat food cooked by Hindus or Christians, though tradition permitted them to take food brought by non-Muslims by uttering *bismilla* ('In the name of God') over it.

All Indians ate with their hands, sitting on the floor. Sometimes food was served in new earthenware platters, for the flavour it imparted.

Muslims, especially of the lower class, usually took food from a common plate, and they sat kneeling on their knees to eat, unlike Hindus, who sat cross-legged. 'They all eat with the right hand,' says Manucci about upper-caste Hindu eating habits, 'and may not touch anything with the left, not even the plate or leaf from which they have eaten, nor the spoon with which they sup a concoction by way of wine, which is some water boiled with pepper. But a vessel of cold water they lift with the left hand, at the same time never putting the vessel to the mouth. They hold their mouth open and raised to catch the liquid they pour into it.'

'Monks, ascetics, Brahmans, and the learned before eating wash their hands and bodies,' notes Manucci. 'Then they put upon their foreheads, stomach, shoulders, knees and sides a little ash mixed in water . . . Next they enter the house, finding its floors all rubbed over with cow-dung . . . They bind round their body a piece of cloth, and sit down with their legs crossed, or upon a small mat of about one cubit length. Before them is placed the large leaf of certain trees, or smaller leaves of other trees stitched together, not with needle and thread, but with rushes. Upon this leaf is put first of all a pinch of salt and two drops of butter, with which they anoint or rub the leaf. This ceremony completed, they deposit on this platter some rice cooked in water without salt, followed by a little vegetables and some green stuff. When this is eaten, they throw upon the rice left on the said leaf a little sour curds or some whey. When all this food has been swallowed, they rise from the place and move to a courtyard or garden, if there is one in the house where they live. If there is not, they go into the street, and there bathe their hands, mouth, and feet. They do not return to their dwellings till the leaves they have eaten have been removed, and the ground has been rubbed over afresh in the way already mentioned. For they say that if they did so their bodies would be as polluted as the house.'

HINDUS CONSIDERED COW-DUNG, as well as cow's urine, purificatory. 'Although these people hold it an abomination to eat of the cow, they believe, however, that it is a venerable thing, and one worthy of praise, to drink that animal's urine,' writes Manucci. They receive cow's urine in two hands 'of which they take a drink. Then turning the tail into a sort of holy-water sprinkler, they immerse it in the said liquid, and with it they daub their faces. When this ceremonial is over, they declare they have been made holy.'

Bernier is more perceptive than Manucci about Hindu practices.

Though he notes the religious reasons usually given for the veneration of cows, he goes on to maintain that 'this superior regard for the cow may more probably be owing to her extraordinary usefulness, as being the animal which supplies them with milk and ghee (a considerable part of their aliment), and which may be considered the source of husbandry, consequently the preserver of life itself . . . Perhaps the first legislators in the Indies hoped that the interdiction of animal food would produce a beneficial effect upon the character of the people, and that they might be brought to exercise less cruelty toward one another when required by a positive precept to treat the brute creation with humanity.'

Rituals dominated the lives of caste Hindus, and to some extent those of Muslims as well, and these would persist well into the twentieth century with little change. And so would the customs and manners of the people. The common people of India, unlike the Persianized elite who were elaborately ceremonious, were largely indifferent to social graces. It was, says Manucci with smug prejudice, 'delightful to see a Brahmin on a visit to another man, for without the slightest salutation he seats himself . . . When he takes his leave he goes off . . . without being any more polite on going away than on entering.'

There are a few references in Mughal writings to Indian funeral customs. 'All Hindus burn their dead, except the infamous sect of the Lingam . . . ,' says Manucci. 'No Brhaman, however rich he may be, is allowed to die within his house, for in their belief all within it would be thereby defiled. This is the reason that before he expires they carry him into a courtyard, and there place him under a sort of gallery, which every house has for the purpose. Should it happen that the Brahman dies a sudden death within the house, they carry the body at once, with all imaginable haste, and place it under the gallery alluded to. Then, breaking all the earthen vessels in the house, all the inmates quit it, and do not re-enter it until it has been well rubbed over with cow-dung, and until . . . the interdict has been removed by a number of ceremonies, used by them for this purpose.'

'When a Brahman dies, all his female relations and female friends stand in a circle, and with their stomachs bared beat themselves severely with their two hands, weeping for the dead; and, moving round, they sing a song learnt for the purpose,' continues Manucci. 'It is extremely well suited to the condition of the time and place in which they find themselves. After they have been round three times in this fashion, they bathe the body, dress it in new clothes, put some ground sandal-wood on the forehead, and then deposit it in a sort of coffin which is quite open . . .

made just as our hand-barrows for manure, constructed like them from pieces of wood tied together with straw. Then four Brahmans carry the body to the burning-ground ... After the body has been burnt, the Brahmans bathe their bodies, and wash the pieces of cloth which they used for clothing themselves. All dripping as they are, they put these on again and return home, They then proceed to the house of the deceased, where a feast is given ...'

Among the Rajputs, before the dead body was taken away to be burnt, they 'shave his head, his beard, his whole body, anointing it with essence of roses, binding it up in fine cloth smeared with different jasmine oils mixed with saffron. The body is laid upon lathes of sandal and aloes wood, bound together in the shape of an open bier. The women who are to be burned with him follow,' notes Manucci.

'Most Gentiles burn their dead; but some partially broil the bodies with stubble, near the side of a river, and then precipitate them into the water from a high and steep bank,' says Bernier. Sometimes a dying man would be floated into the Ganga, his relatives inserting him feet first into water, then slowly lowering him up to his neck, and finally, when he was about to expire, immersing the whole body, and leaving him there, 'after violently clapping their hands, and crying out with great vehemence. The object of this ceremony ... is that the soul may be washed, on taking its flight, from all impurities which it may have contracted during its abode in the body.' But these were the privileges of the upper class. As for the common people, in death as in life, they were 'dealt with as mere animals,' says Manucci.

Upper-caste Hindus (as well as upper-class Muslims) were fetishistic about physical cleanliness. 'They are verie clean on their Bodies, for everie day they wash themselves all their bodies over, as often as they ease themselves or make water, both men and women, like Moores and Mahometans,' says Linschoten. 'They wash themselves with the left hand, because they eate with the right hand, and use no Spoones.' Special attention was given to oral hygiene. 'Every Beggar ... rubs his Teeth every Morning betimes with a Stick, and spends two Hours at that Work, according to the Custom of the Country,' says Careri, no doubt calculating time relativistically.

INDIANS, IN THE opinion of Bernier, lacked physical vigour, because of the enervating climate of the subcontinent. But they had, according to Manucci, a ravenous sexual appetite. 'All Mahomedans are very fond of women, who are their principal relaxation and also their only pleasure,' he writes, and goes on to state that Hindus too 'know no higher delight in the world than consorting with women.' Among the nobility, the pursuit of carnal pleasure was presumably a refinement, another expression of their lifestyle of conspicuous consumption, but for the common people, with no cultural interests to divert them, procreation was their only recreation.

'During the short time I was with their army, I got no time to rest,' says Manucci, 'for everybody pestered me, as their way is, for medicines, even those who had no need for them. They would say as a reason, "I have no appetite; give me some medicine to make me eat like an elephant, or like a camel, or at any rate like a horse." And all these brute-like demands simply to have strength to slake their sensuality!'

In the eyes of medieval European travellers, the people of Kerala were especially promiscuous—they were, says Linschoten, 'the most Lecherous and unchaste Nation in all the Orient, so that there are verie few women Children among them even seven or eight years old, that have their Maidenheads . . . They (Nair men) may freely lie with Nayros Daughters, or with any other that liketh them, what women soever they be, yea though they be Married women. When the Nayro hath a desire thereunto, he entereth into a house where he thinketh good, and setteth his Armes in the street without the doore, and goeth in and dispatcheth his businesse, with the good Wife or the daughter, the doore standing wide open, not fearing that any man should come in . . .' Of Bengalis, Thevenot says: 'The People (for the most part) are extraordinarily voluptuous; they have a captious and subtil wit, and are much given to pilfering and stealing: The Women themselves are bold and lascivious, and use all Arts imaginable to corrupt and debouch Young Men . . .'

Similar tales could no doubt be told about the rural and tribal folk in any part of medieval India, but Muslims were on the whole strict in segregating the sexes and cloistering their women. Even then, women often managed to wriggle free, sometimes using pilgrimages to holy places to have illicit liaisons, one ardour concealing another. Such deceptions were an old problem in India, and were so endemic in fourteenth century India that Sultan Firuz Tughluq had to ban women from visiting shrines! Even puritanical, scholarly Badauni once fell victim to the seduction of such an environment. 'In this year a dreadful event happened to the compiler of this epitome,' he writes. While visiting a shrine, he was 'captured in the net of desire and lust . . . and committed a terrible piece of impropriety.' Retribution was immediate. The relatives of the girl involved surrounded and attacked Badauni, inflicting 'nine sword wounds in succession on my head and hand and back.'

Homosexuality, though prevalent among the Mughal amirs, seems to have been rare among the common people in India. Hindus were largely untouched by the vice—they, according to Albiruni, considered it as revolting as eating beef. But a few cases of incest are noted in Mughal chronicles. Nizamuddin Ahmad reports that when an incestuous brahmin was brought before Akbar, the emperor ordered 'that the organ of generation and the means of his vice and wickedness should be cut off from the root and should be roasted before his eyes. That eternally accursed and forever condemned man ate that thing with great appetite, under the belief that he would probably be released after this punishment.' But the next day Akbar sentenced the brahmin to death, though his daughter, who was his sexual partner, repented and was set free.

Such aberrations were probably rare, for there was not much cause for sexual frustration in Mughal India, at least for men. Mughal society was tolerant towards the dalliances of men, and there was no odium among Hindus or Muslims in maintaining concubines or visiting harlots. There were large colonies of prostitutes in all major towns, and even in villages, along caravan routes, the comforts of travellers were provided for. In the early seventeenth century, Nicholas Withington once came across a village of prostitutes in Gujarat. 'This towne the King's father (ould Accabaa) after the conqueste of Guyseratt, cominge thether, gave to a company of women and theire posteritie for ever, uppon condition to teache and bringe upp theire children in theire owne profession, which is dauncing, etc. At our beeinge here, the women from the towne came into our caravan and daunced, everye man givinge them somethinge; and afterwards they asked openlye: Whoe wants a bedfellow. Soe shamelesse they were.'

Lahore had, according to Manucci, 'six thousand houses of ill fame', from which a weekly tax was collected by the Kotwal. Similar practices were prevalent in Vijayanagar, as indeed they were in ancient India under the Mauryas. In the Delhi Sultanate, Alauddin Khilji, while fixing the prices of other commodities, also fixed the rates of prostitutes. 'Most governors . . . doe allow that any woman . . . unmarried may lawfully turne common whore . . . and take her habitation among other whores in small villages . . . payeing so much per mensem to the governor,' writes Thomas Bowrey about the conditions in eastern India in the mid-seventeenth century.

In Hyderabad, according to Tavernier, there were 20,000 'common women' who were licensed to engage in their profession. 'Without . . . licence it is not lawful for any woman to profess the trade,' says Tavernier. 'They pay no tribute to the King; only they are obliged to come, a certain number of them, with their governess, and their music every Friday, and present themselves before the balcony. If the King be there, they dance before him. If he intend not to come, an eunuch comes into the balcony, and makes them a sign to retire. In the cool of the evening they stand at the doors of the houses, which are for the most part little huts; and when night comes, they set up a candle or a lighted lamp for signals: then it is also that they open all the shops where they sell Tari (toddy); which is a certain drink made of the juice of a tree and is as sweet as our new wines.'

Apart from common prostitutes, all the major Mughal towns had troupes of dancing girls called Kanchanas or Luliyanis in Hindustan, accomplished entertainers who had an essential—and respectable—social function, as they were an obligatory part of wedding entertainments. 'They are not indeed the prostitutes seen in bazaars,' says Bernier, 'but those of a more private and respectable class, who attend the grand weddings of Omrahs and Mansebdars, for the purpose of singing and dancing. Most of these Kenchens are handsome and well dressed, and sing to perfection; and their limbs being extremely supple, they dance with wonderful agility, and are always correct in regard to time.'

The Mughal attitude towards prostitution varied from emperor to emperor. Akbar set up a separate colony for prostitutes outside Fatehpur Sikri under the charge of royal officers, with whom the women's customers were required to register, but Shah Jahan, a voluptuary himself, was indulgent towards them. 'In the reign of Shahjahan female dancers and public women enjoyed great liberty . . . and were found in great number in the cities,' says Bernier. Aurangzeb prohibited dancers from entering the seraglio, though, 'complying with long established usage, [he] does not object to their coming every Wednesday to the Am-Kas, where they make the salaam from a certain distance, and immediately retire.' As for common prostitutes, Aurangzeb ordered that they must either marry or clear out of the realm. 'This was the cause that the palaces and great enclosures where they (prostitutes) dwelt went to ruin little by little; for some of them married and others went away, or, at least, concealed themselves,' says Manucci.

Hermaphrodites, called Hijras, 'a crowd of worthless profligates', as Monserrate describes them, were common in Mughal India. The Jesuits pleaded with Akbar to banish them from his kingdom, at which the emperor 'laughed . . . and retired, saying that he would attend to the matter,' says Monserrate. Hijras, notes Thevenot, were required 'to wear upon their Heads a Turban like Men, though they go in the habit of Women.'

AND SO LIFE went on in Mughal India. Outwardly there was little in common between the amirs and the commoners. It was as if they were two entirely different species. Yet, basically there was little difference. All were driven by the same passions, devastated by the same tragedies, singed by the same frustrations, the pains and the pleasures of the common man in his mud hovel exactly the same in their subjective effect as those of the amir in his fragrant mansion. But the amirs had comforts to cocoon their sorrows, the commoners could only lick their wounds.

Chapter Four

GILDED
AND
OTHER CAGES

The Imperial Harem

IN THE PALACE of the Mughal emperor, there was a closely guarded wing known as the harem, meaning, in Arabic, a sacred or prohibited place. That was where the begums lived, in a vacuum-sealed world of their own.

There were similar annexes in the mansions of the ruling elite everywhere in India, among Hindus as well as Muslims. Traditionally, there was no purdah (seclusion and veiling of women) in India, till the Rajputs adopted the custom in imitation of Muslim aristocracy. Purdah then became a status symbol among Hindus, but only among the ruling classes, and even among them it was not enforced as rigorously as among Muslims.

Brahmin women did not veil themselves, and Fitch describes them going about singing in groups in Agra, on their way to perform their rituals at the river. In the Deccan, even among Muslims, except in the leading families, few observed purdah. Further south, among the matrilineal communities of Kerala, women not only enjoyed considerable freedom, but great power as well. Lower-class Muslims nowhere observed strict purdah, for the Koranic rule was: 'Women can move about and earn their living but they have to cast down their eyes and to conceal those parts of their body that are apt to excite passions and not to display their ornaments.'

Among the poor, life was so minimal that it could not possibly be divided into separate spheres for men and women. Among them, there was no seclusion of women, nor any veiling. They wore hardly any clothes, in fact. But ruling class women, by and large, lived in a world quite distinct from that of men, cloistered in the inner apartments of mansions, guarded zealously, and, in the case of Hindu wives, sometimes burned alive with their dead husbands. For the nobles, there was no greater duty than guarding the honour of their women, protecting them from public exposure and preventing them from falling into the hands of the enemy. In extreme peril, Rajputs saved the honour of their women by slaying them, and so did Hindu chieftains elsewhere, as in Karnataka, where the

Rayal's men, when routed in battle, slaughtered their women, just as they spiked their cannons to deny them to the enemy.

Women were property, but valued property. And to be valued thus, it would seem, was in many cases what the women themselves desired, as so many eyewitness accounts of sati, jauhar and other similar customs show. By long cultural habituation, women had come to view their bondage and seclusion as privileges.

Purdah was strictly observed by the Muslim aristocracy in Hindustan. Outside the harem, women had to wear the burka, a loose, shapeless garment covering the whole body, with only a veiled opening for the eyes, and they had to travel in covered litters or howdahs. No structure that would overlook the harem was permitted to be built on the street by the side of the harem, and elephants were not allowed to pass along the way. At camps, no tent could be pitched close to a harem tent. 'The Mahometans,' writes Terry, 'who have most wives and women, are most jealous, and their jealousy such, as that they will not suffer the brothers, or fathers of their wives to come to them, or to have any speech with them, except it be in their presence.'

It would be divorce or death for a begum who even accidentally unveiled herself in public. Thus Amir Khan, the governor of Kabul, divorced one of his wives when she inadvertently broke the purdah in the street while running to save herself from a rampaging elephant. And a soldier once slew a tax collector for looking into the litter where his ladies were sitting. He slew the ladies too—honour demanded no less!

Purdah was strictest in the imperial harem. Many of the royal women were even nameless to the outside world, and they presumably considered that a high honour. 'Ever since the reign of the Emperor Akbar, it had been ordained that the names of the inmates of the seraglio should not be mentioned in public,' says Inayat Khan, 'but that they should be designated by some epithet, derived either from the place of their birth or the country or city in which they may have first been regarded by the monarch with the eye of affection.'

THE MUGHAL HAREM was an immense establishment. Akbar, according to Abul Fazl, had 'more than five thousand women' in his harem, wives, concubines, female relatives, administrators, guards, cooks and menials. Lady officers in Akbar's harem received stipends varying from twenty-seven to 1610 rupees a month, according to Shireen Moosvi in her brilliant study of the Mughal economy at the close of the sixteenth century. These were very high salaries—in contrast, an ordinary Mughal cavalryman received a maximum of just thirteen rupees a month under Akbar—and they indicate the high status of the lady officers. The total cash stipends that Akbar paid to the harem women came to 852,000 rupees a year, excluding the pay of eunuchs. Harem salaries rose even higher under later emperors. 'The matrons have generally three, four, or five hundred rupees a month as pay, according to the dignity of the post they occupy,' says Manucci. 'The servants under their orders have from fifty up to two hundred rupees a month. In addition to these matrons, there are the female superintendents of music and their women players; these have about the same pay more or less, besides the presents they receive from princes and princesses.'

The vastness of the imperial harem, its reputed opulence, and the fact that there was little authentic information about harem life, led to a lot of spicy speculation among the public about what went on there, based on the colourful gossip of eunuchs and harem servants. This was the source on which foreign travellers based their reports, and their accounts in turn are the main source of our information on Mughal harem life. Inevitably, their accounts are marred by exaggerations and distortions. Still, there is a good amount of consistency in the reports of various travellers written at widely different times, so that the picture they draw seems credible in general outline, especially as it matches what we know from other sources about Mughal life.

In the wondering eyes of foreigners, the imperial harem was a pagan heaven of extravagant and endless orgies. 'The king (Jahangir) keepeth a thousand women for his own body,' says Coryat credulously. This is incredible. The emperor had plenty of other things to do than dally for-ever in the harem. True, he did maintain a large number of wives and concubines—though not anywhere near as many as Coryat imagined—for there was a functional need for him to be polygamous, to beget as many children as possible, so that at least some of them might survive the prevalent high infant mortality rate and grow into adulthood, to succeed him to the throne and continue the royal line. But this was not the only reason, perhaps not even the main reason, for the emperor to maintain a vast harem—the number of his wives and concubines was often several times more than what was needed to meet the procreative requirements of the dynasty or even to sate whatever gargantuan sexual appetite the emperor might have had.

Many royal marriages were contracted for political reasons, to cement alliances or to show favour. There were other considerations too. 'Just as for other people more than one wife is not suitable, so for great persons more are necessary, so that their dwellings may be more splendid, and a large number of people may be supported,' says Abul Fazl. The imperial harem, Abul Fazl implies, was a part of the pomp and display expected of the emperor—the harem symbolized the power (and potency) of the emperor as the supreme lord. But it was mostly an empty show, for none of the emperors, despite their many women, produced very many children to prove their virility. Evidently, contrary to common myth, the arduous life of the emperor left him with little leisure for amorous play.

There were other similar misconceptions about the emperor's women. 'In wiving, he respects fancie more than hounour,' says Terry, 'not seeking affinitie with neighbour princes, but to please his eye at home.' This was only partly true. Though the Mughal emperors, unlike the kings of Europe, did not enter into matrimonial alliances with other sovereigns, and their wives were either their own cousins or the daughters of amirs and vassal rulers, all from within India, Terry was wrong in believing that the emperor chose his wives only 'to please his eye'. He could no doubt marry any beautiful woman he fancied, but it was more in his concubines than in his wives that he looked for beauty, charm and accomplishments. In fact, he did not even have conjugal relationships with all his wives, for as Aminai Qazvini says of Shah Jahan, except for Mumtaz Mahal, the other wives of the emperor 'enjoyed nothing more than the title of wifeship.' Invariably, the older queens were sexually neglected. Observes Terry: 'The King and his great men . . . little affect them after thirtie yeares of their age.'

'THE SERAGLIO CONTAINS beautiful apartments, separated, and more or less spacious and splendid, according to the rank and income of the females,' writes Bernier. 'Nearly every chamber has its reservoir of running water at the door; on every side are gardens, delightful alleys, shady retreats, streams, fountains, grottoes, deep excavations that afford shelter from the sun by day, lofty divans and terraces, on which to sleep coolly at night . . . The eunuchs speak with extravagant praise of a small tower, facing the river, which is covered with plates of gold . . . and its apartments are decorated with gold and azure, exquisite paintings and magnificent mirrors.'

The emperor was the only adult male who lived in the harem. 'There lodge none in the Kings house but his women and eunuches, and some little boyes which hee keepes about him for wicked use,' says Terry. Each of the great ladies in the royal harem had her own apartment, her own allowance and set of servants. 'Ordinarily, there are within the *mahal* two thousand women of different races,' records Manucci. 'Each has her office or special duties, either in attendance on the king, his wives, his daughters, or his concubines. To rule and maintain order among this last class, each one is assigned her own set of rooms, and matrons are placed over them. In addition, each has usually attached to her ten or twelve women servants, who are selected from the above-named women.' Even in the harems of nobles, says Pelsaert, 'each wife has separate apartments for herself and her slaves, of whom there may be 10, or 20, or 100, according to her fortune. Each has a regular monthly allowance for her *gastos* (expenditure). Their food comes from one kitchen, but each wife takes it in her own apartments . . .'

The royal harem, being also the residence of the emperor, was tightly guarded. Within, it was guarded, says Abul Fazl, by 'sober and active women; the most trustworthy of them are placed about the apartments of his Majesty. Outside the enclosure the eunuchs are placed; and at a proper distance, there is a guard of faithful Rajputs, beyond whom are the porters of the gates. Besides, on all four sides, there are guards of Nobles, Ahadis, and other troops, according to the ranks.' Uzbeg, Tartar and Ethiopian women were preferred for harem duty; eunuchs came mainly from Bengal, a large number of them from the district of Sylhet.

Admission into the harem was strictly regulated. The eunuchs who guarded the harem doors, says Manucci, 'search everything with great care to stop the entry of *bhang*, wine, opium, nutmegs or other drugs which could intoxicate, for all women in *mahals* love much such beverages. Nor do they permit the entry into the place of radishes, cucumbers, or similar vegetables that I cannot name.' Coryat is more explicit. 'Whatsoever is brought in of virill shape,' says Coryat, 'as instance in reddishes, so great is the jealousie, and so frequent the wickednesse of this people, that they are cut and jagged for feare of converting the same to some unnaturall abuse.' This no doubt was bazaar gossip, but not necessarily untrue.

'When women come to pay a visit or otherwise, if they are not known they are searched, no respect being paid either to the position or rank of the person,' continues Manucci. 'What forces eunuchs to such strict measure is the continual fear . . . that some young man in disguise might enter in female dress. When masons or carpenters, or other workmen are wanted to carry out any job, their names are registered at each gate they pass through; the descriptive marks of their faces, and so forth, are taken down. A paper showing all this is delivered to other eunuchs, who are required to conduct them out in the same way, and to take care that they are the same persons with the same physiognomy and same personal marks. All this for fear of anyone remaining inside, or any change being made.'

Apart from eunuchs, there were women attenders at the doors of the harem—usually Kashmiri women, says Manucci, who 'do not veil themselves to anybody'—to carry messages or materials into the harem or bring them to the door. All entrances except the main door of the harem were locked at sunset and seals attached to them, and the main door, though not locked, was closely guarded, with torches kept burning there all night. The zenanas of the great amirs too were guarded with equal rigour. 'All the nobles exercise the same exact supervision of their women that the king does,' notes Manucci.

THE EMPEROR SPENT a good part of his working day in the harem—Akbar was there for about six hours—but he spent it working, for it was here that he did some of his most confidential work. The harem was his residence-cum-private office, and it was run like a full-fledged government department, with its own budget, administrators and accountants, headed by the Mahaldar, the lady superintendent. 'Just as the king has his officers outside, he has the same among the fair sex within the mahal,' says Manucci. 'Among these ladies are some who occupy the same offices that are held by grandees outside; and it is by the mouth of these illustrious persons, when the king does not come forth, that the officials outside receive the orders sent to them from within. All the persons employed in those offices are carefully selected; they have much wit and judgment, and know all that is passing in the empire. For the officials outside are required to send written reports into the *mahal* of all that the king ought to know. To these reports the women officials reply as directed by that prince. And to carry this out there are eunuchs who take out and bring back the sealed letters written from one side to the other on these matters.'

There was no ranking system for the emperor's wives and concubines, but there was a pecking order. The harem was usually headed by the emperor's chief queen, but at times the first lady was the royal mother, as Hamida was in Akbar's harem, or even a grandmother, like Aisan-daulat Begum in the early years of Babur, or a daughter, as in the case of Jahanara in the harem of Shah Jahan after the death of Mumtaz Mahal, or a sister, like Raushanara in Aurangzeb's harem for some years. The first lady had her own formal seat in the hall of the zenana, on which, as on a throne, no one else was allowed to sit. This was the practice in the nineteenth century, but it was very likely an old custom, for a painting in *Baburnama* shows Babur's grandmother sitting on a canopied, throne-like seat. The role of the first lady in the affairs of the empire depended on the personality of the begum and on the emperor's regard for her, but it was never an insignificant role. The *uzuk*, the royal signet ring, was usually in her keeping, which gave her a chance to review the final drafts of firmans.

When the affairs of the empire were considered a family matter, it was inevitable that members of the royal family, including women, should be involved in the business of government. The begums, watching and listening from behind the screens of durbar halls, were knowledgeable about affairs of state, perhaps even more than many of the amirs, for they were privy to the secret reports that the emperor received from his intelligence agents, which were opened in the harem. And they, by their daily contact with the emperor and the intimacy of their relationship, exercised considerable influence on the modulation of state policy. Sometimes they even intervened in discussions in the durbar. Once, when Jahangir was discussing with his amirs whether Aziz Koka, Khusrav's insolent father-in-law, should be executed for complicity in the prince's rebellion, Salima Begum, Akbar's senior widow, spoke up from behind the screen, calling the emperor into the harem to hear the views of the women—they wanted mercy to be shown, and Jahangir heeded their advice.

Occasionally, the begums on their own authority issued firmans to officials, to assure them of favour, to give advice, or to call them to duty. Thus Akbar's mother Hamida in September 1587 ordered local officials that 'the cows belonging to . . . Bithaleshar (Vithaleshwar, second son of the Vaishnava sage Vallabhacharya), *zunnardar* (wearer of the sacred thread: brahmin) may graze wherever they are, and that not a single individual of the Khalisa and jagirdar should molest them or prevent them [from grazing, as the emperor had granted the brahmin that privilege].' Several letters from the begums to Raja Jai Singh are extant— Nur Jahan assuring him of favour, Nadira (Dara's wife) congratulating him on his victory over Shuja, Jahanara offering to intercede with Aurangzeb on his behalf, and so on.

The begums were a potent though invisible power behind the throne. Such a role for high-born women was not unusual in Islamic political tradition. Thus, though Prophet Muhammad on his deathbed had decreed that women should not meddle in public affairs, his favourite wife, to whom this advice was given, herself disregarded the injunction. In Persia royal women wielded great power under the Safavids, and Abul Fazl states that once a princess was even offered the throne (which she refused). However, the general trend in medieval Muslim society was to deny women a public role, or at least to keep their involvement quiet and behind the screen. The prevalent attitude, as one sage put it, was *'Zerdastan ra zabardast na kunaid!'*—Don't give the upper hand to those who are under you! Or, as Aurangzeb once wrote, 'A man submissive to women is worse than a woman.'

SUCH BEING THE environment, it was only the exceptional woman, under exceptional circumstances, who made a mark in medieval history. Surprisingly, there were a number of such women. Before the Mughals, in the Delhi Sultanate, several royal women were active in public life, beginning with Raziya, who ascended the throne and led the army in person. And in Mughal history, right at the beginning, Babur's wise and masterful grandmother, Aisan-daulat Begum, was in charge of the affairs of the troubled boy-king. In Akbar's reign, the ouster of Biram Khan was managed by a harem party, and late in his reign, Akbar's mother Hamida and wife Salima played a key role in bringing about a rapprochement between Akbar and Salim. Then there was Nur Jahan, the most remarkable of the Mughal queens. A similar but quiet role was played by Mumtaz Mahal, as Shah Jahan's confidant and adviser. Shah Jahan's daughters, Jahanara and Raushanara too played at politics, and so did Aurangzeb's daughter Zebunnisa. In Kabul, on the death of Amir Khan, the governor, his wife Sahibji took over the administration of the province.

Outside the Mughal empire royal women often exercised power still more openly, like Chand Bibi of Ahmadnagar and Tara Bai of Maharashtra. In the mid-seventeenth-century Golconda, queen mother Hayat Baksh Begum was the de facto ruler during the reign of Abdullah Qutb Shah; in a similar role, Rani Durgavati of Gond led her army in person against the Mughals and died fighting. A Maratha contingent in the Mughal service was commanded by the widow of the Deshmukh of Mahoor. When pressed, Mughal princesses too did not hesitate to enter the battlefield—Prince Azam's wife (she was Dara's daughter) once directed a battle from a covered howdah and routed the Maratha army that attacked her camp during her husband's absence.

That was an unusual proceeding for a Mughal princess. Normally royal women confined themselves to the battle of wits in court politics, which gave a certain edge to their otherwise sedate lives. Many of them had fabulous incomes, which they could deploy in any enterprise of their choice. Mumtaz Mahal, for instance, had an annual allowance of one million rupees; that apart, she periodically received extravagant presents from the emperor and the amirs, so that when she died—arid she died young—her wealth, according to Inayat Khan, was estimated at 'upwards of one crore (ten million) rupees'. Sometimes jagirs or specific taxes were assigned to the begums, such as the customs dues of Surat allotted to Jahanara.

A good part of the immense resources of the begums was spent on luxuries, but a fair amount was also spent on the patronage of culture, on charities, or on the construction of monumental buildings such as the exquisite mausoleum of Itimad-ud-daula built by Nur Jahan in Agra, and the great serai built by Jahanara in Delhi. Exchanging gifts was an engaging diversion for the begums. On royal birthdays and other festival days, especially during the Nauruz celebrations, 'ladies of the court are obliged to attend at the palace to make their compliments to the queens and princesses ... ,' says Manucci. 'They remain at the court until the end of the feast. The dancing women and singing women receive on these occasions handsome presents from princesses and other great ladies ... When the ladies attend there they never go in with empty hands, but always carry costly presents to be offered.' And when they leave, 'their hands are filled with *kichari*'—not the rice and vegetable preparation, but 'a mixture of gold and silver coins, with all kinds of precious stones and pearls, large and small'.

Occasionally, the great begums indulged in the gamble of international trade—Jahangir's mother, Maryam Zamani, for instance, conducted extensive overseas trade, and so did Nur Jahan and Jahanara, and there were several others like them. The business affairs of the begums were managed by officers called Nazirs, who were, says Manucci, in charge of the 'property, lands and income [of the begums]. All the officials, servants, and slaves are bound to account to the Nazir for all they do, and for whatever they have in their hands.'

The royal ladies also played an important role in the patronage of officials, and amirs courted them assiduously, sending them presents and seeking their advice and support. The begums knew all the top officers, having watched them through the grille in the durbar hall. 'These ladies are ... very liberal in making presents to the nobles of the court, and most industrious in obtaining appointments and promotion for those that they esteem,' writes Manucci. 'Very rarely is any service done them or any civility shown that they do not acknowledge it in one way or another, subject, of course, to treating everyone according to his merit, or, rather, according to how he touches the heart of the lady.'

There could be, of course, no direct contact between the begums and the amirs, and they had to communicate with each other through eunuchs. In exceptional cases, the emperor might confer on a senior amir the freedom to enter the harem, as a gesture of high favour and great intimacy. 'On this day I honoured Itimad-ud-daula as an intimate friend by directing the ladies of the harem not to veil their faces from him,' writes Jahangir about his father-in-law. 'By this favour I bestowed everlasting honour on him.' When Shah Jahan in rebellion was hounded by imperial forces, he took aged Abdur-Rahim, the Khan-i-khanan, into his harem and made him *maharem-sakth* (one who had the privilege to enter the harem) to bind him to his cause.

Similarly, a begum, when she desired to bind an amir to her cause, would send him a little milk drawn from her breast to drink, or some token of that, to make him her surrogate son. Thus Dara's wife, when she wanted to secure the loyalty of Raja Sarup Singh to her husband's cause, 'offered him (because she had no milk in her breast) water to drink with which she had washed her breasts,' says Manucci. The raja drank the water and swore allegiance—and promptly deserted to Aurangzeb!

The Gilded Cage

A BLESSED WORLD of perfect contentment and happiness—that was how the royal harem would have seemed to outsiders. The begums were shielded from everything unpleasant in life, even from intimations of mortality. 'Through all the palaces such a thing (death) is never mentioned, nor anything to bring it before the eyes or mind,' says Manucci. They were pampered with every material comfort a woman could dream of, had any amount of money to squander in any manner they fancied, and did not have a care in the world.

Yet the harem was a smouldering world of private misery, of unspeakable loneliness and unsated love, the deprivation in fact of all the primary satisfactions of life—the pleasures of sex, the happiness of love and family and children—which no luxury in the world could compensate. The begums had everything and more. But they missed life.

Under Babur and Humayun, when the harem was relatively small and the princesses were allowed to marry, the royal household was rather like an extended family, a happy world. Under Akbar, the scene changed. Not only was there now an exponential growth in the size of the harem, but its organization was made formal and rigorous. Further, though Akbar had initially allowed one of his daughters to marry, he later decreed that princesses should not marry, as no man was considered worthy of a Mughal alliance. Also, it was feared that if they married, the royal sons-in-law also might become contenders for the throne. The princesses (as well as the neglected wives and concubines of the emperor) were thus forced into a life of dreary, involuntary chastity—until Aurangzeb repealed the rule and married off his daughters and nieces.

The begums filled the vast emptiness of their days with incessant gossip and petty palace intrigue. Or they gorged themselves on delicacies—'the food allowed to the women of the seraglio commences to be taken from the kitchen in the morning, and goes on till night,' says Abul Fazl. Or they spent endless hours adorning and perfuming themselves. Writes Manucci: 'If they (the begums) have any ... thought, it is to regale themselves with quantities of delicious stews; to adorn themselves magnificently, either with clothes or jewellery, pearls et cetera; to perfume their bodies with odours and essences of every kind.' Women taking their own time to dress was an annoyance even to emperors; Gulbadan says that once when the royal family was setting out on an excursion and Humayun was ready to mount, the begums 'were still putting on their head-to-foot dresses', and Gulbadan had to go and hurry them up.

Many occupied themselves with embroidery, stitching, painting, palace decorations and illuminations, setting off fireworks, or watching acrobats, jugglers and magicians. At other times they flew kites and pigeons or enjoyed falconry. 'To this must be added,' says Manucci ironically, 'that they have permission to enjoy the pleasure of the comedy and the dance, to listen to tales and stories of love, to recline upon beds of flowers, to walk about in gardens, to listen to the murmur of the running waters, to hear singing, and other similar pastimes.' Music and dance were important diversions, but tinged with guilt, because of the Islamic prohibitions against them.

The begums also played a variety of indoor and outdoor games. 'Twelve players had each twenty cards and twenty *shahrukhis*. Whoever lost, lost those twenty *shahrukhis*,' says Gulbadan of a card game they played. Occasionally they went out on picnics, or to hunt or play polo. Says Gulbadan of a night picnic in Kabul: 'It was a moonlit night. We talked and told stories, and . . . [the reciters] sang softly, softly.' Fairs and pilgrimages also provided Muslim women a means of temporary escape from their dreary seclusion. 'Under the pretext of a pilgrimage,' says Pelsaert, 'they used to come without reproach to see, and perhaps even speak to their lovers. Assignations were made in the gardens . . . and there passion was given the food for which it hungered.' Sometimes the begums went on pilgrimage to Mecca—as was done by Gulbadan, Salima Begum and other great ladies of Akbar's harem—which took several years to complete.

A few begums occupied their time with political, religious, business or philanthropic activities. Some sublimated their frustrations into cultural pursuits: Jahanara and Zebunnisa were writers of note and generous patrons of culture. And, of course, the harem ladies managed the household and social functions of the royal family. But mostly they idled about, narcissistically admiring themselves in the tiny ring mirror each lady wore on her right thumb. 'They live in this way, with no cares or anxieties,' notes Manucci, 'occupying themselves with nothing beyond displaying great show and magnificence, an imposing and majestuous bearing, or making themselves attractive, getting talked about in the world, and pleasing the king.'

A high point of the year for the royal women was the Meena Bazaar, a new year amusement fair held in the citadel, in which the begums of the amirs played hucksters and the emperor (the only male participating) and princesses played customers, all haggling over prices and joshing each other and having the time of their lives in a mirthful, flirtatious, mildly bacchanalian fiesta. The objective of the fair was fun, not shopping, though the occasion also served, according to Badauni, to arrange 'important affairs of the harem people, marriage contracts, and betrothals of boys and girls.' The fair lasted a week. 'These eight days were observed in the palace with festivity, dancing, music, acting and other amusements. The fortress remained shut, with no man inside but the king,' says Manucci.

The idea of a fancy fair for women was originally conceived by Humayun who, according to his sister Gulbadan, held it for the first time at 'the house of feasting' on the banks of the Yamuna in Agra, during the celebrations to commemorate his accession. Similar fairs in Akbar's reign was called Khushroz, Joyful Day Fair. But these differed from the later fairs in that the stalls there were run by merchants, not begums. It was probably Akbar who started the custom of holding the annual Meena Bazaar. Badauni, censorious and rigidly orthodox, saw it as a deliberately heretical move. 'In order to direct another blow at the honour of our religion, His Majesty ordered that the stalls of the fancy bazaars, which are held on New Year's day, should, for a stated time, be given up for the enjoyment of the Begums and the women of the harem, and also for any other married ladies.'

Jahangir, says Coryat, had an amorous motive in holding the fair: 'By this meanes hee attaines to the sight of all the prettie wenches of the towne.' Shah Jahan also had a similar purpose, says Manucci. In Delhi, the fair was held in the gallery of the royal harem, and attracted, according to Manucci, as many as 30,000 women from outside the citadel. It was, says Bernier, 'a whimsical kind of fair . . . conducted by the handsomest and most engaging of the wives of the Omrahs and principal Mansabdars. The articles exhibited are beautiful brocades, rich embroideries of the newest fashion, turbans elegantly worked on cloth of gold, fine muslins worn by women of quality, and other articles of high price. These bewitching females act the part of traders, while the purchasers are the King, the Begums or Princesses, and other distinguished ladies of the Seraglio. If any Omrah's wife happens to have a handsome daughter, she never fails to accompany her mother, that she may be seen by the King and become known to the Begums.' Says Manucci: 'Each one brought what merchandise she could. But the best piece of goods she could produce was her own body . . .'

'The charm of this fair,' continues Bernier, 'is the most ludicrous manner in which the King makes his bargains, frequently disputing for the value of a penny. He pretends that the good lady cannot possibly be in earnest, that the article is much too dear, that it is not equal to that he can find elsewhere, and that positively he will give no more than such a price. The woman, on the other hand, endeavours to sell to the best advantage, and when the King perseveres in offering what she considers too little money, high words frequently ensue, and she fearlessly tells him that he is a worthless trader, a person ignorant of the value of merchandise; that her articles are too good for him, and that he had better go where he can suit himself better, and similar jocular expressions. The Begums betray, if possible, a still greater anxiety to be served cheaply; high words are heard on every side, and the loud and scurrilous quarrels of the sellers and buyers create a complete farce. But sooner or later they agree upon the price, the Princesses, as well as the King, buy right and left, pay in ready money, and often slip out of their hands, as if by accident, a few gold instead of silver roupies, intended as a compliment to the fair merchant or her pretty daughter. The present is received in the same unconscious manner, and the whole ends amidst witty jest and good-humour.'

'THE CONSUMPTION OF fine cloths of gold, and brocades, silks, embroideries, pearls, musk, amber and sweet essences' in the Mughal harem, says Bernier, was 'greater than can be conceived.' The dresses of the begums 'are superb and costly, perfumed with the essences of roses,' says Manucci. They changed their clothes several times a day, especially in summer, when they 'put on such exceeding thin raiment that their skin shows through.' Confirms Tavernier: their clothes were so fine that you could 'see all the skin as though it were uncovered.' Continues Manucci: 'Ordinarily they wear two or even three garments each weighing not more than one ounce, and worth from forty to fifty rupees each. This without counting the gold lace that they are in the habit of adding.' Their dresses, says Bernier, were 'so delicately fine as frequently to wear out in one night. This article of dress, which lasts only a few hours, may cost ten or twelve crowns, and even more, when beautifully embroidered with needlework.'

The gossamer muslin that the begums wore had such romantic names as *ab-i-rawan* (running water), *shabnam* (night dew), and *daft hawa* (woven air). 'Of this, the Sultanesses, and the great noble men's wives make their shifts and garments in hot-weather: and the king and the great lords take great pleasure to behold them in those shifts, and see them dance with nothing else upon their bodies,' says Tavernier.

'They sleep in these clothes . . . and never put them on again, but give them away to their servants,' says Manucci. While sleeping, the only apparel put aside was the *dupatta*, a cloth worn over the head, sometimes reaching down to the knees, made of the finest muslin and woven with gold thread. In the cold season, in addition to the usual dress, they wore a long open gown of fine wool and a woolen shawl which, says Manucci, was 'so thin that . . . [it] can be passed through a small finger-ring.'

The ordinary dress of Muslim women was virtually the same as that of men, but with some charming variations. 'The Mogul Women . . . are Cloathed almost like the Men,' says Thevenot; 'however the sleeves of their Smocks, as those of the other Indian Women, reach not below the Elbow, that they may have liberty to adorn the rest of their Arm with Carkanets (chains) and Bracelets of Gold, Silver and Ivory, or set with Precious Stones, as likewise they do the small of their Legs.' Raushanara, according to Manucci, was fond of wearing the sari, the traditional dress of Hindu women. Royal ladies sometimes wore a cap called Taj Kulah, or, with the emperor's permission, a turban adorned with an aigrette of gems, which, says Manucci, 'is extremely becoming, and makes them look very graceful. During entertainments . . . there are dancing-women who have the same privilege.'

European hats became popular among the begums during the reign of Jahangir—an English merchant (Keridge) in 1614 asked his principals in England for 'half a dozen of coloured beaver hats, such as our gentlewomen use . . . for the king demanded for such things of me for his women to wear a-hunting.' Roe also notes that Jahangir asked for hats for women. Women were usually barefooted, 'even princesses and queens', says Manucci.

Upper-class Hindu women usually wore, along with the sari, an *angiya*, a tight-fitting short bodice, often 'made to fit the bust with great exactness' and fastened behind. At home, the upper end of the sari was wrapped around the shoulder, but when going out or speaking to a person deserving respect, it was drawn over the head. Sometimes at home they wore no bodice but covered their breasts with the end of the sari, or wrapped the sari end around the waist so they were naked from waist up. In some areas of western and central India, women wore skirt and blouse instead of sari.

As for the dress of ordinary women, 'it is very indifferent, and little can be said about it,' says Manucci. The poor, men as well as women wore nothing more than a loin cloth in most parts of India. Banjara women too went naked from waist up, but were so heavily tattooed that, says Tavernier, 'it seems as though their skin was a flowered fabric'.

The begums were heavily bejewelled. Manucci claims that on his visits to the harem for treating the inmates, jewels were sometimes brought to him in trays for his appraisal, or as an opening for conversation. Some of the stones, he says, were 'of an extraordinary size, and strings of pearls very equal in size . . . there were strings of rubies pierced and strung together just like the pearls, and about the size of a nut . . .' The begums wore gem-studded necklaces ('like scarves,' says Manucci) and three or five strings of pearls round their neck hanging down to their lower abdomen; they also wore earrings and several other ornaments, such as the jewel that hung down from the top of the head to the middle of the forehead, which, says Manucci, 'suits them exceedingly well'.

'They wear on their arms, above the elbow, rich armlets two inches wide, enriched on the surface with stones, and having small bunches of pearls depending from them,' continues Manucci. 'At their wrists are very rich bracelets, or bands of pearls, which usually go round nine or twelve times. In this way they often have the place for feeling the pulse covered up that I found it difficult to put my hand upon it. On their fingers are rich rings, and on the right thumb there is always a ring, where, in place of a stone, there is mounted a little round mirror, having pearls around it. This mirror they use to look at themselves, an act of which they are very fond, at any and every moment. In addition they are girded with a sort of waistbelt of gold two fingers wide, covered all over with great stones; at the ends of the strings which tie up their drawers there are bunches of pearls made up of fifteen strings five fingers in length. Round the bottom of their legs are valuable metal rings or strings of costly pearls. All these princesses own six to eight sets of jewels, in addition to some other sets.'

Zinat Kausar, a modern researcher who has taken the trouble to catalogue the various ornaments of the Mughal ladies, lists eight head ornaments, sixteen for the forehead, thirty-one for the ears, fifteen for the nose, one for the teeth (gold or silver studs fitted to the front teeth), twenty-nine for the neck, sixteen for the arms, twenty-four for the wrists, three for the palms, nine for the fingers, nine for the waist, fifteen for the feet and ankles, and five for the toes. The begum was a walking treasure house.

Hindu women too wore a great quantity of jewels, and even the poor were avid for jewels, gilding their wretchedness. Hindus believed that there should be at least a speck of gold on a person for ceremonial purity; Muslims held that gold offered protection against the evil eye and malevolent spirits. Says Fryer: 'The rich [women] have their arms and feet fettered with gold and silver, the meaner with brass and glass and tuthinag (tutenag: nickel silver), besides rings in their noses, ears, toes and fingers.' Says Careri, 'All the Gentiles bore their Noses to put Rings through, as they do to Buffaloes in Italy.' Says Fitch, 'Here the women weare upon their armes infinite numbers of rings made of elephants teeth, wherein they take so much delight that they had rather be without their meate then without their bracelets.'

'Their main Cost is expended upon their Women, who ambitiously affect a Gayety in their Dress and Cloathing,' says Ovington. 'Jewels and Ornaments are the very joy of their Hearts . . . with which they are deckt from the crown of the Head to the very feet. Their Toes are adorn'd with Rings, and their Legs with Shackles of Gold, or Silver, or some other Metal, which are sometimes above two Inches in Diameter, wreath'd and hollow. The Women that carry the Water about the Streets, will not walk abroad without these Ornaments upon them. Some tie up the Hair of their Heads, and put it under a hollow large piece of Silver, rais'd somewhat like a Bell, gilt, and neatly embellisht on the outside, and fasten'd to the Crown of their Heads. Some wear Earrings all round their Ears, which for Ornament's sake will dangle sometimes almost down to their Shoulders, and have Bracelets about their Necks and Arms, and Rings about their Wrists, and on every Finger. Some adorn themselves with Breast Jewels, form'd in Fashion of a Heart, compos'd of variety of Diamonds, Rubies, Saphiers, and other Stones of Esteem; and on their Fore-heads wear a Gold Bodkin, broad at the end, beset with glittering Diamonds, or some other precious Stones. And as they are much taken with this gaudy Attire, and delight in these splendid Ornaments themselves, so they think them a kindness to the very Brutes; and shew their Affection to a Darling Cow, or Favourite Goat, by fastening large Rings of some Metal or other about their Legs. Nor will they spare their Ornamental Favours to the Fruit-Trees in their Gardens, but shew them their profuse Respect in adorning them with Painting of divers Colours.'

The begums, for all their fine dress, jewels and perfumes, were somewhat backward in their ablutions, retaining the habits of their distant ancestors in Central Asia—though there were hammams (Turkish baths) in the harem, instead of having a bath every day, the begums only washed their face, hands and feet, perfumed themselves and applied cosmetics (but were not allowed to go out of the harem after applying scents). On Fridays they had an obligatory bath—and they bathed in rose-water. They cleaned their teeth with a twig and a tooth-powder prepared with crushed pearls, musk, amber, aloeswood and camphor. Their lips were coloured red, by chewing paan, or they applied *missi* (black powder) to lips and gums, and occasionally to the teeth—as Zebunnisa often did—to blacken the rims of their teeth, to set them off, like pearls.

Ladies invariably applied a beauty spot to the chin, and blushed their cheeks with red powder; henna coloured their palms, nails, fingertips, toe nails and soles. 'All women in India,' says Manucci, 'are in the habit of scenting their hands and feet with . . . *mendy* (henna), which colours the hands and feet red, in such a way that they look as if they had on gloves.' They applied collyrium and antimony to the eyes to add lustre to them and to make them seem larger—'Large, rolling eyes were regarded beautiful,' says Terry. Joined eyebrows were admired. Sometimes, imitating Hindu women, the begums decorated their foreheads with moon and stars of gold or silver dust. Their hair was worn long, never cut, and the parting of the hair adorned with gold or silver dust and decked with pearls. Some dyed their hair or used false hair. 'Their hair is always very well dressed, plaited, and perfumed with scented oil,' says Manucci.

THE IMPERIAL HAREM is described by Mughal chronicler Nizamuddin Ahmad as 'the pavilion of chastity'. Every possible precaution was taken to ensure the virtue of the begums. Yet everything in the harem, unlike in a nunnery, exuded sensuality; only its consummation was forbidden. The begums lolled erotically in the soft, voluptuous luxury of their perfumed garden palace, their fantasies spiced with the romantic tales they read and re-read, the amorous verses they learned and sang, and the lascivious gossip ever resonating through the palace chambers. 'In the midst of so much idleness, enjoyment, and grandeur, they cannot fail to get their minds loaded with the impurity of many vices,' says Manucci.

With so many women around, the competition among the royal wives and concubines to attract the attention of the emperor, the only male around, was intense—not merely to slake sexual thirst, but to fulfil themselves by bearing children, and possibly to gain the status of the first lady of the empire. Conditions were no different in the harems of the amirs, where also many wives and concubines vied for the attention of their lord. 'Sometimes to heighten their Master's Lusts they give him

Compositions of Pearl, gold, Opium and Amber; or else much Wine that he may require Company in Bed,' says Careri. Manucci says that 'the wife of Asad Khan, the Vizier, her name was Naval Bae, . . . she told me that her only thoughts were to imagine something by which she could please her husband and hinder his going near other women.'

Pelsaert has a rather fanciful account of the amir in his harem: 'Each night he visits a particular wife, or mahal, and receives a very warm welcome from her and from the slaves, who, dressed specially for the occasion, seem to fly, rather than run, about their duties. If it is the hot weather, they undress the husband as soon as he comes in, and rub his body with pounded sandalwood and rosewater, or some other scented and cooling oil. Fans are kept going steadily in the room, or in the open air, where they usually sit. Some of the slaves chafe the master's hands and feet, some sit and sing, or play music and dance, or provide other recreation, the wife sitting near him all the time. They study night and day how to make exciting perfumes and efficacious preserves, such as *mosseri* or *falonj*, containing amber, pearls, gold, opium, and other stimulants; but these are mostly for their own use, for they eat them occasionally in the day-time, because they produce a pleasant elevation of the spirit. In the cool of the evening they drink a great deal of wine, for the women learn the habit quickly from their husbands, and drinking has become very fashionable in the last few years. The husband sits like a golden cock among the gilded hens until midnight, or until passion, or drink, sends him to bed. Then if one of the pretty slave girls takes his fancy, he calls her to him and enjoys her, his wife not daring to show any signs of displeasure, but dissembling, though she will take it out on the slave-girl later on.'

Sexual intrigue was rampant in the harems. Also prevalent were auto-eroticism, lesbianism, affairs with eunuchs—and dangerous liaisons with men. Sometimes, if gossip is to be believed, men were smuggled into the royal harem, but this obviously could be done only by women in the very highest positions. Jahanara, according to Bernier, once had a lover 'of no very exalted rank' who, on being discovered by Shah Jahan in the harem, was stewed to death in a water cauldron in which he had hidden; later, she was said to have had another lover, a Persian youth of high birth, whom Shah Jahan disposed of with poisoned paan. Bernier further says— Manucci also reports the story—that he was once told by an old, half-caste Portuguese woman, who had been a slave in the harem for many years, that Raushanara had once admitted two men into the seraglio, who were caught and punished by Aurangzeb. Sir Thomas Roe notes that a royal concubine was once caught 'in some action with a Eunuch' and that she was ordered to be buried up to her shoulder for three days, to be pardoned if she survived, and that the eunuch was trampled to death under an elephant. The queen of Bidar, according to Bernier, once created quite a scandal by having affairs with sailors on the Dutch ship on the way to Mecca on pilgrimage.

There probably were also some incestuous susceptibilities in the harem, as was rumoured about Jahanara and Shah Jahan, for after all the princesses could be intimate with no men except their fathers and brothers, on whom they naturally focused all their love. It is possible that this sometimes slid imperceptibly towards incest, especially in the case of Shah Jahan, who, after Mumtaz Mahal's death, was himself emotionally vulnerable.

PHYSICIANS WERE WELCOME visitors in harems, for they were the only outside male contacts that the begums could legitimately have, however fleeting and inconsequential the contact might be. 'There are some who from time to time affect the invalid,' says Manucci, 'simply that they may have the chance of some conversation with, and have their pulse felt by, the physician who comes to see them.' Usually, the sick were taken to the entrance of the harem to be examined, but physicians were allowed into the harem to treat ladies too ill to be moved. On such occasions great care was taken to ensure that the privacy of the harem was not violated. When Bernier was once called in to treat 'a great lady so extremely ill that she could not be moved to outward gate', a Kashmir shawl was thrown over his head, covering him from head to toe, and a eunuch led him in by the hand, 'as if I had been a blind man'. The shawl was removed only at the bedside of the patient, who, whether young or old, still remained out of sight behind a curtain, extending or exposing only the appropriate limb through the curtain for the physician to examine.

Sometimes the doctor would be allowed to put his hand inside the curtain, which, claims Manucci, gave the lady a chance for gentle mischief. When the physician 'stretches out his hand inside the curtain, they lay hold of it, kiss it, and softly bite it. Some, out of curiosity, apply it to their breast, which has happened to me several times; but I pretended not to notice, in order to conceal what was passing from the matrons and eunuchs then present, and not arouse their suspicions. The physicians are well treated by these ladies, and they too, on their side, maintain much discretion both in their way of acting and in their speech, which is always restrained and polished.'

Male physicians were not permitted to examine women of royal blood 'without the express permission from the king', says Manucci, who goes on to claim that he used to bleed Aurangzeb's wife Nawab Bai twice every year regularly. 'She put her arm out from the curtain, but wrapped up, leaving only one little spot uncovered, about as wide as two fingers, close to the veins . . . It is just the same when they want themselves bled in the foot, or have any wound or fistula dressed. Nothing is ever shown but the part affected, or the vein they wish opened. When I bled the wives and daughters of Shah Alam, each of them gave me two hundred rupees and a *sarapa*.'

The harem had its own infirmary. 'When these ladies chance to fall ill, they are carried away to a very pretty set of rooms in the palace, which they style the *bimar-khanah*, or house of the sick,' notes Manucci. 'There they are nursed and tended with all possible exactitude, and they only come forth either well or dead. When the latter is the case, the king seizes the wealth of the defunct. If the patient is one esteemed by the monarch, he goes to see her at the beginning of her illness, and if she does not recover promptly, he does not go back to her again, but he sends from time to time a slave to ask after the state of her health.'

IN THE HAREMS of amirs, the eunuchs were the only regular links of the begums with the outside world, and they were pampered by the ladies, to keep their guilty secrets from their husbands. The women 'allow the eunuch to enjoy them according to his ability, and thus gratify their burning passions when they have no opportunity of going out; but otherwise they spare no craft or trouble to enable them to enjoy themselves outside,' says Pelsaert. 'These wretched women wear, indeed, the most expensive clothes, eat the daintiest food, and enjoy all worldly pleasures except one, and for that one they grieve, saying they would willingly give everything in exchange for a beggar's poverty.'

'Some of the nobles . . . have chaste wives, but they are too few to be worth mentioning,' continues Pelsaert; 'most of the ladies are tarred with the same brush, and when the husband is away, though he may think they are guarded quite safely by his eunuchs, they are too clever for Argus himself with his hundred eyes, and get all the pleasure they can, though not so much as they desire.' The women, says Mandelslo, 'brook so ill [the restraints imposed on them], that in those parts a man would think Polygamy should rather be permitted to women than the men.' Says Ovington, 'The Watch is neither so careful, nor their Modesty so blameless, but that they sometimes will look abroad for Variety, as well as their roving Husbands do.' Adds Careri, 'These Women are committed to the custody of Eunuchs, but it is delivering up the Sheep to the Wolves; so lascivious are the Women.'

Sometimes the eunuchs, themselves got emotionally involved with women. A maid of Nur Jahan was once discovered in sexual play with a eunuch, upon which 'another capon that loved her killed him'. In another instance, Didar Khan, one of the principal eunuchs of the seraglio, became enamoured of the sister of a Hindu neighbour—proving, says Bernier, 'the fallacy of an opinion entertained by myself, as well as by others, that he who is entirely deprived of virility cannot feel the passion of love.' The brother caught the eunuch and the woman one night in the same bed and stabbed them both dead. The whole seraglio then wanted the man executed, but Aurangzeb merely required him to become a Muslim—in atonement!

The Woman's Lot

'WE HAVE HEARD that prosperity and bad luck depend on four things: first, upon your wife; second, upon your slave; third, upon your house; fourth, upon your horse,' says Jahangir in his memoirs. Jahangir was lucky, particularly in his wife, Nur Jahan. Not so fortunate was Sultan Husain Mirza, Babur's uncle, whose wife, Bega Sultan Begum, 'was very cross-tempered and made the Mirza endure much wretchedness, until driven at last to despair, he set himself free by divorcing her,' says Babur, and goes on to quote a Persian couplet:

A bad wife in a good man's house
Makes this world already his hell.

Shrews were probably uncommon among the genteel ladies of the Mughal harem, though Aurangzeb's first wife, Dilras Begum, was reputed to have been irascible. But the common women in Mughal India loved to brawl. It was their pastime. There was, says Terry, a virago at the residence of English ambassador Sir Thomas Roe, 'a laundress . . . who had such a freedome and liberty of speech that she would sometimes scould, brawl, and rail from the sunrising to sun-set'—but she more than met her match in Thomas Coryat, the eccentric Englishman who could out-nag anyone in any number of languages, and had mastered Hindustani during his short stay in India. 'One day he undertook her in her own language, and by eight of the clock in the morning so silenced her that she had not one word more to speak,' says Terry.

The woman's side of the story, unheard, could be quite different in all these instances. Mere appendages in a man's world, women normally had no life of their own in Mughal India. Even at the lowest stratum of society, where gender inequality had little meaning, their life was bleaker than that of men. Wretchedly poor and undernourished, their health broken by intermittent childbearing, weighed down by endless household drudgery, often in addition to working alongside their men in the fields, there was not much more to their lives than bare existence. In the next layer of society, in the families of traders, artisans, and peasants in comfortable circumstances, things were easier for the housewife, for she had servants to do the chores, but her life too was empty of any real worth. Their 'principal business is to tell stories and eat betel,' says Manucci about middle-class women. They had no cultural interests beyond their blind and routine devotions, had no social life outside the circle of their extended families, no role in society.

Their word carried little weight. It took the word of two women to match that of one man in judicial decisions in Muslim society. Similarly, the shariah, the Muslim customary law, allotted to daughters only half the share of parental property that was allotted to sons, and even this portion was denied to them from the eighteenth century on. The lives of Hindu women were still worse, because of the disabilities imposed on widows and the practice of sati.

There were of course exceptions to all this. Mothers were generally revered by Hindus as well as Muslims. There were a few women writers of repute in Mughal India, even a few women sages. But literate women were extremely rare, for it was only among the aristocracy and a few upper-caste families that the education of girls was given any attention at all, and even among them the schooling of girls was of short duration, limited to reading and writing, and the study of the Koran among Muslims and of the *Ramayana* and the *Mahabharata* among Hindus. After this rather basic education, most women concentrated on acquiring the skills essential for survival in a polygamous household.

In these skills, upper-class women were great virtuosi, especially Hindu women, because of the relative lack of sexual inhibitions among them. Some of these women, like Rupmati of Malwa, were legendary figures, immortalized in song and dance. In ancient India, the high-class courtesan was a cultured, talented woman, expert in 'sixty-four arts', and some of those skills seem to have survived into Mughal times. The caresses of the 'dancing *lulis* and charmers of India . . . would captivate the hearts of angels,' says Jahangir, a connoisseur of feminine charms. Even dour Aurangzeb once fell victim to the witchery of a Hindu siren. Indian dancing girls, says Ovington, 'set themselves off with such advantage by a Rhetorical look . . . that a grave European will scarce adventure himself in the sight of their insinuating temptations.'

These were backhanded compliments, as much rebuke as praise. Even in the best of circumstances, the woman's lot in medieval India was grim. In this environment, it is no surprise that daughters were not favoured. Among the Rajputs, the birth of a daughter was considered a curse—if a woman gave birth to two daughters in succession, she could even be divorced—and female infanticide was widespread. Similar practices prevailed in other parts of India. 'When a daughter is born to a man without means, they put her to death by strangulation,' notes Jahangir. In some parts of India, unwanted babies were hung in a cloth cradle on a tree, where birds pecked at their eyes, says Tavernier; in Bengal, and presumably elsewhere too, if the child did not take the mother's breast, it was exposed to death. These were common, accepted social practices, and did not horrify anyone. Daud Khan, the Mughal general, for some reason routinely killed all his babies, and no one ever questioned his right to do so.

In the imperial household, the tradition was that the whole court celebrated the birth of a prince, while the birth of a princess was celebrated only by the ladies. Akbar changed this custom. Thus when a daughter was born to Salim, Akbar, says Abul Fazl, 'contrary to the usage of contemporaries, had an assemblage to render thanksgivings, and there was a great feast in the house of Maryam Makani (Akbar's mother), and there was a presentation of gifts, and there was largess.' When a second daughter was born to Salim, that too, 'was made an occasion for rejoicing.'

MARRIAGE WAS THE most important event in the life of women in Mughal India, as they had hardly any life outside the home. 'To their idea, there is not in this world anything to compare in importance with getting married,' says Manucci. Men too attached the greatest importance to marriage, for a man's life was considered incomplete without a wife. 'It is a maxim of the Hindus that no good deed can be performed by men in the social state without the partnership or presence of the wife whom they have styled the half of men,' writes Jahangir.

Girls—boys too, for that matter—had little choice in the selection of their life partners, though nominally their assent was sought, at least among Muslims, as the formal, explicit consent of the couple was necessary to perform *nikah*, the marriage ceremony. Akbar, says Abul Fazl, maintained that 'the consent of the bride and bridegroom, and the permission of parents, are absolutely necessary in marriage contracts.' Among Hindus, the prevalence of child marriage made the question of consent largely irrelevant. Aristocratic Rajput women however enjoyed considerable freedom in choosing their husbands, sometimes even demanding that the groom prove himself by some act of valour.

Occasionally, Muslim girls too spiritedly asserted themselves—Hamida thus rebuffed Humayun initially, and a princess of Bijapur, while being escorted to marry Akbar's son Daniyal, took advantage of the confusion of a night storm to run away.

Most upper-class households in Mughal India, among Hindus as well as Muslims, were polygamous, because of the need to have a large number of children as an insurance against high infant mortality. Hindus do not seem to have had any rules regarding the number of wives a man could have; it was the man's capacity, sexual as well as financial, that determined the number of his wives. Muslims had rules, but they were ambiguous and their interpretations conflicting.

Muslim convention on the number of permitted wives was based on an enigmatic statement of Prophet Muhammad: 'Marry what seems good to you of women, by twos, or threes, or fours: and if ye fear that ye cannot be equitable, then only one, or what your right hand possesses.' This statement was interpreted in different ways by different authorities—one scholar added two and three and four and got nine wives, another got a total of eighteen by doubling two and three and four and adding the results. In addition to the 'permanent' wives taken in *nikah* marriage, some authorities, especially among Shiahs, permitted any number of temporary wives to be taken under *mutah* marriage; there was also no limit to the number of concubines a man could have. It was a man's world.

The normal Muslim practice was not to have more than four wives at a time, but a man could have any number of wives in succession, by divorcing his earlier wives. Akbar did not even bother to divorce them but married some three hundred wives—an act of royal kindness, according to Abul Fazl—though later he decreed that 'one woman sufficeth for one man'. Akbar's foster brother Mirza Aziz had a droll explanation as to why a man needed four wives: 'A man must marry one woman of Hindustan to rear up children; one wife from Khurasan to do the household work; one woman from Iran to keep company and talk.' And the fourth? 'Why? One woman from Transoxiana to whip the other three and keep peace!' Aziz cracked.

The laxity in the number of wives and concubines, and the freedom for men and women to divorce and remarry, often made Muslim families proliferate confusedly. Badauni writes of the predicament of a poor Muslim who had the following categories of sons at home: his sons by his former wives, his wife's sons by her former husband, and his sons by his present wives—burdened by such a large family, the man was obliged to seek financial relief from the emperor!

Unlike polygamy, polyandry was rare in India, confined to parts of the Himalayan tracts, and among a few tribes in other parts of India. According to Tavernier, a merchant community in Multan practised polyandry, with several brothers sharing one wife, and the eldest brother being considered the father of all the children. Among some communities—like the Nairs of Kerala—a matrilineal system also prevailed.

Child marriage was common among Hindus in India—girls being considered a burden, parents were anxious to pass on the burden early, an anxiety that was intensified by the religious injunction that to keep a girl unmarried after she attained puberty was a sin. Sometimes the groom was very much older than the bride, but Manucci's statement that 'ordinarily the marriage is between a little child and a grown man' seems an exaggeration. Withington reports that he was told that children were married off young so that in case the parents died early, the child would have other parents to take care of her.

Such anxieties do not seem to have troubled Muslims, among whom child marriages were rare. In the royal family, marriages were seldom performed before the late teens, though sometimes betrothal was arranged earlier. Akbar disapproved of marriage of boys before sixteen and of girls before fourteen—'He (Akbar) abhors marriages which take place between men and women before the age of puberty,' says Abul Fazl—as well marriage between close relatives, which was common among Muslims as well as Hindus, except brahmins.

The guilt-free, permissive sexual ethos of India generally favoured cohabitation among children as soon as they were ready for sex—and in the steamy, tropical climate of India, children were apparently ready for sex earlier than in cold countries. 'Indians of both Sexes are capable of engendering much sooner than any other Nation: so that there are not any but are fit for the work of generation at ten or twelve years of age,' says Mandelslo. 'In . . . India men are active to form this union at a tender age, and this introduces the leaven of evil,' says Abul Fazl. 'And when the children come to bee ten yeares ould, they lye together,' says Withington, but Thevenot says that 'there are places in the Indies where the young Married couple are not suffered to lye together before the Man be fourteen Years old.' If Indian women began to have sex early, they also left off early. 'The women who have children so young soon leave off child bearing and commonly do not conceive after thirty years of age, but become extremely wrinkly,' says Thevenot.

Some sort of an exchange of cash, goods or property, or the promise of that, was part of the medieval marriage process. Among Hindus it took the form of dowry, by which the bride's father endowed her, just as he would later bequeath his wealth to his sons. The dowry was a settlement on the girl; it belonged to the girl. Muslims had no dowry system, but Muslim women had the right to a share of their parents' wealth, and were provided with additional financial security in the form of *mehr*, an ante-nuptial settlement, by which the groom agreed to pay a certain amount to his wife in case he divorced her. The bride also received gifts from her father, depending on his wealth and status, but this was entirely voluntary. The amount of the *mehr* depended on the status of the girl's family, and it was usually kept high to prevent frivolous divorce. Among the affluent, the amount was given as a settlement on the wife at the time of marriage; it was in any case the first charge on the husband's property. *Mehr* was not bride money; the amount belonged to the girl, not to her parents. The custom of purchasing a bride from her parents, however, existed among certain Indian communities.

NORMALLY MARRIAGES WERE arranged within the same community, and in the case of Hindus by observing the various caste and clan taboos. 'No one marries but in his own trade or profession,' notes Bernier, 'and this custom is observed almost as rigidly by Mahometans as by the Gentiles, to whom it is expressly enjoined by their law. Many are the beautiful girls thus doomed to live singly, girls who might marry advantageously if their parents would connect them with a family less noble than their own.' The one major exception to the traditional Hindu marriage conventions was that Rajput princesses were given in marriage to Mughal emperors and princes—but only to emperors and princes, not to amirs and their sons, who had to content themselves with taking Hindu concubines of lower social status.

Among kings and aristocrats, weddings were elaborate, fabulous affairs, involving vast expenditure—for Dara's wedding with Parvez's daughter, for instance, Shah Jahan, according to Inayat Khan, spent in all 3.2 million rupees. 'At a wedding the feasting lasts fifteen days,' says Manucci.

The ceremonies began on the day preceding the wedding, when the ritual of *hennabandi* (dyeing the groom's hands and feet red) was held. The henna for this came from the bride's home in a grand procession, and with it came various presents, including a set of clothes for the groom, sugar-candy, perfumes, betel leaves and fireworks. After applying henna, the groom was dressed in the apparel sent by the bride's father, sprinkled with perfumes and fed sugar-candy for good luck. This was followed by a reception for male guests, who were entertained with song and dance and fed a sumptuous dinner.

The date and time of the wedding were in all communities fixed by astrologers, and the ceremony held at any odd hour determined as auspicious. In the case of Aurangzeb's marriage with Dilras Banu Begum, it was held at four hours to dawn. Before setting out for the wedding ceremony, Aurangzeb was taken to pay his respects to Shah Jahan, who gave the prince rich presents, and with his own hands tied the groom's turban and the *sehra*, the veil of strings of pearls and precious stones falling over his face. The marriage procession, with the princes and the grandees mounted on caparisoned horses, then wound its way through the streets of the capital to the bride's home, to the accompaniment of music and the discharge of fireworks. Shah Jahan himself arrived separately, by boat, at the bride's mansion, and the Kazi married the couple in his presence. *Mehr* was fixed at 400,000 rupees. The bride's father, as was the custom, kept away from the wedding ceremony. After the wedding, a reception was held at Aurangzeb's mansion, which was attended by the emperor, who there gave wedding gifts to amirs.

Marriage brokers were common in Mughal India. Among Hindustani Muslims, marriage negotiations were usually initiated by the groom's family, and when settled, the bridegroom, says Pelsaert, 'sends a ring to the bride, with his compliments. She sends in return some betel, with a handkerchief or something of the kind, though the unfortunate bridegroom is not allowed to meet the lady, still less to see if his future bride is white or black, straight or crooked, pretty or ugly; he must trust to his mother and friends. From this time on begins much merry-making . . . with music and singing . . . and this goes on continuously, night and day, with drums, pipes and other noise, provided by both parties, so that the whole neighbourhood is drowned in noise.'

The wedding usually took place a couple of weeks after engagement, to give time for the families to organize the festivities. Three or four days before the wedding day, says Pelsaert, the groom with his parents and their entire clan went to the bride's house to the accompaniment of music, bearing 'large ornamented wooden dishes, full of confectionery, sugar, almonds, raisins and other fruits,' and also money for wedding expenses in the bride's family. The next evening, the bride's family went in procession to the groom's house with similar presents.

On the marriage day, continues Pelsaert, the bridegroom was 'dressed

in red, and so garlanded with flowers that his face cannot be seen . . .'
and was led in procession on horseback to the bride's house, to the
accompaniment of fireworks, music, and dancing by *kenchens*. 'The women
follow in palanquins and carts, covered with the finest cloth that can be
provided.' At the bride's house, the groom 'may not speak till the marriage
is complete, but sits as if he were dumb.' Music and dancing went on till
a quarter of the night was gone. Then the Kazi arrived, said a prayer,
and joined the couple in marriage without the bride being present—the
ceremony consisted merely of registering the marriage in the Kazi's book.
Feasting followed, accompanied by singing and dancing, and it 'lasted
the whole night till the morning.'

The newly married couple then went in procession to the groom's
house, the bride travelling in a palanquin. 'His house is ready; he goes
in, and his wife is brought to him, who he now sees for the first time, and
he may congratulate himself if she happens to be pretty, or to suit his
taste. The marriage must be consummated at once,' says Pelsaert, 'while
the ladies sit and sing at no great distance; otherwise the bridegroom
would be deeply disgraced, and the married ladies would send him the
spinning-wheel. When the marriage has been consummated, the mother
and an old woman enter, and after their investigation, they begin to
scream or sing 'Mubarak' or Good Luck! as if a great victory had been
won. Then the bridegroom goes to his apartments for the day, and the
bride to hers; and the friends take their leave and depart, after each has
received the gift of a piece of cloth, the men from the bridegroom and the
women from the bride.' (Among orthodox Hindus, marriage was
consummated only on the fourth day after marriage.)

THE WEDDING DAY was the only time in a woman's life when she was
the queen of the day. Thereafter, among the common people, she slid into
the drab, oppressive routine of the Indian housewife. 'It is the custom of
the Hindus,' says Manucci, 'that when the bride comes to her husband's
house she acts as servant to all the house—sweeps, cleans, cooks, and
performs all the other work. She never opens her mouth, keeps her head
down, enduring the importunate demands of her mother-in-law. When
she is in child-bed she has little liberty, and during her periods she has to
retire to a separate room kept for this special purpose, where no one
speaks to her. Her food is left at a distance; no one approaches her.'
Corroborates John Fryer: 'The women are conformable to the wills of
their husbands, being truly no more than their chief slaves, dressing the

victuals and waiting till their Lords have dined, before they eat themselves.'
The couple did not even sleep together. 'Here man and wife do not sleep
together,' says Pelsaert, 'but the man calls his wife when he wants her in
the night, and when he has finished she goes back to her own place or
bed.'

Divorce among caste Hindus was extremely rare, because marriage
was a sacrament, but among the lower classes both marriage and divorce
were casual affairs. Among sudras, according to Manucci, 'when the
husband is tired of his wife he gives her a straw called turumbo (*turumbu*).
By the giving of this straw the marriage is broken.' It was literally the
last straw—but a woman also could force her husband to give her the
straw.

Among Muslims too divorce was easy, because marriage was only a
civil contract, not a sacrament. The contract could be terminated instantly
and irrevocably by the husband pronouncing *talaq* ('divorce') thrice in
succession. But there were also more cautious forms of divorce among
Muslims, which took effect only after a three-month period of separation,
during which the process could be aborted. A woman too could divorce
her husband, but in that case she had to give back the *mehr*. Divorce by
mutual consent was also prevalent.

In the midst of all their miseries, Indian women had one blessing:
their ease in child-bearing. Says Terry: 'The women in those parts have a
great happinesse above all I know, in their easie bringing forth of children;
for it is a thing common there, for women great with childe one day to
ride, carrying their infants in their bodies, the next day to ride againe,
carrying them in their arms.' Confirms Thevenot, 'These Indian Women
are easily delivered of their Children; and sometimes they'll walk about
the Streets next day after they have been brought to Bed.'

Linschoten describes what seemed to him an extraordinary incident:
One day when he was out on a walk in the fields, feeling thirsty he went
into a hut of a 'Canarin' for a drink of water. 'I stooped downe and thrust
my head in at the doore, asking for some water, where I espied a Woman
alone within the house, tying her cloth fast about her middle, and her
having a wooden Trough full of Water, where shee stood and washed a
child, wereof as then she had newly beene delivered without any helpe:
which having washt, she laid it Naked on the ground upon the great
Indian Figge leafe, and desired me to stay and she would presently give
me water.' Linschoten fled.

Such a minimal, almost animal level of existence was the lot only of
people at the lowest stratum of society, but it was a very broad group, to

which almost all but a tiny segment of people of medieval India belonged. Among them, the lot of Hindu women was the bleakest of all. The position of Muslim women was on the whole better, at all levels of society. The Muslim husband had no right to take anything away from his wife, including what he had given her, and she had (at least until the eighteenth century) the right to a share of her father's and husband's properties, which she could dispose of as she pleased. There were no disabilities on widows and divorcees among Muslims, and remarriage of both was common. And, of course, they were not burned with their dead husbands.

'IT IS THE CUSTOM among the Hindus,' writes Jahangir, 'that after the death of their husbands women burn themselves, whether from love, or to save the honour of their fathers, or from being ashamed before their sons-in-law.' Jahangir exaggerates. Sati, the custom of widows immolating themselves on the funeral pyres of their husbands, was not widespread among Hindus, but was largely confined to the Hindu ruling classes, especially the Rajputs. Even among the Rajputs, it was by no means universal. 'There are hundreds, or even thousands, who do not do it,' says Pelsaert, who notes that in Agra in the reign of Jahangir sati occurred only 'two or three times a week'. The practice was exceptional enough for the sati site, and the ash from the sati pyre, to be considered sacred.

Sati was an ancient tradition in India, prevalent perhaps even in Vedic times; the epics mention it, and so do Greek writers of the fourth century BC. By about the fifth century AD, the custom had become fairly common among kshatriyas (the warrior caste) in Hindustan, but in South India it was very rare till about AD 1000, and was uncommon later also, even among the Marathas. In Mughal times, a few non-kshatriya communities, like brahmins in eastern India, practised sati; occasionally, though rarely, lower-caste Hindus, and even the Sikhs despite its express prohibition by the Gurus, performed sati.

The normal practice of sati was for the widow to burn herself with her husband's body on the same pyre, but if the husband died in battle, as often happened among the Rajputs, his women, says Manucci, 'immolate themselves with still greater alacrity on receiving the turban sent them as a sign of their husband's death. With it in their hands they are cremated.' Withington once saw a young widow of ten, wife of a soldier who had died in action, being burned with her husband's clothes. When Raja Bhao Singh died in the Deccan (in his case, not in battle, but from excessive drinking) 'two wives and eight concubines burned themselves in the fire of fidelity for him,' records Jahangir. Sometimes even betrothed girls committed sati on the funeral pyres of their fiances, as Manu, the ancient Indian lawgiver, had decreed that a woman should be considered a widow if her groom died before marriage.

Sati was usually voluntary. Pelsaert flatly states that 'the deed was done not under compulsion but out of sheer love', and Manucci records an instance in which, even after the widow had mounted the funeral pyre, her consent was re-confirmed before lighting the pyre. 'The woman is then spoken to by her name,' Manucci reports, 'and three times distinctly she is called on to say whether she consents to go to heaven. To this she replies in the affirmative.' Terry also states that sati was not performed under compulsion.

There are, however, numerous recorded incidents of forced sati. 'In Lahore I saw a most beautiful young widow sacrificed, who could not, I think, have been more than twelve years of age,' reports Bernier. 'The poor little creature appeared more dead than alive when she approached the dreadful pit: the agony of her mind cannot be described; she trembled and wept bitterly; but three or four of the Brahmens, assisted by an old woman who held her under the arm, forced the unwilling victim toward the fatal spot, seated her on the wood, tied her hand and feet, lest she should run away, and in that situation the innocent creature was burnt alive.' Abul Fazl states that, though normally the Hindu wife 'gives herself to the fire with an expanded heart and an open brow, . . . if from wickedness and love of life she refrains from doing this, her husband's relatives assemble and light the flame, whether she be willing or unwilling.'

'I have known some of these unhappy widows shrink at the sight of the piled wood,' says Bernier, 'so as to leave no doubt on my mind that they would willingly have recanted, if recantation had been permitted . . . [by the men, who] excite or astound the affrighted victims, and even thrust them into the fire. I was present when a poor young woman, who had fallen back five or six paces from the pit, was thus driven forward; and I saw another of these wretched beings struggling to leave the funeral pile when the fire increased around her person, but she was prevented from escaping by the long poles of the diabolical executioners.' Even when the sati was voluntary, when the fire reached the women, they 'naturally move and begin to shriek. They are soon choked by the smoke, while the men surrounding the pyre raise a great noise with drum and gongs and loud shouts, while the burners skillfully force them to lie down by thrusting at them with poles,' says Manucci, but adds: 'I have seen some die with their husband's body in their arms without making a sign or movement.' Terry says that when the fire was lit, 'all the people assembled shoute and make a noyse, that the screeches of this tortured creature may not bee heard.'

Often it was the parents of the widow, not the family of the dead man, who forced the woman to commit sati. Says Withington: 'The kyndred of the husband that dies never force the wife to burne her selfe, but her owne kyndred, houldinge it a great disgrace to theire familie if shee should denye to bee burned; which some have done, but verye fewe . . . Nowe, if any one of them purpose to burne and (after ceremonies done) bee brought to the fyer, and there, feelinge the scorchinge heate, leape out of the fyer, her father and mother will take her and bynde her and throwe her into the fyer and burne her per force; but such weaknesse seldome happeneth amongste them.'

Instances of forced sati were probably rare. It amazed Akbar that Hindu wives should show such ardour. 'Since you reckon the reverencing of women as part of your religion, and allow not more than one wife to a man, it would not be wonderful if such fidelity and life-sacrifice were found among your women,' Akbar once said to the Jesuits in his court. 'The extraordinary thing is that it occurs among those of the Brahman religion. There are numerous concubines, and many of them are neglected and unappreciated and spend their days unfructuously in the privy chamber of chastity, yet in spite of such bitterness of life they are flaming torches of love and fellowship.' Marvels Abul Fazl:

> Being saturated with love, they burn together,
> Like two wicks caught by one flame.

This is poetic fancy. Burning love was rarely the fire that lit the sati pyre. The stoicism of the widow committing sati was, says Manucci, induced by the administration of 'certain beverages—*bhang*, opium, and such like, which entirely stupefy them'. Another factor, as Bernier perceptively notes, was cultural conditioning, 'the effect of early and deeply rooted prejudices. Every girl is taught by her mother that it is virtuous and laudable in a wife to mingle her ashes with those of her husband, and that no woman of honour will refuse compliance with the established custom. These opinions men have always inculcated as an easy mode of keeping wives in subjection, of securing their attention in times of sickness, and deterring them from administering poison to their husbands.' The rationale of sati as a means to deter wives from poisoning husbands is also mentioned by Withington and Ovington.

Whatever its rationale, sati offended Mughal notions of social propriety. However, not even Akbar considered it prudent to ban sati, for that would have been a provocative intervention in the customs of Rajputs, his valued allies. Instead, Akbar sought to mitigate its evil by decreeing that no woman should be burned against her will, and that a woman of 'tender years' should not be burnt at all. Once, when he heard that the widow of Jai Mai, a cousin of Raja Bhagwan Das, was being forced to commit sati (by her son!), Akbar personally rode out to save her. Jahangir also imposed restrictions on the practice of sati, and Aurangzeb, according to Manucci, banned it altogether, but probably without much effect.

In the imperial capital, sati could be performed only with royal permission, and each case had to be brought before the emperor. 'When these commeth, hee doth perswade them with many promises of gifts . . . if they will live, but in my time no perswasion could prevaile, but burne they would,' says Hawkins about the practice under Jahangir. In the provinces, the governor's permission was necessary to perform sati. 'No woman can sacrifice herself without permission from the governor of the province in which she resides,' notes Bernier, 'and he never grants it until he shall have ascertained that she is not be turned aside from her purpose: to accomplish this desirable end the governor reasons with the widow and makes her enticing promises; after which, if these methods fail, he sometimes sends her among his women, that the effect of their remonstrances may be tried.'

These indirect controls seem to have had some effect, for, according to Bernier, the incidence of sati was steadily declining in Mughal India. Says Ovington: 'Since the Mahometans became Masters of the Indies, their execrable Custom is much abated, and almost laid aside, by the Orders which the Nabobs receive for suppressing and extinguishing it in all their Provinces. And now it is very rare, except it be some Rajahs Wives, that the Indian Women burn at all; and those that do, obtain the liberty by costly Presents and powerful Applications to the Governors . . .' Tavernier notes that sometimes the governor was bribed to get permission to commit sati.

THE INCIDENCE OF sati, though declining in Mughal India, was still common enough for travellers to have seen and recorded many incidents. The practice had a few minor regional variations. In Gujarat and Uttar Pradesh, sati rite was usually performed in a specially built wooden hut, while in the Deccan, Rajasthan and Western India, the sati pyre was built in a deep pit.

Once, while travelling through Rajasthan, Bernier heard that a sati was about to be performed near the place where his caravan had halted. 'I ran at once to the spot,' writes Bernier, 'and going to the edge of a large and nearly dry reservoir, observed at the bottom a deep pit filled with wood: the body of a dead man extended thereon; a woman seated upon the pile; four or five women, tolerably well dressed, holding one another by the hand, singing and dancing round the pit; and a great number of spectators of both sexes.

'The pile, whereon large quantities of ghee and oil had been thrown, was soon enveloped in flames, and I saw the fire catch the woman's garments, which were impregnated with scented oil, mixed with sandalwood powder and saffron; but I could not perceive the slightest indication of pain or even uneasiness in the victim, and it was said that she pronounced with emphasis the words five, two, to signify that this being the fifth time she had burned herself with the same husband, there were wanted only two more similar sacrifices to render her perfect, according to the doctrine of transmigration of souls . . .

'But this was only the commencement of the infernal tragedy. I thought that the singing and dancing of the five women were nothing more than some unmeaning ceremony; great therefore was my astonishment when I saw that the flames having ignited the clothes of one of these females, she cast herself head-foremost into the pit. The horrid example was followed by another woman, as soon as the flames caught her person: the three women who remained then took hold of each other by the hand, resuming the dance with perfect composure; and after a short lapse of time, they also precipitated themselves, one after the other, into the fire.'

A governor once tried to dissuade a handsome widow of eighteen from committing sati by offering her 500 rupees a year as long as she lived, says Pelsaert, but she said that 'even if she could have all the King's treasures in this world, they would be of no use to her, for she meant to live with her husband.' When the governor finally gave reluctant consent for her to perform sati, 'she hurried off with a light step, as if she might be too late.' She was, continues Pelsaert, wearing 'her finest clothes, her jewels, and the best ornaments she has, adorning herself as if it was her wedding day.' At the pyre, she distributed her jewels and clothes among her friends, 'keeping only an undergarment. Then she took a handful of rice and distributed it to all the bystanders; this being done, she embraced her friends and said her last farewells; took her baby, which was only a year old, kissed it, and handed it to her nearest friends; then ran to the hut where her dead husband lay, and kissed and embraced him

eagerly.' The pyre was then lit, with the crowd chanti[...]
and 'when the burning was over, everyone took a little o[...]
bones, which they regard as sacred, and preserve.' In Patna, [...]
and very beautiful woman, scarcely more than 22 years of age', on[...]
demonstrated to the governor her resolve to commit sati by holding 'her
hand firmly in the flame without the least grimace . . . till it was . . .
scorched,' says Tavernier. And in Machilipatnam, a woman once hanged
herself when the Kotwal denied her permission to commit sati.

The calm of the widow committing sati was astounding to the observer.
Bernier speaks of 'the brutish boldness, or ferocious gaiety depicted in the
woman's countenance; of her undaunted step; of the freedom from all
perturbation with which she conversed, and permitted herself to be washed;
of the look of confidence, or rather of insensibility which she cast upon
us; of her easy air, free from dejection; of her lofty carriage, void of
embarrassment . . .'

'It is a memorable thing to see these women . . . surround the corpse,
and calling out thousands of praises of their husband, the good life he led,
and the pleasures he enjoyed here below,' says Manucci. 'Feeling under
an obligation for so many favours received, they look forward in the next
life to receive still greater delight in his society there. All this is carried
out with much joy and animation, they being richly clad, oiled and
perfumed. Reaching the place of death, they . . . assist in lifting the bier
on to the heap of wood. This stands in a pit. The principal wife among
them places herself on one side, embracing the corpse and uttering
innumerable praises; the others range themselves round the body in the
same way. The burners set fire to the wood all round, and dexterously
empty on it pots of oil and butter to increase the rapidity of the cremation.'
Sometimes the widow herself, sitting on the pyre, with the 'deceased
husband's head in her lap, took up a torch, and with her own hand lighted
the fire,' notes Bernier.

The plight of widows who did not burn themselves was pathetic. 'If
they will not burne (yt beeinge in theire choyce), then shee muste shave
her hayer and breake her jewells, and is not suffred to eate, drinke, or
keepe companye with anye bodye, and soe liveth in this case, miserablye,
till her death,' says Withington. Confirms Fitch: 'The wives here doe
burne with their husbands when they die; if they will not, their heads be
shaven, and never any account is made of them afterwards.'

To avoid such a fate, some widows become courtesans, says Manucci.
Sometimes, says Bernier, if the family of the deceased was unimportant,
sweepers (*halal-khors*) help the widow to escape—but thereafter she had

to lead a low life, sometimes as a prostitute.

In the eighteenth century, as the Mughal empire collapsed, sati became rampant again—it was widely prevalent at the close of the century, and between 1815 and 1828, in Calcutta division alone, there were as many as 5099 incidents of sati. Sati was abolished in British India in 1829 by Governor General William Bentinck, but it continued to be legal in princely states for some more time. The last incidence of a legal sati was in Udaipur in 1861, but stray incidents of sati continued to take place even into the last quarter of the twentieth century.

Chapter Five

PRODUCERS
AND
PREDATORS

The Poor Rich Country

IN THE SEVENTEENTH century, in the eyes of Europe, India was a land of fortune. Throughout the previous century, there had been a steady trickle of Europeans braving their way into India, travelling by sea or land, in pursuit of adventure or fortune—or to spread the gospel of peace, sometimes at the point of the sword. Through the letters, journals and books of these men, a legend had spread in Europe about the incredible wealth of India, fuelling greed and spawning a million fantasies.

The legend was not all myth. Nowhere else in the world was there such a fabulous display of wealth as at the Mughal court, or such a lavish lifestyle as that of the Mughal amirs. Bullion from all over the civilized world had been pouring into India for many centuries—ancient Romans used to fret about the drain of wealth into India—and now the stream, after nearly drying up during the Dark Ages in Europe, was in flood again. 'Many silver streames runne thither, as all rivers to the sea, and there stay, it being lawfull for any nation to bring in silver and fetch commodities, but a crime not lesse than capitall to carry any great summe thence,' says Terry. 'All nations bring Coin, and carry away commodities for the same; and this Coin is buried in India, and goeth not out,' says Hawkins. Bernier makes the same point: 'Gold and silver, after circulating in every other quarter of the globe, come at length to be swallowed up . . . in Hindustan.' Grieved Sir Thomas Roe: Europe 'bleedeth to enrich Asia.'

The wealth enjoyed by the Mughal emperor was so immense as to be almost incomprehensible. The royal hoard at the time of Akbar's death, according to Pelsaert, consisted of seven million gold *muhrs*, 100 million silver rupees and 230 million copper *dams*, and a vast treasure of gems, ornaments, gold and silver bullion. So vast was Akbar's stock of gold and silver that in 1597, when he was celebrating the festival of the sun in Lahore and a great fire burned down a part of his palace, molten gold and silver were said to have 'streamed into the streets'. Jahangir's diamond chest, according to Hawkins, was 'three spannes long and a spanne and halfe broad, and a spanne and halfe deepe, full of diamants of all sizes and sort.' Jahangir, says Roe, 'was so rich in jewelles that I must confesse

I neuer saw togither so unvaluable wealth.' And Shah Jahan, according to Manucci, had caves built under his palace to store huge bars of gold and silver. The monarchs of Europe were almost destitute in comparison to the Mughal emperor—for instance, the revenue of the king of England at the close of the seventeenth century was only about one-seventeenth of Akbar's revenue of the same period.

Mughal nobles too had prodigious incomes and lived more opulently than most monarchs elsewhere in the world. Shah Jahan's Vizier Asaf Khan, for instance, had a net annual income of five million rupees, and on his death left assets worth twenty-five million rupees in cash, bullion and jewellery, apart from his several mansions and estates in Agra, Lahore, Kashmir and other places. Mir Jumla, another grand amir of Shah Jahan, according to Thevenot, 'had the wealth of a Prince . . . He had twenty Mans of weight of Diamonds, which make Four hundred and eight pounds of Hollands weight.' It was riches such as these that spawned the myth about the wealth of the Indies. As Robert Clive would say in the mid-eighteenth century, India was 'a country of inexhaustible riches'. But the land of gold and gems was not the land of milk and honey. Not for the common people.

MUGHAL SOCIETY WAS starkly unequal and pitilessly exploitative. In the reign of Shah Jahan, 36.5 per cent of the entire assessed revenue of the empire was assigned to sixty-eight princes and amirs, and a further twenty-five per cent to the next 587 officers, so that 61.5 per cent of the total revenue of 220 million rupees of the empire was arrogated by just 655 individuals. The distribution of income was even more unequal in the reign of Akbar, when the top twenty-five took over thirty per cent of the total revenue. The largest share of the revenue of course went to the emperor, whose personal income, from crown lands and tributes, ranged from a minimum of five per cent to a high of twenty-five per cent of the total revenue of the empire.

The magnitude of these appropriations astounds us all the more when we consider that the revenue claim of the state was between one-third and one-half of the gross national product of the empire—which meant that in the reign of Shah Jahan at least about a quarter of the gross national product of the Mughal empire was appropriated by less than 700 persons out of a population of over 120 million! The people of India, says Sir Thomas Roe, 'live as fishes do in the sea—the great ones eat up the little. For first the farmer robs the peasant, the gentleman robs the farmer, the greater robs the lesser, and the King robs all.'

Undoubtedly, some of the richest men in the world in Mughal times lived in India. So did many of the poorest. 'Although this Empire of the Mogul is such an abyss for gold and silver . . . the inhabitants have less the appearance of moneyed people than those of many other parts of the globe,' says Bernier. Says Pieter van den Broeke: 'When I was travelling in [India] . . . I wondered whence such large sums [as accumulated by rulers] could be obtained, for the people are very poor and live miserably.'

Conditions were no different elsewhere in India. Says Athanasius Nikitin, a Russian merchant, about Vijayanagar late in the fifteenth century: 'The land is overstocked with people; but those in the country are very miserable, while the nobles are extremely opulent and delight in luxury.' The common people around Goa, says Linschoten, a sixteenth-century traveller, 'are so miserable that for a penny they would endure to be whipped, and they eat so little that it seemeth they live by the air.'

The coexistence of fabulous wealth and abject poverty was not surprising, for there was, paradoxical though it might seem, a causal connection between poverty and wealth in India—it was not the prosperity of the economy that made the ruling class rich; rather, they fattened by churning the country and gathering all the cream in it. The people were poor, the country was poor, only the emperor and the amirs were rich. Even the much lauded flow of precious metals into India was more a sign of economic debility than of vitality—bullion flowed into India for there was little else that could flow into India, the common people being too poor to want foreign goods and the aristocracy minuscule. True, India did export large quantities of textiles, but only because most Indians went virtually naked, and not because of any superiority of its production technology. In a sense, the flow of bullion into India was irrelevant to the Indian economy, for much of the gold and silver, especially gold, was simply buried or turned into trinkets; it did not lead to any significant capital formation to fuel economic growth, nor to any improvement in the standard of life of the people.

The wealth of Mughal India, it thus turns out, was an illusion created by the opulence and ostentation of the ruling class. 'In the palaces of these lords dwells all the wealth there is, wealth which glitters indeed, but is borrowed, wrung from the sweat of the poor,' observes Pelsaert. 'Consequently their position is as unstable as the wind, resting on no firm foundation, but rather on pillars of glass, resplendent in the eyes of the world, but collapsing under the stress of even a slight storm.'

THE SINGLE MOST appalling fact of life in Mughal India was famine, a spectre present at the turn of every season. Famine was of course an old problem in India, mentioned even in the Jataka tales of ancient India, but the graphic descriptions of famine horrors in medieval writings scorch even in cold print. 'The author with his own eyes witnessed the fact that men ate their own kind, and the appearance of famished sufferers was so hideous that one could scarcely look upon them,' says Badauni about the famine that ravaged Hindustan in 1555.

One of the worst famines in India in Mughal times was the one that swept through Gujarat and the Deccan early in the reign of Shah Jahan, in which some three million people are said to have perished. 'Life was offered for a loaf, but none would buy,' writes Lahori; 'rank was to be sold for a cake, but none cared for it . . . Destitution at length reached such a pitch that men began to devour each other, and the flesh of a son was preferred to his love.' Writes van Twist, a Dutch merchant in the Deccan during the famine: 'So little rain fell that the seed sown was lost and no grass grew. Cattle died. In towns and villages, in fields and on roads, men lay dead in great numbers, causing such a stench that it was terrible to use the ways. For want of grass cattle fed on corpses . . . As the famine increased, men abandoned towns and villages, and wandered helplessly. It was easy to recognize their condition: eyes sunk deep in the head, lips pale and covered with slime, the skin hard, with the bones showing through, the belly nothing but a pouch hanging down empty, knuckles and knee-caps showing prominently . . .

'Men deserted their wives and children. Women sold themselves as slaves. Mothers sold their children. Children deserted by their parents sold themselves. Some families took poison, and so died together; others threw themselves into the rivers. Mothers and their children went to the river-bank, and drowned themselves hand in hand, so that the rivers flowed full of corpses. Some ate carrion flesh. Others cut up the corpses of men, and drew out the entrails to fill their own bellies; yes, men lying in the street, not yet dead, were cut up by others, and men fed on living men, so that even in the streets, and still more on road-journeys, men ran great danger of being murdered and eaten.'

'Terrible tragedies were seen every day,' continues van Twist. It was reported that 'a mother had killed and cooked her only son . . . that husbands had eaten their wives, wives their husbands, children their parents . . . Some of our Dutchmen, coming from Ahmadabad, found some people sitting at a little fire where hands and feet were cooking, a terrible thing to see. Even worse was it in the village of Susuntra, where human flesh was sold in open market.'

When at last the rain fell, prices began to drop, but the relief was short-lived, for soon 'locusts, rats, mice, and other vermin' ravaged the young crops, and finally, to cap the misery, 'continuous heavy rain when the crops were ripening caused much grain to perish in the fields; flooded rivers caused much grain loss in towns, villages, and country; and prices rose higher than ever. Thus famine lasted throughout the year, and pestilence and fever followed, so that scarcely a healthy man could be found,' concludes the Dutchman. 'The dead lay scattered in the streets. Corpses lay for days in the houses, because men could not be paid to carry them out. Wood could not be had for the pyres and unburnt corpses were buried or thrown into the river.'

The veracity of the gruesome picture of famine drawn by van Twist is confirmed by Mustaid Khan in his description of a famine that devastated the Deccan during Aurangzeb's siege of Golconda: 'Kos after kos (mile after mile) the eye fell only on mounds of corpses. The incessant rain melted away the flesh and the skin . . . After some months when the rains ceased, the white ridges of bones looked from a distance like hillocks of snow.' Says Manucci about yet another famine towards the close of Aurangzeb's reign: 'In those two years (1702–04) there expired over two millions of souls; fathers, compelled by hunger, offered to sell their children for a quarter to half a rupee, and were yet forced to go without food, finding no one to buy them.'

In the face of famine, the Mughal emperor undertook relief measures— public kitchens were opened, taxes remitted, and money allotted for 'gratuitous relief'; sometimes, as Akbar once did, additional soldiers were recruited during famine, to give relief to the poor, virtually putting them on the dole. During the 1630–32 famine, Shah Jahan distributed 5,000 rupees a week for five months to the poor, giving away a total of 100,000 rupees; tax remissions of nearly seven million rupees were granted by imperial revenue officers, and similar reliefs were given by amirs in their jagirs. These were, however, only token and random measures, at best palliatives. The amounts spent on famine relief were trivial compared to the extravagant personal expenses of the emperor and the amirs—for instance, the 100,000 rupees disbursed by Shah Jahan for famine relief was a mere one-tenth of the annual pin-money of Mumtaz Mahal!

The Mughal indifference to the woes of the people was not callousness, but culture. It was the same everywhere in the medieval world. Human misery was not seen as misery by medieval rulers, but merely as the common lot. Even if the emperor had viewed it differently, and had wished to help, there was not much that he could do, for he did not have the administrative capability for effective famine relief. There was not much scope for market forces to redress famine scarcities either, for the high cost of transport made it impossible to supply deficit areas from a distance.

For the emperor, famine relief was charity, desirable but not obligatory. His primary concern was to preserve and extend his power, and he would not even suspend military operations to provide famine relief. The attitudes of Hindu monarchs were the same. Thus, 'while people died with the word "bread" upon their lips,' Hemu, the Hindu revivalist, 'valued the lives of a hundred thousand men at no more than a barley-corn,' says Badauni; 'he fed his five hundred elephants upon rice, sugar, and butter. The whole world was astounded and disgusted.' For a monarch it was more prudent to feed elephants than people.

CAPRICIOUS MONSOONS, too much or too little, were the main cause of famine in India, but the wars that raged continually in Mughal times were also a major factor, for medieval rulers—Sher Shah being the lone notable exception—invariably employed a scorched earth mode of warfare. Thus the Mughal army invading Bijapur in 1636 was ordered by Shah Jahan 'to ravage the country from end to end', and they accomplished this task so consummately that, gloats Inayat Khan, 'there was now scarcely a vestige of cultivation left in that part of the country.' Even worse were the Marathas, who never carried any provisions with them on their campaigns, but lived off the land, on plunder. The defenders were often as guilty as the invaders in devastating the countryside, for they destroyed crops, poisoned wells and ponds, demolished the embankments of lakes, even felled trees, to deny the invaders the resources of the land. No one spared a thought for the plight of the common man: he was irrelevant in a world where might was the only right.

The greatest devastation of war during the Mughal period was in the Deccan, for peace generally prevailed in Hindustan after Akbar subjugated and pacified the region. Such was the havoc caused by war in the Deccan that by the mid-seventeenth century, the number of peasants and artisans in the northern and central regions of south India fell to a quarter of their former number, and by the end of the century, the situation got so bad that the English found it difficult to secure the supply of cloth they needed for export. 'The frequent Revolts in India render those parts very miserable, and reduce the Inhabitants to a very distressed State . . . Which makes Fear and Distress, Poverty and Famine the universal Air and Genius of those unquiet Abodes,' says Ovington about the conditions in the Deccan in the late seventeenth century. 'The lands of the Dakhin, which are so vast, and once seemed like a terrestrial Paradise are nowadays uncultivated, unproductive, and uninhabited,' says Manucci.

Even when a region was not directly affected by war, the very movement of an army through the land caused damage to property and unsettled life, so people invariably fled from the army's path, like gazelles at the scent of the tiger. They fled even when Akbar marched within his empire. The advance of a vast horde of several hundred thousand men, spread out across a front of some three kilometres and stretching out behind over several kilometres, was like a locust invasion: they simply ate up everything on their path or trampled down standing crops. The greatest damage was done by camp followers, the rabble that constituted the bulk of the Mughal host, who stripped whatever they found on the way.

Sher Shah used to enforce stern discipline in the army to protect cultivation; he would not allow peasants to be harmed even in enemy territory, considering them politically neutral and blameless. The Mughals were not so thoughtful, though within the empire they did take some care not to ruin agriculture. According to Nizamuddin Ahmad, Akbar used to assign an officer 'to protect the cultivated land in the vicinity of the camp; and besides that, trustworthy men were appointed to carefully examine the land after the camp had passed, and were ordered to place the amount of any damage done, against the government claim for revenue. This practice became a rule in all his campaigns, and sometimes even bags of money were given to these inspectors, so that they might at once estimate and satisfy the claims of the ryots and farmers . . .' Akbar's successors continued these benevolent practices, at least in form, but none of the Mughals had any inhibition about desolating enemy territory.

Life was not very much better for the common man during times of peace either, for he was then subject to other kinds of despoliation. The fief-holders, local officials, zemindars and other predators always had the productive people—the farmer, the trader and the artisan—by the throat to force them to regurgitate whatever little they had managed to put away.

THE MUGHALS LIVED by aggression and pillage. As Jadunath Sarkar puts it, 'War . . . [was] the only trade they . . . [had] a natural aptitude for, and peace . . . [meant] to them unemployment, vice and downfall.'

From their own subjects, the Mughals seized nearly all the surplus wealth by extortionate taxation or by direct confiscation; against their neighbours they followed a policy of inveterate belligerence, to plunder, annex or exact tribute. There was no sustained nourishing of the economy by the Mughal rulers, scarcely any public works to promote agriculture, or incentives to foster trade and industry, but only relentless arrogation of the fruits of other people's labour. 'Almost throughout India the tendency was to reduce the reward of production to a point where it ceased to offer an adequate incentive,' says Moreland. The Mughals were, as it were, pulling out the tree by its roots to gather its fruits.

Inevitably, the oppressed had to bear the cost of their oppression. 'The country,' says Bernier, 'is ruined by the necessity of defraying the enormous charges required to maintain the splendour of a numerous court, and to pay a large army maintained for the purpose of keeping the people in subjection.' By the reign of Aurangzeb, the Mughal army and bureaucracy, feeding voraciously on the vast and growing revenue of the expanding empire, had grown so monstrously bloated, that it seemed as if a good number of the emperor's subjects were following him around, clinging to and feeding on him like so many millions of leeches. It is estimated by Tapan Raychaudhuri that in the mid-seventeenth century, towards the close of Shah Jahan's reign, those who depended for their livelihood on the Mughal 'armed services and associated activities', directly or indirectly, wholly or partly, numbered, along with their families, some twenty-six million people—about twenty-one per cent of the population of the empire. To this has to be added the 'army of prayer'— Muslim religious personages and ecclesiastical officers—that the emperor had to maintain as a theocratic obligation. It is thus probable that nearly a quarter of the total population of the Mughal empire lived off the state!

Astonishingly, despite the withdrawal of such a vast number of people from productive work, enough was produced in the country to clothe and feed the people—but this again was not a sign of economic vitality, for the bulk of the people subsisted on meagre food and went practically naked. 'Weavers, naked themselves, toiled to clothe others. Peasants, themselves hungry, toiled to feed the towns and cities,' says Moreland.

Productivity in Mughal India, compared to that of contemporary Europe, was low, and was declining further, for neither the peasant nor the artisan was left with sufficient surplus to encourage productive endeavour, but only with just enough to survive. Sometimes not even that. 'No adequate idea can be conveyed of the sufferings of the people,' says Bernier. 'The cudgel and the whip compel them to incessant labour for the benefit of others; and driven to despair by every kind of cruel treatment, their revolt or their flight is only prevented by the presence of a military force.'

Driven beyond endurance, the peasant at times abandoned his fields to seek refuge in other domains, or to join the army, or to chance his luck in towns. During times of political instability he often took to robbery— this too was part of the medieval culture: the peasant toiled on the land when he had to, but took to thieving when he had the opportunity. It was better to be a predator than a producer.

Traders were on the whole better off than peasants and artisans, because they operated mainly in relatively secure urban centres, and the aristocracy needed their services to maintain its lifestyle. But they had their own problems, mainly to circumvent the pervasive corruption and inefficiency of the Mughal government. Writes Roe in his report to the East India Company: 'You can neuer expect to trade here vpon Capitulations that shalbe permanent,' because 'the Gouerment depends vpon the present will.' Often it was the very men charged with the protection of the people, the imperial officers and the local chiefs, who harried the people. Corruption was so rampant in the Mughal empire that traders had to pay bribes or other illegal fees to secure even such basic government services as police and judicial protection.

The effect of all this was ruinous to the Mughal economy. 'Production,' says Moreland, 'was ceasing to be worthwhile, because the life of the producer was ceasing to be worth living.' The attitude of the peasant and the trader was, as Bernier puts it, 'Why should I toil for a tyrant who may come tomorrow and lay his rapacious hands upon all I possess and value, without leaving me, if such should be his humour, the means to drag on my miserable existence?'

PEOPLE, BY AND LARGE, endured the miseries of war and exploitation with the same bleak fatalism with which they endured everything else in life. The poverty of the people was, says Pelsaert, 'so great and miserable that the life of the people can be ... accurately described only as the home of stark want and the dwelling-place of bitter woe. Nevertheless, the people endure it patiently, professing that they do not deserve anything better; and scarcely anyone will make an effort, for a ladder by which to climb higher is hard to find, because a workman's children can follow no occupation other than that of their father, nor can they intermarry with any other caste.'

The Hindu caste system had served a useful purpose in the old, static, self-contained Indian society, by neatly organizing people into hereditary functional groups to ensure social stability—but it also fossilized society and desiccated the human spirit. By its very nature, the caste system discouraged innovation, for it had a vested interest in preserving the existing social order and its political, economic and technological foundations. This was a major impediment to progress in Mughal India.

Muslims too were mired in archaic values. As the master race in India, they disdained agriculture as plebeian, and though the emperor and a few amirs did take an interest in horticulture, it was for them only a self-indulgence, an extension of their interest in exotic fruits and ornamental gardens, not a productive activity. Trading was more acceptable to Muslims, especially overseas trade, because of its prestige and aura of adventure, and Muslim traders dominated the great port cities of India. Sometimes the Mughal amirs, occasionally even members of the royal family—the begums and the princes, even the emperor himself, Shah Jahan, for instance—were involved in overseas trade, but usually through agents, not directly.

The preferred career of Muslims in India was government service, to obtain a share of the imperial pie. They, as a community, considered themselves the ruling class, therefore the leisure class, and abhorred productive work. A good number of them managed to live without toil in religious sinecures funded by government. Productive work in agriculture, industry and local trade was largely left to Hindus. This, however, was not a privilege conferred on Hindus but an onus laid on them, for the productive class laboured mainly to feed the ruling elite, which was predominantly (though not exclusively) Muslim.

The effete values and parasitic practices of Indian society were reinforced by (or were perhaps the cause of) the archaic modes of production of Indians in agriculture and industry, and their timid practices in trade. There was hardly any improvement in agricultural and industrial technologies from what they were in ancient India, nor any significant change in trade practices. In general, Indians passively accepted their given environment and adjusted themselves to it, rather than attempting to transcend it through innovation and enterprise.

There was undeniably some economic progress under the Mughals. Population had grown, and with it the area under cultivation. There was significant growth in urbanization. Monetization of the economy did make substantial progress, because of the increased production of cash crops and the Mughal preference for cash payment of agricultural tax. Inter-regional trade had grown, and the tenuous web of the economic integration of India was beginning to form, facilitated by the political unity the Mughals imposed over the subcontinent. The adoption of the opulent Mughal lifestyle by the elite throughout India, and the consequent growth in the demand for comfort and luxury goods, stimulated trade and industry, and so did the new trade links with Europe. These developments did make a difference in the Indian economy, but not enough of a difference to lift India out of the medieval rut. The swell was too gentle, the trough too deep.

WHAT INDIA PRODUCED in abundance was people. And that, in medieval perception, was an asset. Babur thought so. More people meant a larger productive force, more land under cultivation, more revenue for the state, more men for the army and, therefore, overall, more power for the emperor.

Unfortunately, that was not quite how it worked out in practice. In social dynamics, unlike in physics, a large mass did not necessarily yield great energy. On the contrary, more people meant, in Mughal India at any rate, overall inefficiency and lower per capita productivity, especially in towns and cities, where there were far too many servants doing too little. 'Servants are exceedingly numerous in this country,' says Pelsaert. There were swarms of them everywhere. Some amirs had as many as 500 torch-bearers in their employ, and even the lowest soldier had a couple of menials serving him. Each royal elephant had four to seven attenders, and Jahangir had four men to look after his favourite dog. The royal stable even had an officer whose sole duty 'was to burn certain seeds to guard against the evil eye'.

This incredible proliferation of servants led to a pointless division of labour, specializations so minute as to be utterly absurd, which, instead of boosting efficiency, directly led to inefficiency, as work spread to occupy the available number of servants. In the imperial stables, for instance, servants were organized into fourteen different categories under three groups of supervisors, each category with its own privileged and exclusive segment of work. A servant assigned to a particular task, says Bernier, would 'consider it a sacrilege to touch the work of another servant'. Productivity was deplorable. 'For work that could be done by one man they have ten here . . . A job which one man would do in Holland here passes through four men's hands before it is finished,' says Pelsaert. An English worker, says Hawkins, would do the work of three Indians.

If productivity was low, so were wages: the lowest category of servants in Mughal India received just one dam (one-fortieth of a rupee) a day, and even skilled workers got no more than seven dams. Low productivity justified low wages, and low wages justified low productivity, completing the vicious circle. It debased human labour, denied the worker self-respect, encouraged sloth in the master, sloth in the servant. 'The Moguls call this population *zulum-parast*—that is, tyranny adorers,' says Manucci, for it was only the whip that could get any work out of them. 'If the common people here have four rupees, they are quite high and mighty and decline service . . . It is only when they have nothing to eat that they take service.' Says Careri: 'No sooner have they got as much Rice as will keep them a Week, but they give over Work, living Idly as long that lasts.'

The Indian work ethic, as Europeans saw it, was dismal. 'For the Mahometans . . . there are many of them idle, and know better to eat than work,' says Terry; 'and these are all for tomorrow, a word common in their mouths, and their word *Sub-ba*, which signifies tomorrow, and when that day comes, tomorrow; and so still tomorrow, they will set down upon their business tomorrow, will do anything you would have them to do tomorrow, they will bestow anything upon you *Sub-ba*, tomorrow.' The work attitudes of Hindus, we must assume, were no different.

THE SLOTH OF commoners was matched by the prodigality of the aristocracy. The royal family spent incredible amounts of money on dress, jewels and entertainment, and so did the amirs—the emperor had a couple of thousand sets of dress made for him every year (mostly for giving away as robes of honour to courtiers); the ornate chair in which Shah Jahan sat in durbar (the Peacock Throne) was valued at ten million rupees for materials alone; the diamond studded slippers of the wife of Aurangzeb's Vizier Jafar Khan were said to be worth 100,000 rupees; Akbar's confidant Abul Fazl had 100 dishes served to him at every meal, and he gave away his entire wardrobe to servants every year, and made fresh clothes. Such extravagance was integral to the lifestyle of the ruling class, who considered saving, investment and productive work as unmanly. The orgiastic consumption by amirs turned the Mughal economy into a trinket economy, even though the trinkets were priceless jewels.

The only thing the amirs could think of doing with their immense wealth was to spend it prodigally. They seldom saved anything, rarely invested wealth productively, to breed wealth from wealth. They had not laboured to produce the wealth, but had merely grabbed it from those who had laboured, and therefore had no respect for wealth, or for the labour that produced wealth. The wealth that was acquired without productive endeavour was squandered unproductively. Besides, the amirs had no incentive to save and accumulate wealth, for their properties invariably reverted to the state on their deaths. Some amirs (Asaf Khan, for instance) did leave vast fortunes, but it was merely for the vainglory of leaving a vast fortune; such legacies had no economic or social consequence. Unlike in late medieval Europe, there was no great accumulation of wealth in any class in India, no major investment in agriculture, trade or industry, no stirring of an agrarian or industrial revolution.

The commoners of course did not have the means, or the heart, to live extravagantly, and they simply buried what little savings they could squirrel away, or turned them into jewels. There was little else the rural folk could do with money anyway. Money in the traditional agrarian economy had no energy; it was not mobile and had nowhere to go except into the earth. It was thus in a way fitting that peasants should bury wealth, though they did it actually to hide it from vultures. 'They must not let the . . . [wealth] be seen,' says Pelsaert, 'or they will be the victims of a trumped-up charge, and whatever they have will be confiscated in legal form . . . These poor wretches, who, in their submissive bondage, may be compared to poor, contemptible earthworms, or to little fishes, which, however closely they may conceal themselves, are swallowed up by the great monsters of a wild sea.' Confirms Tavernier, 'If their governors know that they have anything about them, they seize it either as their right, or by force.'

None of the buried gold sprouted. Equally sterile were the gold and silver turned into jewellery. It was just so much good capital left fallow. Not only that, the practice of hiding wealth and living low maimed the very character of the people, turning them timid and cringing, altogether lacking the spirit essential for enterprise. To live low was to have low aspirations. Like a wretched miser, the average Indian curled into himself, a grub in endless toil.

There was presumably some saving and investment among Indian traders, but not enough to make any difference in the economy as a whole. India did not generate the kind of high and secure mercantile profit that fuelled industrial revolution in Europe. The only person who could, and did, accumulate substantial wealth, and did not have to be coy about it, was the emperor, but he too squandered wealth—or buried it! According to one estimate, Shah Jahan spent 28.9 million rupees on his buildings, and several times that amount on his wars, his futile Central Asian and Kandahar campaigns alone costing some 160 million rupees. Apart from such unproductive expenditures, the emperor withdrew a part of the revenue of the empire from the economy and put it in the royal hoard.

Hoarding treasure was an old Indian royal custom. When Babur gave away 'the treasures of five kings [that] fell into his hands', he was, says Gulbadan, told that 'in Hindustan it was thought disgraceful to expend the treasure of bygone kings, and that people rather added to it.' Notes Abul Fazl: 'It is not the custom that the Rajah should use the accumulations of his predecessors.' Indians 'must be reduced to an extreme pinch' before they would dig into their inheritance, says Thevenot. In Vijayanagar, according to Paes, it was the practice to seal the treasury of each monarch on his death, which would be opened again only in an extreme emergency, and it is said that the royal family of Vijayanagar, while fleeing from the victorious Muslim army after the battle of Talikota, carried away treasures valued at more than a hundred million sterling. Enormous wealth also lay buried in temples. During the Khilji invasion of South India in the early fourteenth century, the loot in gems and gold was so immense that soldiers threw away silver articles as not worth carrying.

A STUPENDOUS HOARD of wealth was thus unproductively locked away in Mughal India, or spent equally unproductively on luxuries, ostentatious buildings and jewels, or on ruinous wars. The basic reason for such barren practices was, according to Bernier, the absence of private property. Viewing that 'the right of property . . . is the basis of all that is good and useful in the world', Bernier argues: 'Take away the right of private property in land, and you introduce, as a sure and necessary consequence, tyranny, slavery, injustice, beggary and barbarism: the ground will cease to be cultivated and become a dreary wilderness; in a word, the road will be opened to the ruin of Kings and the destruction of nations. It is the hope by which a man is animated, that he shall retain the fruits of his industry, and transmit them to his descendants, that forms the main foundation of everything excellent and beneficial in the sublunary state; and if we take a review of the different kingdoms in the world, we shall find that they prosper or decline according as this principle is acknowledged or contemned . . .'

Bernier was not entirely right in believing that there was no private property in land in India. The Indian peasant certainly owned his land, and he could alienate or bequeath it, subject of course to unpredictable and arbitrary action by the emperor and the officials. The peasant's ownership of land was however worth nothing, for he did not own the produce of his land, as the state took away what it pleased of the produce, leaving him with only just enough to carry on husbandry. The issue in Mughal India was, therefore, not the peasant's right to own land but his right to a fair share of its produce, the yield of his labour. The denial of that fair share nullified the advantage of the peasant owning land. Therefore, Bernier's thesis about the Indian economy, though technically faulty, was nevertheless valid.

What bothered Bernier however was not so much the plight of the peasant, as the absence of a stable landed aristocracy in India, as in Europe. He regarded the presence of such a class as essential for the stability and prosperity of the state, and attributed its absence in India to the ruthless and unjust application of the law of escheat by the emperor. 'The land throughout the whole empire is considered the property of the sovereign; there can be no earldoms, marquisates and duchies,' says Berruer, echoing what Roe had said earlier, that the Mughal was heir to all his subjects.

Here again, technically Bernier was wrong. The reason why Mughal amirs did not own great estates was not because the king was the sole proprietor of land, but because the land mostly belonged to cultivators. Nor was escheat the problem. The amir's jagir was not his personal estate, but only a revenue assignment given to him by the state in lieu of cash salary; such assignments were periodically shuffled for various administrative reasons, and when the service of an amir to the state finally ceased on his death, his salary too ceased and his jagir reverted to the state—not because all the land belonged to the state, but because all the land revenue belonged to the state.

The private property of the amir, including his land holdings, did not revert to the state on his death, and the emperor could not legitimately take them over without compensation. Escheat applied only when an amir died without an heir. Nevertheless, confiscation of the private property of the amir on his death was commonplace in Mughal India. Ostensibly, this was done to recover from the amir's estate what he owed to the state by way of repayment of loans and other dues, but it was often a mere cover for arbitrary seizures. Normally, therefore, the amir could bequeath to his children only what he could hoard in cash or jewellery and gift secretly.

Mughal amirs were helpless against such tyranny, for they were almost entirely an official aristocracy. Their status, power and wealth depended on their offices, which in turn depended on royal favour. The only amirs with quasi-independent status were the rajas, who had hereditary revenue rights, which they could bequeath to their successors, though the successors themselves had to be approved by the emperor. The rural gentry (zemindars and chaudhries) too enjoyed similar revenue rights, though the land itself in all cases belonged to the cultivator. It was not, therefore, the absence of private property but the unconscionable exploitation of cultivators that was ruinous to the economic health of Mughal India.

Such exploitation of peasants was inherent in the Mughal practice of assigning land revenue to officers in lieu of cash pay, and leaving it to them to collect the revenue. The bulk of the land in the empire (land yielding as much as ninety-five per cent of the total land revenue under Jahangir) was held by amirs as jagirs, and the common attitude of the amir was, as Bernier puts it, 'Why should the neglected state of this land create uneasiness in our minds? and why should we expend our own money and time to render it fruitful? We may be deprived of it in a single moment, and our exertions would benefit neither ourselves nor our children. Let us draw from the soil all the money we can, though the peasant should starve or abscond, and we should leave it, when commanded to quit, a dreary wilderness.'

This savage despoliation of the land by amirs did not unduly bother the emperor, for his concerns were as much of the short term as those of the amirs. And in the short term it was rather the intensification of exploitation than the expansion of production that gave the highest returns to the state. In the long run, of course, such a policy was detrimental to the stability and prosperity of the empire, and therefore detrimental to the interests of the emperor himself. A prosperous and stable empire could not be built on the shoulders of a crippled and ruined people. Says Bernier, 'The kings of Asia grasp at everything, until at length they lose everything.'

THE LACK OF economic dynamism and social mobility also hampered the rise of the bourgeoisie in India. There were merchant and artisan castes in India, and a number of very wealthy merchants too, but there was no merchant or industrialist class. Bernier speaks of the mansions of rich merchants in Delhi, but they were dependent on royal or aristocratic patronage for their incomes as well as for the protection of their lives and properties. Unlike merchants in Europe at this time, they had no independent standing, and played no political role. The Mughals did not value the economic contribution of merchants and accorded them little respect, but subjected them to periodical extortion. Under the circumstances, productive endeavour seemed futile to many. 'Few are the men who will voluntarily endure labour and anxiety, and incur danger, for another person's benefit—for a governor who may appropriate to his own use the profit of any speculation,' says Bernier. It was only in great port cities like Surat, far away from political centres, that merchants enjoyed security and wielded power.

In general, for all practical purposes, there was in Mughal India no avenue other than imperial service for a man to get ahead in life. Outside the ruling elite, life was dismal for most Indians. 'Men and women, living from season to season on the verge of hunger, could be contented so long as the supply of food held out: when it failed, as it so often did, their hope of salvation was the slave-trader, and the alternatives were cannibalism, suicide, or starvation,' writes Moreland. 'The only way of escape from that system lay through an increase in production, coupled with a rising standard of life, but this road was barred effectively by the administrative methods in vogue, which penalized production and regarded every indication of increased consumption as a signal for fresh extortion.'

The enormous burden of poverty that Indians carried pinioned them, like a worm impaled on a nail, helpless and immobile in their predicament—a poverty so oppressive and seemingly irredeemable that the people had long given up struggling against it. There was no light at the end of the tunnel. In such an environment of hopelessness there could be no enterprise, and trade and industry, even agriculture, could barely endure, hardly flourish. The best that the people could hope for was to somehow survive, and that was the limit of their dreams.

The Peasant's Lot

'THE LAND WOULD give a plentiful, or even an extraordinary yield, if the peasants were not so cruelly and pitilessly oppressed,' says Pelsaert about Mughal India. Bernier saw India differently: 'Of the vast tracts of country constituting the empire of Hindustan, many are little more than sand, or barren mountains, badly cultivated, and thinly peopled.' These divergent views are in fact complementary. The fertility of soil in India varied greatly from region to region, from the sandy deserts of Rajasthan and frigid Himalayan wastes to the tropical forests of the Western Ghats and the lush river basins of the Indo-Gangetic Plain.

As the land was varied, so were the crops grown—Abul Fazl lists cereals (rice, wheat, barley), millets (johar, bajra, chena, etc.), pulses (gram, lentils, peas, etc), oilseeds, sugar cane, cotton, hemp, indigo, opium, betel leaf, and a variety of minor crops, including vegetables, spices and fruits. Mango was India's very own special fruit. Babur introduced into India a few new fruit varieties from Kabul, and many more fruits and other crops were brought by the Portuguese from South America: corn, tobacco, chilli, potato, cashew, pineapple, papaya and guava. Chilli probably had been introduced into India in the seventeenth century, but its farming would be taken up only in the eighteenth, and of potato and guava even later. Coffee was probably grown in a small way in Karnataka in Mughal times, but tea cultivation was unknown, though the plant grew wild in the hills of Assam.

Tobacco cultivation began in India in the sixteenth century, but it was slow to gain ground till the hookah was introduced into the Mughal court at the beginning of the seventeenth century. The smoking habit thereafter spread rapidly, and with it the cultivation of the plant. By 1623, tobacco had become a noted item of export from Surat, and by the last quarter of the century, a major crop cultivated throughout the country. Opium too was cultivated on a large scale, particularly in Malwa, and was a valued crop, and so was betel leaf. Toddy, the mildly intoxicating sap of the palm tree, was tapped extensively in many regions of India.

Cotton was a major traditional crop, and was grown in most parts of

India, especially in the splendidly congenial black soil of the Deccan. Indigo, which was needed for dyeing cotton white, was cultivated extensively in Hindustan. Kashmir and western Rajasthan were the principal producers of wool, while raw silk came mainly from Kashmir, Bihar and Bengal. Saffron was the speciality of Kashmir, spices of Malabar—the most expensive spice in Mughal India was clove, which in Akbar's time cost sixty dams per seer (1.5 rupees for about a kilogram) compared to cardamom which cost fifty-two dams, cinnamon forty dams, and cumin seed two dams. Fishery was common along the sea coasts, but not in the interior; pearl-fishery off the Tamil Nadu coast was a major enterprise, with as many as 60,000 persons engaged in it at times.

The inadequacies of the medieval transport system hampered local specialization in agriculture, so the tendency in India was to grow all essential crops everywhere. Specialization was limited to a few luxury items. Most farmers were poor and cultivated for their own consumption; only the rich produced for the market, and generally it was only they who farmed the cash crops, as such crops required larger investments and involved delayed realization of revenue.

The Indian farmer, for all his conservatism and inertia, was willing to follow the market and take up new crops for which there was a ready demand. The classic example of this was the spread of tobacco cultivation. Similarly, corn that was introduced into Maharashtra in the seventeenth century rapidly spread to Rajasthan. And in Bengal, responding to the Dutch demand for raw silk for export to Japan, farmers diverted large tracts of paddy fields to sericulture in the mid-seventeenth century, though sericulture was unknown in Bengal before the fifteenth century. After a famine, farmers usually diverted land from commercial crops to food grains, to take advantage of the high price of grain.

The prime agro-industries in Mughal India were the manufacture of jaggery, sugar (the best sugar came from Bengal), various alcoholic beverages (both spirits and fermented liquors), oil-pressing, cotton-ginning, and the processing of tobacco and indigo. The products of India's extensive forests—lac, timber and aromatic woods like sandalwood—were also a rich source of wealth; Malwa was a major source of lac, which was used for making bangles, varnishing wooden furniture and painting cloth, and was among the items exported from India by the English and the Dutch.

India had fairly good reserves of mineral wealth, but not much of them were exploited in Mughal times. Coal, India's largest mineral resource, was not mined at all. As for gold and silver, only negligible quantities were mined in India, and the reserves were small. Abul Fazl's claim that gold was found in abundance in several parts of the country is a lyrical fancy; most of the vast hoard of gold and silver in India came from outside. Iron was not present in India in the metallic state; the ore had to be smelted, so its production was dependent on the availability of fuel, and smelting was done in small furnaces as a cottage industry. Copper was mined in Hindustan, but there was a shortfall in supply, which was met with imports from China. Copper was an expensive metal in Mughal times, one pound of it costing as much as eighty-four pounds of wheat. Diamonds were mined along the basin of the Krishna river.

India produced all the salt it needed, from sea water as well as from the salt lakes of Rajasthan and the salt rocks of Punjab. The price of salt was high in Mughal times, and its per capita consumption low; salt was about two and a half times costlier in Mughal India than it was in the early twentieth century. Saltpetre, used in making gunpowder and a major item of export, came mainly from Berar, though the region around Agra and Patna also yielded large quantities.

THE INTRODUCTION OF new crops and the increased export demand for some of the agricultural produce, along with the growth in population, would have, it has to be conjectured, led to some increase in gross agricultural production and an expansion of the area under cultivation in India in Mughal times. But the growth was not conspicuous. This is not surprising, for the population of India, periodically decimated by famine and pestilence, was growing by only about 0.14 per cent at this time. Not enough people were clearing new land and moving out, and the marginal growth in population was at least partially negated by the withdrawal of an increasing number of people from productive work, either by being drawn into government service or driven off the land by oppression.

It is likely that agricultural production per farmer was higher in Mughal times than later, because, land being freely available, only the best land was cultivated. A 1630 report of Dutch merchants in Gujarat states that he 'who wants to cultivate the land, goes to the headmen of the village, who are called muqaddam, and asks for as much land as he wants, at the place which suits him. This is rarely refused, but almost always granted, because here not one-tenth part of the land is cultivated, and so anyone can easily obtain his choice, and the area he needs; and he may sow as much as he can till, on condition of paying the dues to the lord.'

The peasant probably also had a larger stock of cattle—they were cheaper to maintain, as wasteland for grazing was plentiful—and so was able to plough a larger area. Abul Fazl records that under Akbar the number of cattle allowed tax-free for each plough were four bullocks, two cows and one buffalo, which was substantially higher than what the average peasant had in the early twentieth century, when the pressure of population began to tell on the peasant's productivity.

But while the average Mughal farmer produced more than in later times, he most probably produced less than in earlier times. On the whole, the Mughal period was marked by agricultural stagnation, if not slump. The per capita yield was declining, and the average man in Mughal India probably had less to eat than before. 'The surplus income left to the peasant was tending to decrease, where it had not already vanished,' says Moreland. 'The provinces,' says Pelsaert, 'are so impoverished that a jagir which is reckoned to be worth 50,000 rupees, may sometimes not yield even 25,000, although so much is wrung from the peasants, that even dry bread is scarcely left to fill their stomachs.' Agricultural decline was especially marked in the war-ravaged Deccan. In Rajapur in southern Maharashtra, which had once produced 1500 *candy* (about 340 metric tons) of pepper, the yield fell to one tenth by 1685, after the area fell to the Marathas, and the town itself became 'a miserable poor town', according to the report of English merchants in Surat.

Another indication of the decline in agricultural productivity in Mughal India is that while Akbar's officers preferred jagir assignments over cash salaries, by the reign of Aurangzeb their preference had turned to cash, because of the fall in farm productivity, the overvaluation of jagirs, and the growing administrative difficulties in collecting revenue. Though the revenue statistics of Mughal India give the impression that there was an increase in agricultural production, on closer examination it turns out to be an illusion created by the overvaluation of the jagirs and the rise in the prices of agricultural produce.

ONE REASON FOR the slide in agriculture was that the number of people engaged in farming, as a percentage of the population, had fallen in Mughal times, while the percentage of economic parasites had grown. War was another disruptive factor, along with the perennial problems of drought, famine and pestilence. Says Badauni about the conditions in India on the eve of Akbar's accession: 'What with the scarcity of rain, the famine and desolation, and what with uninterrupted warfare for two years, the whole country was a desert and no husbandmen remained to till the ground.' It took many years for an area to recover fully from the blight of famine, sometimes as many as fifteen years, as happened in Gujarat after the famine of 1630–32.

The Indian farmer lived on the verge of destitution even in normal times, with no buffer of savings, and he usually keeled over at the first blow of misfortune. His mode of cultivation was primitive compared to that of contemporary Europe or of even China, Japan and Persia; his implements (mostly of wood, for iron was expensive) were rudimentary, just 'the bare minimum required', as Moreland puts it; and his spirit had been crushed by chronic poverty. He had therefore no financial, technological or psychological resilience to withstand calamity.

There were hardly any major irrigation canal systems in Mughal India. Cultivation was largely monsoon-dependent. 'The Mussouns are the only Season for watering of their Fields, their meadows, and Arable Land,' says Ovington. There were some old canals along both the Indus and the Ganga-Yamuna basins, but they were mostly in disrepair, and their economic value was negligible. Abul Fazl mentions only wells as the means of irrigation, and does not speak at all of canals. Even for well irrigation, Indians generally used the primitive plane and bucket method, instead of the Persian-wheel—the Greeks had noticed this technological backwardness in ancient India, and the scene had changed little in nearly 2000 years. Though Babur mentions seeing the Persian-wheel in use in Punjab, its adoption was slow, and even by 1660, only 1.7 per cent of the wells in Merta in Rajasthan used the Persian wheel.

In the Deccan and South India, the rivers were all rain-fed, so there was not much scope for riverain irrigation canals. There were, however, several major reservoirs and dams in the region, constructed by Hindu chieftains; there was also some temple-related rural development. The spread of farming into new areas was also probably facilitated by the political fragmentation of the region and the proliferation of power centres. Yet, with all that, the total land brought under irrigation in south India was modest—even by the beginning of the nineteenth century, only three to seven per cent of the cultivated area was irrigated in most parts of South India, except in Thanjavur, where about fifty per cent of cultivated land was irrigated.

Not much is known about the Mughal practices in manuring the fields, but the use of cattle manure was probably higher in Mughal times than later, as farmers had more cattle; sometimes sheep and goats were hired to spend several nights on the field to manure it. In some regions of India, fish was used as manure.

Fields were tilled, as in early medieval India, with the help of landless labourers, whose status was similar to that of serfs; they were by custom bound to particular land-owning families, and were often transferred with the land when it was sold. Farm labourers were not normally paid wages, but were fed and clothed and taken care of, just as the farm animals were taken care of. But then, the average farmer too could not have had much more than just enough to feed and clothe himself, for most landholdings were small. Wealthy peasants, who produced for the market, not for just subsistence, were few in Mughal India.

THE MUGHAL AGE was not a good time for peasants. Their problem was not with government policy but with official practice. The policy was exemplarily benevolent. Among Akbar's orders recorded by Abul Fazl is one in which he directed a provincial governor that he 'should turn his attention to the increase of agriculture and the flourishing condition of the land and earn the gratitude of the people by the faithful discharge of his obligations and account the befriending of the agriculturists as an excellent service to the Almighty.' 'Be a friend of the agriculturist,' was Akbar's advice to revenue collectors.

Akbar's successors too professed similar worthy policies. Shah Jahan, says Rai Bhara Mal, was 'constantly directing his generous attention towards the improvement of agriculture and the collection of the revenues of the state . . . The *chakladars* who, by carefully cultivating their lands, aided in increasing the revenue, received marked consideration, and vice versa.' Shah Jahan disbursed money from the treasury to stimulate agriculture in Kashmir, says Inayat Khan. Aurangzeb in his firman to the Diwan of Gujarat in 1668, advised that imperial officers 'should practice benevolence to cultivators . . . so that they may joyfully and heartily try to increase the cultivation, and every arable tract may be brought under cultivation.' It was not, of course, altruism but royal self-interest that was behind such policy pronouncements, for peasants were the primary source of state revenue.

Occasionally, during times of scarcity, the state made tax remissions, initiated relief measures, and advanced money to the farmer—*taqavi* (strength-giving) loans—to buy seed, to be repaid at harvest. Similarly, to encourage agricultural expansion, they charged lower taxes on land newly brought under the plough, and introduced differential tax rates that favoured the cultivation of high-value crops. Such measures were however haphazard; they depended on the whim of the ruler, and were never on a scale adequate to make any significant difference in the economy or in the lives of the people. On the whole, in spite of commendable policies, and the revenue benefit to the state in promoting agriculture, the Mughal rule was ruinous to peasants, because of the laxity and corruption of the administration and the ruthless exploitation of peasants by jagirdars.

The basic Mughal orientation was towards reaping, not sowing. They built hardly any major irrigation systems, and they allowed even the canals dug during the Sultanate period to fall into disuse. Thus the 100-kilometre-long canal from the Yamuna to Safidon, built by Firuz Tughluq, though it was repaired during the reign of Akbar, soon after, 'for want of repairs . . . again stopped flowing', notes Inayat Khan. When Shah Jahan built his citadel in Delhi, he had the canal repaired and extended by another 100 kilometres to Delhi, but to water his city, not for irrigation. 'No person is found willing and able to repair the ditches and canals for the conveyance of water,' says Bernier, 'so it happens that the whole country is badly cultivated, and a great part rendered unproductive from the want of irrigation.'

The only major irrigation work undertaken by the Mughals was the canal system built in Punjab by Ali Mardan Khan during the reign of Shah Jahan, to bring water from the Ravi for Lahore and incidentally to irrigate the land along the way. The relative importance the Mughals attached to public works can be gauged from the fact that even this 'major' canal work cost the emperor only 100,000 rupees, an insignificant amount compared to what he spent on the Peacock Throne (which cost at least 100 times more in materials alone) and his Delhi palace complex (which cost sixty-five times more), and what he granted as annual personal allowance to Mumtaz Mahal (which was ten times more).

Despite such low investment in public works, the Mughal tax rates were high, compared to what they were before the Mughals and what they would be later, under the British. The normal Mughal tax claim was one-third or more of the gross produce, and in addition the state collected various special cesses from time to time. Peasants also had to bear the burden of several illegal exactions, so that in the end they were probably left with less than half their gross produce. Not only was the Mughal tax rate high, its effective incidence was even higher, as the state's share of the harvest was frequently valued at a price higher than the market rate, and the farmer was forced to pay the amount in cash. Inevitably, peasants cheated, and were for that reason often tortured by revenue collectors.

The most pernicious aspect of the Mughal government, from the point of view of the peasant, was the jagirdari system. The jagirdar had no permanent interest in the land assigned to him; his only concern was to squeeze as much out of the land as quickly as possible, before his jagir was transferred to someone else. He was, therefore, savagely oppressive towards peasants. Sometimes local officers simply appropriated to themselves the prime lands of farmers. Imperial officers routinely treated peasants 'as Turks treat Christians, taking from them all they can get by their labour, leaving them nothing but their bad, mud-walled, ill-thatch-covered houses and a few cattle to till the ground, besides other miseries,' says Peter Mundy. The peasant had no incentive to expand cultivation, for whatever extra he produced was seized by officers on some pretext or other. The tyranny, says Bernier, was 'often so excessive as to deprive the peasant and artisan of the necessaries of life, and leave them to die of misery and exhaustion.'

STILL, IN NORMAL times the rural folk in Mughal India probably had enough to eat, given their simple needs. Provisions were cheap. A kilogram of wheat cost only about a dam, one-fortieth of a rupee. In Akbar's time a sheep could be bought for about a rupee and a half; and one rupee bought thirty quarts of milk. 'I have seen good mutton sold for the value of one shilling, foure couple of hennes at the same price, one hare for the value of a penny, three partridges for as little, and so in proportion all the rest,' says Terry about the conditions in Jahangir's India. Fish, he says, was so cheap that it was not worth valuing. In Coromandel, says Thevenot, provisions were 'very cheap . . . The people of our Caravan had a Sheep for Twelve pence, a Partridge for Half penny, and a Fowl for less than Two pence . . .'

During times of scarcity, however, prices skyrocketed, though Manucci no doubt exaggerates when he says that 'without exaggerating, I bought one chicken for thirteen rupees', and 'I bought two calves for six hundred rupees, and paid one rupee for every ounce of butter'. According to English traders in Gujarat, the price of wheat, which was normally one rupee for eighty-five pounds, rose during the 1631 famine to one rupee for six pounds, a fourteenfold increase. 'The famine was so severe that the price of one *maund* of grain shot up to one hundred and twenty copper *tankas*, equal to six rupees,' says Muhammad Arif Qandahari. Firewood was scarce and expensive in most parts of India at all times. 'Firewood is very dear, and is sold by weight, 60 lbs. for from 12 to 18 pice (or 5 stivers), making a serious annual expense for a large household,' says Pelsaert. 'The poor burn cow-dung, mixed with straw and dried in the sun, which is also sold, as peat is sold in Holland.'

The peculiar predicament of the peasant was that in times of plenty as well as in times of scarcity he was at a disadvantage. 'The peasant,' says Moreland, 'is the last person to benefit by a rise in price, while he is the first to suffer from a fall.' In some years prices fell so low that farmers were unable to pay the cash dues to the state, so Akbar had to remit the tax claim by one-sixth, notes Abul Fazl, though correspondingly tax claims were raised when prices ruled high.

On the whole, the lot of the peasant in Mughal India was pathetic, and sometimes, unable to bear oppression and adversity, he fled from the land. Records of Aurangzeb's reign indicate a scarcity of cultivators and a decline in agricultural production. 'A considerable portion of the good land remains untilled from want of labourers, many of whom perish in consequence of the bad treatment they experience from the Governor,' says Bernier. 'The ground is seldom tilled otherwise than by compulsion.' Says Pelsaert: 'Some peasants abscond to escape their tyranny, and take refuge with rajas who are in rebellion, and consequently the fields lie empty and unsown, and grow into wilderness. Such oppression is exceedingly prevalent in this country.' Confirms Tavernier, 'You may see in India whole provinces like deserts, from where the peasants have fled on account of the oppression of the governors.'

The Whip and the Artisan

THE PREDICAMENT OF the artisan in Mughal India was not very much different from that of the peasant—he too was crippled by the same oppressions, yoked to the same flaccid values, blindly grinding on in the same old rut as his ancestors had in ages past. His caste and karma allotted to him a particular lot, and he accepted it with abject passivity.

It is very rarely that we hear of a revolt by artisans or traders in Mughal India, even rarer than revolt by peasants. In 1669, the Baniyas of Surat closed business to protest against the injustice of the local Kazi; earlier, in 1630, weavers in Bharuch (Borach) had rioted to protest against the English buying up cotton yarn; another time weavers in Baroda deserted the city to protest the Mughal governor's tyranny; in 1686, Indian traders and artisans in Madras observed a hartal over a tax levied by the English. These were rare incidents. Ordinarily, the artisan endured his fate with meek fatalism.

This attitude of passivity, though it was not conducive to innovation and enterprise, inculcated in the artisan the virtues of humility and patience, and enabled him to hone his traditional skills to perfection through endless repetition. 'There are ingenious men in every part of the Indies,' says Bernier. 'Numerous are the instances of handsome pieces of workmanship made by persons destitute of tools, and who can scarcely be said to have received instruction from a master. Sometimes they imitate so perfectly articles of European manufacture that the difference between the original and copy can hardly be discerned.'

'The Weaver of Silk will exactly imitate the nicest and most beautiful Patterns that are brought from Europe,' says Ovington. 'And the very Ship-Carpenters at Suratt will make the Model of any English Vessel, in all the Curiosity of its Building . . . as exactly as if they had been the first Contrivers . . . The Tailors here fashion the Cloaths for Europeans, either men or Women, according to every Mode that prevails; and fit up the Commodes, and towering Head-Dresses for the Women, with as much Skill, as if they had been an Indian Fashion, or themselves had been Apprentices at the Royal Exchange.' Says Oxenden: 'These carpenters are growne soe expert and masters of their art that here are many Indian vessails that in shape exceed those that come out of England or Holland.' Concludes Bernier: 'Want of genius, therefore, is not the reason why works of superior art are not exhibited in the capital. If the artists and manufacturers were encouraged, the useful and fine arts would flourish.'

There was no such general encouragement. Even though there was greater patronage of arts and crafts by the ruling class in Mughal times than in the preceding several centuries—as much as sixty-seven per cent of the imperial household expenditure went to the craft sector, according to Moosvi's estimate—and the small number of artisans who served the emperor did well for themselves, the Mughal ruling class usually 'treated [the artisan] with harshness, and inadequately remunerated [him with] . . . the pittance that shall supply him with a piece of bread,' says Bernier. As for the common people, they were either too poor or too parsimonious to demand quality goods. These circumstances, along with the low level of common culture, primitive technology, and the rigidity of the caste system, made conditions in Mughal India on the whole unfavourable to any improvement in the status of the artisan or in his mode of production.

The artisan himself showed little interest in technological innovations. Technology was not of course 'altogether stagnant' in Mughal India— there were some improvements in dyeing and printing cloth, as well as in carpet weaving, rope-making and shipbuilding—but these changes were minor and superficial, not systemic. The technological environment of India did not change. Nor did the values of the artisan. In many instances, where Indian craftsmen expertly copied European products, they copied blindly, without absorbing and internalizing the technology, perhaps without even understanding the product.

The adoption of new technologies required investment of both energy and capital, neither of which the Indian artisan had any to spare. Moreover, labour was cheap in India, so there was no incentive to adopt labour-saving technologies. Sometimes, in fact, superior modes of production were suppressed to protect old trades, as when the authorities in Coromandel banned the efficient new method of producing cannonballs introduced by the Dutch.

Thus in almost every sphere of production Indian 'technology was remarkably backward in comparison with the other advanced civilizations of the period, especially western Europe and China,' writes Tapan Raychaudhuri, a modem economic historian of India. 'Her world-famous textiles were produced without the aid of multi-spindle wheels known to China from at least the early fourteenth century and, of course, she had nothing to compare with the water-powered throwing mills with 200 spindles of the Italian silk industry. Her sea-going vessels were devoid of virtually all modern nautical instruments with the probable exception of the astrolabe. The massive Mughal monuments were constructed without the use of even such elementary aids to human labour as the wheel-barrow. India did not know of the uses of coal, and had no proper cast-iron, was unfamiliar with the techniques of deep mining and her chemical industry was, at best, primitive . . . Even such elementary objects as screws with proper grooves essential for most mechanical processes were not produced. Watermills and windmills, in use for centuries not only in China but in neighbouring Iran as well, were peripheral to the technology of the period.' Mechanical clocks and watches, common in Europe at this time, were largely ignored by Indians, who preferred to let time run medievally.

Mughal India was in no hurry for anything. There were no social or intellectual pressures in India to force technological innovation. Though there was some interest in European science and technology among the elite in Mughal India, it was mere idle curiosity, and was not intense enough, or sustained or widespread enough, to energize the transformation of India. The overall Mughal ambience was not congenial to scientific or technological revolution, not only because of the despotic-theocratic nature of the Mughal government and the depressed state of the Indian economy, but also because of the pre-existing institutions, folk ways and values of India that desiccated human spirit and throttled enterprise.

By and large, artisans in Mughal India continued to make what they had been making for centuries, using the same old tools and the same old processes. The use of primitive tools kept productivity low and made standardization impossible, and these were major problems for European traders seeking to market Indian goods worldwide. Curiously, contact with European traders, instead of stimulating innovation in production, actually tended to reinforce the Indian artisan's resistance to change, since whatever he produced, by whichever process, had a ready market. And when European traders tried to enforce quality and standardization, Indian suppliers sought to get around the problem by delivering close to the shipping date, so there would be no time to reject and reorder the goods.

BY SUCH PRACTICES the Indian artisan was foreclosing his future. While in Europe the profits of the trader and the artisan fuelled economic transformation, there was no such prospect in India. The wages of Indian artisans were dismally low, and for most of them life was a grim struggle for survival. Methwold reports that on the Coromandel coast master-craftsmen were paid threepence a day, their assistants one penny or less; according to Pelsaert, in Agra when workers were paid monthly wages, the month was reckoned as forty days. As for self-employed artisans, they seldom had money to buy raw materials for production, and were invariably caught in the debt trap of middlemen who advanced them money or material. Weavers, observes Moreland, were 'living on a dead level of poverty throughout the country.' The artisan, says Bernier, 'feels it no trifling matter if he have the means of satisfying the cravings of hunger and covering his body with the coarsest garment.'

Such was their predicament in normal times. Often it got a lot worse. Periodically the entire manufacturing activity of a region would collapse under the stress of famine, and then the routine misery of the artisan would turn into stark tragedy. Thus during the Gujarat famine of 1630–31, so many weavers abandoned home and trade, and so many died, that English factors were unable to procure cargo for their ships for quite a while, and had to nurture the industry back to health by supplying weavers with corn. Even then it took several years for the industry to recover fully. Further, famine lowered the level of skill in society, because of the death of master craftsmen and that too retarded economic recovery.

Apart from natural calamities, the artisan also had to contend with oppression by chieftains and imperial officers, who sought to mop up all the available surpluses in the economy through various exactions, legal and illegal. The Mughal, says Terry, had 'officers that spread over his Empire to exact money out of all the labours of that people who make the curious manufactures.' Tavernier found that in Varanasi weavers had to get each piece of cloth they produced stamped by the tax farmer before it could be sold.

These circumstances blighted the growth of craft and industry in India, but the most crucial disability of the Indian manufacturing system was not external to it, but intrinsic. Like everything else, production was organized along caste lines in Hindu society, with castes specializing in particular professions or products as, for instance, in weaving different varieties of cloth. Furthermore, castes tended to divide and multiply into sub-castes, with each sub-caste specializing in some absurdly minute but sacrosanct segment of production. There were, according to one Mughal list, as many as sixty-six castes among 'urban artisans and service groups'. Normally, none could change his occupation, just as none could change his caste. Craft guilds in Mughal India were really caste associations.

The caste-based organization of industry, though it ensured the preservation of minimum professional skills and provided security to craftsmen, barred competition and thereby precluded the build-up of the creative tension that is essential for the pursuit of excellence through innovation. Castes had a vested interest in their particular products and modes of production, a quasi-religious sanction for them, and therefore a prejudice against change. Further, the caste exclusiveness of professions led to professional secretiveness, which not only inhibited the dissemination of skills through society, but occasionally led to the secret of perfection in a craft dying with a master craftsman, unless he taught it to his son or disciple towards the end of his life.

Yet another disadvantage of the caste system was that it prevented skills from spreading across the country, for castes were localized, and their members were generally reluctant to move from their traditional habitats, as the East India Company discovered when they failed to entice silk weavers from Bengal to move to Madras despite the offer of high wages. Likewise, the caste system, because of its taboos and social rigidity, curtailed the entrepreneurial potential of society. Thus high-caste men in Mughal India altogether avoided involvement in any manufacturing activity, while in Europe patricians readily moved into trade and industry and formed strategic alliances with the bourgeoisie.

THE ORGANIZATION OF production in India at this time, as in medieval Europe, was primarily domestic. The home was the workshop, the paterfamilias the master craftsman, and the family members the work force. Artisans and manufacturers seldom employed wage labourers. The only large manufacturing facilities in India were those which produced goods exclusively for the royal family. There were several such establishments in Mughal India, in the imperial capital as well as in the provinces, employing numerous expert craftsmen. In the Delhi fort, for instance, 'large halls are seen in many places, called Kar-kanays (*karkhanās*), or workshops of artisans,' notes Bernier. 'In one hall embroiderers are busily employed, superintended by a master. In another you see goldsmiths; in a third, painters; in a fourth, varnishers in lacquer-work; in a fifth, joiners, turners, tailors, and shoemakers; in a sixth, manufacturers of silk, brocade, and those fine muslins of which are made turbans, girdles with golden flowers, and drawers worn by females . . . The artisans repair every morning to their respective Kar-kanayas, where they remain employed the whole day; and in the evening return to their homes.'

Other than the emperor, the major patrons of artisans in India were European trading companies. They had the whole world as their market and therefore required Indian products in large volumes. At times they hired an entire village of weavers to produce cloth for export, or they induced artisans to settle near their commercial centres, though even in the seventeenth century they had also to scour the villages for goods to export.

Such organized production, whether of luxury goods for the court or of export goods for European traders, was, for all its prominence in the records of the age, peripheral to the Indian economy. The preponderant bulk of manufactures in Mughal India was produced in villages, not towns, and was for local consumption, not for the market. Manufacturing in rural India was essentially an extension of farming; it had as yet no distinct identity of its own. Sometimes peasants doubled as artisans, to produce some of the items they needed, cloth for instance, and artisans presumably did some cultivation of their own. Village artisans were usually maintained by the village collectively, and were given a share of the village produce for their service, though they were at this time also beginning to produce some for the market, in addition to meeting their obligation to the village.

As from time immemorial, cotton textiles were the main item of manufacture and trade in Mughal India. Cotton was woven throughout India, but there were some regional specializations. Fine muslin was the speciality of Bengal—the area around Dacca, says Fitch, produced 'the best and the finest cloth made of cotton'. The Coromandel coast was the major production centre for calico and chintz (plain and printed cotton) till the depredations of the Marathas ruined the industry. Gujarat specialized in fabrics of cotton-silk mix.

India was the biggest exporter of cotton textiles in the world in Mughal times. But the value of the exports could not have been very high, considering the low volume of international trade at this time and the fact that the bulk of the people in the African and Asian countries within the immediate reach of Indian goods went nearly naked, as they did in India itself. Pyrard's often-quoted saying, that 'every one from the Cape of Good Hope to China, man and woman, is clothed from head to foot' in the products of Indian looms, was metaphoric rather than factual.

Silk weaving was a minor industry in India at this time, and was largely confined to Gujarat, Kashmir and Bengal, though there was some production in Agra and Lahore and possibly in other cities as well, mainly for local consumption. A small quantity was exported, mainly to South-East Asia. Silk yarn was produced in Kashmir and Bengal, but not enough to meet the demand, so yarn had to be imported from China and Persia. Curiously, India also exported a good amount of raw silk, from Bengal to Japan by the Dutch. Indian aristocrats (Muslims, despite religious taboo) favoured silk, but the silk woven in India was not sufficient in quantity, or good enough in quality, to meet the demand, so superior silk was imported from the Far East, Central Asia, Persia and the Eastern Mediterranean region. Says Terry about Indian silk: 'The best of them, for richness and goodness, come not near those which are made in parts of Italy.'

Very little woollen cloth was produced in Mughal India, except in Kashmir, and the local woollen, according to Terry, was coarse. The woollen used by the emperor and the nobles was imported from Turkey, Persia and Italy. There was some carpet weaving in Agra, Lahore and Kashmir, but Persian carpets dominated the market. India also made a variety of minor products: gilded glass and perfumed pottery in Patna, paper in Lahore, lac bangles in Gujarat, and so on. There was a great amount of boat building in Sind and Bengal, and shipbuilding in Gujarat. And of course India also produced numerous items of everyday use.

There was thus considerable manufacturing activity everywhere in Mughal India, and a great many varieties of products were made, but most of the activity was inertial, and lacked the dynamism to transform the economy.

Hamstrung Trade

MUGHAL INDIA WAS a self-contained world. It produced nearly everything it needed. What it needed, however, was little. The vast majority of the people being wretchedly poor, their needs were basic, and were met in each locality almost entirely by what was produced in the locality. The kings and nobles, of course, needed goods from different parts of India and from other lands, but the quantity of luxury goods required by this minuscule group, for all its extravagance, was marginal to Indian economy. There was thus no great scope in Mughal India for inter-regional trade or for imports from other countries.

There was, however, a good amount of local trade in essential commodities, mainly in foodgrains and cloth, brought to urban markets from the surrounding villages. There was also some movement of agricultural produce from surplus areas to deficit areas, as for instance rice from Bengal to Coromandel and Kerala. Banjaras—an ancient tribe of nomadic traders, their name a corruption of the Sanskrit word *vanijyakara*—carried vast quantities of provisions across India, but their main business was to provision armies on the march, a perennial and assured market in Mughal times.

There was, we must assume, some growth in trade in India at this time, generated by the normal swell of human advancement. Certainly, exports grew in Mughal times, owing largely to the enterprise of European traders. While India's traditional trade with the Middle East and East Africa continued to flourish, European traders revived and expanded India's defunct direct trade with Europe, stimulated the declining trade with East Asia, and opened, though in a small way, an entirely new market for Indian goods in the Americas.

But whatever the extent of the growth in trade, and however great the volume of trade in absolute terms, inter-regional and overseas trade had little effect on the Indian economy as a whole, which was sustained primarily by local production and local trade. What is even more significant is that the quantitative growth in trade did not lead to any qualitative changes; among Indians, there was no new energy in trade, no new dynamism, only a slight bloating. By and large, India continued to produce and sell what it had been producing and selling for centuries, with no significant changes in production techniques, trade practices or markets.

In fact, organizationally, trade in Mughal India was weaker than in ancient India. The complex network of guilds and craftsmen's cooperatives, which had once given the Indian economy its vitality, had long vanished, presumably in the chaos of the early Middle Ages; there are only stray references to them in Mughal chronicles and in the journals of foreign travellers. There were caste organizations of artisans and merchants, and members of different communities or castes did on occasion act in concert in their common interest, but there does not seem to have been any standing organization of merchants or artisans in Mughal India.

Local trade was, however, well organized. Town markets were regulated by government officials, who checked prices, weights and measures. Metropolitan cities like Agra, Delhi and Lahore had thriving markets selling products from all over India and abroad. 'You cannot desire any thinge butt you shall find itt in this cittye,' says Jourdain about Agra. 'Every great towne or citie of India hath markets twice a day: in the coole season presently after the sunne is risen, and a little before setting,' says Terry. Peddlers abounded in towns. In Surat, Ovington saw 'multitude of Bannians and other Merchants [in the bazaar, standing] . . . with Silks and Stuffs in their Hands, or upon their Heads, to invite such as pass by to come and buy them.' Tavernier says that 'even in the smallest villages rice, flour, butter, milk, beans, and other vegetables, sugar and other sweetmeats, dry and liquid, can be procured in abundance', while in the large villages even 'sheep, fowl and pigeons were on sale'.

The most vivid account of an Indian bazaar in Mughal times is given in the chronicle of Akbar's envoy Asad Beg, who found in Bijapur 'a bazaar of great extent', as much as 27.5 metres wide and nearly 6.5 kilometres long. 'Before each shop was a beautiful green tree, and the whole bazaar was extremely clean and pure,' writes Asad. 'It was filled with rare goods, such as are not seen or heard of in any other town. There were shops of cloth-sellers, jewellers, armourers, vintners, bakers, fishmongers, and cooks . . .

'In the jewellers' shops were jewels of all sorts, wrought into a variety of articles, such as daggers, knives, mirrors, necklaces, and also into the form of birds . . . all studded with valuable jewels, and arranged upon shelves, rising one above the other. By the side of this shop will be a baker's, with rare viands, placed in the same manner, upon tiers of shelves.

Further on a linendraper's, with all kinds of cloths, shelved in like manner. Then a clothier's. Then a spirit-merchant's, with various sorts of china vessels, valuable crystal bottles, and costly cups, filled with choice and rare essences, arrayed on shelves, while in front of the shop were jars of double-distilled spirits. Beside that shop will be a fruiterer's, filled with all kinds of fruit and sweetmeats, such as pistachio-nuts, and relishes, and sugar-candy, and almonds.

'On the other side may be a wine-merchant's shop, and an establishment of singers and dancers, beautiful women adorned with various kinds of jewels, and fair-faced choristers, all ready to perform whatever may be desired of them. In short, the whole bazaar was filled with wine and beauty, dancers, perfumes, jewels of all sorts, palaces, and viands.' There were no doubt a few other similar centres of affluence and elegance in India in Mughal times, but they were rare, like oases in a vast desert of squalid poverty.

THESE OASES OF wealth were mostly seats of political power, but a few commercial cities were also coming into prominence at this time, such as Goa, Calicut, Madras, Machilipatnam (Masulipatam), Hugli, and of course Surat, which was by far the richest and most prominent port city in the Mughal empire.

The traders at these ports were a cosmopolitan lot—Europeans, Arabs, Persians, Armenians and Jews, apart from various Indian trading communities like the Baniyas, Bohras and Parsees of Gujarat, Chettis and Komatis of the Coromandel coast; Marwaris of Rajasthan who operated throughout India, and Khattris of Hindustan. Most Indian trading firms were family-owned, though sometimes partnerships were formed by traders of the same caste. There were no Indian joint stock companies. Inter-community trade links, as between Hindus and Muslims, were rare, but Muslim-owned ships were used by all communities, and Hindus and Jains served Muslim traders as bankers, clerks and accountants. The Muslim amir and trader, says Fryer, kept 'a Scrivan of the Gentues: on which account it is the Banyans [who] make all Bargains, and transact all Money-business.'

Port cities like Surat were dominated by Indian merchant princes, who were held in high esteem in international trading circles. The most prominent Surat merchant in the mid-seventeenth century was Virji Vohra, who was reputed to be the richest merchant in the world in his time, and could deploy as much as eight million rupees in trade. He had branch offices or agencies at Ahmadabad, Agra, Burhanpur, Golconda and Malabar, and he dominated and controlled the markets in which he operated. Often the syndicate which he led bought up entire cargoes of ships valued up to a million rupees. He also lent money on interest—the English often borrowed from him, a couple of hundred thousand rupees at a time—on no security other than the creditworthiness of the borrower and the assurance of strict adherence to the agreed terms.

Haji Said Beg and Haji Qasim were the other Croesuses of Surat. Shantidas Jawhari, a Jain jeweller and banker of Ahmadabad, was yet another prominent merchant of Gujarat. He had considerable influence at the imperial court, sufficient to discomfit even imperial princes, as Aurangzeb once learned to his sorrow—when Aurangzeb, as the governor of Gujarat, seized the temple Shantidas had built and converted it into a mosque, Shantidas petitioned Shah Jahan and got the temple restored to him. Aurangzeb himself, on his accession, took care to conciliate Shantidas. Likewise, Surat merchant Rustam Manak successfully petitioned Aurangzeb to secure for Parsees exemption from jizya. Similar prominence was enjoyed by Mir Jumla of Golconda, Malay Chetti and Kasi Viranna of Coromandel, and several others like them.

Some of these merchants were wealthy enough to advance loans to princes—and independent enough to deny them even to the emperor. Thus when Murad set out on the war of succession, he borrowed ten million rupees from the merchants of Surat by issuing a bond guaranteeing repayment. When Murad lost the war of succession and was executed by Aurangzeb, the creditors petitioned Aurangzeb to redeem the bond—though, when the emperor conceded the claim, they said that they were only interested in proving their claim, and requested the emperor to treat the amount as a gift. But later, when Aurangzeb, in acute financial stringency at the end of his life, sought an interest-free loan from the bankers at the imperial camp, they refused, on the ground that it would set a bad precedent, and that the governors too, if they came to hear of it, would ask for interest-free loans.

Sometimes, though rarely, amirs were involved in trade, the most distinguished of them being Mir Jumla, who had begun his career *as* a trader. Mir Jumla owned ten ships and a large fleet of carts to transport his goods; he also had the weavers of an extensive tract of land working exclusively for him, and had once, having fallen out with the Dutch, proposed a partnership with the English to monopolize east coast trade. Muqarab Khan, the governor of Surat under Jahangir, was also a prominent and successful trader. 'It is the principal trade of the nobles of

India to place their money on vessels in speculations,'. says Tavernier. Amirs seldom handled trade directly, to avoid the stigma of being branded Baniyas, but acted through merchant agents, who operated under their protection.

Trade, including international trade, was also a hobby of the royal ladies; they had plenty of idle money in their hands, and their royal connections enabled them to acquire valuable monopolies. Sometimes the emperor himself created monopolies. Thus, in 1633, Shah Jahan made indigo a royal monopoly, requiring its sale throughout the empire to be channelled through a particular merchant, who was given a loan from the treasury to finance the trade and was required to share the profit with the emperor. In 1655, Shah Jahan set up a monopoly in saltpetre, and in 1640–41, he and his Vizier Asaf Khan commandeered the entire textile industry in Ahmadabad for exporting cloth to the Middle East. Salt was a royal monopoly under the Mughals.

Even when no formal monopoly was created, when a member of the imperial household entered a trade, it had the effect of creating a monopoly, as few traders were brash enough to compete with them. Sometimes the local governor stepped in as a buyer or seller, 'and when it occurred, it meant that competition was for the time being displaced by force,' says Moreland. Shayista Khan, the governor of Bengal, was notorious for such interventions. 'The Nabob's (Shayista Khan's) officers oppress the people, monopolize most commodities, even as low as grass for Beasts . . . firewood, thatch, etc, nor do they want ways to oppress those people of all sorts who trade, whether natives or strangers,' notes a report of English merchants. Mughal amirs (princes too) sometimes took forced loans from merchants, which were not always repaid, though even the most powerful amir had to provide security for taking loans. Also, occasionally amirs forced loans on merchants at exorbitant interest rates, as Shayista Khan did in Bengal. According to Peter Mundy, when Parviz took over as the governor of Patna, merchants immediately concealed their wealth and lay low, uncertain of what to expect from the prince.

Sometimes even non-intrusive royal activities disrupted trade. Thus when Shah Jahan was building his palace complex in Delhi, all the carts in the region were taken over to transport materials for construction, and the goods that the carts were carrying were 'by the King's officers cast down in the fields', where they lay for months for lack of transport. Paradoxically, even the political unity that the Mughals imposed on India, though it facilitated trade, also somewhat restricted its pattern and direction, as wealth and power, instead of being diffused in many centres, were now concentrated at one centre, so that trade in luxury goods had only one main channel to flow through.

BY WHATEVER CHANNEL trade in India flowed, the flow was never smooth. All along the route, trade was impeded by numerous quasi-legal and illegal payments that traders were coerced to make. Thevenot, travelling through the Deccan in the early part of Aurangzeb's reign, noted that on the road between Aurangabad and Golconda, over a distance of just twenty-three leagues (111 kilometres), there were sixteen posts where transit dues were collected—one every seven kilometres! Mughal roads were insecure (as roads were everywhere in the medieval world) so local officers and chieftains collected a toll (*rahdari*: road-guard tax), usually one-tenth of the value of goods, from merchants and travellers for the protection they offered. Often they preyed on merchants and traders, instead of protecting them.

Traders were also harassed for trade tax. This tax, called *pandari*, says Khafi Khan, was collected 'throughout the imperial dominions' from 'every tradesman and dealer, from the butcher, the potter, the greengrocer, to the draper, jeweller and banker. Something was paid to the government . . . for every bit of ground in the market, for every stall and shop.'

The collection of these tolls was an old and well-established custom in India, which the Mughal emperors were unable to ban effectively, though they routinely issued orders against it. 'The royal prohibition had no effect,' says Khafi Khan about Aurangzeb's decree against illegal tolls. The situation in fact got worse. Local authorities, continues Khafi Khan, 'by force and tyranny now exact more than ever from the traders and poor and necessitous travellers . . . By degrees matters have come to such a pass that between the time of leaving the factory or port and reaching their destination, goods and merchandise pay double their cost price in tolls. Through the villainy and oppression of the toll-collectors and zemindars, the property, honour, and the lives of thousands of travellers and peaceful wayfarers are frittered away.'

Corruption was rampant in Mughal India. At the seaports, customs officers were strict, even harsh, with travellers and traders, searching not only their baggage but even their pockets. The purpose of the severity was not however to enforce the law, but to put the squeeze on the victim. Though customs duty was low in Mughal India, sometimes as low as two per cent and never higher than five per cent, the effective duty worked out much higher, because of corruption. Mughal officers, according to English merchants, 'will do nothing without bribes, which, however extorted, is made a continual custom, enforced as a duty.' The valuation of goods was in the hands of officers on the spot, and they fixed it according to their pleasure. The customs officer, says Fryer, would not clear goods unless his 'Fist is mollified'.

Such extortions applied to exports too. The Dutch at Machilipatnam complained in 1606 that though the official rate of duty was moderate, local officers claimed for themselves, as a consideration, sixteen per cent on exports. Traders, like peasants, were sometimes tortured or otherwise persecuted by officers, and even so eminent a merchant as Virji Vohra once had to suffer imprisonment at the hands of the local governor. It cannot be assumed of course that merchants were always, or ever, innocent, but most often they were squeezed only to extort money from them, not to bring them to book. Occasionally, but rarely, traders rose to resist such oppression—once the merchants of Surat observed hartal, at another time the merchants of Bagnagar; in Ahmadabad, a merchant chief, Kapurchand Bhansali, once even organized a private army to resist illegal exactions. But generally merchants survived by slinking low.

APART FROM THE problems that traders had with government officials, the flow of trade in India was also hampered by the prevailing confusion of coins, and weights and measures, though it was not as bad under the Mughals as it was before them. Coins were seldom accepted at their face value, although Mughal coins, especially those issued by Akbar and Jahangir, were of high quality and superior to contemporary European coins. Standards fell later. 'Sales are, in general, conditional on payment being made in money coined during the current year,' says Tavernier; 'and if you paid in old pieces you must submit to loss, according to the time they have been coined.' Often coins were accepted only after testing them for purity and weight, as forgeries were common. 'Coins,' says Moreland, 'were not at this period regarded as fixed standards of value, but rather as a form of merchandise . . . a particular kind of barter.' This was especially true of foreign coins, which were accepted only at the value of the metal.

There was, as in everything else, widespread cheating in currency in Mughal India. Badauni states that counterfeit coins circulated even during the reign of Akbar. The penalty for counterfeiting was relatively light; in the reign of Aurangzeb, it involved only the chopping off of a finger of the culprit, and that risk could not have deterred many. The prevalence of counterfeit coins and the general debasement of currency so lowered the acceptability of Mughal coins in the reign of Aurangzeb that the English in Bombay had to mint their own coins—because, as they told Khafi Khan, 'the coins of Hindustan are of short weight and much debased'.

But more than all these, what impeded the growth of trade in India was the general poverty of the people. In rural India there was hardly any money circulation, for almost the entire rural labour force was made up of virtual serfs, who were merely fed and clothed by farmers. In the towns, to which the rural folk sometimes drifted to seek a living, there was a labour market—Terry writes about seeing men standing about in the market-place to be hired—and these daily workers were paid in cash, at least in part. But that did not make any great difference in the economy, for the wages of urban labourers were so low that their condition was little better than that of the rural serfs. They too, like the serfs, were often taken forcibly to work, says Pelsaert: 'The man is not asked if he is willing to come, but is seized in the house or in the street, well beaten if he should dare raise any objection, and in the evening paid half his wages, or nothing at all.'

The best paid workers in Mughal India were those in the service of the emperor. Their wages, as fixed by Akbar, were two dams (one-twentieth of a rupee) a day for unskilled labourers, three to four dams for superior labourers, three to seven dams for carpenters, and five to seven dams for builders. The monthly salary of sweepers was sixty-five dams, of camel drivers sixty dams, and of wrestlers seventy dams. The lowest grade slave got a dam a day—three-fourths of a rupee a month—which probably was just enough for him to survive. Wages rose somewhat under later rulers. Even then, domestic servants during the reign of Jahangir, 'working from morning to night ... [could] earn only 5 or 6 tankas (10 or 12 dams)', says Pelsaert, and adds that in the households of amirs servants were paid after many deductions, such as fines for mishaps, and wages were usually three or four months in arrears, 'and then paid in worn-out clothes and other things'. The service conditions of ordinary soldiers were not much better: they too lived at the bare subsistence level.

In the area around Surat, a servant was paid only about two rupees a month, says Terry. Della Valle mentions a wage of three rupees a month, while de Laet mentions the wage as between three and four rupees, all of which struck European travellers as very low. But they were, in terms of real wages, clearly adequate for subsistence. Terry says that the servant who was paid two rupees a month could save half his wage and send it home. However that may be, the wage-earning labour class in Mughal India was too small in number and too weak in economic power to have any great effect on the market.

Nor was there much of a middle class in Mughal India to stimulate trade, though Bernier exaggerates when he says that 'in Delhi there is no middle state; a man must either be of the highest rank or live miserably.' In the great cities of Mughal India, there were a good number of men in the middle-income group—lower government officials, traders, artisans, professionals—but they too lived like the poor, because of the general tendency of the common people to live humbly. Inter-regional trade, therefore, depended largely on royal and aristocratic patronage. The market was very narrow, and had little scope for growth.

THESE NEGATIVE FACTORS, by and large, cancelled out the advantages to trade in the positive developments in Mughal India. The Mughal environment was on the whole unfavourable to the trader, and he had to be sly and devious to survive. His orientation was therefore towards caution rather than enterprise, and he was jittery about security. An extreme instance of this was the practice of some Baniya shopkeepers who, according to Manucci, never kept their shops open as a precaution against looting, but sold their goods through a hole in the shop door, 'through which they receive the money and hand out what is wanted'. When thieves got around this hurdle by grabbing the hand of the trader and, putting a knife to it, demanded money and goods, the Baniyas began to use a wooden spoon, 'and on no account would they put their hand through the hole'.

Merchants kept a low profile in Mughal India, hiding their wealth and living in houses of modest frontages, for fear of the vultures who preyed on the rich. 'There are very many private men in cities and towns, who are merchants or tradesmen, that are very rich: but it is not safe for them that are so, so to appear, lest that they should be used as fill'd sponges,' says Terry. The Baniyas usually held their wealth in cash and jewels, not in real estate, and this made them extremely vulnerable to predators. 'This ... awes them to great secresie in their Commerce, especially in their receiving, or Payments of Money, for which they either make use of the darkness of the Night, or the obscurity of the Morning, in conveying it to the place of Payment,' says Ovington. 'For should the Mughal's Officers see the Chests and Bags of Gold and Silver carried as publicly here, as they are in the Streets of London, they would be apt to change their Owner, and be deliver'd to him who calls himself the Original Proprietor.'

Traders lived humbly because they dared not live well, and not because of spiritual indifference to worldly comforts. Besides, they were by nature miserly. 'They are mainly addicted to prosecute their Temporal Interest, and the amassing of Treasure; and therefore will fly at the securing of a Pice, tho' they can command whole Lacks of Roupies,' says Ovington. 'I know those among them computed to be worth an Hundred Thousand Pounds, whose Service the Prospect of Sixpence Advantage will command to traverse the whole City of Suratt. For they are always upon the Thoughts of increasing their Wealth, and plodding for Gain . . .' Tavernier speaks of the 'extreme parsimony of shroffs . . . and of all Indians in general'.

Baniyas were a nonviolent people, and the battle of wits was the only battle they would fight. 'They are most innocent and obsequious, humble and patient to a Miracle,' says Ovington; 'sometimes they are heated into harsh Expressions to one another, which is seldom; and this Tongue-Tempest is term'd there a Bannian Fight, for it never rises to Blows or Blood-shed.' Says Manucci, 'By nature these Baniyas are very timid, and object to carry arms . . . They are very careful about the answers they give to questions . . . it is their habit to dissemble even when someone asks them what day it is.'

INDIANS WERE GENERALLY passive traders. They seldom took any initiative to expand production to meet demand, none at all to develop their markets. It was the buyer, not the seller, who had to take the initiative. Such attitudes hampered the growth of trade: timidity and enterprise do not go well together. 'This debasing state of slavery obstructs the progress of trade and influences the manners and mode of life of every individual,' writes Bernier. 'There can be little encouragement to engage in commercial pursuits, when the success with which they may be attended, instead of adding to the enjoyments of life, provokes the cupidity of a neighbouring tyrant possessing both power and inclination to deprive any man of the fruits of his industry. When wealth is acquired, as must sometimes be the case, the possessor, so far from living with increased comfort and assuming an air of independence, studies the means by which he may appear indigent: his dress, lodging, and furniture, continue to be mean, and he is careful, above all things, never to indulge in the pleasures of the table. In the meantime, his gold and silver remain buried at a great depth in the ground.'

Surprisingly, even in the drab, slinking world of traders, there were a few who defied convention and lived in great opulence. 'A few individuals . . . who derive their income from the King or from the Omrahs, or who are protected by a powerful patron, are at no pains to counterfeit poverty, but partake of the comforts and luxuries of life,' says Bernier. In Agra, a merchant prince named Sabal Singh Sahu is said to have lived like a prince, while Khemchand, another great merchant, is said to have allotted 1.5 million rupees for the marriage of his daughter, an incredible sum, considering that Shah Jahan spent only 3.2 million on the marriage of Dara. Yet another merchant of Agra was escorted by 500 soldiers when he went on a pilgrimage to Puri; he had 500 porters to carry his baggage, and he distributed 500 rupees in alms every day.

These were exceptional cases. In any case, traders in Mughal India, unlike traders in Europe, seldom played politics, however rich they were and to whatever community they belonged. It was dangerous to do so, as Surat merchant Ahmed Chelabi, who maintained some 2000 men as retainers, found out; he had to pay with his life for his presumption. The only great merchant in Mughal times who was also conspicuously successful in politics was Mir Jumla.

Merchants generally enjoyed greater freedom and security in port cities than they did in the interior, and rich Muslim merchants were on the whole more open in their lifestyle than rich Hindus. Even greater freedom was enjoyed by foreign merchants, for they came from a different socio-cultural environment, and their ways were tolerated with amused indulgence by local authorities. It was also less risky for foreign merchants to take on authority, as the most they stood to lose were the goods in their immediate possession, not their whole wealth. 'You shall be sure of such privilege as any stranger, and rights when the subject dares not plead his,' Roe advised the East India Company.

IN COPING WITH their hostile environment, Indian traders developed acute survival skills. Baniyas were, according to Finch, 'as subtle as the devil'. Says Tavernier, 'All the Jews who occupy themselves with money and exchange in the empire of the Grand Seigneur (Sultan of Turkey) pass for being very sharp; but in India they would scarcely be apprentices to these [money] Changers.' Pieter van den Broeke, who was in Surat in the third decade of the seventeenth century, considered Baniyas as 'the craftiest and most knavish people in all India'.

These are left-handed compliments, for foreigners, ignorant of the ways of India, were often victims of Indian businessmen, and their bitterness warped their perception. Says Fryer of the Baniyas of Surat: 'Lying, Dissembling, Cheating are their Masterpiece.' Says Manucci about Indians in general: 'Money is their only passion . . . not a native of this country has any loyalty, or gratitude or power to keep a secret.' Tavernier too speaks of cheating by Indian traders. And a Jesuit missionary has this catholic complaint: 'The gentiles regard neither Pope nor Faith where money is concerned.'

Yet, even in their deceits Indian traders were orthodox, and operated within a conventional commercial code, sometimes surprising foreign traders by not taking advantage where advantage could have been taken. Commercial morality, however, was only morality within the trading community, their rules of the game—the same as honour among thieves— and did not mean socially responsible behaviour. Traders were usually fair to each other, but not to the public. And they had no hesitation in exploiting any opportunity whatever, including the misery of famine, for making profit. As one European merchant put it, 'they for little profit to themselves, still wish famine to the world.'

During famine, prices rose by many times, and no trader could resist the seduction of the immense profits that could be made from it. Such pitiless avarice also possessed the begums. Thomas Bowrey, writing towards the close of the seventeenth century, reports that in Patna during the famine of 1670, 'the Nabobs Chiefe Wife had Several large Storehouses full of graine, and would not dispose of any for less than the equal weight of silver for rice and wheat'. Sometimes, when nature failed to oblige them with opportunities, traders created artificial scarcity, cornering the grain market. Adulteration too was an accepted trade practice; indigo, for example, was often mixed with sand, oil and wood shavings, the amount of additive rising with the demand. Now and then the government took stern action against adulterators—the governor of Ahmadabad once decreed death on them—but traders usually took such risks in their stride, as professional hazards. Their greed was greater than their fear of death.

Traders of course, like everyone else, cheated the government, which was not considered cheating at all. When Aurangzeb decreed that Muslims could bring in small value items free of duty, 'the revenue officers . . . reported that Musulmans had adopted the practice of dividing their goods into small parcels in order to avoid the duty, and that they passed the goods of Hindus in their names,' says Khafi Khan. Manrique records that the passport issued to him as an ecclesiastic to travel from Lahore down the Indus was used by a merchant in his caravan to evade various tolls along the way.

There was a good amount of smuggling into Mughal India. 'As regards gold, the merchants who import it use so much cunning in order to conceal it,' writes Tavernier. If caught, they had to pay double the duty, ten per cent instead of five per cent, but this was hardly a deterrent. Foreign ambassadors, especially those from poor Muslim kingdoms, often misused their diplomatic status to take goods into India without paying customs duty, where they sold the goods, bought Indian goods with the sales proceeds, and took them out without paying duty.

The Indian commercial world was for the foreign trader a maze of booby-traps, and he needed help to negotiate his way through it. Such help was provided by brokers, who were indispensable as middlemen between traders and producers, and as clearing and selling agents. Often however the brokers themselves took advantage of foreigners. Says Roe about Jadu Das, a broker of English merchants: he was 'sufficient in all but his honesty, wherein there is little choice'. In course of time, brokers, mostly Hindus, became ubiquitous at Indian ports, and some of them amassed vast fortunes, investing no capital other than their business acumen.

THE SYSTEM OF financing trade was fairly sophisticated in Mughal India. Hindu financiers dominated the scene, serving as moneylenders, bankers and money-changers, and issuing *hundis*, bills of exchange. They even provided some sort of trade insurance, covering war risks and 'overdue market'. Bills of exchange, rather than cash, were increasingly used in large commercial transactions in Mughal India. 'In this country the rule is that when one desires to have money conveyed without expense and trouble of transit to distant places, he makes it over to a man of means who thereupon gives a writing,' writes Abul Fazl. 'This is conveyed to the desired place, and the person there pays the money on seeing the document. The singular thing is that seals and witnesses are not required. The writing is called *hundi*.'

Most of the money transactions in Mughal India were handled by shroffs, money-changers, who, along with merchants, also served as bankers, accepting deposits on interest, the interest being around 7.5 per cent in the mid-seventeenth century. There were no exclusive bankers in Mughal India. 'In India a village must be very small indeed if it has not a money-changer, called Shroff, who acts as banker to make remittances of money and issue letters of exchange,' says Tavernier.

Mercantile credit was provided by shroffs and merchants in their role as bankers, as well as by amirs, sometimes even by the emperor, Shah Jahan, for instance. Lending rates in Mughal India varied considerably from place to place and from time to time but were, on the whole, much lower than in ancient India—where the rates ranged from fifteen per cent to an incredible 240 per cent per annum—though higher than the four per cent rate prevailing in contemporary England. The minimum interest rate for foreign trade recorded was six per cent, and the highest thirty-six per cent; in Golconda, high government officials were known to charge as much as sixty per cent, but these were probably not regular commercial loans, but were like the high-interest loans that Shayista Khan as governor forced on merchants in Bengal.

The high rates of interest indicate the high profits that could be earned in trade—and also the high risks involved. Many traders grew rich rapidly, many others collapsed as rapidly into bankruptcy, and it was seldom that the fortunes of a great mercantile family endured for more than four generations. No great stigma was attached to bankruptcy in Indian society; it was treated more as misfortune than as failure. The bankrupt trader, according to Manucci, simply 'lighted two candles in the morning as a sign that he had become bankrupt', a symbolic pyre for a dead business.

Bankruptcy was common in Mughal India because, apart from the hazards of war and natural calamities that the trader had to face, the bulk of trade in medieval times was highly speculative, for markets, as Moreland notes, 'were exceedingly narrow; the arrival of a single ship might convert scarcity into glut.' An even greater risk was in transporting goods—on land, robbers (and the equally predatory government officers) lay in wait for trade caravans; the seas and rivers were infested with pirates.

Overland, traders travelled in large caravans of a hundred or two hundred wagons, each wagon guarded by four soldiers paid by the owners of the merchandise, two on each side. The only secure caravans were those of the Banjaras, nomadic grain dealers who provisioned armies on the move; they were considered neutral and enjoyed the right of transit through all lands, and their property was respected by all. The Banjaras travelled in immense caravans of ten or twelve thousand laden oxen, each ox carrying about 150 kilograms of weight, and it was, says Tavernier, quite a sight to see them on the move across the plains, in a rolling cloud of dust.

Transport, apart from being risky, was also expensive. According to Moreland's calculation 'the cost of carrying 100 lb. a distance of 100 miles in Northern and Western India ranged between half and three-quarter of a rupee, exclusive of anything required for payment of armed guards and inland customs duties'—which meant that agricultural produce from the Agra region, if transported to Gujarat, would have cost five to eight times as much as in Agra. The feasible radius of foodgrain trade in Mughal India was therefore well under 300 kilometres, unless it was transported by sea, as rice was from Bengal to Kerala. The high cost of transport was one of the reasons why famine in one province could not be relieved with provisions from another province. River transport was much cheaper, but its scope was limited.

The bulk of goods in India was carried on pack animals, mostly oxen and camels, but seldom horses. 'For the Carriage of their Goods, the Indians seldom make use of Horses,' says Ovington. Because roads were few and badly maintained, carts were used only for valuable articles. Carts drawn by oxen could be hired for a rupee a day. The camel was the most important draught animal after the ox. In the hill country, porters (men and women) were used for transporting goods. Sometimes provisions were loaded on goats.

There was not much river traffic in India, except down the Indus and along the Yamuna-Ganga system, as navigable rivers were few. Boats usually travelled together in large numbers for safety against river pirates, for waterways were no more secure than roadways. Thus when Fitch travelled by river to Bengal, it was in the company of 'one hundred and fourscore boats laden with Salt, Opium, Hinge (asafoetida), Lead, Carpets, and divers other commodities.'

Pirates swarmed the seas too—the sea dogs of Malabar, the Marathas, and the most ruthless of all, European buccaneers—so that even the Portuguese coastal merchant fleet had to travel in sea caravans of several hundred oar-propelled small boats escorted by warships. Even then they sometimes fell victim to buccaneers. Vessels normally sailed from Surat at night, so that 'they might not be discovered by Malabars', says Thevenot.

A DEVELOPMENT OF great significance in Mughal times was the growing presence of European traders in India, but its full impact would be felt only in the nineteenth century. The European connection did not bring about any change in the dynamics of Mughal economy or any evident quickening of its tempo, though undeniably it led to some increase in production and overseas trade. Superficially, India had an advantage over Europe, as the balance of trade continued to be in India's favour, and would remain so till the mid-twentieth century. But balance of trade was not everything. Economic vitality was. There was, however, no vitality in Mughal economy. The future of Indian economy therefore depended little on what Indians did, for they did precious little on their own. It would be external forces that would shape India's economic future.

All that was in the distant future. In Mughal times, the volume of India's foreign trade, imports as well as exports, was small, and of that European traders accounted for only a small percentage. Long distance overseas trade linking nations and continents was only just then beginning its explosive growth, and there was yet no great demand for European goods in India or for Indian goods in Europe. Nor did the traditional Afro-Asian market for Indian goods have much potential for growth, to benefit from European trade initiatives. It was only in the late seventeenth century, with the marketing of new Indian products like saltpetre and silk, and the opening of European markets for Indian textiles, that Indian exports would grow noticeably.

'I see no Comoditye that will proue staple and certaynly vendable, able to returne a ship yearly,' stated Roe about the prospect of marketing European goods in India. He was equally sceptical about marketing Indian goods in Europe: 'I thought all India a China shop, and that I should furnish all my Frendes with rarietyes; but [India] is not that part.' It was only in cotton goods export from India that Roe saw any future: 'The trade here will doubtlesse in tyme bee very profitable for your Majesties Kingdomes, and may vent much cloth.'

For a century and half after the appearance of Europeans on the Indian scene, the bulk of India's foreign trade, except for the direct trade with Europe in pepper, continued to be with the old, established markets in Asia and Africa, and in the old, established products. There was however a partial change in the carriers of this trade, as Europeans snatched away some of the business from Arabs and Indians. Even then, most of India's overseas trade remained in the hands of Indian merchants, and was carried by Indian ships—Europeans ruled the Indian seas, but they did not have the freight capacity to monopolize the sea trade.

In the beginning, the Portuguese tried to interdict Indian ships from plying on certain routes, primarily to East Africa and the Spice Islands; they also reserved certain commodities (pepper mainly) as their monopoly to carry, and further required all ships in the Indian Ocean to call at a Portuguese port in the region, pay a duty on their cargo, and obtain a pass (*cartaz*), which listed the ports the ship was allowed to visit and the articles it could carry. Ships without passes were treated as prizes of war, seized, plundered and burned. These restrictions did hurt Indian maritime activity for a while, but did not cripple it, as Indian merchants managed to get partially around the controls by forming conniving trade partnerships with corrupt Portuguese officers engaged in unofficial private trade. The main victims of Portuguese action were Arab traders, and their discomfiture proved advantageous to Indian traders, as it enabled them to move strongly into the Red Sea, to make up for the loss of the South-east Asian trade. The collapse of Indian maritime activity would begin only in the eighteenth century.

THE CHIEF IMPORTS into Mughal India were bullion, a few metals in short supply in India (copper, lead, tin, zinc and mercury), borax, sulphur, amber and coral; musk and porcelain were imported from China; fruits came from Central Asia, coffee from Arabia, rhinoceros horn (a supposed aphrodisiac), ivory and slaves from Ethiopia, spices from the East Indies, horses from the Middle East and Central Asia, a few elephants from Sri Lanka and Myanmar, sea-shells from the Maldives—'used in Bengal, and other places, as a species of small money,' says Bernier—pearls from Bahrain, and so on. From Europe was imported a small amount of high-quality woollen, silk, velvet, wines and spirits, glassware and fancy items; high quality tobacco was imported from America.

The main items of export from India remained virtually unchanged from the previous centuries—cotton textiles (from most parts of India), pepper (from Kerala), rice and sugar (from Bengal). India also exported a good amount of indigo, some pulses, wheat and oil, as well as lac, wax, coconut products and lesser spices like ginger and turmeric. The only new export items were saltpetre to Europe, raw silk (from Bengal) and skins (from Coromandel) to Japan. There was also some slave trade by the Dutch and the Portuguese, and occasionally by the English too.

The Middle East and South-East Asia were the main markets for cotton goods, India's chief export product; Africa and the Far East took some, and the Americas and Europe took small quantities. Calico was traditionally exported to South-east Asia and East Africa; the Portuguese extended this trade to West Africa, and also to Brazil which had a large number of African slaves. The established markets for fine muslin were Persia, Arabia and Egypt, and in this too, the Portuguese extended the market to North-west Africa. There was good market in South-east Asia for Indian fancy textiles, like painted and patterned cloth, chintzes, short-dyed calico and cotton-silk interwoven cloth.

Indian cotton began to penetrate into Europe in the second decade of the seventeenth century, initially the coarse cloth because of its cheapness, and later the finer varieties. In the beginning, the volume involved in this trade was negligible, but it rose sharply in the second half of the century, and by the 1680s, the value of Indian cotton goods sold in Europe by the East India Company amounted to eighty-three per cent of the total value of the company's trade. Towards the close of the seventeenth century, there was also some increase in the export of silk, taffeta and brocades from India to Europe, as a result of improvement in the quality of these products after the English brought in expert weavers and dyers from England to supervise production. In the course of time, the popularity of Indian textiles spread throughout Europe, thanks to the enterprise of English and Dutch traders.

Still, a good amount of the Indian goods carried by the English and the Dutch in Mughal times was for sale in the Afro-Asian markets, especially in South-east Asia. The profit from this trade was essential for Europeans to finance the purchase of spices from South-east Asia for export to Europe, for there was at this time a prejudice in Europe against exporting precious metals, and not enough bullion was available for foreign trade. Moreover, the economy of the Moluccas, the main source of spices, was not sufficiently monetized at this time, so traders had to barter Indian goods, especially textiles, for spices.

These activities of European traders certainly boosted India's exports, and competition among Europeans enabled Indian producers to get good prices for their products. The volume involved in this trade was nevertheless small. According to Moreland's estimate, at the time of Akbar's death, 'the total volume of Indian foreign trade was probably less than 60,000 tuns . . . roughly equivalent to from 24,000 to 36,000 net tons of the present day.' Exports grew but slowly, and it was only by the first decade of the twentieth century that the net tonnage rose to 6.75 million tons—it took 300 years to achieve a 200-fold increase.

Despite the low volume of Indian exports, bullion continued to flow into India. 'The importation of . . . articles into Hindustan does not . . . occasion the export of gold and silver; because the merchants who bring them find it advantageous to take back, in exchange, the production of the country,' says Bernier. 'Supplying itself with articles of foreign growth or manufacture, does not, therefore, prevent Hindustan from absorbing a large portion of the gold and silver of the world, admitted through a variety of channels, while there is scarcely an opening for its return.'

This flow of bullion into India did not however vitalize the economy, as much of the new wealth was mopped up by the ruling class or was buried secretly. Though the European connection enriched some regions and some groups of producers and traders, India, on the whole, could not benefit from it because of the 'economic parasitism' that ate away the vitals of the Indian economy.

A NEW FEATURE of India's foreign trade during Mughal times was the gradual displacement of traditional overland trade routes by new sea routes. The two main land routes out of India were from Lahore to Kabul and from there to China and Europe, and from Multan to Kandahar and from there to Persia. 'Down to Kabul every year come 7, 8, or 10,000 horses and up to it, from Hindustan, come every year caravans of 10, 15, 20,000 heads-of-houses, bringing slaves, white cloth, sugar-candy, refined and common sugars, and aromatic roots,' says Babur. 'Many a trader is not content with a profit of 30 or 40 on 10. In Kabul can be had products of Khurasan, Rum (Turkey), Iraq and Chin (China); while it is Hindustan's own market.'

These overland trade routes, though in use since ancient times, swarmed with brigands, so traders had to travel in large caravans under escort, and they sometimes had to wait for a few months for a caravan to form up. Further, caravan traffic was seasonal—there was no traffic during the rainy season when the roads were impassable, and the traffic was thin in summer when fodder was scarce. The volume of goods carried by the land route therefore could not have been high, probably only a tenth of what went by sea in the seventeenth century. The future belonged to sea trade.

Sea traffic was of course entirely seasonal, borne by the winds. During the south-west monsoon, from June to September, no ship could safely enter or leave any Indian port; thereafter the winds gradually changed direction and became northerly, which favoured departures from India, but made it difficult for ships to reach the northern ports. The ideal time for ships to arrive in India was therefore around September, after the fury of the south-west monsoon had abated; they could then leave by January, taking advantage of the northerly winds. September to January was thus the busy shipping season in India, though sailings to the east could be made till April. But even in the best of seasons, the sea passage between Europe and India was perilous—only half of the thirty-three carracks that sailed from India for Portugal between 1590 and 1599 survived the journey.

Before the arrival of the Portuguese, the Indian Ocean, especially the Arabian Sea, was dominated by the Arabs. 'Pagans do not navigate much, but it is the Moors who carry the merchandise,' says Ludovico di Varthema, who was in India in the first decade of the sixteenth century. Once the Portuguese arrived on the scene, they easily dominated the seas, using force to control trade. The Arabs were no match for the Portuguese on the high seas. For a short while the Portuguese in the Arabian Sea were harried by Kunj-Ali, a pirate chief operating from a lagoon in north Kerala with the connivance of the Zamorin, the local ruler. Kunj-Ali styled himself as the 'Lord of the Indian Seas' and issued sea licenses in the Portuguese style; once he even defeated a Portuguese naval force sent against him, but he was finally captured by the Portuguese and possibly executed by them in Goa.

The Mughals did not pay much attention to what happened on the seas around India. It was not important to them. Says Della Valle, who was in India in the first quarter of the seventeenth century: 'The Mogol is a very great and wealthy King, whose Revenues arise from his own Lands and not from the Sea; and one to whom that little which is to be had from the Sea . . . is nothing . . . because it accrues rather to some small Captain of his, as the Governor of Surat, and the like, than to the King himself.' According to the estimate of Sarkar, the gross revenue from import duties in the Mughal empire was 'probably less than three million rupees a year (out of which two-fifths came from Surat), so that customs yielded less than one per cent of the total revenue of the state.'

Europeans were minor players in India at the time of Aurangzeb's death. But the scene would change dramatically within decades. The Mughal empire would crumble. And the British would seize the political and economic destiny of India. But this potential, like the secret of a giant tree hidden in a tiny seed, was not evident at the close of the seventeenth century.

Chapter Six

MASTERS
AND SLAVES

The Alien Face

'THE GREAT MOGOL is a foreigner in Hindoustan, he finds himself in an hostile country, or nearly so'—so wrote Bernier early in the reign of Aurangzeb.

Bernier was mistaken. No one in the seventeenth century considered the Mughals as foreigners or questioned their right to rule in India. The legitimacy of their imperial authority, in fact, became so rooted in the political psyche of India that an alternative to it seemed inconceivable even in 1857, a century after the collapse of the empire, when the rebels against British rule proclaimed the phantom emperor, Bahadur Shah, as their sovereign. In Mughal times, there was no sharp sense of Indianness by which to segregate the foreigner. There was no xenophobia against the Mughals. Their imperial expansion was of course resisted by their victims, but not because they were foreigners. The concept of the nation state, by which Bernier was judging the Mughals, would rise in India only two centuries later, in the mid-nineteenth century.

The Mughal rule was alien only in the sense that the ruler and his subjects together did not constitute a stable political entity. There was no emotional bond, no sense of nationhood. But then, this was true of all medieval Indian kingdoms, Muslim as well as Hindu. The people had no loyalty towards their rulers, and the rulers no regard for their subjects. The people were prey, the rulers predators.

The establishment of Muslim rule in India at the close of the twelfth century introduced a few additional elements of antagonism into the prevailing alienation between rulers and subjects, as the Turko-Afghans were separated from their subjects by race, language and religion, especially religion. This polarization however had become less marked by the time the Mughals arrived in India, as a certain amount of cultural interchange had taken place between Muslims and Hindus over the centuries.

Yet, curiously, the chasm between the monarch and his subjects appeared greater under the Mughals than under the Delhi Sultans. This was largely because of the forbiddingly monolithic and adamantine nature of the Mughal monarchy. In the Delhi Sultanate, because the ruling dynasty changed every few generations, and the empire itself periodically broke up and re-formed, the sultans never came to acquire the kind of Pharaonic stature that the Mughal emperor would enjoy. Power in the Delhi Sultanate was diffused, which made its political system permeable, allowing the folkways and traditions of the local people to seep into it everywhere. Beneath the skin of their alien rule, a complex web of neural connections integrated the Turko-Afghans with India and its people. This was even more evident in the Deccan sultanates, where there was a virtual sharing of power with the local elite. In contrast, in the Mughal empire, there was an insurmountable barrier between the emperor and his subjects, even between the emperor and his amirs.

Such overwhelming concentration of power in the hands of the emperor did not matter much to the common people. The manner in which political power was organized in the state, or even who the rulers were, was primarily of concern only to the power elite. For the people, it made little difference whether they were ruled by Turks or Afghans, by Mughals, Rajputs or Marathas. They were all rapacious. Being ruled by Hindu kings was not necessarily a blessing for Hindus. As the Jesuits noted about the Bijapuri occupation of Thanjavur, 'The people have submitted to the yoke of a conqueror from whom they get less cruelty and more justice than from their own sovereigns.' It was only the benevolent efficiency of individual rulers like Sher Shah or Akbar that gave the people respite from oppression.

THE MUGHAL ADMINISTRATIVE system was the creation of Akbar. In the beginning, when Mughal power was confined to the principality of Kabul, governance was a simple affair for Babur, as the frontiers of his domain were, so to speak, within his sight, and his subjects within the range of his voice. He could rule the kingdom directly. This was not possible in India. But Babur's reign in India was too short for him to deal with the administrative problem. Humayun had grand plans, but was unable to execute them. So it was left to Akbar to build Mughal administration,

Akbar did more than just set up an administrative machinery; he also created a unique and almost supernatural aura around the Mughal dynasty, so that for about three centuries, even after the disintegration of the empire, his descendants enjoyed the exclusive, never-ever-questioned prerogative to occupy the throne of Delhi. Unlike in the Delhi Sultanate, there would be no dynastic changes in the Mughal empire. Furthermore, the emperor enjoyed, at least until the second decade of the eighteenth century, absolute and untrammeled personal sway.

Akbar, for all his liberalism, was an absolute autocrat. Though he prominently associated Hindus with his administration, he did not share power with them, or with anyone else. His nobles were merely his servants. He was not dependent on them: they were dependent on him.

This was not an entirely new development. Though Babur and Humayun generally treated their amirs as comrades in arms, and not as lackeys, it is significant that Babur took the title Padshah (emperor) while his ancestors were content to call themselves Mirzas (princes). Akbar completed the process by assuming the title Shahanshah, king of kings.

Early Islam, reflecting the values of the tribal society in which it developed, had no strong monarchical tradition, but gradually, under the influence of pre-Islamic Persian culture, the idea that the king was divinely ordained and that he was the shadow of god on earth began to take root in Muslim political thought. Persian poet Firdawsi thus spoke of monarchs as divine agents endowed with *farr*, a supernatural effulgence, and Spanish-born scholar Turtushi spoke of the king's divine right to rule, ranking him next only to prophets and angels. Balban, the first theoretician of Muslim monarchy in India, maintained in the late thirteenth century that 'the king's heart is the mirror of the divine attributes'. Wrote Abul Fazl: 'Royalty is a light emanating from God, and a ray from the sun, the illuminator of the universe, the argument of the book of perfection, the receptacle of all virtues.'

Thus the king came to be looked on as *zill-i-subhani*, the shadow of god, whose power could not be questioned. Wrote Sheikh Abdul Haqq during the reign of Jahangir: 'No rank is higher than that of a king . . . The order and arrangement of worldly affairs depend upon the king.' And Sheikh Ahmad Sirhindi, Abdul Haqq's contemporary, wrote: 'The sultan in relation to the world is like the soul in relation to the body. If the soul is healthy, the body is healthy, and if the soul is sick, the body is sick. The integrity of the ruler means the integrity of the world; his corruption, the corruption of the world.'

The alternative to monarchy was chaos, it was held. As a common Muslim saying had it, 'If there was no Sultan, people would devour each other.' Even a tyrannical, rapacious ruler had to be obeyed, just as 'the eating of carrion in time of dire need' is permitted, argued Barani, a fourteenth-century Indian scholar. Tyranny was considered a visitation of god. In support of such views Muslim jurists quoted a saying attributed to Prophet Muhammad: 'Whoever obeys me, verily and truly will have obeyed God and whoever obeys the Imam, that is to say, the sultan, will have obeyed me, and whoever rebels against me will have rebelled against God, and whoever rebels against the sultan, verily and truly he will have rebelled against me.'

The power that Muslim jurists granted to the sultan had its corresponding obligations, and he was required to function within the ambit of Islamic law and convention. In theory, he had only executive and judicial functions, no legislative powers, for the law had already been laid down by the Prophet and elaborated by Muslim tradition. In practice, however, he had considerable freedom of action. This was because the interpretation of Islamic law varied greatly, and the king could always find some conniving jurist to validate his decisions. Virtually, therefore, the will of the emperor was the law. 'As regards the laws,' says Pelsaert, 'they are scarcely observed at all, for the administration is absolutely autocratic.'

Autocracy did not necessarily mean tyranny, and by and large the Mughal emperors strove to provide good government, within the constraints of the prevailing political environment. None of them was systematically vicious or tyrannical. All of them professed high ideals. 'It is the repose and prosperity of my subjects that it behoves me to consult; nor are these to be sacrificed to anything besides the demands of justice, the maintenance of royal authority, and the security of the State,' maintained Aurangzeb. However, since it was the emperor himself who decided what was good for the people, he could by and large do exactly as he pleased.

In fact, for all the professed high-mindedness of the Mughal emperor, his subjects suffered brutal oppression, though the fault was more in the system—and the tyranny of officials—than in the arbitrariness of the emperor. Charges Manucci: 'As to their government . . . there could be nothing more tyrannical, and . . . there are slaves in Turkey whose condition is preferable to that of the free people in this country.' The Mughal emperor did not have the administrative means to control his vast empire effectively and ensure good government. Nor was it a priority with him to have that kind of control—he was alert to the developments that threatened his throne or curtailed his power, but the sufferings of the people were a subsidiary concern to him.

THE MUGHAL EMPIRE, like all medieval Muslim states, was theocratic. The state existed to enforce the laws of god. This meant that the laws of the state had to be in conformity with the canons of Islam, and that anyone who violated the laws of Islam violated the laws of the state too. The Muslim state was a community of believers, so only Muslims could be its citizens. Non-Muslims, merely by being non-Muslims, offended the law. Heresy was crime; apostasy, treason.

To permit non-Muslims to live and practise their religion in an Islamic state was, therefore, from the orthodox point of view, to connive with crime as well as sin. It was a religious and political obligation of Muslim rulers to extirpate the infidels within the state and to wage holy wars (jihad) against infidel states, thus to turn *dar-ul-harb*, the land of infidels, into *dar-ul-Islam*, the land of Islam. Strictly speaking, the only options for infidels in a Muslim kingdom were to accept Islam or to suffer death.

Such was the theory. The practice was quite different. As the Arab empire expanded into the lands of other established religions, it became impossible to enforce the death-or-Islam rule, as infidels in the new territories were too firm in their own faith to accept Islam, and too numerous to be killed. Moreover, the subject people were needed to do the productive work which Muslims, as the ruling class, usually shirked. To accommodate this new reality, Islam introduced the concept of the *zimmi*, the protected non-Muslim, who could be, on certain conditions, permitted to live and work and practise his religion in a Muslim state. Initially, this concession was given only to the people of the faiths related to Islam—Christians, Jews and Zoroastrians—but was later extended to Hindus as well, though some theologians argued that Hindus, being of a totally alien religion, could not enjoy protected status and had to be put to death if they did not accept Islam.

In any case, the protection offered to non-Muslims in a Muslim state was, in theory, only a transitional arrangement, a reprieve given for them to reform and change faith. Their lives were spared only provisionally; they were permitted to live only on sufferance. And as long as they remained infidels, they had to suffer numerous humiliating disabilities—they were required at all times to be respectful and submissive to Muslims; they were not to wear fine clothes, ride horseback or carry arms; their dress had to be distinctive, so that they might not be mistaken for Muslims. They must not build houses in Muslim residential areas; there should be no noisy lamentations to mourn their dead. In practising their religion, they had to take care not to give offence to Muslims, and they were not allowed to propagate their religion; they were permitted to retain their old temples, but not allowed to repair them or build new ones. The public celebration of their fairs and festivals was restricted.

They had to pay jizya, the poll tax, and pay all other taxes at double the rate which Muslims had to pay.

Under such constrictive measures, it was hoped, Hinduism would desiccate and perish. That did not happen. Yet there was no alternative in India but to accommodate Hindus. There was therefore never any frenzied general destruction of temples by sultans in India, nor any wanton slaughter of Hindus, even in the worst of times. It was, however, common to demolish the chief temple of a captured city and erect a mosque on its site, to demonstrate that the victor had triumphed not only over the enemy's army, but over the enemy's gods as well. To destroy Hindu temples was to prove the powerlessness of Hindu gods—it was the medieval equivalent of capturing the enemy's standard. Similarly, though Muslim rulers setting out against an infidel or heretic kingdom habitually spoke of their campaign as a holy war, it was often just a convenient fig-leaf to cover the shame of naked aggression. The pursuit of power, not the propagation of faith, was the motive force of military and political action by Muslim rulers in India, even by Aurangzeb.

Much of the theocratic fire-breathing and sabre-rattling by Indian sultans was just theatricality, while in practice they quietly compromised on many of the orthodox proscriptions against infidels, to meet the exigencies of the Indian situation. But they had to be careful in pursuing liberal policies, for to dilute theocracy was to dilute the power and wealth of the Muslim ruling class and alienate them.

The most radical measures to liberalize the Muslim state in India were taken by Akbar, who treated Hindus as equal citizens, instead of excluding them from power and wealth. In 1562, Akbar banned the forced conversion of prisoners to Islam, and followed it with the abolition of the pilgrim tax and jizya. Further, he permitted re-conversions from Islam to Hinduism, allowed Hindu girls forcibly married to Muslims to be restored to their parents, repealed the death penalty for blasphemy, and sought to modify Muslim and Hindu personal laws through various decrees.

Akbar's liberal policies were continued by Jahangir, who ordered that no one 'should . . . force Islam on anyone'. With Shah Jahan, however, the policy began to change, and Aurangzeb reverted the empire to theocracy. But even Aurangzeb appointed Hindus to top positions—a Hindu, Raghunath, was for a while his assistant revenue minister, and there were more Hindu mansabdars in his service than that of any other Mughal emperor. On the whole, there was much more religious freedom in India than in contemporary Europe (with its inquisition, religious massacres and witch-hunts) or in any Muslim state outside India. Says

Thomas Coryat, the British eccentric who publicly blasphemed Prophet Muhammad in India: 'If I had spoken thus much in Turkey or Persia against Mahomet, they would have rested me upon a spitt.' Says Terry: 'All religions are tolerated, and their priests held in good esteeme.' It was only in contrast to the passivity and broad tolerance of Hinduism that Islam seemed virulent.

In any case, the bulk of India's population was little affected by theocracy, as most of its disabilities, except jizya, were directed against the Hindu ruling classes. Even Aurangzeb's temple demolitions did not greatly affect the common people, because the demolitions were largely confined to urban centres—in the rural areas, where the vast majority of Hindus lived, there were no great temples to be demolished, only small shrines, and there were hardly any Muslims around to do the demolition either. What hit the common people, and hit them hard in the stomach, where it hurt them most, was the imposition of jizya.

Jizya was a pre-Islamic tax, collected by the Byzantine and Sasanian rulers from conquered people. The Arab empire gave it an exclusively religious cast and imposed it on its non-Muslim subjects as a commutation tax, to spare their lives and to let them practise their religion. In India it was first collected during the Arab invasion of Sind in the early-eighth-century; when the Turks established the Delhi Sultanate nearly 500 years later, it was imposed in Hindustan.

The history of the tax thereafter was haphazard. It is not even certain that jizya was systematically collected by the Delhi sultans. In Kashmir, which came under Muslim rule in the mid-fourteenth century, jizya was imposed late in the century, but was abolished almost immediately afterward, when even cow slaughter was banned for a while in deference to Hindu sentiments; in the Deccan, jizya was abolished in Golconda in the mid-sixteenth century; and in the Mughal empire, Akbar abolished it in 1564. Akbar, says Abul Fazl, abolished jizya 'in spite of the disapproval of statesmen, and of the [loss of] great revenue and of much chatter on the part of the ignorant'. Aurangzeb reimposed it 105 years later, in 1679. His great-grandson Farrukh-siyar reversed the policy in 1713, but was compelled to reimpose jizya four years later. Finally, another great-grandson of Aurangzeb, Muhammad Shah, abolished it in 1720.

Anatomy of the Empire

AMONG THE MUGHALS, the sabre decided succession. This enabled the fittest to survive and rule. Though the custom among the Turks and the Mongols of Central Asia was to divide the kingdom among the sons of the monarch—with the throne and the main portion of the kingdom going to the eldest son, and the younger sons holding autonomous but subsidiary charge of their realms—such divisions were often nullified subsequently by wars among the brothers. In India, Babur and Humayun divided their kingdom among their sons, but the question did not arise with Akbar, as Jahangir was the only son to survive him. On Jahangir's death, the issue of division was pre-empted by Shah Jahan liquidating all rival claimants. During the war of succession at the end of Shah Jahan's reign, there was some talk about partitioning the empire, but Aurangzeb's usurpation thwarted the move; Aurangzeb in his will is said to have asked his sons to share the empire, but Muazzam ignored the suggestion and won the throne in a war of succession.

The struggle for power among the Mughals was not just between brothers, but at times between father and son. It was an occupational hazard of the Mughal emperor that he could not reign without forever looking over his shoulder to keep track of the movements of his brothers, cousins and sons. Akbar, Jahangir, Shah Jahan and Aurangzeb all had to face rebellions by their sons. In the political arena, the Timurids played to win, no matter who their opponent was, not allowing kinship or sentiment to sway political or military decisions. The Mughal motto, as Jahangir once stated, was: 'A king should deem no one his relation.'

Jahangir acted on that precept, blinding and imprisoning one rebel son (Khusrav) and driving another (Shah Jahan) into exile; Shah Jahan and Aurangzeb cold-bloodedly exterminated their brothers, cousins and nephews, and even Akbar found it necessary to execute his cousin Abul Kasim, Kamran's son. 'It is,' says Shah Jahan's chronicler Muhammad Salih Kambu, 'entirely lawful for the great sovereigns to rid this mortal world of the existence of their brothers and other relations, whose annihilation is conducive to the common good.'

Eternal vigilance was the price of power. 'The art of reigning is so delicate, that a King's jealousy should be awakened by his very shadow,' maintained Aurangzeb. He had no illusions about his sons, and kept a constant watch over them, at one time or other imprisoning three of his sons and driving a fourth into exile. 'The distrust among these princes is so acute that father does not trust the son, nor the son his father,' says Manucci. In the royal family, a brother was not merely a rival but a mortal enemy. That was how it was nearly everywhere at all times in royal households—it was by wading through a pool of the blood of his brothers that the great emperor Asoka, according to Buddhist sources, seized the Maurya throne in ancient India, and that was how Rana Sanga of Mewar too came to power. Bloody successions were common in Vijayanagar. And in Khandesh in Mughal times, says Faizi Sirhindi, 'it was the established custom . . . that the reigning potentate kept his sons, brothers, and other relations in confinement, to guard against attempts upon the throne; so these unhappy persons, with their wives and families, passed all their lives in confinement.' At one time, there were as many as fifty princes of Khandesh confined in the Asirgarh fort.

IN THIS CLIMATE of distrust and insecurity, the critical requirement for the effective exercise of power by the emperor was for him to keep himself fully informed about what was going on in the empire. The Mughals were particularly thorough about it. Intelligence reports from an army of public and secret reporters and spies flowed into the royal court in a continuous stream from every corner of the far-flung empire, informing the emperor about the state of the provinces and what the princes and the great amirs were saying and doing. 'In every quarter of the empire there are officials who keep an eye on everything,' says Manucci. Ambassador Norris noticed, while visiting the governor of Surat, that there was 'ye Mogulls secretary who tooke minutes of all yt was saide & passd, & others likewise of ye same nature yt wrote down their Remarks, all wch is sent to ye Mogull.'

No secrets could be kept from the emperor. 'Aurangzib,' says Manucci, 'had such good spies that they knew (if it may be so said) even men's very thoughts. Nor did anything go on anywhere in the realm, above all in the city of Delhi, without his being informed.' But just as secrets could not be kept from the emperor, the emperor could not keep any secrets either. Says Hawkins: 'There is no matter passeth in the Mogols court in secret, but it is knowne halfe an houre after, giving a small matter to the writer of that day, for there is nothing that passeth but it is written, and writers appointed by turnes.'

India had a good communication system even under the Delhi Sultans, and Babur built on that to set up an express link with Kabul, stationing post horses at regular intervals. Sher Shah and Akbar elaborated and refined the system further, covering Hindustan with a network of roads, caravanserais and communication centres. Runners supplemented horsemen in carrying the post—runners in fact were quicker over rugged terrain, and were known to cover the distance of 900 kilometres between Delhi and Ahmadabad in twelve days. 'In India all the letters which Kings, Generals of Armies, and Governors of Provinces send by footmen go much faster than by horsemen,' says Tavernier. Says Monserrate: 'They [the runners] practise running in shoes made of lead, or train themselves by repeatedly lifting their feet and moving their legs till their heels touch their buttocks.' Akbar is said to have had as many as 4,000 runners in his employ. But this postal system was only for official use; market couriers and hired runners carried private mail.

'The King's letters or firmans to the chief lords or princes are transmitted with incredible speed,' writes Pelsaert, 'because royal runners are posted in the villages 4 or 5 *kos* (about 12 or 16 kilometers) apart, taking their turns of duty throughout the day and night, and they take over a letter immediately on its arrival, run with it to the next village in a breath, and hand it over to another messenger. So the letter goes steadily on, and will travel 80 *kos* (about 250 kilometres) between night and day. Further the King has pigeons kept everywhere, to carry letters in time of need or great urgency.' To withstand hunger and fatigue the runner ate opium and *bhang*, says Pelsaert, and he wore 'a plume on his head and two bells at his belt', to distinguish his office and to claim the right of way. 'Throughout India the sides of most of the roads are planted with avenues of trees, and where there are no trees planted, at every 500 paces small pieces of stone are fixed, which the inhabitants of the nearest villages are bound to whiten from time to time, so that the letter carriers can distinguish the road on dark and rainy nights.'

'For the Security of Letters sent abroad to the principal Ministers, or the Emperor, they are inclos'd in a large hollow Bambou of a Foot length, at one end of which is a Head or Cover two Inches long, which after the Letter is put in, is join'd close to the Bambou, and upon that joining the Seal is fixt, to prevent taking out the Letter without breaking the Seal,' notes Ovington. 'This preserves the Letter neat and clean, unsullied by Rain or Dust, on being carried from Hand to Hand . . .' The imperial firmans issued to potentates, rajas and princes bore 'the royal seal with the impression of the [emperor's] hand in saffron colour,' says Manucci; firmans to other officials were attested by the royal seal only, 'with the countermark of the chief vizier'. The Muslim custom was that a person should affix his seal at the top of the letter while writing to an inferior, but should place it at the bottom while writing to a superior, and at the back of the letter while writing to an equal.

The Mughal intelligence and communication system, like everything else, showed a marked decline in standards in the second half of the reign of Aurangzeb. The news reporters, says Manucci, 'being at a distance from the court, do not acquit themselves of their duty as loyal subjects ought.' Confirms Bernier: 'The Great Mogol sends a Vakea-Nevis to various provinces; that is, persons whose business it is to communicate every event that takes place; but there is generally a disgraceful collusion between these officers and the governor, so that their presence seldom restrains the tyranny exercised over the unhappy people.' Sometimes provincial officers terrorized news-writers. Thus, when a news-writer reported to Aurangzeb that Amin Khan, the governor of Gujarat, had held court while drunk, 'the governor in open durbar ordered the moustaches and beard of the news-writer to be pulled out and flung into the air,' says Hamiduddin Khan Nimacha.

The decline of the intelligence and communication system under Aurangzeb was a symptom of the general decline of Mughal administrative efficiency. And the disruption of communications aggravated the inefficiency, as decisions then had to be made on the basis of misleading or incomplete information. Says John Fryer, a late-seventeenth-century traveller, 'While the Generals and Vocanovices consult to deceive the emperor, on whom he depends for the true state of things, it can never be otherwise but that they must be misrepresented, when the Judgment he makes must be by false perspective.'

Still, the rivers of communication continued to flood unabated through the reign of Aurangzeb. The Mughal government was a *kaghazi* raj, a paper government. From the reign of Akbar on, copies of all state communications were systematically preserved, along with a vast number of records and accounts, and the daily log of all that the emperor said and did. In the course of time, a mountainous pile of documents accumulated at the imperial capital. Unfortunately almost all of it was lost in the chaos of the eighteenth century, leaving only fragments in the provincial archives.

THE MUGHAL EMPIRE had, at the end of Aurangzeb's reign, twenty-one provinces, and was the largest empire in the history of India. For the effective administration of this vast territory, the empire was divided into a number of graded units, in the first instance into Subas (provinces), each headed by a Subedar (governor), who was, says Abul Fazl, 'the vicegerent of His Majesty. The troops and people of the province are under his orders . . .' Initially, the Subedar was in overall charge of the province, but Akbar towards the close of his reign took revenue powers away from the Subedar and vested them with the provincial Diwan, who functioned directly under the imperial Diwan. In other respects, the provincial government was a scaled-down replica of the central government, except that the governor had no power to impose capital punishment or mutilations, save in a military emergency. The Subedars reported directly to the emperor, while the provincial Diwans routed their communications through the imperial Diwan.

Each Suba was further divided into two separate sets of units, one for revenue collection and the other for military administration. The boundaries of the revenue and military units were not always identical, as the rationales for their composition were different, but such bureaucratic over-refinements, instead of promoting efficiency, often led to complications, especially as revenue officers invariably had to seek the help of military officers to enforce payment of taxes.

For revenue purposes, the Suba was divided into Sarkars (districts) and then again into Parganas (sub-districts), while for military administration, it was divided into Faujdaris (under Faujdars), which were again divided into Thanas, military outposts commanded by Thanedars. The Faujdar was responsible for the maintenance of law and order in his district and for the suppression of rebels. 'These Faujdars have to supervise the roads,' says Manucci, 'and should any merchant or traveller be robbed in daylight, they are obliged to pay compensation. If robbed at night, it is the traveller's fault for not having halted earlier, and loses all, without his complaint being heard.' The Faujdars and even some of the important Thanedars were appointed directly by the central government, while lower officers were appointed by the Subedars. All senior local officers were periodically rotated to prevent them from developing vested interests in their territory.

The basic administrative unit of the state was, as it has always been, the village, which was in most matters self-administering. Indian villages generally had clan homogeneity, and functioned under a headman chosen according to the custom of the clan. Where a village was made up of different clans, the headman was usually appointed by an external authority.

MAJOR TOWNS AND cities, though nominally under the local governor, had their own administrative set-up under Kotwals (town prefects) whose functions were nearly identical to those of the Nagaraka in the ancient Mauryan empire. The term Kotwal was derived from *kotpal*, commander of the fort, but in Mughal times his functions were of civilian administration, to regulate everyday life in the town. He was assisted by subordinate officers in charge of the wards (*mohallas*) into which the town was divided.

The Kotwal was, according to Abul Fazl, required to 'engage the citizens in a pledge of reciprocal assistance, and bind them to a common participation of weal and woe.' Thevenot speaks of the officer as 'Cotwal, who is the Criminal Judge', but Badauni describes him as the chief of police. 'The chief of police,' says Badauni, 'was to take cognizance of the streets and houses of the city one by one, and to require of the heads and chief persons of every street a bond that he would perform the following duties: That he would keep a close watch on every one who came in or went out, of whatever degree he might be, whether merchant, soldier or otherwise; that he would not allow troublesome and disorderly fellows or thieves to take up their abode in the city; that if he saw any one whose expenditure was greater than his receipts, he would follow the matter up, and represent to the Emperor, through the chief police officer, that this extravagance of his was probably paid for with money irregularly acquired; that he would inform the chief of police of all rejoicings and feasts, and mournings and lamentations which might take place, especially marriages, births, feasts and such like.' The Kotwal, through his assistants, had to keep 'in every street and lane and bazaar, and at every ford of the river' a trustworthy person to gather information about 'everything that went on, whether good or bad'.

The Kotwal was also required to set the idle to work, fix wages and prices, control weights and measures, and organize conservancy work. Further, according to Abul Fazl, the Kotwal had to keep track of the properties of those who died intestate, keep out fanatics and cheats from the town, organize the illumination of the town during festivals, protect the honour of women, prevent forced sati, demarcate areas for burial grounds and quarters for butchers, enforce the emperor's social regulations, and so on. 'He should direct that no ox or buffalo or horse or camel be slaughtered, and forbid the restriction of personal liberty and the selling of slaves,' notes Abul Fazl. He was also required to prepare a register of the inhabitants of his area, listing their professions and activities. It was the Kotwal's responsibility to control guilds, and to ensure that there were no illegal exactions.

The gates of walled cities were closed at sunset. Tavernier says that if a traveller planned to leave the town at night, he should leave before sunset, for the gates were closed then, and no one would be let out after that. The Kotwal was responsible for robberies, and if he was not able to recover stolen goods, he had to make good the loss.

THE MUGHAL IMPERIAL system was strong in serving the primary interests of the emperor—in preserving his power and in collecting revenue—but was weak in providing good government. As the empire grew in size, it became increasingly difficult to prevent oppression by provincial chiefs, who often raised all sorts of difficulties in executing imperial orders. Says Manucci about the conditions under Aurangzeb: 'Those who are at a distance pay very little attention to his (the emperor's) orders.' In one extreme instance, local officials ignored Aurangzeb's written order to restore to a woman the lands confiscated from her, and they continued to raise difficulties in implementing the order though Aurangzeb repeated it seven times. So when the woman approached Aurangzeb for the eighth time, he told her that 'as they (local officers) would not obey, he could do nothing, and she must lay her plaints before God.' Similarly, when William Norris told provincial officials that he had Aurangzeb's permission to carry goods without paying customs duty, the Faujdar said that 'the king's orders were worth nothing in this matter'. And when Peter Mundy invoked the authority of the emperor and the governor against being charged tolls near Allahabad, the local officers not only disregarded the plea but went on to abuse the emperor and the governor in obscene language.

Such problems were there even during the reign of Jahangir. Writes Pelsaert: 'Whereas each governor ought to protect the people under him, they have in fact by subtle means drained the people dry, because they know very well that poor suppliants cannot get a hearing at the King's court; and consequently the country is impoverished, and the citizens have lost heart.' Jahangir notes in his memoirs of 'having again heard that the amirs on the borders interfere with authority in matters that do not concern them.' Says Bernier, 'Thus do ruin and desolation overspread the land. The provincial governors . . . are so many petty tyrants.'

'Every man honours the king, but no man obeys him'—that was how the English merchants in India saw the Mughal emperor's predicament. 'He is to be regarded as King of the plains or the open roads only,' says Pelsaert about Jahangir; 'for in many places you can travel only with a strong body of men, or on payment of heavy tolls to rebels . . . [In the hill country] they recognize only their Rajas . . . Jahangir, whose name implies that he grasps the whole world, must therefore be regarded as ruling no more than half the dominions which he claims, since there are nearly as many rebels as subjects . . . The Governors are usually bribed by the thieves to remain inactive, for avarice dominates manly honour, and, instead of maintaining troops, they fill and adorn their *mahals* with beautiful women, and seem to have the pleasure-house of the whole world within their walls.' The general tendency of local chieftains and provincial officials in Mughal India, indeed, even of the common people, was to defy authority whenever they could get away with it—and often they did get away with it.

Part of the emperor's difficulty in maintaining effective control over the provinces was that the empire was too diverse in people, language and customs, so that no single set of rules could apply in all parts of the empire. As Erskine puts it, 'India, in reality, was rather a congeries of little states under one prince, than one regular and uniformly governed kingdom.' Not only that, different parts of the empire were in different degrees of subordination to the emperor—the Rajput rajas, for instance, were semi-autonomous; they only paid a fixed tribute, though the revenue and general administrative regulations of the empire applied, in theory at any rate, in their dominions, and only the imperial currency was permitted to be used in them. In the hill tracts, tribal chieftains were virtually independent.

THE MUGHAL EMPEROR, despite his administrative limitations, considered himself the lord of the whole of India, and would not recognize any other ruler anywhere in the subcontinent, even those well outside the Mughal frontiers, as independent. Oddly, most of the rulers in India, including the inveterate rebel Shivaji, usually acknowledged the emperor as their suzerain, at least nominally. Even the raja of the obscure principality of Kochi at the southern extremity of the subcontinent is believed to have paid him homage.

Only the kingdoms beyond the Afghan frontier were recognized by the Mughals as sovereign states. They maintained a close though somewhat patronizing relationship with Central Asian rulers—emissaries bearing gifts from India periodically trekked to Central Asia to announce Mughal victories—but they acknowledged only the monarchs of Turkey and Persia as their peers. With Turkey, which was too far away, they had no regular contact, but they cherished their relationship with Persia, keeping up, as was the custom, ambassadorial courtesies even when hostilities broke out between them. Says Manucci, 'When two rajahs are at war they retain ambassadors not only at the court, but often in the army which is opposed to them . . . [so] every intention and every design of an enemy is known to his opponent and to everyone else—so much so, that when an ambassador dispatches a letter to his rajah, it is read out by him in public . . .'

The relationship of the Mughals with European kingdoms was on an entirely different plane from that of their relationship with Asian kingdoms. The power of European states was unknown to the Mughals, and was made suspect by the slander and recriminations the agents of different European nations flung at each other—the Portuguese, for instance, consistently described the English as a petty nation of thieves.

The Mughals considered Europeans more as traders—which in fact was what they were in India—than as political or military entities. Jahangir therefore scornfully dismissed Roe's plea for a trade treaty with England, considering it unbecoming to the stature of the emperor. Nor did William Norris in the reign of Aurangzeb fare any better in negotiating a trade treaty.

European powers no doubt dominated the seas, but as the Mughals did not consider the sea around India as part of their domain, they did not pay much attention to what went on there. European naval interference with pilgrim traffic from Surat to Arabia, and piracy on the high seas, were of course annoyances to the Mughals, but no more than that. Of greater concern to the Mughals should have been the fact that European nations had, in addition to dominating the seas, sunk sucker roots into the Indian soil and anchored themselves at a number of places along the long shoreline of India. But the rudimentary neural network of the Mughal mammoth was not sensitive enough to respond to this intrusion.

Curiously, the earliest warning of the danger of a European conquest of India was sounded during the very first contact between a British trader and the Mughal emperor. When John Mildenhall, the trader, arrived at Akbar's court, the Jesuits entrenched there spread the rumour (as Mildenhall told the emperor) that 'under colour of merchandise wee (the English) would invade your countrey and take some of your forts and put Your Majestie to great trouble.' Later, Jahangir was also similarly cautioned by the Jesuits. The warnings were not taken seriously. The Mughals did not foresee—nor did Europeans themselves foresee—that the European domination of the Indian seas would lead to the European domination of India itself.

All the Emperor's Men

FOR NEARLY TWO centuries after the accession of Akbar, the Mughal empire faced no threat whatever to its existence from any external power. Its fate depended entirely on what happened within the empire, on its spirit and organizational strength, in a sense, on the valour and ability of the emperor. He was its nucleus: everything revolved around him. All the power in the empire radiated from him, and all its resources converged on him.

The administrative system through which this radiation and convergence took place was manned by a group of ranking officers called mansabdars. Unfortunately, the system and the men did not match—the system was complex, its procedures elaborate, but the men who operated it were non-specialists, haphazardly chosen and randomly assigned.

There was nothing like a structured administrative service in the Mughal empire, not even any separation of civil and military services—officers were casually assigned to different posts, and who held what position and with what powers and responsibilities depended entirely on the whim of the emperor. Anyone could be called on by the emperor to perform any duty at any time: sent to organize the revenue administration of a province at one time, then ordered to lead an army into battle, or recalled to do some work at the court. Even poets and theologians were at times assigned to command armies. Some, like Todar Mal, were equally good at finance, general administration and military command, but such officers were rare, and random assignments meant wastage of talent in a talent-scarce environment.

The emperor did not even have a regular council of ministers. The highest officer of the empire was the Vakil, royal deputy, but it was not a regular office, and only two had ever held the position under the Great Mughals, Biram Khan under Akbar, and Asaf Khan under Jahangir and Shah Jahan. The second highest officer was the Vizier, but his functions were ill-defined; at times he functioned as the chief executive officer of the empire, and at times merely as a figurehead. There were even times when there was no Vizier. A jewelled ink-pot was the insignia of his office.

The next ranking officer was the Diwan, the finance minister, whose office was often combined with that of the Vizier. Then came the Mir Bakshi (paymaster-general, who was also the controller of mansabdars and the administrator of the army), the Khan-i-saman (in charge of the royal household and establishments), Chief Sadr (chief ecclesiastical officer-cum-chief justice, who was also in charge of charitable and religious endowments), the Chief Kazi (the expounder of canon law), and the Muhtasib (the regulator of civic life, who controlled the market and enforced Islamic injunctions). There was also a chief of intelligence and communications. An army of mansabdars made up the further rungs of the official hierarchy, and beneath the mansabdars was a host of soldiers, clerks and menials, who held no rank.

There were no racial, national, religious or class criteria for admission into the Mughal service. However, the preponderant majority of Mughal officers were Muslims, and most of the top positions were held by Persians. Nearly seventy per cent of Akbar's mansabdars, according to Moreland's calculation, were foreigners who came to India with Humayun or later. This was inevitable, for the Mughals themselves had only just then settled in India. Moreover, Persia was the role model of the Mughals, so they preferred officers with a Persian background. In the mid-seventeenth century, during Shah Jahan's reign, nearly eighty per cent of the posts of the rank of commander of 500 and above were held by Muslims, of whom non-Indian Muslims constituted over sixty-four per cent of the total, with Persians and Turks together taking nearly fifty-two per cent.

The percentage of foreigners in the Mughal service declined during Aurangzeb's reign, especially in the top echelons of administration. Thus while 62.7 per cent of the officers of the rank of commander of 5000 and above were foreigners in the first half of Aurangzeb's reign, in the second half their percentage dropped sharply to 30.3, according to the calculation of Athar Ali, a modern authority on the Mughal mansabdari system. In contrast, there was at this time a significant and surprising increase in the number of Hindu mansabdars—while Hindus constituted only 22.5 per cent of all officers above the rank of 500 at the end of Akbar's reign, and their position remained at about the same level during Shah Jahan's reign, their percentage rose to 31.7 in the second half of Aurangzeb's reign; the increase in their numbers was even more dramatic in the ranks above 5000, where their percentage rose from 14.3 under Akbar to 32.9 under Aurangzeb.

Hindus, as the subject people, were mostly in the lower strata of Mughal administration, but they had access even to the top posts, though not to the topmost post. No Hindu was ever appointed Vizier. It was not politic for Muslim rulers to push the patronage of Hindus too far, because of the risk of alienating Muslim amirs. Under Akbar there were only 21 Hindu officers of the ranks above 500, and all but four of them—Todar Mal and his son (Khattris) and Birbal and his son (brahmins)—were Rajputs. Later, during the reigns of Shah Jahan and Aurangzeb, an increasing number of Marathas entered the Mughal service. Most of the Hindu officers serving the Mughals came from martial castes, which was natural, given the military character of Mughal government.

UNLIKE IN CONTEMPORARY China, there were no tests or qualifications for admission into Mughal service, nor were there any rules for promotion. It was not even necessary for officers to be literate. Though common soldiers (and even horses) taken into the imperial service were carefully chosen, there was no selection procedure for the appointment of mansabdars. All that was required was for the candidate to catch the emperor's eye, and to have a godfather to push his claim.

It was essential for an officer to have a patron at the court, to advance his career and to counteract the intrigues of his rivals. Often officers had to 'bribe . . . the headman, or make presents to his chamberlains, door-keepers, and sweepers, in order to get their blanket out of the mire,' says Badauni. Ultimately, of course, a mansabdar's fortune depended on the emperor's will. 'The Mogol raises them to dignities, or degrades them to obscurity, according to his own pleasure and caprice,' says Bernier. Seniority counted little, for, as Abul Fazl puts the gloss on imperial whim, 'in the code of just sovereignty, weight is given to wisdom and not to years, and reliance is placed upon abundance of loyalty, not upon age.' Being out of royal favour wrecked careers and ruined lives—Jahangir reports that one of his nobles, whose claim for promotion was long overlooked, took to asceticism.

To rise in service was to rise in the emperor's favour. Artful sycophants thrived in this environment. Though the Mughal emperors were generally clear-eyed enough to see through the fog of adulation that enveloped the court, and pick out true talent—'the numbers of flatterers are unlimited . . . [but] the wise prince holds firmly the thread of discrimination and prudently gives them the go-by,' says Abul Fazl—still, to get ahead in imperial service, it was necessary for an officer, however talented he might be, also to have the talent to win and hold the emperor's favour. On the whole, those who did well at the Mughal court were ambidextrous men, who could please the emperor as well as perform well in office. Thus Todar Mal, who was both competent and courtly, flourished, while Shah Mansur, who did not have courtly graces though he was brilliant as finance minister, lost his life.

The Mughal amirs, except for the few Hindu rajas, were fortune hunters from many lands, who were totally dependent on royal favour for their power and wealth. Being the emperor's creatures, they were entirely obsequious towards their creator. Even the rajas were servile. As British ambassador Norris noted, none of the amirs dared to move a step without the emperor's leave. And they who were servile towards the emperor demanded similar servility from their own subordinates, and so it went all the way down the Mughal hierarchy, everyone obsequious towards his superiors and everyone tyrannical over his subordinates.

Hardly anyone had any loyalty. The only concern of the amir was to be on the winning side. Even so eminent a commander as Jai Singh had no hesitation in abandoning Dara for Aurangzeb in the midst of the succession war, nor did he or any other amir ever raise his voice against Shah Jahan's overthrow and imprisonment. There were occasions when amirs defected to the enemy in the midst of battle, as Abdullah Khan did during the rebellion of Shah Jahan; sometimes they even re-defected, as Jaswant Singh did during Aurangzeb's reign. At lower levels there was even less loyalty. 'The want of order being so great, desertions are very numerous,' says Manucci, 'for today a soldier will be serving in one army and tomorrow in an opposing force; then, when it pleases him, he will rejoin his first service without any hesitation, and as often as not may even be promoted.'

Usually, employment in the imperial service provided lifelong security, provided of course the officer did not offend the emperor. Occasionally, though rarely, there were retirements, sometimes even resignations. Often the emperor persuaded the retiring or resigning officer to stay on, and few could refuse the honour of being indispensable to the emperor. If an officer retired from service, 'the king as a favour continues always to pay to him an allowance for his support. But there is no fixed rule,' says Manucci. Sometimes aged amirs were allowed to shift from active service to honourable sinecures. Thus when an old retainer of Jahangir petitioned that he might be transferred from military service and 'enrolled in the army of prayer', the emperor graciously agreed.

Top amirs were given the privilege of carrying 'drums, trumpets, and other instruments of music . . . before them, together with hands in silver' as symbols of power, says Manucci. The immense gains in power, wealth and honour to be made by being in the emperor's favour, and the loss and disgrace to be suffered by being out of favour, kept the amirs in a flutter all the time. It was safest for them to stay at the court, where they could be in the emperor's eye and could keep a watch on their rivals, but it had the disadvantage that they had to constantly dance attendance on the emperor. In the provinces, on the other hand, they were virtually their own masters, but it had the disadvantage of rendering them vulnerable to the machinations of their rivals at the court. It was tempting for the amir to stay away from the court, but dangerous to do so.

Even the intimates of emperors sometimes had to face the uncertainties of court life. Abul Fazl says that he once got into trouble because of the ill will of Salim. In that predicament, says Abul Fazl, 'I withdrew my hand from everything and tucked my foot into my shirt. I shut my door in the face of both stranger and acquaintance.' During this time he had, he says, 'sometimes meditated my own destruction, and sometimes I thought of becoming a vagabond'. Even when Akbar summoned him, Abul Fazl was reluctant to resume his duties, saying that his heart was not in it. Akbar however finally persuaded him to return. 'If there is a place of repose for mortals, and you can always retire there, why are you so much troubled . . . ?' Akbar asked, and went on to advise, 'The tongues of ill-wishers cannot be stopped. Do you take the right path so far as you know it. Your choice is to do God's work; what matter it about this man or that man.'

THE GENERIC TERM mansabdar, by which Mughal officers were known, meant 'holder of rank'. The rank was always expressed in military terms, as a commander of so many cavalrymen, even if the officer was a non-combatant, like a musician or a poet. And all were, in theory at least, obliged to maintain a certain number of troopers, and were liable to be assigned to active military duty, as were Abul Fazl (scholar), Birbal (poet) and Hakim Abul-Fath (physician). Some however received *inam* (reward) commissions, in which pay was not linked to any particular service.

The Mughal mansabdari system was the creation of Akbar, who in his eighteenth regnal year grouped imperial officers into thirty-three ranks *(zat)*, from commanders of ten to 10,000. The ranks above 5,000 were normally reserved for princes, but were occasionally opened up for top amirs like Todar Mal and Raja Man Singh. Those below the rank of 500 were simply called mansabdars, while those holding ranks between 500 and 2500 were called amirs (nobles), and those of 3000 and higher ranks were dignified as amir-i-azam (great noble). The premier noble of the empire bore the title Amir-ul-umra or Khan-i-khanan.

Each rank of mansabdars was further divided into three classes (first, second and third), on the basis of whether the cavalrymen (*sawar*) a mansabdar was required to maintain were equal to, half or less than half of the number indicated by his *zat* rank. Thus an officer of 1000 *zat* rank belonged to the first class in his rank if he maintained 1000 horsemen; to the second class, if he maintained 500 horsemen; to the third class if he maintained fewer than 500 horsemen.

The mansabdari rank was thus in effect a dual rank. This was a refinement that Akbar introduced in his fortieth regnal year. Till then there were only single rankings, which, as Moosvi points out, were 'directly related to the size of the military contingent' mansabdars were required to maintain. Under the new system, the *zat* rank indicated an officer's grade in the official hierarchy, and his personal remuneration and perks. The *zat* rank obliged an officer to maintain a certain number of horses, elephants, transport animals and carts, for the maintenance of which he was given a supplementary allowance. His *sawar* rank, on the other hand, indicated his trooper ranking, which specified the number of cavalrymen he was required to maintain. The officer drew an additional allowance for the maintenance of the cavalrymen assigned to him.

Ranks did not indicate functions. The actual duties an officer performed depended on what the emperor assigned to him from time to time, which could be important or trivial, though normally it was appropriate to his rank.

The Mughal amirs drew fabulous salaries. At the close of the sixteenth century in the reign of Akbar, all the mansabdars together, just 1671 persons, appropriated '82 per cent of the entire net revenue resources of the empire', with the top twenty-five mansabdars pocketing as much as 30.29 per cent, according to the calculation of Moosvi. The pattern of revenue appropriation was about the same under Akbar's successors. In a sense what the amir received was not just a salary but a share of the riches of India that the Mughals had seized.

The remuneration of an officer was broadly based on his rank, but his actual pay was calculated on the basis of complicated and confusing schedules, and involved elaborate bureaucratic procedures. His pay depended first of all on his *zat* rank, then on his *sawar* class, but that was not all—the rank and class only indicated his pay on paper; what he actually got depended on a number of other factors and was usually considerably less.

The government often made various deductions from the officer's pay, alleging irregularities, so that, according to Vincent Smith, the officer's pay 'was seldom, if ever, drawn for the whole year, and in some cases only four months' pay was allowed.' The officer, on his part, seldom maintained the troopers, animals and equipment assigned to him, and what he saved on this added to his net income. In the beginning, Akbar insisted on officers maintaining the actual number of troopers allotted to them, but few could meet their quotas—for instance, historian Badauni, a mansabdar of twenty, could not meet his troop commitments. Akbar therefore relaxed the rule towards the end of his reign. Later emperors required mansabdars to furnish only one-third of their quota in Hindustan, one-fourth in the Deccan, and one-fifth in Central Asia. The emperor, says Manucci, 'allows them to keep up no more than the quarter of the number.'

Even these adjusted trooper demands were seldom met by officers. Says Manucci, 'Those who ought to keep fifty horses, more or less, very frequently have no more than six or eight.' At the same time, as the empire grew and the number of mansabdars multiplied several-fold, the ranks of amirs were extravagantly inflated, to match the prestige of the emperor and the high dignity of the amirs. In the eighteenth century there were even commanders of 50,000. But such lofty ranks bore little relation to the actual pay received by amirs. 'The rank the soldiers receive is high in name, but as for the pay it is never more than half of what the rank indicates,' says Manucci. The pay of mansabdars was as illusory as the military contingents they maintained. Hardly anything in the Mughal empire was what it appeared to be.

The different modes of paying the mansabdar's remuneration introduced yet another complication. When the salary was paid in cash, as Akbar did for a while, there was no problem. But when the mansabdar was paid by a jagir assignment, there was uncertainty about the yield of the jagir, which was often inflated by revenue officers, but could be altered through influence or bribery. Frequently, the posting had to be obtained by offering presents or bribes to high nobles or to the emperor, and the interest on the money borrowed for this also had to be taken into account in calculating the net income of the officer.

There was furthermore always an inordinate delay—long enough for a boy to become an old man, notes Khafi Khan caustically—between the formal allocation of a jagir and its effective possession by the mansabdar. During the interval, the mansabdar had to borrow money, either from the treasury or from moneylenders, to meet his immediate expenses, the interest liability of which also cut into his real income. Often local officers intervened to obstruct mansabdars from taking possession of their jagirs. Royal 'orders are of little use,' says Manucci, 'because the governors and faujdars turn out the grantees unless a present is made to them.' As for the revenue actually collected from the jagir, it depended on the rapacity of the mansabdar and the caprice of nature.

The Mughals paid some officers in cash and others with jagir assignments. 'The whole country, with the exception of those lands held immediately from the Crown (the Khalisa lands) were held by the amirs as jagir,' says Badauni. For a while Akbar paid all mansabdars in cash, but that seems to have been a temporary measure necessitated by the confusion then prevailing about the revenue valuation of the empire. After Todar Mal's reforms firmed up the revenue administration, and reliable revenue data became available, Akbar reverted to the jagir system, though some mansabdars continued to be paid in cash. Akbar's successors continued the mixed payment system—of the 14,449 mansabdars in the service of Aurangzeb, 7000 were jagirdars, while the rest were paid in cash. But whether an officer was paid in cash or by jagir assignment, his remuneration was always stated in money, with the revenue valuation of his jagir matching the remuneration. Jagirs were assigned only to mansabdars; all subordinate personnel, including ahadis (royal guards), were paid in cash.

During Akbar's reign, mansabdars preferred jagir assignments, because of the delay in getting cash out of the treasury, but they preferred cash payments in Aurangzeb's reign, as jagirs at that time seldom yielded the specified revenue, because they were vastly overvalued to provide for the greatly increased number of mansabdars. Further, by the late seventeenth century, it had become difficult to collect taxes from the people, because of weakened political authority, especially in the Deccan. Sometimes rival jagirdars tried to collect dues from the same place, in disregard of royal orders.

THE JAGIR SYSTEM relieved the government of the burden of revenue administration over large tracts of the empire, and shifted to mansabdars the uncertainties and risks involved in revenue collection, but it added immeasurably to the burden of the common people, as jagirdars ruthlessly wrung out all their surplus income. Sometimes they simply grabbed the prime lands of farmers for their own use—the practice was so common that Jahangir once had to issue a general warning 'that the officials of the

Crown lands and the jagirdars should not forcibly take the ryots' lands, and cultivate them on their own account.' On the whole, the effect of the jagir system was ruinous to the economy, and in the long run it undermined the very health of the empire.

The ruination of the land did not in the least trouble the mansabdar, for he was only in temporary possession of the jagir. He seldom lived in his jagir, and rarely had any administrative responsibility there, except to collect its revenue through his agents. The arrangement was further complicated by the fact that the jagirs assigned to an amir were not congruous with the revenue and administrative divisions of the empire, and could even be scattered in bits in different places, though some care was usually taken to assign to him jagirs near the place where he was posted. Moreover, the jagirs were periodically shuffled, the normal duration of assignments being three or four years, but was sometimes as short as one year. Changes in the ranks of amirs and their transfers from one part of the empire to another also necessitated shuffling of jagir allocations.

An indirect consequence of the jagir system was that it prevented the emergence of a strong landed aristocracy in India, and this was a major factor in shaping the Mughal political destiny. It was land that gave stability and strength to the aristocracy, for the ownership of land in a way made the aristocrat resemble the king: he possessed land just as the king possessed territory. As Bernier perceptively observed, a landed aristocracy, had it existed in Mughal India, would have fostered the prosperity of the land, served as the buttress of royal authority, and at the same time checked the excesses of royal absolutism.

In a narrow sense, it was an advantage for the emperor not to have a class that would check and balance his power, but the absence of a landed aristocracy meant that there was no one (except the poor peasant) in Mughal India with a permanent interest in the land. There were therefore no permanent defenders of the land. The Mughal amirs had no enduring interest in the empire, and being unstable themselves could not provide any stable support to the emperor. Indeed, as Bernier argued, the absence of an independent, landed aristocracy was 'injurious to the best interest of the Sovereign himself'.

The only solution to the evils of the jagir system was for the state to collect all the revenue directly from the cultivators and pay cash salaries to all officers. But the Mughals did not have the administrative capability to do this. Nor could they create a landed aristocracy by making the jagirs bequeathable, for then they would have had to make the offices too bequeathable—which was impractical—as otherwise they would quickly run out of jagirs to allot to their new officers.

Even as it was, the Mughals often faced a shortage of jagirs. The problem existed even during Akbar's reign, for Biram Khan had liberally given away large land assignments to officers, to attract talent. The shortage of jagirs was sought to be made up by the ruse of arbitrarily raising the valuation of jagirs in the register of the valuation of the empire (which showed the revenue potential of each segment of the empire) to meet, on paper, the remuneration allotted to amirs. This caused considerable discontent among amirs, so the register was revised in 1566 to reflect the true revenue of jagirs. But this list too, being corruptly falsified, turned out to be worthless. So, in 1573, Akbar resumed all jagirs and paid cash salaries to all officers. Six years later, after Todar Mal's revenue reforms, a fresh register of the valuation of the empire was prepared, and the system of paying officers with jagir assignments was reintroduced.

The difficulty in finding land for jagirs grew even more acute under Akbar's successors, as the bureaucracy grew at a rate faster than the empire itself. There was an acute shortage of jagirs during the second half of Aurangzeb's reign, when, after the fall of Bijapur and Golconda, the emperor inducted into Mughal service 'countless Deccani and Maratha nobles with inflated ranks', says Khafi Khan. Inayetullah Khan, the Diwan, warned Aurangzeb: 'The retinue of officers who are daily paraded before your Majesty is unlimited, while land for being granted as jagirs is limited.'

A GOOD NUMBER of the Mughal amirs were retained at the court, to wait on the emperor. At the court, they were required to attend the durbar twice daily and be ready to perform any task that the emperor might assign to them. 'Every Omrah at court is obliged, under a certain penalty, to repair twice a day to the assembly, for the purpose of paying his respects to the King, at ten or eleven o'clock in the morning, when he is there seated to dispense justice, and at six in the evening,' notes Bernier. Also, the amirs by rotation had to mount guard at the royal citadel. A few amirs (like Bernier's employer, Danishmand Khan, the scholar administrator of Delhi) were exempted from attending court regularly, because of the nature of their offices; on the other hand, some nobles had no work other than to adorn the court and sing the praises of the emperor.

Away from the court, in the provinces, the amirs came into their own, and generally behaved as if they were potentates themselves. Still, they had to be careful not to let the freedom and power they enjoyed in the provinces go to their heads, for there were royal intelligence officers around all the time to report to the emperor all that the amir said and did. As an English gunner in the service of Aurangzeb told Norris, 'The old Kinge is very cunninge & has spys upon every body & soe good intelligence yt nobody can move a step or speake a word but he knows it.'

Even princes were subject to constant surveillance. Thus Prince Muazzam was repeatedly reprimanded by Aurangzeb on the basis of reports from intelligence officers, for committing such offences as encroaching on the exclusive privileges of the emperor by holding elephant fights, by setting-up screens while praying in the Friday mosque, and by sitting on a high platform to hold court, to punish which last transgression Aurangzeb sent mace-bearers (sergeants-at-arms) to make the prince get down from his seat 'in open court' and dismantle the platform. Jahangir had to admonish provincial governors periodically for arrogating royal prerogatives like sitting at the jharokha, granting titles to their servants, requiring *kornish* and *taslim* salutations to be performed by their servants, and for meting out unauthorized punishments. Aurangzeb often castigated presumptuous amirs for having kettledrums and bandsmen attend on them without royal authorization, for sitting on couches while holding court, for riding in palanquins while going to the Friday mosque, and so on.

In exercising such controls, the emperor's concern was to protect royal prerogatives, and not to prevent the oppression of the people—the stress was on regulating the amir's relationship with the emperor, not the amir's relationship with the people. The emperor did now and then issue warnings to officers against misgovernment, but the fact that emperor after emperor had to issue these orders, and that the orders were invariably issued at the beginning of a reign, exposes the symbolic and token nature of such exercises. Royal controls were not effective, for, as Bernier points out, royal intelligence officers often colluded with provincial officers to conceal the actual state of affairs from the emperor.

THE IMMENSE POWER and wealth enjoyed by the Mughal amir brought a steady flow of high talent from all over the Muslim world to India, especially in the early Mughal period when the empire was expanding rapidly and vast career opportunities were opening up. But gradually this flow began to dry up, for the Mughal bureaucracy became dense with coteries, which made it hard for outsiders to push their way in. Khanahzad, as the hereditary officers of the empire called themselves, closed ranks to prevent the entry of outsiders, so as to secure office and promotion for themselves and their children.

The emperors themselves favoured such succession to office. Thus when one of Aurangzeb's senior officers died, the emperor wrote to his Vizier, Asad Khan: 'You should write to me about the condition of his sons . . . so that each may be favoured according to his merit.' Of the 486 mansabdars above the rank of 1000 during the 1658–78 period, 213 were children or relatives of other mansabdars, according to Athar Ali. The Khanahzad looked on new entrants with contempt, and thwarted their progress. By the late seventeenth century, not many foreigners were in any case seeking Mughal service, as the empire had lost its elan and its financial foundations were crumbling. Sadly, while the flow of foreign talent was thus drying up, the Rajputs, whose military skills had helped to build the empire, also became alienated from the Mughals, because of Aurangzeb's narrow political and religious policies.

THE ALIENATION OF the Rajputs and the ebbing of the flow of talent from Persia and Central Asia into India accelerated the administrative decline of the Mughal empire. At the same time, there was an abnormal, almost incredible, proliferation in the number of mansabdars—from a total of 1866 in 1596, it rose by 64 per cent to 3057 in 1620, and then in just twenty-seven years leapt by 165 per cent to 8099 in 1647, and finally by another 78.4 per cent to a preposterous 14,449 by 1690. This wild, monstrous bloating, instead of adding strength to the empire, actually debilitated it and directly contributed to its administrative collapse, as work stretched thin to occupy the men available, and the work ethic fell precipitously.

It is significant that the number of amirs who held commands of over 3000 after nearly doubling from sixty-three under Akbar to 112 under Jahangir, fell to ninety-nine under Shah Jahan, indicating the constriction of talent at the top. This decline in the number of ranking officers took place at a time when the total number of mansabdars had grown to more than four times what it had been under Akbar. So it came to be that there were far too many junior officers and far too few commanders in the Mughal service. Further, as the number of mansabdars grew, their quality declined. The emperor, says Bernier, 'is surrounded by slaves, ignorant and brutal; by parasites raised from the dregs of society; strangers to loyalty and patriotism; full of insufferable pride, and destitute of courage, of honour and of decency.'

There were still a few men of great ability around, but they found it increasingly difficult to function in an environment vitiated by the parasites, who, being men of no merit, could progress only by pulling down or pushing aside others, especially those of merit, for the greatest obstruction to the progress of mediocrities was the presence of an officer of true ability in their midst. Further, while in the early Mughal period the amirs generally worked together as a team, and often held consultations among themselves before taking important decisions, this cooperative spirit disappeared in later times, and officers constantly endeavoured to thwart each other's careers, viewing the failure of others as the means of their success. Their attitude, as a Persian saying had it, was: 'The death of the great has made me great.'

The officers cooperated with each other only in cheating the government. Thus, instead of maintaining their full complement of troops, the mansabdars borrowed men and horses from each other or mounted the bazaar riff-raff on baggage ponies, to pass the muster. Akbar tried to end the sham by preparing descriptive rolls of soldiers and by branding horses, as Sher Shah and Alauddin Khilji had done before him, but that led to a revolt by mansabdars—to assert their right to cheat the government! The revolt was quelled, but the amirs still did not mend their ways. 'Notwithstanding the new regulation,' reports Badauni, 'the condition of the soldiers grew worse . . . They (the amirs) put most of their own servants and mounted attendants into soldiers' clothes, brought them to the musters, and performed everything according to their duties. But when they got to their jagirs they gave leave to their mounted attendants, and when a new emergency arose, they mustered as many "borrowed" soldiers as were required, and sent them away again, when they had served their purpose.'

Eventually it was Akbar who had to make the compromise. Towards the end of his reign he eased the rigour of government controls, and they were further slackened by his successors. In the eighteenth century, some of the Mughal amirs kept no troopers at all. 'Lutfullah Khan Sadiq, although he held the rank of 7,000, never entertained even seven asses, much less horses or riders on horses,' notes William Irvine, an early modern historian of the Mughal army.

A thick pile of red tape covered and hid most official misdemeanours in the Mughal empire. The Mughal bureaucrat, like bureaucrats everywhere, was snug in the folds of red tape, but it snarled up the ponderously turning wheels of the government. Consider, for instance, the procedure for appointing a new officer, as described by Abul Fazl: when the emperor made an appointment, it was first recorded in the diary of the court, in which all transactions had to be entered. After the diary was checked and verified, an extract of the imperial appointment order was made, which had to be authenticated by three officials. The extract was then handed over to the copying office, where an abridged order was prepared, which in turn had to attested by four officials and then sealed by ministers.

The order was thereafter dispatched to the military office, which then called for the estimates and descriptive rolls of the troops to be furnished by the newly appointed officer. When these were submitted, a salary statement was prepared, which, after having been entered into various records, was forwarded to the finance department. The finance department then made the necessary entries in its records, and submitted a report to the emperor, who had to finally approve the payment of allowance to the officer. A pay voucher was then prepared, which again had to be cleared by the finance minister, the paymaster-general and the military accountant. The military accountant then prepared the pay order, which in turn required six signatures from three separate departments, before it would be accepted by the treasury as authorization for the payment of the salary.

The emperor's order thus had to pass through some nineteen stages, requiring innumerable signatures and entries into records, before it could be put into effect. Aurangzeb often wailed that his orders were not being carried out. They could not be. There were procedures to be followed!

Such bureaucratic tangles were not, however, an exclusively Mughal phenomenon. The bureaucracy was the same everywhere. In the court of the Zamorin of Calicut, a petty chieftain on the Kerala coast, Pyrard, who visited India in the first decade of the seventeenth century, was amazed 'to see the great number of men who have no other business and do nothing else all day long but write and register. Their position is very honourable ... Some write down the goods which come for the King, others the taxes and tributes paid day by day, others the most noteworthy events from day to day at Court or in the rest of the kingdom, and in short all the news; for everything is registered, and each has its own place. They register also all strangers who arrive, taking their names, and their country, the time of their arrival, and the object which brings them, as they did in our case; and it is a surprising thing to see their number, the good order kept among them, and how quickly they write ... The King has similar clerks in all the towns, seaports, harbours, and routes of the kingdom; they correspond with the clerks in the palace, and everything is organized, the former obeying the latter, and also having superiors among themselves. They have the same method of writing and the same organization all along the Malabar Coast.'

THE COILS OF red tape were an ideal environment for corruption to thrive. Officials harvested the public like a farmer harvests his field. Every favour, indeed every official action, had its price. Each class bled the one below. The emperor himself connived with the ministers and courtiers who took bribes for securing royal favour. 'It is a custom established throughout India that without friends and without interest nothing can be done,' says Manucci. 'Even princes of the blood royal, if they want to carry any purpose, cannot do so without paying. It is such a usual thing to give and to receive that when any eunuch or any princess asks the king for something as a favour to some general or officer, be it an appointment or some other favour of any consequence, the king never omits to ask how much has been received. The other side ordinarily admits the exact amount, which the prince is aware of, and leaves a portion with the intercessor and takes the rest himself, sending it to be locked up in the treasury.'

An honest government officer was, as the saying goes, as rare as a horned rabbit. According to Manucci, when British ambassador Norris was given sanction for the English to establish factories on the Coromandel coast, he was told that 'in order to obtain the necessary documents he must present to the king two hundred thousand rupees, and one hundred thousand to the officials.' Bernier says that the officers authorized to affix the emperor's signet to pay orders 'scruple not to receive bribes for the quick issues of these documents'.

It does not seem that Mughal officers saw such payments as bribes. Presents (or bribes—the distinction was vague) were looked on by the receiver as a tribute due to him, and by the giver as a customary means to promote his interests. It was all done in the open. 'In the taking of bribes . . . [Itimad-ud-daula] certainly was most uncompromising and fearless,' says Muhammad Hadi about Jahangir's Vizier. Itimad-ud-daula's son Asaf Khan, the Vizier of Shah Jahan, was also audaciously venal. And Asaf Khan's son, Shayista Khan, is said to have amassed 380 million rupees during the thirteen years he was the governor of Bengal, no doubt by the usual Mughal means. British merchants at Hugli had this to say of him: 'So dishonourable and covetous a person never came into these parts for a Governor.'

Says Badauni about an amir in Akbar's court: 'In his sect bribery and corruption were considered as a duty . . . and making profit on bonds for debt, and on signing judicial decrees, as a positive command.' Corruption was so endemic in the Mughal empire that when Roe came across an officer who was 'no briber, reported honest,' he made a note of that as something singular. Norris was once told by an English gunner in the Mughal service: 'Ye Top to ye bottom there is nothinge but cheatinge & Treachery & basenesse in ye Highest degree.' Norris could find only one honest minister in Aurangzeb's court, Ali Beg—in the 'midst of ye most base vitious & corrupt court in ye Universe this minister alone is virtuous,' writes Morris. 'The sole businesse of all other ministers is gripe squeeze all ye money they can from all people by ye basest & Indirect meanes Imaginable openly & barefaced.'

The amirs had at least the merit of being dignified in their bribe taking, but common government employees were almost like beggars. When Norris came out of the durbar after his first audience with Aurangzeb, he was surrounded and pestered for gratuities by palace attendants. Amirs had to tip all royal messengers, even the bearers of food from the royal kitchen. And when the emperor gifted an elephant or a horse, the stable men collected bridle-money. Significantly, when Jahangir put a stop to the practice, instead of taking action against his servants, he paid them money from the treasury to compensate them for what they lost as bridle money. Rather than tackling corruption and inefficiency, the Mughal system simply adjusted itself around it.

Ecclesiastical officers too were notoriously corrupt. Aurangzeb's Chief Kazi, Abdul Wahab, writes Sarkar, 'sold the subordinate Qazi-ships of the cities for money and took bribes in every case he tried. At the same time he made profit by engaging in secret trade in rich stuff and jewellery.' One of Aurangzeb's officers was said to have amassed a fortune of 1.2 million rupees, apart from valuables and real estate, in just two and a half years of personal attendance on the emperor. Official appointments were openly sold during Aurangzeb's reign, the standard premium being six and a half times the annual salary of the post, one-fourth of which had to be paid on receipt of the deeds of office and the balance in instalments. It was thus with considerable justification that Aurangzeb's rebel son Akbar charged:

> The officials trade, buying and selling offices at court;
> Today, when done eating, they break their
> salt-cellar and pay him with ingratitude.

Much of this corruption was within the official circle itself, but it affected the common people also whenever they had anything to do with a government official. Land assessment, for instance, was generally taken to mean loot. Even Akbar's social reform measures provided opportunities for corruption. His regulations about marriage age, for instance, enabled 'a host of profits and perquisites surpassing all computations, guess, or imagination . . . [to find] their way into the pockets of those in office, especially certain police officers, and effete Khan-lings and other evil oppressors,' says Badauni.

Sums up Manucci: 'Nothing can be more surprising than the way things go in the Mogul Empire. The king, the princes, the governors, and the generals have each their own line of policy, calculated for securing success to their own designs . . . Down to the very smallest officer there is not one who is not a past master in the art of enriching himself prodigiously. They flinch from nothing in their pursuit of wealth; they ignore even the loyalty due to their sovereign.'

THERE WAS NOTHING that could be done about corruption in the Mughal empire, for corruption was the lubricant essential for its administrative machinery to run smoothly. If any officer had uneasiness about taking bribes or performing any misdeeds, he could look to the emperor himself for reassurance. Aurangzeb, for example, once instructed his governors that they might take false oaths to serve the interests of the state, to erase the sin of which it was enough for them to feed ten people. Those who lied and cheated for the state, also lied and cheated for their own interest; what was legitimate in one instance was legitimate in the other too. No one would trust anyone in the Mughal empire. 'These people are as base as corrupt; because they are made of falsehood themselves, they believe there is no Truth in any one else,' says Norris. 'They distrust everybody because they are conscious themselves are not to be trusted.'

Offering presents to one's superiors and to those from whom favours were sought was obligatory in Mughal India. Akbar made it mandatory for those who called on him to offer him a tribute according to their means. 'He . . . issued a general order, that every person from the highest to the lowest should bring him a present,' says Badauni. The motive of the order was not material gain, but to establish a proper relationship between the subject and the monarch—the subject by making an offering acknowledged the emperor as his lord, and the emperor by accepting it took the subject under his wing.

'In Asia, the great are never approached empty-handed. When I had the honour to kiss the garment of the great Mogol Aurengzebe ... I presented him with eight rupees,' says Bernier. 'There is no man that commeth to make petition who commeth emptie-handed,' says Hawkins. 'By the gift you give him he knoweth that you would demand some thing of him.' Tavernier claims he gave presents worth a total of 23,100 rupees to Aurangzeb, his sister and his nobles. Says Thevenot, 'The first time one goes to wait upon the Governor, as soon as they come they lay before him, five, six or ten Roupies, every one according to his Quality; and in the Indies the same thing is done to all for whom they would shew great respect.'

Sometimes—or perhaps often—these presents (or tributes) to the emperor took the colouration of bribes. Thus, in 1627, European merchants in Surat sent instructions to their agents in Lahore to obtain enforceable orders from the emperor—'Otherwise we will bribe no more to have the King's farmans,' they warned. Was it a present or a bribe that the chieftain in Solapur gave to Aurangzeb when he offered 50,000 rupees for being designated as a raja? And was not Aurangzeb soliciting a bribe when he asked a title aspirant, 'Your father gave to Shah Jahan one lakh rupees for adding *alif* to his name and making him Amir Khan. How much will you pay me for the title I am giving you?' When Aurangzeb was in the Deccan, amirs even paid him to secure transfers to Hindustan!

The amirs who had to make presents to the emperor, the begums and top officials, in turn tried to make good their investments by taking presents from those below them, and so it went all the way down. Governors, says Terry, 'looke for presents from all which have occasion to use them, and if they be not often visited aske for them; yea, send them backe for better exchange.' James Bridgman, an officer of the East India Company in Bengal in the mid-seventeenth century, wrote to his superiors in London: 'Presents must be given occasionally to the Prince (Shah Shuja) and Governors of the towns; and so a few rarities of low price should be furnished for the purposes, such as globes, glasses, multiplying glasses, and four or five good substantial home clocks.' Writes Hawkins, 'Without gifts and bribes nothing would either goe forward or bee accomplished.'

The rationale for taking presents and bribes was simple—the favour-seeker would gain by the favour, so why should not the favour-giver gain too, especially as the favour-giver had himself to bribe to secure his own posting? 'At all times, but especially on the breaking out of an important war' governorships were sold 'for immense sums in hard cash,' says Bernier. 'Hence it naturally becomes the principal object of the individual thus appointed Governor, to obtain repayment of the purchase-money, which he borrowed as he could at a ruinous rate of interest. Indeed whether the government of a province has or has not been bought, the Governor, as well as the *timariot* (jagirdar) and the farmer of the revenue, must find the means of making valuable presents every year, to a Visir, a Eunuch, a lady of the Seraglio, and to any other persons whose influence at court he considers indispensable.'

Such practices were common elsewhere in India too. Thus in Golconda, English factors called for 'Persian horses, English mastiffs, Irish greyhounds and water spaniels; fair large looking glasses; a piece of fine scarlet; crimson and violet satins; our King's Majesty's picture, large, in Parliament robes; a good buff coat; an excellent perspective and multiplying glass; a large pair of globes; and a suit of fine light armour, if possible musket-proof' for presenting to the sultan. When the agent of the East India Company visited Shivaji to seek trade concessions, he held up a diamond ring to draw the attention of the raja. The French are also on record of having made presents to Shivaji—the raja, it is said, made light of their presents, but they excused themselves saying that they 'were not very rich'. 'With the Rajah (Shambhuji) down to the plowman the infection of *peshkash-ing* (present-taking) is so prevalent that nothing can be well done without it,' noted the English merchants at Karwar.

THE MUGHAL OFFICERS were, says Bernier, 'men who extract oil out of sand'. Aggrieved subjects could, of course, seek redress from the emperor against the tyranny of local officials, and occasionally such appeals were successfully made, as by the merchants of Surat, but such cases were extremely rare. For most people in the provinces, it was practically impossible to appeal to the emperor, because of the great distances involved, and the hazards of travel made more hazardous by the officials against whom the complaints were being preferred.

Everything about the Mughal mansabdari system promoted inefficiency and corruption, from the mode of appointment and promotion of officers to the mode of paying salaries and the kind of royal controls exercised over them. The system however had two advantages: it simplified revenue administration through the jagir system, and it simplified military administration by shifting to mansabdars the task of recruiting and maintaining the bulk of the army. Its only disadvantage was that it ruined the people. And in the long run it ruined the empire too.

'Whoever has money, whether loyal or disloyal, can get his business settled as he likes by paying for it,' Sher Shah had said about the Mughal government during the reign of Babur; 'but if a man has no money, although he may have displayed his loyalty on a hundred occasions, or be a veteran soldier, he will never gain his end.' Conditions only got worse with the passage of time. 'They were wicked and rebellious . . . and amassed wealth . . . [and] had no leisure to look after the troops, or take an interest in the people,' says Badauni about Akbar's officers. Akbar introduced several regulations to discipline the officers, but not with much success. 'The amirs did as they pleased,' says Badauni curtly.

'In these days . . . everybody's only thought is to steal,' says Manucci about the conditions in India towards the close of Aurangzeb's reign. 'But whatever happens, it rarely reaches the king's ears, for he being old . . . and also taken up with this war against the [Marathas] . . . , his empire, too, being such a vast extent, he is unable to put a stop to all this injustice and misrule, which his ministers carry on with impunity.'

Sacred Laws, Profane Justice

THE MUGHALS, AUTOCRATS though they were, also claimed to be totally just. Said Akbar: 'If I were guilty of an unjust act, I would rise in judgment against myself. What shall I say then of my sons, my kindred and others.' Indeed, only an absolute monarch could render absolute justice, as he was beholden to no one, and did not have to moderate justice with expediency.

By medieval standards, the Mughals showed a commendable concern for justice. Humayun's drum of justice and Jahangir's belled chain were not empty symbols, but assertions of the royal will to render justice. Says Monserrate about Akbar: 'The King's severity towards errors and misdemeanours committed by officers in the course of government business is remarkable, for he is most stern with offenders against the public faith . . . For the King has the most precise regard for right and justice in the affairs of government . . . by King's direction all capital cases, and all really important civil cases also, are conducted before himself. He is easily excited to anger, but soon cools down again. By nature moreover he is kindly and benevolent, and is sincerely anxious that guilt should be punished, without malice indeed, but at the same time without undue leniency.'

Manucci records a story he had heard in the late seventeenth century, that Jahangir 'kept at his court an official with several baskets full of poisonous snakes. He would order that in his presence they should be made to bite any official who had failed to administer justice, leaving the culprit lying in his presence till breath left him.' The venomous should die of venom—in Muslim judicial practice, it was essential that the punishment should match the crime.

Shah Jahan often fretted that not enough supplicants were approaching him for justice, though he obligingly swallowed the glib explanation of his courtiers that this was because of the excellence of his government that left little scope for complaint. Aurangzeb, with his reputation for orthodoxy and saintliness, was particularly strict about adhering to the letter of the law, though he had little compunction in insidiously violating its spirit.

Aurangzeb was cold and deliberate in action, but his predecessors often administered 'justice' on the high surge of passion. Akbar once had a poor lamp-lighter flung over the ramparts of the fort for the minor infraction of falling asleep near the royal couch. Similarly, Jahangir ordered the execution of a groom who disturbed his game during a hunt—when he was about to shoot a nilgai, Jahangir writes, 'suddenly a groom and two bearers appeared, and the nilgai escaped. In a great rage I ordered them to kill the groom on the spot and hamstring the bearers and mount them on asses and parade them through the camp.'

Usually, however, Mughal emperors were considerate towards common people, and even such a haughty monarch as Shah Jahan would take their rebukes with good humour—they were no threat to the throne, and being attentive to the lowly was an essential element of the semi-divine royal aura. Thus when Shah Jahan ordered the widow of a rich Baniya, on a complaint from her estranged son, to pay 50,000 rupees to the son, and 100,000 rupees to the royal treasury, she, while conceding that the son had the right to claim his patrimony, asked the emperor in the open court: 'What kinship there may have been between your Majesty and my deceased husband to warrant the demand of one hundred thousand rupees?' At this, says Bernier, Shah Jahan burst out laughing, and let her enjoy the wealth undisturbed.

It is, however, important to note that if Shah Jahan had at that moment taken offence and ordered the widow's punishment, no one would have accused the emperor of injustice. Whatever the theory, in practice, the royal will was the law. Crime was what offended the emperor. Similar arbitrariness also prevailed at the lower levels of the Mughal judicial administration. There were no uniform laws applicable throughout the empire, no codified procedures, no system of recording evidence, so that judicial decisions were invariably ad hoc, though ostensibly within the perimeter of religious law and social conventions. What therefore prevailed was not the rule of law, but the rule of men, so the quality of justice depended on the quality of the person administering justice. And that meant, in the Mughal environment, injustice and tyranny.

From the point of view of the common people, the one great advantage of the medieval government was that it did not have the capacity to routinely intrude into their lives, especially in rural India. In everyday matters, the local bodies—the village or caste or guild council—administered justice according to their customs and practices, as they had been doing for centuries, caring for the welfare of the individuals in the group, resolving disputes and punishing deviants and criminals. The imperial government was hardly involved in it.

IN THEORY, THE Mughals were expected to abide by the shariah, but the emperors, except Aurangzeb, ruled without much reference to it, so that it often seemed as if there was no law at all in Mughal India, other than the emperor's will. 'The Great Mogul is so absolute, that there being no written Laws, his will in all things is a Law, and the last decision of all Causes, both Civil and Criminal,' says Careri. 'Lawes they have none written: the kings judgement binds,' says Roe. 'I could never heare of law written amongst them; the King and his substitutes will is law,' says Terry.

These views are misleading. The shariah bound all Muslim rulers. And the shariah was immutable, being based on Koranic injunctions, the traditions about Prophet Muhammad, and the established conventions of Islam. There could be no amendment to the shariah, no fresh legislation.

But while the shariah was immutable, life was not. So shariah had to be interpreted by jurists (Mujatahids) to apply it to emergent situations, and since there were nearly as many interpretations as there were jurists, monarchs had considerable freedom in deciding what was right and wrong. Thus when it turned out that Akbar had taken far more wives than custom permitted, willing jurists reinterpreted the rules to validate the extra marriages. And when some Kazis refused to legitimize Aurangzeb's usurpation, the prince was able to persuade jurist Abdul Wahab to declare that, since Shah Jahan was physically unfit to govern, the throne could be deemed as vacant and therefore it was legal for Aurangzeb to occupy it. For that peerless exposition, the emperor made Abdul Wahab the Chief Kazi of the empire, who then went on to acquire an appropriately peerless reputation for corruption. Another time, to conform to Aurangzeb's will, judicial officers sanctioned the execution of Muslim and Hindu prisoners captured during the siege of Satara, revising their earlier judgement against execution.

The jurisprudence that the Mughal emperors generally followed was that of the Hanafi school, but they acknowledged other schools too, to gain flexibility in policy and action. 'Praised be God! there are four schools [of Sunni theology, each] . . . according to the particular age and time,' exclaimed Aurangzeb. Babur had written his own treatise on Muslim law, and Aurangzeb had his officers compile a comprehensive compendium of Muslim law, the *Fatawa-al-Alamgiriyya*.

In general terms, there were three categories of crimes under Muslim law: crimes against god (theocratic crimes), crimes against the state (fraud, default, etc.), and crimes against private citizens (murder, theft, etc.). Of these, the crimes against god were the most heinous, and there could be no mercy in punishing such offenders, but the crimes against the state and against individuals could be punished according to the pleasure of the emperor or compounded by paying blood money or other compensations. In the crimes against individuals, action could be taken only if complaints were made, as there was no public prosecutor in the Mughal judicial system.

If Muslim law was thus complex and variable, Hindu law was even more so, as each community and caste had its own conventions, which were so region-specific that they could be administered only by local bodies like the caste or village panchayats. The reach of royal judicial authority was therefore limited, but that did not unduly perturb the emperor, for the only crime that really concerned him was the crime against the state, which was in effect crime against the emperor.

PEOPLE IN MUGHAL India were generally careful to conform to the customary law of their caste or village, but they would obey the laws of the state only under coercion. Zemindars were a source of perennial disturbance. And so were ordinary peasants. 'The villagers and cultivators on the other side of river Yamuna,' writes Jahangir, 'had not given up stealing and highway robbery, and, passing their time in the shelter of thick jungles and difficult strong places in stubbornness and fearlessness, would not pay their rents to the jagirdars.' When royal forces were sent against them, villagers often put up stout resistance, and sometimes even routed them. During the last years of Aurangzeb, when the authority of the state loosened, peasants in droves took to robbery, especially in the Deccan, where farming had become impossible due to incessant wars.

Thieving tribes abounded in India. Writes Babur: 'If one goes into Hindustan the Jats and Gujurs always pour down in countless hordes from hill and plain for loot in bullock and buffalo. These ill-omened people are just senseless oppressors.' In a sense, these tribes were not criminal, only backward—they had not evolved much beyond the ways of ancient tribes, for whom cattle-lifting was a routine civic activity.

Even the normally peaceful communities of Mughal India were liable to turn into marauders at the slightest tremor of weakness in royal authority. Thus villagers hounded Humayun along the way when he was retreating from the battle of Kanauj, and disturbances broke out throughout the empire when Akbar was struck down by a mysterious illness in 1578, and again when Shah Jahan fell ill in 1657. The next year, when Dara, routed by Aurangzeb, fled from Agra, the city rabble immediately looted his palace, even though Shah Jahan was resident in the city at that time. In Vijayanagar, ruffians and jungle folk went rampaging in Hampi the moment they heard of the raja's defeat at Talikota.

The authority of the state prevailed only where it was present in armed strength. Along the highways, bandits lay in wait of the unwary. 'The country is so full of outlawes and theeves that almost a man cannot stirre out of doores throughout all his [Jahangir's] dominions without great forces,' writes Hawkins. India 'swarms with rebels and thieves,' says Peter Mundy. On the outskirts of large cities, chor minars, towers built of the severed heads of thieves, were a common sight. William Finch, travelling from Surat to Agra in 1609, found roads infested with thieves, and near Panipat saw 'the heads of some hundred theeves newly taken, their bodies set on stakes a mile in length'.

THE CHAOS IN Mughal society was compounded by the chaos in the Mughal judicial organization. All Mughal courts, from the lowest to the highest, were courts of first instance, though the courts of the provincial Kazi and governor, as well as of course the court of the emperor, were also courts of appeal. The various courts, located at different administrative divisions of the empire or having different purviews, were not clearly segregated or hierarchically organized; their jurisdictions overlapped, their powers were ill-defined, and the laws they were to enforce were variable. Consequently, there was a great amount of confusion in the Mughal judicial system, and it was shot through and through with corruption.

At the top of the Mughal judicial organization stood the emperor. He was not merely the final arbiter of justice, but its very fountainhead, and it was to him that common people looked up as their saviour from oppressions and calamities. For the peasant, the artisan and the trader, the tyrant was the government official in their village or town with whom they had to deal, but they believed the far-away emperor to be just.

And in a way he was. The emperor was accessible to all his subjects, and could be approached for justice during any of his two or three daily public appearances. 'At any of these three times, any sutor, holding up his petition to be scene, shall be heard,' says Terry. There was, notes

Abul Fazl, a master of petitions for each shift. The emperor began his day by receiving petitions from the public and attending to their grievances during the morning darshan. Ordinarily, he would be prompt to offer relief to supplicants, but sometimes he would refuse to take up a case. Thus when a land dispute was brought before Aurangzeb, he declined to deal with it saying, 'Cases about land are settled on the land itself.'

Apart from being accessible to petitioners at his public appearances, the emperor set aside one day in the week exclusively for the administration of justice, when the durbar was converted into a court of justice, and only law officers, jurists and a few nobles who attended on the emperor were allowed into the durbar. Says Roe about Jahangir's custom: 'On Tuesday at the Jarruco (jharokha) he sits in Judgment, neuer refusing the poorest mans Complaynt, where hee heares with Patience both parts.' According to Bernier, Aurangzeb reserved one day of the week to hear the appeals of persons 'selected from the lower order, and presented to the King by a good and wise old man'.

Taking disputes to the emperor sometimes assumed a bizarre form, in which the complainant took on himself the roles of the judge and the executioner, right before the emperor. Thus Salabat Khan, the Mir Bakshi, was assassinated by an aggrieved Rajput in the durbar of Shah Jahan, and there was a similar incident during the reign of Aurangzeb. Even Adham Khan's murder of Atga Khan in the reign of Akbar could be deemed as a perilous exercise of the right of retaliation. Such outrages presumably took place in the lower courts too. Taking the law into one's own hands was a recognized right in medieval society—the right of self-defence, not just of life, but of honour too. And in matters of honour, it was not enough merely to slay the offender; he had to be slain in public, in the royal court, if possible.

Next to the emperor, the highest judicial officer in Mughal India was the Chief Kazi. The Kazi's jurisdiction was primarily over Muslim religious and personal law—marriage, divorce, inheritance and the like—but his authority often randomly stretched over other areas too, and he tried many criminal cases. But political and administrative offences, such as rebellion or embezzlement, and offences under secular and common law, were normally outside his purview; these cases were tried by the governor and other officers at various levels. The actual role that the Chief Kazi played in government depended on his relationship with the emperor; Abdul Wahab, Aurangzeb's Chief Kazi, for instance, enjoyed enormous powers, because of his closeness to the emperor, and he often meddled in matters which were no concern of his.

Under the Chief Kazi, subordinate Kazis administered justice in the provinces, districts and other subdivisions of the empire. Apart from presiding over their courts, the Kazis officiated at marriages, appointed guardians for the property of orphans, arranged the marriages of Muslim widows and orphan girls, and generally looked after the interests of the Muslim community; further, the Chief Kazi and the provincial Kazis often doubled as Sadrs and administered religious and charitable endowments. The Kazis were in their judicial work assisted by jurists (Muftis), who expounded the law.

Proceedings in Mughal courts were entirely oral. 'Everything is done verbally,' says Monserrate. According to Manucci, clever investigative methods were used by rulers to trap criminals, but he does not specify what those methods were. There were no lawyers in Mughal courts; the plaintiff had to plead his case in person, and was required to prove his claim through the testimony of witnesses. Usually two men of good reputation were required as witnesses, but women also could be called as witnesses, in which case the evidence of two women was considered as equal to that of one man. Cross examination of witnesses was not permitted, but their character, and therefore their credibility, could be questioned.

WITNESSES PLAYED A crucial role in the Mughal judicial process, but they were also its bane, for 'false witnesses . . . [were] always to be had in great numbers, at a cheap rate, and [were] never punished,' says Bernier. The empire, says Manucci, 'is overrun with men whose only profession is to act as false witnesses or to forge signatures.' One of Aurangzeb's Chief Kazis, Sheikh-ul-Islam, the upright son and successor of the venal Abdul Wahab, often refused to pass judgement in the cases that came up before him, but asked the disputants to settle matters out of court, saying that 'in this age of lying witnesses, God alone knows the truth!'

Akbar was wary of witnesses. He 'places no reliance on testimony or on oaths, which are the recource of the crafty,' says Abul Fazl, 'but draws his conclusions from the contradictions in the narratives, the physiognomy, and from sublime researches and noble conjectures,' and he directed judges too not to depend on witnesses, but to pursue truth 'by manifold inquiries, by the study of physiognomy and the exercise of foresight.'

Torture was a common investigative method in Mughal India, to get at the truth, or at least to get a confession. Mughal ingenuity in applying torture is not recorded, but trials by the use of hot iron and boiling oil are mentioned. There was also trial by water. 'While they shot an arrow and brought it back,' writes Badauni, 'he (the accused) should dive into water, and if he put his head out of the water before they returned, the defendant should satisfy the claims of the plaintiff.' The truth was in the lung power of the accused, or in the nimbleness of the retriever.

In the use of torture, the trial itself was a form of punishment, and it is unlikely that Akbar would have favoured it, for he had laid down humane rules for awarding punishments. His advice to judicial officers, according to Abul Fazl, was that they should 'reclaim the criminal by good counsels', failing which they should 'punish by reprimands, threats and imprisonment', and should resort to mutilation only in the most serious cases.

In the matter of capital punishment, Akbar initially advised his officers that it should be awarded only with 'utmost deliberation', but later, in 1582, he altogether prohibited its imposition by officers, and this practice was followed by his successors. 'The King reserves that Power to himself,' says Thevenot about the custom early in the reign of Aurangzeb; 'and therefore when any Man deserves death, a Courier is dispatched to know his pleasure, and they fail not to put his Orders in execution so soon as the Courier is come back.' The emperor himself exercised the power of awarding capital punishment with caution, and under Akbar, according to Monserrate, 'the guilty are, by his own direction, not punished until he has given order for the third time that this shall be done.' Jahangir says that after a hasty execution that he later regretted, he 'directed that whenever an order was given for anyone's execution, notwithstanding that the command were imperative, they should wait till sunset before putting him to death.'

These high-minded professions were often violated in practice by the emperors themselves. Jahangir, says Terry, was impelled by 'his will and passion, not justice'. Medieval justice was, generally speaking, pitiless and rough-and-ready, even in punishing trivial offences. Often passion, or the arrogance of power, overrode caution and concern for fair play. 'Tryals,' writes Terry, 'are quicke, and so are executions: hangings, beheading, impaling, killing with dogges, by elephants, serpants, and other like, according to the nature of the fact.'

Matching punishment to crime sometimes resulted in bizarre judgements, such as those passed on deserters by Humayun, beheading the headstrong and chopping off the hands and feet of the indiscreet (who could not 'distinguish between their feet and hands'). Similarly, Akbar once had a man's feet hacked off for stealing a pair of slippers, and Jahangir had a man's thumbs cut off for chopping down a tree. Mughal punishments were usually deterrent; they had to be, for that was the only way to maintain some semblance of law and order in those wild times. For this reason, and also in order not to deprive the rabble of their gory entertainment, executions were usually carried out in the marketplace.

The prescribed Mughal punishment for adultery was stoning to death, but it was only 100 lashes for fornication; one who falsely accused a married woman of adultery would get eighty lashes, which was also the punishment for drinking wine; the highway robber would have his hands and feet cut off; the murderer would get the death penalty, and so would the apostate. Public degradation was a common punishment in Mughal India, as in many other lands: head shaven, dressed in rags and wearing a garland of old shoes, the culprit would be seated on a filthy donkey facing its tail, and paraded through the streets with loud music. In the crimes against individuals, the aggrieved had the right to claim retaliation or blood money. In civil cases, judges could imprison debtors and sureties, and, says Terry, even 'men of power for payment will sell their persons, wives, and children; which the custome of the land will warrant.' Sometimes criminals were let off if they became Muslims, says Bernier.

THE CORRUPTION OF practice, not the insufficiency of precepts, was the problem with the Mughal judicial system. 'They are not altogether destitute of good laws . . . ,' says Bernier. 'But of what advantage are good laws when not observed, and when there is no possibility of enforcing their observance?' Laws could not be enforced because the enforcers were corrupt. Aurangzeb's Chief Kazi, Abdul Wahab, was notoriously corrupt, and the subordinate Kazis vied with each other to emulate their chief, so that it became a maxim of the age that 'to trust a Kazi is to court misfortune'. Shah Nawaz Khan, Aurangzeb's father-in-law, and one of his most perceptive critics, says of the Kazis of the time: 'Those who sell religion for worldliness regard this noble office as a very easy one and spend money in bribes (to obtain the office), in order that by doing away with the rights of men they may extort a hundred times more. They consider *nikahana* (fees on marriages) and *mahrana* (fees on dowers) as more their due than their mother's milk.'

As a Mughal saying had it, one favour of the judge was better than a thousand witnesses. Manucci cites the case of a merchant who bribed a judge with 5000 rupees (no small amount those days) to obtain a favourable judgement. The difference between a fine and a bribe was vague in Mughal India. Pelsaert notes that criminals were rarely executed unless they were poor; others bought their freedom from judges. On the other hand, there were advantages too in being a destitute litigant. 'In Asia, if justice be ever administered,' says Bernier, 'it is among the lower classes, among persons who, being equally poor, have no means of corrupting the judges, and of buying false witnesses.'

Under Aurangzeb, Kaziship tended to be hereditary, and that greatly lowered judicial standards. There were even illiterate judges at this time, like the Kazi of Jodhpur. Inevitably, the Kazi became the butt of much ridicule and contempt in Mughal India, as reflected in a parable of the age: 'When the Kazi's bitch died, the whole town was at the funeral; when the Kazi himself died, not a soul followed his coffin.'

'One must indeed be sorry for the man who has to come to judgment before these godless "un-judges",' writes Pelsaert in a scorching condemnation of the Mughal judicial system; 'their eyes are bleared with greed, their mouths gape like wolves for covetousness, and their bellies hunger for the bread of the poor; everyone stands with hands open to receive, for no mercy or compassion can be had except on payment of cash. This fault should not be attributed to judges or officers alone, for the evil is a universal plague; from the least to the greatest, right up to the King himself, everyone is infected with insatiable greed . . .'

What one got in the Mughal court was not justice, but one's fate.

The Royal Revenue Squeeze

'ALL UNDERTAKINGS DEPEND upon finance,' maintained Kautilya, the ancient Indian political sage. 'Hence foremost attention should be paid to the treasury.' This was a precept that the Mughals understood well. The Mughal administration was, in fact, not so much a system of governing the state, as a system of gathering revenue.

Yet, curiously, the Mughals were improvident in finance. They concentrated on collecting revenue but neglected to nurture the source of revenue, parasitically ravaging the very body that sustained them. This, apart from being counterproductive in the long run, also violated the principle of reciprocity implicit in the relationship between the monarch and his subjects—that the monarch, in return for the taxes paid by the people, had the obligation to protect the lives and property of the people and to promote their welfare. But there was little that people could do to defend their rights against such violations. This was especially so in the case of peasants, who were the main victims of the royal tax squeeze, for though they were the primary creators of wealth in medieval society and therefore the chief source of the revenue of the state, they were themselves wretchedly poor and weak. Monarchs often treated peasants as bonded labourers, obliging them to work on the land and provide revenue for the king, in return for being permitted to keep a part of their produce for their sustenance.

But monarchs had to be careful not to push peasants too far, for there was more arable land in medieval India than there were peasants to cultivate it, so peasants, if oppressed too hard, could always migrate to more hospitable domains, leaving the land fallow and the treasury impoverished. The peasant and the monarch had to cooperate with each other to make agriculture worthwhile for either. The land by itself had no value to the government unless the peasant made it productive; conversely, the land had no value to the peasant unless he could enjoy its yield, which was possible only if the government protected his life and property.

In this, the primacy of obligation was on the peasant, for unless he cultivated the land and paid taxes, the government could not function, and without a government there could be no state, no society—Hindu law, in fact, emphasized the peasant's obligation to make the land productive and pay revenue. From the point of view of the state, there was not much difference between refusing to cultivate the land and refusing to pay the tax: both were acts of rebellion. The monarch could indeed force peasants to till the fields, just as he could put lazy artisans to work. Such coercive measures were often employed by the Mughals—in 1632, an English trader reported that a Mughal governor cleaved a village headman into two for not sowing his fields; in 1658, Aurangzeb instructed his revenue officers to flog peasants if necessary to force them to expand cultivation.

BUT WHOSE LAND was it anyway? Bernier says that the Mughal emperor was 'the proprietor of every acre of land in the kingdom, excepting, perhaps, some houses and gardens which he sometimes permits his subjects to buy, sell, and otherwise dispose of, among themselves.' Says Terry: 'No subject in this empire hath land of inheritance, nor have other title but the King's will.' In such views Bernier and Terry were apparently misled by the absence of manorial landholdings in India, as in Europe. In India it was the peasant who owned the land, not the lords and squires. Certainly not the emperor. He no doubt had absolute political and military authority over all the land, but the land itself, as an economic asset, belonged to the cultivator to whom it was assigned by the clan that cleared the wilderness and established the village, and he could dispose of his land as he liked, subject to his obligations to the village and the state. The amirs too owned some land, though not extensive estates, and the rajas and zemindars had the right to a share of the revenue of their ancestral domains, though the land itself belonged to the cultivator.

The emperor could not justly take over any land without compensating its owner. Says Jahangir about a land transaction in Kabul: 'An excellent plot of land came to view, which I ordered to be bought from the owners,' so he could lay out a garden there. Similarly Shah Jahan felt obliged to compensate Raja Jai Singh, from whom he acquired the site for building the Taj, even though the raja offered the property as a present to the emperor. And when a plaza was constructed in front of the Delhi fort, Shah Jahan had to pay for the property he acquired for it. 'The ground on which the chauk and mosque were to be constructed belonged chiefly to the royal domains,' says Inayat Khan. 'And as for the little which was the property of others, some of the owners were gratified by receiving 10 or

15 times the actual value, and the others by grant of neighboring estates out of the crown lands.' Likewise, when Aurangzeb wanted to acquire a farm to meet his personal expenses, he had to buy the land.

Clearly then, the emperor was not the owner of all the land in Mughal India. As Aurangzeb put it, though in a different context, 'A kingdom is not a hereditary private property.' The cultivator certainly owned the land; the government only had the first claim on its produce. This was the legal position. Sometimes however officials did arbitrarily seize the lands of peasants, as indicated by Jahangir's order prohibiting the practice.

Under Islamic law, infidels could be dispossessed and their lands distributed among the faithful, but this was neither practicable nor necessary in India. Muslims in India were a predominantly urban people and they were content to let Hindus own and cultivate the land. There was no point in expropriating the peasant unless he failed to cultivate the land or pay taxes. There was, therefore, no great change in the ownership of land in India, or in the life of the peasant, following the establishment of Muslim rule.

LAND IN THE Mughal empire fell into five revenue categories. First of all, there was the khalisa, crown lands, the revenues of which were reserved for the emperor. These were prime properties, and were scattered all over the empire; the entire province of Kashmir and a good part of Bengal were reserved as crown lands. The size of the khalisa and the revenue from it varied from reign to reign—while Akbar towards the end of his rule reserved about one-fourth of the total revenue of the empire for himself, the share fell to one-twentieth under Jahangir, then rose again to one-seventh under Shah Jahan. In 1647, during the reign of Shah Jahan, the aggregate land revenue of the empire was 220 million rupees, of which the revenue from the khalisa was thirty million.

The bulk of the empire was given away as jagirs, which constituted the second land category. The jagirdars managed their lands in different ways; while some employed salaried officers to collect revenue, others handed over the collection to speculative revenue farmers, from whom they often collected the tax in advance. Akbar, like Sher Shah before him, disliked the jagir system but could find no alternative to it. For a short while he converted the entire empire, except the hereditary lands of rajas and zemindars, into khalisa lands, and paid officers in cash directly from the treasury. But that only further vitiated revenue administration, for, as Abul Fazl puts it, 'the imperial clerks increased immoderately the assessments of the territories, cities, towns and villages and opened the hand of embezzlement in raising and diminishing them.' Akbar therefore reverted to the jagir system, after his administrative reforms furnished a clear revenue profile of the empire.

Watan-jagirs, the ancestral lands of subordinate rulers in Rajasthan and the Deccan, constituted the third category of land. These jagirs were bequeathable, but the emperor had the right to nominate the successor raja. Besides, the rajas had to adopt, at least outwardly, the Mughal pattern of administration in their domains, as they were a part of the empire.

Similar to watan-jagirs were the altamgha lands. The altamgha was a Central Asian form of land grant, by which the emperor honoured a deserving officer by giving him hereditary possession of an estate, usually in his native district. Such was the grant of a village given by Shah Jahan to the physician who cured Jahanara's burn wounds. Altamgha grants were rare till the eighteenth century, but the successors of Aurangzeb gave them away capriciously.

Zemindari land, belonging to hereditary revenue collectors, was the fifth category of land. Zemindars too, like the rajas and altamgha grant holders, had bequeathable land rights. The Persian term zemindar, meaning a landholder, had been in use in India from the fourteenth century, and referred to the chief of a territory who had the right to a share of the produce of farmers. The zemindar was generally held responsible for revenue collection in his lands, in return for which he received a certain percentage of the revenue (ten per cent in Bengal) as his commission or was compensated with an allotment of rent-free land. A semi-military class, zemindars derived their power from settling a village, distributing its land, and offering local protection to peasants. In this political role, they also claimed the right to evict peasants and other similar powers. All the zemindars of a region usually belonged to the same caste.

Gradually, the status and rights of zemindars began to change, and they converted their right to a share of the produce of the land into an absolute property right. Form the seventeenth century on, a small number of Mughal mansabdars also began to invest their savings in acquiring zemindari rights. The zemindars, who had forts and militias of their own, were a counterpoise to the power of the emperor, but only at the local level. Says Abul Fazl: 'The custom of the majority of the zemindars of Hindustan is to leave the path of single-mindedness and to look to every side and to join anyone who is powerful or who is making an increasing stir.' They were usually oppressive towards itinerant merchants and travellers, but protective towards their own tenants.

The sixth category of land was the freehold, land assigned free of revenue obligations, as charity or favour, usually for learned men to run seminaries and schools. Even non-Muslims received such grants, especially under Akbar. Freehold grants, like all grants, were sanctioned by the emperor, but were given under the authority of the Chief Sadr. They were normally hereditary grants, but were sometimes given only for a lifetime or for a specific period; in all cases they could be reduced or resumed by the emperor.

There was, as in everything else, much corruption in the administration of charity in the Mughal empire. Akbar, ever vigilant in such matters, took action against the abuses, curtailing the powers of Sadrs, and sometimes, as in Gujarat in 1595, reducing all freehold grants by half. Further, he specified that half the freehold grants should be wasteland, so that cultivation could expand, and revenue loss reduced.

REVENUE ASSESSMENT AND collection in Mughal India was a battle of wits between the government and the people. Sher Shah was the only ruler in Mughal times who had seen the workings of the revenue system in all its facets, from the side of the taxer as well as of the taxed, as he had worked his way from outside the government to the inside, and then all the way from the bottom to the top. He could therefore effectively control and reform the system in all its aspects, to serve the interests of the state and yet promote the welfare of the people.

Before Sher Shah, revenue assessment was a haphazard process, largely based on information provided by the Qanungo (the Pargana officer who maintained farming records) and settled with the village or Pargana as a whole. Sher Shah revamped the whole system, drawing on the administrative practices of Alauddin Khilji and expertly adapting them to serve his needs.

Sher Shah first divided arable land into three broad categories (good, middling and poor) on the basis of their fertility, and then for each crop worked out the average yield per unit of the standard category of land, probably by stating that so much of good, middling or poor land made one unit of standard land. Finally, the land under each crop was measured and categorized, its yield determined, and tax assessed as a portion (usually one-third) of the yield. As far as possible Sher Shah made the revenue settlement with individual cultivators, instead of with the whole village as was previously done.

This was Sher Shah's preferred mode of revenue assessment, but he kept his administration flexible enough to accommodate the diversities of custom in his empire. In some outlying regions—in Multan, for instance—he did not enforce the measurement of land, but adopted the older method of sharing the actual produce. And, though he preferred to settle revenue directly with cultivators, he also sometimes dealt with intermediaries like jagirdars and zemindars. Similarly, though he favoured cash payment of salaries to officers, he also made jagir assignments.

Sher Shah's revenue system, despite the shortness of his reign, apparently worked well, for his reputation for administrative efficiency endured long after him. Akbar initially built his revenue administration on Sher Shah's model, and then modified it by a process of trial and error that went on till nearly the end of his reign. First of all, he stipulated that tax should be paid in cash, by calculating the value of the tax portion of the produce at prices fixed by him. In the beginning there was only one price for each crop for the whole empire, but that was inefficient, as market prices varied considerably from place to place. Therefore, in the tenth year of his reign, Akbar introduced the system of calculating the tax demand on the basis of the actual prices prevailing in each region for each season. But that procedure turned out to be too complicated and was abandoned after three years, and a system of largely summary assessments was introduced as a temporary measure, while a thorough reform of the revenue administration was initiated.

IT WAS AT this point that Todar Mal entered the scene. He is usually credited with crafting the Mughal revenue system, and it is possible (but not certain) that he had served under Sher Shah. In 1570, Akbar appointed Todar Mal to assist Muzaffar Khan, the Diwan, in preparing a fresh revenue assessment of the empire, as part of the general overhaul of administration that Akbar undertook around that time.

Under the new revenue system that was then introduced, Akbar reverted to Sher Shah's practice of assessing tax on the basis of the estimated average yield per unit of land, with the added refinement that yield averages were worked out separately for each pargana, to provide for local variations in productivity. The tax, assessed as a share of the produce, was stated in cash as before, by calculating the value of the assessed crop at prices determined by the emperor separately for each crop in each region in each season, based on the reports of local prices. The revenue settlement was made directly with the cultivator (ryot), so the system came to be known as the ryotwary system.

This system with its numerous variables—several categories of land, the productivity of each category of land varying from Pargana to Pargana, and from crop to crop, and the price of crops too varying from place to place and from season to season—was appallingly complicated, and required an enormous amount of computing and record maintenance for each summer and autumn crop. This was beyond the capacity of non-specialist Mughal officers to administer efficiently, despite the very detailed instructions given to them. Its very complexity opened a thousand avenues for corruption. Further, with the emperor constantly on the move in a rapidly expanding empire, price fixing by the emperor often got inordinately delayed. Says Abul Fazl, 'When . . . the empire was enlarged in extent, it became difficult to ascertain each year the prices current and much inconvenience was caused by the delay. On the one hand, the husbandmen complained of excessive exaction, and on the other, the holder of assigned lands was aggrieved on account of the revenue balances.'

Despite its forbidding complexity, the system remained in operation for ten years. In 1580, Akbar abandoned the custom of calculating tax on the basis of seasonal prices, and introduced in its place fixed cash rates. For each crop in each region, the tax claim was now fixed as so many rupees per standard unit of cultivated land, on the basis of the average prices of crops in the previous ten years. These rates remained unchanged from year to year, probably till the end of Akbar's reign.

Concurrently, Akbar also made certain modifications in the organization of the empire to facilitate revenue administration. At the base of the structure was the village under its headman (Muqaddam), who was assisted by a hereditary registrar (variously called Patwari, Talati, Kulkarni or Karnam) who kept track of land and revenue transactions. Several villages were grouped together to form the Pargana, which was headed by a Chaudhri. The Chaudhri's role in administration is not clear, but his assistant, the Qanungo, had clearly defined functions—he was the registrar-accountant of the Pargana and the expounder of local customs and traditions, and was paid by the state either a monthly salary (20 to 50 rupees under Akbar) or a percentage of the revenue of the Pargana, and was assisted by an accountant and a treasurer. In each Pargana, the Qanungo prepared a *dasturu-l amal*, a manual which recorded a whole variety of information about the Pargana (including land tenures) to serve as a guide to administrators. The Parganas were grouped together into Sarkars 'on the basis of agricultural homogeneity'.

Every season, when the crops sprouted, revenue officials visited each village to categorize and measure (with the help of the Patwari) the area under cultivation for various crops. They then issued tax demand slips to farmers, noted the assessments in a tax demand register, and filed a copy of the register with the local Diwan. After harvest, the village headman collected the tax (either in cash or kind, but he always issued receipts for cash) from the cultivators and paid the revenue into the local treasury in cash. For his labour, the headman received a 2.5 per cent commission on the revenue, but only after the state had realized its full dues from the village. If there were any arrears, they were reported to the Diwan, and their collection formed the first charge on the next season's harvest.

In the case of damage to crops after measurement, adjustments were made in the tax claim. Established cash rates were also sometimes raised or lowered in abnormal situations—during Akbar's long stay in Lahore, when the prices in the region rose sharply, cash tax rates were raised by twenty per cent, but were brought back to the norm after Akbar left Punjab; similarly, when prices of agricultural produce fell sharply in the Delhi-Allahabad region because of very good harvests in five consecutive years between 1585 and 1590, extensive remissions in cash rates were granted. Remissions were also routinely granted during natural calamities and famines.

The main advantage of Akbar's long-term revenue settlement was that it assured reasonable financial stability to the peasant as well as to the government. As long as the area under cultivation and the crops cultivated remained stable, both the peasant and the government knew in advance what the tax dues were, irrespective of the fluctuations in yield or price from season to season. The system favoured the peasant in good years or if he improved the yield of the land or if prices rose; it favoured the state in bad years or if the peasant neglected the land, or if prices fell. The general thrust of Akbar's revenue reforms was to encourage the peasant to intensify and expand cultivation.

REVENUE COLLECTION OFTEN involved the use of force, for people generally, and especially zemindars, 'paid tax only at the point of the sword'. Tax on the winter harvest (rabi) was collected on the day of Holi in March, and on the rainy season harvest (kharif) on the Dasehra day in October. In each province, the revenue was remitted into the provincial treasury, from where funds were transferred to the imperial treasury.

Akbar's standard tax rate was one-third of the gross produce, which was high compared to the rate that generally prevailed in the Delhi

Sultanate. But the actual burden on the farmer was probably not more than in earlier times, as Akbar abolished all sorts of other imposts, and checked the oppression of peasants by middle men. In addition to regular taxes, however, the cultivator occasionally had to pay special cesses, such as the cess which Akbar imposed—at the rate of twenty-five pounds of grain on each acre of land cultivated—to pay for the construction of the Agra fort.

In 1575, even while he was busy implementing conventional tax reforms, Akbar introduced a daringly innovative experiment in revenue administration, the Karori system. 'In this year an order was promulgated for improving the cultivation of the country, and for bettering the condition of the ryots,' writes Badauni. 'All the Parganas of the country, whether dry or irrigated, whether in towns or hills, in deserts and jungles, by rivers, reservoirs, or wells, were all to be measured, and every such piece of land as, upon cultivation, would produce one karor (crore: ten million) of tankas (500,000 rupees), was to be divided off, and placed under the charge of an officer to be called Karori, who was to be selected for his trustworthiness . . . So that in the course of three years all the uncultivated land might be brought into cultivation, and the public treasury might be replenished.'

The primary objective of the reform was to expand cultivation, and thus to increase the revenue of the government. 'As much of the land of the extensive country of Hindustan was lying uncultivated but which still was capable of being cultivated,' special officers were assigned by Akbar to bring the land under cultivation, and they were given three years to achieve the target, says Nizamuddin Ahmad.

The Karori system was simplicity itself, and seemed to be the perfect solution to the revenue problems of the empire, as it streamlined assessment and collection, promoted the expansion of cultivation, and assured a steady revenue for the state. Yet the system failed, probably because the Karoris concentrated on the collection of revenue rather than on the expansion of cultivation. 'Regulations were circulated, but eventually these regulations were not observed as they ought to have been,' says Badauni. 'A great portion of the country was laid waste through the rapacity of the Karoris, the wives and children of the ryots were sold and scattered abroad, and everything was thrown into confusion. But the Karoris were brought to account by Raja Todar Mal, and many good men died from the severe beatings which were administered, and from the tortures of the rack and pincers.'

After five years of operation, Akbar abandoned the Karori system in

1580, when he introduced the long-term cash settlement. With this the main phase of Akbar's revenue reforms came to an end. After this, there was only one major modification in revenue administration, in 1596, when Akbar introduced 'administrative dyarchy' in the provinces, by separating revenue administration (diwani) from general administration (faujdari), and requiring the provincial Diwan to report directly to the imperial Diwan, instead of to the provincial governor.

The revenue reforms of Akbar, like those of Sher Shah, initially applied only to the central provinces of the empire, where they applied equally in the crown lands as well as in the jagirs. In the outlying provinces, the older local systems continued to prevail, though generally Akbar's reforms tended to spread into new areas. The Mughal empire was too vast and diverse to be administered under one uniform code, and in any case, Akbar was not pursuing abstract perfection, but doing what was practicable in his given situation.

THERE IS LITTLE information on how Akbar's revenue system worked under his successors, but both Shah Jahan and Aurangzeb are known to have taken active measures to encourage agriculture. There were substantial increases in revenue under them, partly due to the growth of the empire, and partly due to the effective gathering of all the surpluses in the land by the state.

A major deviation from the practices of Akbar, evident from the reign of Shah Jahan, was to assess the village as a unit, represented by its headman, instead of dealing with peasants individually, as Akbar preferred. In the group assessment system, the dues of individual peasants were fixed by the village headman; the peasants paid the headman, who paid the government. Revenue assessment with the village as a unit was probably a pre-Muslim practice which had never entirely disappeared, but was now extensively revived, as the growth of the empire and the decline of its administrative efficiency made it difficult to make settlements with individual peasants. Under Aurangzeb, annual cash assessments on villages became increasingly common.

From the reign of Shah Jahan, tax rates also tended to rise, from the one-third that was the norm under Akbar to sometimes as high as one-half of the gross produce, leaving hardly any surplus with the peasant. In the eighteenth century, the fifty per cent rate would become common, and Aurangzeb's reign marked the transition towards that. Further, according to Manucci, peasants were often forced to pay for the state's share of the harvest at a price higher than the market price, and that added to their tax burden. In addition, when the administrative system weakened under Akbar's successors, all sorts of illegal levies were extracted from the people by local officers and chieftains, so that the peasant may have ended up paying out as much as 'nearly three-quarters' of the produce of his land, as de Laet claims.

However, as the rate of tax increased, the rate of tax evasion also increased. Peasants often evaded tax payments on grounds (usually fictitious) of crop failure and other calamities, and were tortured by officials to get them to pay up, says Manucci. 'Villages which, owing to some small shortage of produce, are unable to pay the full amount of the revenue-farm, are made prize, so to speak, by their masters or governors, and wives and children sold, on the pretext of a charge of rebellion,' says Pelsaert. Aurangzeb periodically ordered strict action against defaulting peasants. And peasants, driven to desperation, often abandoned their fields, sometimes to take to robbery. Agriculture began to decline.

Aurangzeb, perhaps next only to Akbar, was most earnest about revenue administration, to realize the rightful dues of the state, to prevent corruption, and to ensure a fair deal to the cultivator. In 1665, the eighth year of his reign, he issued a classic firman, which specified the guidelines to be followed by revenue officials. The firman, addressed to a high revenue officer in Bihar by name Rasikadas, probably a Diwan, instructed that the officer should 'strive for progressively populating the desolate villages and getting the cultivable land cultivated . . . Wherever there is a well that is out of repair, he should repair it and also dig new ones. He should make assessment of jama (revenue) in such a manner that the whole peasantry receives its due and the authorized land revenue is realized in time, and not a single peasant is subjected to oppression . . . [Revenue officers] should use praiseworthy endeavour and much effort at soothing and conciliation, to gather cultivators from all sides and directions. As for cultivable wasteland, they should impose such revenue rates on it as to enable it to be brought under cultivation.'

Aurangzeb especially emphasized the need to protect the cultivator from middle-men. 'If the Chaudhri, or Muqaddam, or Patwari is involved in oppression, he (the imperial officer) should, comforting the cultivator, let him have his due, and take away the gain from the dominant ones,' he ordered. He also thoughtfully advised that in the case of hardships caused by natural calamities, tax remissions should be made to individual peasants, not to the village or Pargana as whole, so that the relief reached the peasants, and was not cornered by Chaudhris and others. Further, the

Diwan was told to keep a strict watch against the collection of prohibited cesses, and to dismiss and punish oppressive officers.

Three years later, in 1668, Aurangzeb issued further revenue directives. 'At the beginning of the year inform yourself as far as possible about the condition of every peasant, and whether they are engaged in cultivation or are abstaining from it,' he advised his revenue officers. 'If they have the means to cultivate, ply them with inducements and assurances of kindness, and show them any favour they may desire. But if it be found that, in spite of having the means to cultivate, and of a favourable season, they are abstaining from cultivation, then you should urge and threaten them, and make use of force and the whip.'

THE MUGHAL REVENUE system, despite its imperfections, enjoyed a high reputation throughout India, and was adopted even by Mughal adversaries—Malik Amber adopted it in Ahmadnagar, and so did Shivaji in Maharashtra. The Mughal system was certainly an improvement on what prevailed in some of the other Indian sates. In Vijayanagar, says Numiz, the nobles 'are like renters, who hold all the land from the King . . . the common people suffer much hardship, those who hold the lands being so tyrannical.' Conditions were no different in the Bahmini Sultanate, notes Barbosa.

Traditionally revenue collectors in India were appointed either as *kachcha* (by which collectors were paid fixed salaries and were required to remit to the government all the revenue they collected) or as *pakha* (by which collectors paid a fixed sum to the treasury and retained whatever surplus they could squeeze out of the land). South Indian states generally preferred the *pakha* system. In Golconda, for instance, revenue farms were auctioned every year in July, with even English and Dutch speculators participating in the auction. William Methwold, an English trader in India in the first quarter of the seventeenth century, reports that in Golconda 'the government is farmed immediately from the King by some eminent man, who . . . farmeth out the lesser ones, and they again to the country-people, at such excessive rates that it is almost lamentable to consider what toil and misery the wretched souls (cultivators) endure.'

In the Mughal empire, Akbar preferred to avoid intermediaries, and he generally collected revenue through royal officers. But as the empire grew in size, it became a formidable task for the government to set up its own revenue collection organization and supervise its work, so from the reign of Shah Jahan, the *pakha* system was adopted progressively in crown lands, and it became the norm under Aurangzeb and his successors, especially in Bengal. Large tracts of lands thus came under a small number of revenue farmers, who in the course of time acquired hereditary rights, and came to be treated as zemindars, along with the old chieftains. Even the collection of customs dues came to be farmed out at this time.

Revenue farming was hard on peasants, as those who contracted to collect revenue had no interest in the land other than to recover their investment and make a profit, especially as such contracts were often highly speculative. Says Manucci: 'When any hungry wretch takes it into his head to ruin the Kingdom, he goes to the King and says to him, "Sire! If your Majesty will give me the permission to raise money and a certain number of armed men, I will pay so many millions."' Revenue farming was least oppressive when the farmer's tenure was long, and the rent amount moderate.

When the land was given in jagir, the jagirdar was free to adopt either the *kachcha* or *pakha* system to collect revenue. It is not clear what revenue arrangements prevailed in the domains of the rajas. The Mughal preference would have been to enforce imperial revenue regulations in those regions too, but it is possible that, given the lackadaisical Mughal administrative ethos, the rajas paid only a fixed amount to the government as tribute and collected revenue from their subjects according to their own methods and at their own rates. If the rajas were in the imperial service, the tributes due from them were adjusted against their remunerations. Generally speaking, peasants were better off under rajas and zemindars than under imperial officers or jagirdars, for the rajas and zemindars had a durable interest in the peasants, in whose midst they and their descendants had to live.

APART FROM LAND tax, booty was the main source of revenue for the Mughals—booty in fact was their primary revenue source before Akbar systematized revenue administration, and it remained a major revenue source as long as the empire continued to expand, until the end of Aurangzeb's reign. Plunder was so integral to medieval military campaigns that not to plunder was considered a dereliction of duty, and Akbar once reprimanded Raja Man Singh for not allowing his troops to pillage in Rajasthan. The importance of booty in the medieval state may be gauged from the fact that Nadir Shah in the mid-eighteenth century remitted taxes in Persia for three full years because the spoils of his raid on Delhi had filled his treasury.

For medieval kingdoms, pillage was as legitimate as cattle raids were for primitive tribes. Indeed, Mughal campaigns had at times the appearance of cattle raids. Says Babur about one of his forays: 'Masses of sheep fell to us, more than in any other raid.' Looting, like slaughter, was a crime only for subjects, not for kings. The shariah acknowledged the legitimacy of pillage by prescribing how booty was to be distributed between the ruler and his men: the state could keep one-fifth, but the rest had to be distributed among the soldiers and others.

Monarchs seldom respected such precepts—the Delhi Sultans, for instance, reversed the ratio and kept four-fifths for themselves, on the ground that their army was made up of paid soldiers, not freebooters. Babur however followed the Islamic convention, and sometimes did not even take what he as monarch was entitled to. 'By way of favour, we did not take the Fifth from Qasim Beg and some others,' he writes. His successors usually kept all the booty for themselves, giving only what they pleased as gifts to soldiers and amirs, though soldiers were allowed to keep what they personally plundered. But the shariah principle was not altogether forgotten: Abul Fazl states that one of the responsibilities of the Faujdar was that 'when he had captured the rebel camp, he must observe equity in the division of the spoil and reserve a fifth for the royal exchequer'.

Tributes from subordinate rulers constituted another major source of revenue. Equally important were the presents that the emperor received from his courtiers on celebratory occasions and on being shown some royal favour. The amounts involved in these transactions were not trivial—Shah Jahan, for example, received presents totalling as much as three million rupees one year during the Nauruz celebrations. Even if what the emperor in turn gave to the amirs amounted to half the amount he received, still his gain from presents and tributes over the years was substantial enough for it to require a separate treasurer. 'To refuse presents brought by the nobles before you is a loss to the royal treasury,' Aurangzeb cautioned his son, Prince Azam.

Then there was escheat. Says Pelsaert: 'Immediately on the death of a lord who has enjoyed the King's jagir, be he great or small, without any exception—sometimes even before the breath has left his body—the King's officers are on the spot, and make an inventory of the entire estate, recording everything down to the value of a single pice, even to the clothes and jewels of the ladies . . . The King takes back the whole estate absolutely for himself, except in a case where the deceased has done good service in his lifetime, when the women and children are given enough to live on, but no more.'

Confiscation of the property of the amir on his death was routine in Mughal India until Aurangzeb restricted the practice, but strictly speaking it was not an application of the principle of escheat, except when the amir died without an heir. Says Badauni of the practice under Akbar: 'An inspector and registrar of the effects of those who die or disappear was to be appointed. So that if any one who died had an heir, after it had been proved that he did not owe anything to the imperial exchequer, and was not a Karori or a banker receiving deposits, the heir might take possession of it; otherwise it passed to the imperial treasury; and until they got a receipt from the treasurer, they were not to bury the deceased.' Sometimes, but rarely, the emperor paid the debts of a dead amir, as a gesture of favour. Thus Akbar ordered the debts of Sheikh Muhammad Bukhari and Saif Khan Koka, who fell in battle, to be paid out of the royal treasury. 'Such a fact has not been recorded of any king in books of history,' says Nizamuddin Ahmad.

The legal basis (or pretext) for attaching the property of the deceased was that in many cases the amir on his death owed money to the state on the advances he had taken from the treasury, or because he had not settled his accounts with the government, and his dues to the state were the first charge on his property. In the case of rich merchants, the probable reason for attaching their property was that they usually also served as bankers, and the state had to protect the interests of depositors; furthermore, traders often owed money to the state, either by way of taxes or on advances they had taken from the treasury.

There was thus often good reason for the state to take over the property of the dead, but there was also much abuse of the practice, as Aurangzeb reproached Shah Jahan: 'We have been accustomed,' he wrote, 'as soon as any Omrah or a rich merchant has ceased to breathe, nay sometimes before the vital spark has fled, to place seals on his coffers, to imprison and beat the servants or officers of his household, until they make a full disclosure of the whole property, even of the most inconsiderable jewel. The practice is advantageous, no doubt; but can we deny its injustice and cruelty?'

Aurangzeb in his role as a strict legalist made a show of disallowing such malpractices. 'His Majesty . . . forbade the practice of escheating to the State the property of the dead nobles who had left behind them no debt due to the government, but he let their heirs succeed to their legacy,' says Mustaid Khan. Aurangzeb is also said to have banned the practice of requiring the children of amirs to pay to the state the unrecovered debts of their parents. 'He relinquished the Government claims against the ancestors of the officers of the State, which used to be paid by deduction from their salaries. This money every year formed a very large income paid into the public treasury,' says Bakhtawar Khan.

These pious proscriptions however remained largely on paper, and Aurangzeb himself periodically ordered confiscations. 'You should confiscate the property of the deceased (Ameer Khan) with the utmost endeavour so that ... even a piece of straw is not left ... because the property belongs to the subjects,' Aurangzeb once ordered. On his uncle Shayista Khan's death, he wrote to the imperial Vizier Asad Khan: 'You should write to the finance minister of his province to confiscate his property with great caution and to take into possession as royal property every kind of thing obtainable from his servants with force and strictness.' And on the death of another officer, he hypocritically ordered: 'Confiscate the Khan's property with caution and honesty, because the royal treasury belongs to the public. The king is the trustee (of the people) and the officers are appointed by the king. None but the needy and the weak can claim a share of the property.'

COMPARED TO OTHER revenue sources, taxes on trade were unimportant to the Mughals, though they did collect a variety of trade taxes, such as customs and transit dues, shop tax and so on. The rate of customs duty in the Mughal empire was low, ranging between 2.5 and 5 per cent, so that even Surat, the busiest port in the Mughal empire, yielded a net customs revenue of only half a million rupees a year in the mid-seventeenth century, and in Bengal, the East India Company paid a mere 3000 rupees a year as lump sum customs duty, under an agreement with Shuja. Sometimes reduction in customs duties was granted as a compensation for loss or as a reward. Thus the customs duty in Surat was remitted for one year in 1664, as a relief after Shivaji's raid on the town; at the same time, the English and Dutch merchants of Surat, who had successfully defended themselves against Shivaji, were granted an import duty reduction from 2.5 per cent to 2 per cent which they continued to enjoy for fifteen years.

Customs procedures at ports were thorough, and sometimes it took as much as a month for a person to clear his goods, especially if they were merchandise. Individuals too were carefully searched. 'They feel his Body all over; and handle every the least inch of stuff about him with all exactness,' says Thevenot; 'if they perceive any thing hard in it, they immediately rip it up, and all that can be done, is to suffer patiently.

That search is long, and take up above a quarter of an Hour for every Person severally, though at that time they only examine what they have about them.'

There seems to have been some sort of a tax on bullion trade under Akbar. Says Badauni: 'The price of gold, silver and precious stuffs was to remain fixed, and they were to be bought at the imperial tariff. A fixed profit was to accrue to the imperial treasury.' State monopolies, such as the monopoly on salt, also brought in some revenue. In addition, the state sometimes created temporary monopolies such as in lead, saltpetre and indigo. The royal mint was yet another source of revenue, and so were fines.

APART FROM REGULAR taxes, the Mughals periodically imposed special taxes. For instance, under Akbar there was a tax on marriage; similarly, there were taxes on trees (abolished by Akbar and Jahangir, but revived later), on horses (depending upon the breed), and so on. The most important of these special taxes was jizya, the head tax collected from non-Muslims, which was abolished by Akbar, but reimposed by Aurangzeb.

Jizya was levied on a three-tier income slab. Ishwardas, writing in the reign of Aurangzeb, states that the rich, whose annual income was over 2,500 rupees, paid 48 dirhams (about thirteen rupees) a year as jizya; the middle class, with an income of over 250 rupees, paid twenty-four dirhams (about 6.5 rupees), and the poor, who had an annual income of over 52 rupees 'and was able to support himself, his women and children' paid twelve dirhams (about 3.25 rupees). 'If a person owned no property and his income from labour did not exceed his and his family's necessities, jizya was not be charged from him,' notes a late Mughal chronicler. Still, it was a regressive tax and it hit the poor the hardest. Twelve dirhams were about a month's earnings for the urban labourer, and jizya cut deep into the subsistence income of the poor. The rich, in contrast, got off lightly.

Hitting the poor hardest served a purpose of jizya, to induce conversions. Strangely, brahmins were usually exempted from paying jizya, though they were the spiritual leaders of the Hindu community. This was another one of the compromises that Muslim rulers had to make in India, to accommodate the strong Hindu opposition to taxing brahmins. Also exempted from jizya were women, slaves, children below fourteen, blind men, cripples, lunatics, beggars and paupers. When Aurangzeb reimposed jizya, government officials were exempted from its purview, and jizya on Europeans was commuted by adding one percent to the customs duty they had to pay. The tax had to be paid in advance. On payment, Hindu traders were given 'a receipt to serve as a passport, but when they travel to another kingdom or province of the empire, the said passport is of no value,' says Manucci. 'On their outward and their return journey the same amount is collected.'

Jizya must have been at all times a difficult tax to collect from the vast Hindu population dispersed all over the empire. There is no clear estimate of the revenue from the tax. Abul Fazl claims that when Akbar abolished it, jizya was yielding millions of rupees in revenue, a vague figure from a hyperbolic writer. After Aurangzeb reimposed jizya, in Gujarat it was said to have yielded 500,000 rupees a year (about 3.5 per cent of the total revenue of the province), and in the city of Burhanpur 26,000 rupees a year. Later, when jizya was finally abandoned by Aurangzeb's great-grandson Muhammad Shah in 1720, forty years after its imposition by Aurangzeb, it was estimated to fetch forty million rupees annually. This probably is a vastly exaggerated figure, for it constituted about 12 per cent of the estimated 334.5 million rupees total revenue of the empire under Aurangzeb in 1690, a most unlikely figure.

The probability is that the revenue from jizya, as a percentage of the total revenue of the empire, was about the same as in Gujarat, say about four per cent. It was at that rate that the tax was collected in rural areas, where the practice was to charge jizya on jagirdars and revenue collectors at the rate of four per cent of the land revenue, and leave it to them to collect it from the people. In rare instances jizya was remitted, as was done in the Deccan in 1704 owing to the sufferings of the people due to war and famine. Islamic convention required the revenue from jizya to be lodged in a separate treasury called *khazanah-i-jizya*, to be used for religious charity.

Just as Hindus paid jizya, Muslims also had to pay a religious tax, but a wealth tax, not a head tax. This was zakat, the alms tax. Charity was a religious obligation for Muslims, but people being what they were, charity had to be enforced by the state. Many paid the tax willingly, fearing that they would otherwise face divine wrath, but many others were willing to chance it. Zakat could be charged only on the property that was in the owner's possession for at least one year, so some people found a way around paying it by transferring their property to their wives once a year for a short while. The revenue from zakat was meant to be used only for charity, not for state expenses, but in practice it came to be taken as a regular state revenue. Aurangzeb abolished the tax, to show favour to Muslims. However, the Marathas continued to collect it—but surely not to promote Muslim charity!

IN THE MUGHAL empire it was often difficult to distinguish the legal from the quasi-legal and illegal imposts, as even regular taxes had an element of arbitrariness in their administration, and often a part of the revenue from the 'illegal' levies collected by local officials flowed into the government treasury. Only the periodical prohibitions issued by the emperor marked certain collections as illegal.

Tolls, says Shihabuddin Talish, were exacted from every trader in Mughal India, 'from the rose-vendor down to the clay-vendor'. So tyrannical were the officials that they collected ferry tax from people even for crossing dry river-beds. They also taxed the sale of cow-dung cakes, leaves and brambles used by the poor as fuel. Hindus had to pay a fee for bathing in sacred rivers and for depositing the bones of their dead into the Ganga; there was a tax to be paid on the birth of every male child. Officials at times forced merchants and peasants to buy (or sell) commodities and produce at the prices they specified, and they often collected forced subscriptions and compulsory gifts. Some even demanded from peasants the price of the paper on which they issued tax receipts. Rebels imposed levies of their own. Sometimes even villagers collected illegal taxes, as was done by a village just a few miles from Agra in 1637, during the reign of Shah Jahan.

The most vexatious of these illegal taxes was the inland transit toll (*rahdari*: road-guard tax), which, says Khafi Khan, 'was collected on every highway, frontier and ferry'. Often these tyrannies were practised by the very men appointed to prevent them, the *rahdars* (road guards), who therefore came to be commonly known as *rahzams* (highwaymen), as indeed they were known even in ancient India. 'The severity they exercise upon travellers is great, depriving them of the smallest piece of money to be found upon them, with no tenderness for the poor, taking from them in default of money their shirts, coats and sheets,' writes Manucci. 'On the river highways, if the wind brought it to the ears of the toll-collectors that the stream was carrying away a broken boat without *hasil* (tax), they would chain the river,' says Shihabuddin Talish satirically.

'Excise officers,' says Mustaid Khan, 'used to practice astonishing outrages on the modesty of women in searching their persons,' under the suspicion that they were smuggling tobacco. They oppressed travellers even in the name of zakat, the alms tax. Toll collectors, according to

Shihabuddin Talish, 'considered it an act of unparalleled leniency if no higher zakat was taken from rotten clothes . . . than from mended rags, and a deed of extreme graciousness if cooked food was charged with a lower duty than uncooked grains.' So constant was the menace of these extortionists that in time there came into existence a group of professionals (called *hundikaris* under the later Marathas) who would, for a fee, carry goods evading the transit hurdles!

Most of these tolls were common in India for many centuries; Firuz Tughluq had abolished them in the mid-fourteenth century, but with little success, nor were the Mughal prohibitions any more effective. Among the taxes banned by Akbar, apart from jizya, were the pilgrim tax, taxes on oxen, on trees, on artisans, on the sale of cattle, hemp, blankets, oil and hides, and houses. Similar orders were issued by Jahangir. Aurangzeb on his accession banned, according to Khafi Khan, 'nearly eighty' taxes, including road tax, trade tax, tax on goats, grazing tax, collections made at Hindu and Muslim fairs, 'tax on spirit, on gambling-houses, on brothels, the fines, thank-offerings, and the fourth part of debts recovered by the help of magistrates from creditors. These and other imposts . . . which brought in crores of rupees to the public treasury, were all abolished throughout Hindustan.'

The abolitions were only on paper, concedes Khafi Khan. 'Although his gracious and beneficent Majesty remitted these taxes, and issued strict orders prohibiting their collection, the avaricious propensities of men prevailed, so that, with the exception of *pandari* (octroi), which, being mostly obtained from the capital and the chief cities, felt the force of the abolition, the royal prohibition had no effect, and faujdars and jagirdars in remote places did not withhold their hands from these exactions,' says Khafi Khan.

There was no way for the emperor to enforce his ban on these exactions, for their collection was pervasive, and the officers who were to implement the ban were those who were levying them. It is probable that some of these tolls had become quasi-legal in the reign of Shah Jahan, for Khafi Khan reports that transit dues 'brought in a large sum to the revenue.' Under Aurangzeb, imperial revenue officers tacitly legitimized these illegal collections by adjusting the revenue from them in the accounts of jagirdars, according to Khafi Khan. At the time when Akbar abolished illegal tolls, their revenue, according to Nizamuddin Ahmad, 'amounted to as much as the whole revenue of Iran'. Sarkar estimates that the total amount paid by merchants towards illegal exactions and gratifications must have amounted to ten million rupees a year in the Mughal empire during the reign of Aurangzeb. Oppression by local officers grew steadily worse as the empire expanded and imperial authority stretched thin. At the close of Aurangzeb's reign, people in the Deccan had to bear a double set of taxes, as the Marathas superimposed their own taxes (*chauth* and *sardeshmukhi*) over the Mughal taxes.

ADMINISTRATIVE SLACKNESS, corruption, incessant wars, and the spread of rebellion so debilitated the Mughal empire that by the end of the seventeenth century it had become financially crippled. Akbar alone among the Mughals had kept the empire in robust financial health. According to Moosvi's calculation, in 1595–96, out of a total land revenue of ninety-nine million rupees, payments to mansabdars absorbed 80.95 millions, the central military establishment cost 8.97 million, and the imperial household 4.68 million—a total expenditure of 94.61 million rupees, leaving Akbar an annual surplus of 4.4 million rupees from land revenue alone, in addition to substantial revenues from other sources. The financial health of the empire steadily deteriorated after Akbar.

On paper, the Mughal revenue continued to grow phenomenally till the last phase of Aurangzeb's reign—thus while the land revenue assessment towards the close of Shah Jahan's reign was 220 million rupees, it rose to over 334.5 million by 1690—but the actual collection under Aurangzeb was considerably less than the assessed revenue. The receipts in the Deccan, notes Sarkar, were at times a mere one-tenth of the assessment. These figures refer to land revenue only. In addition, there were revenues from booty, jizya, zakat, customs duties, presents, escheat and so on, none of which can be calculated precisely, so the actual total revenue of the Mughal empire is not known.

Whatever the total revenue, the Mughal government under Aurangzeb was unable to meet its expenses from its income and had to draw on past savings, so that at the end of Aurangzeb's reign there were hardly any cash reserves left, though there was still in the treasury the accumulated hoard of bullion and gems of incalculable value. Says Bernier about Aurangzeb's predicament: 'I admit that his income exceeds probably the joint revenues of the Grand Seigneur and of the King of Persia; but if I were to call him a wealthy monarch, it would be in the sense that a treasurer is to be considered wealthy who pays with one hand the large sums which he receives with the other.'

The Mughal budget was essentially a military budget, the preponderant portion of its revenue being allotted to military and quasi-military expenses.

But war, which was in the beginning a gainful activity for the Mughals and produced vast surpluses, eventually turned out to be entirely wasteful. Shah Jahan's Central Asian and Kandahar campaigns, for instance, cost the empire 160 million rupees with nothing to show for it; the expenses of Aurangzeb's Deccan campaigns proved an unstanchable haemorrhage.

Equally burdensome was the cost of maintaining the teeming bureaucracy—millions of people, as Bernier points out, depended on the emperor's pay for their livelihood. Then there were the theocratic expenses of the state. The emperor had to spend vast sums on charity (to indigent Muslims and fakirs) and on the maintenance of places of worship and other religious institutions (mostly of Muslims, but occasionally of Hindus as well), for which (as well as for favouring nobles) the emperor gave freehold grants, which cut into the state's revenue. Even during Akbar's reign, despite his rigorous financial control, such freehold grants amounted to about four per cent of the revenue of the empire.

A major problem with Mughal finances was that its revenue growth was due to the expansion of territory and the tighter squeezing of the people, and not because of economic prosperity. In fact, indications are that agricultural productivity was declining in the late seventeenth century, despite government efforts to shore up cultivation. Further, towards the end of Aurangzeb's reign the empire had grown too huge for its administrative grid to hold it together; the bindings then began to snap and revenue flow from the provinces began to dwindle, so that the expansion of the empire beyond a point resulted in revenue loss rather than gain.

Financial problems had begun to show up even during Jahangir's reign, when the income from crown lands was found to be not enough to meet the emperor's mounting expenses, so that he had to draw on the reserves in the treasury. Shah Jahan, despite his seeming opulence, had to be careful about his expenses, especially after the futile Balkh and Kandahar campaigns. The crisis deepened under Aurangzeb. He was often so strapped in his last years that he had to borrow money to meet urgent expenses, and had to reject the desperate appeals of his officers for funds to carry out essential repairs to forts. Salary arrears began to mount. The Mughal empire was heading towards bankruptcy.

The Flabby Giant

THE MUGHALS RULED by the drawn sword. The quality of their army was therefore decisive in determining their destiny. Babur invaded India with an absurdly small army, but as the Mughal empire swelled in size, its army too bloated. And it continued bloating, till at last, by the reign of Aurangzeb, it became so obese that it could barely move, a flabby colossus, prey to darting hounds.

What the army gained in mass, it lost in energy. It is significant that while Babur won at Panipat with a small force against a mammoth Afghan army, Humayun lost at Kanauj with a mammoth army against a much smaller Afghan force. And when Humayun won back the empire, it was again with a lean, mean army, proving that discipline, spirit and energy were everything in war, and that a small, sinewy army could smash into a much larger enemy with explosive force and annihilate it.

In Kabul, Babur could exercise direct command over his small army. In India, the Mughals had to marshal their army differently, because of its huge size, but not even Akbar, for all his daring reforms, developed the needed hierarchical organization. Instead, he dealt with the problem of size by simply dividing the army into units and apportioning them to mansabdars to recruit and maintain. In times of war, these various units were brought together—but brought together only physically, without integrating them into a unified fighting force.

Mughal soldiers had no common uniform to make them feel as one army, no drill to weld them together, not even a common fighting style. Each race and clan fought in separate units, the Rajputs by themselves, the Afghans by themselves, and so on, under their own commanders, with their own war cry, with their own preferred weapons, in their own special way of fighting. In effect, what the Mughals had was not an army but an assortment of armies.

A further problem was that Mughal commanders were not full-time military officers, sometimes were not even combatants, as even poets and physicians were at times called to serve in the field. The army had no command structure, only ad hoc assignments, and an amir in charge of one campaign could be a subordinate officer in another or even in the same campaign, if the emperor so decided. The amirs therefore constantly jockeyed for position, thwarting each other's moves to create openings for their own advancement, in reckless disregard for the military objectives of the empire. Further, there was a low proportion of senior officers to men in the Mughal army, one captain for every 5000 or so according to one estimate, which meant that soldiers were barely under control during battle. If a captain died in the midst of a battle, there was no one to take charge of his soldiers, and they usually scattered. Without a command grid to hold it together, the Mughal army was little more than a horde.

THE MAIN DIVISIONS of the Mughal army were the cavalry, infantry, artillery, and elephant divisions. But these were not organized into separate corps with their own commanders; instead, they were distributed haphazardly among high-ranking mansabdars, each of whom had some of each of these divisions, except the artillery. The artillery was a specialized corps, which had its own designated commander, titled Mir Atish. The rest of the army was grouped according to the mode of their recruitment and maintenance, such as the central army directly under the emperor, then the forces maintained by mansabdars and rajas, and finally the local militia to be brought in by zemindars and others for temporary service.

The core of the Mughal army was the central cavalry, a select regiment under the immediate command of the emperor. This was a small force, its strength under Akbar being less than 25,000. This core army had an inner core of its own, made up of superbly equipped gentlemen troopers called Ahadis, the emperor's Praetorian Guards, who were kept in a high state of military preparedness at all times. Bernier notes that Aurangzeb had some two or three thousand fine horse, presumably the Ahadis, 'always at hand in case of emergency'. Later, in the eighteenth century, with the decay of the empire, the status of the Ahadi declined; his post became a sinecure, and the term Ahadi a synonym for idler. The gallant had become the gallivanter.

The soldiers of the central army were recruited with care. All of them, soldiers as well as officers, were individually selected and had to have a guarantor of good behaviour. 'All soldiers, captains, and generals, whatever their birth or position, are obliged to furnish sureties,' says Manucci. 'Without this they will not be taken into the service.' Every horseman in the king's service was required to have a Turkish horse, as the horses reared in India were 'timid and restive'. Periodical reviews of the central army were held by the Mir Bakshi, to check the men, horses and equipment. Anything deficient in a soldier's mount or equipment had to be made good within a specified period of time, otherwise his pay was liable to be docked. If his horse died, he had to produce proof of that on the same day, and was given seven days to buy a new horse.

Similar care was expected to be taken by the mansabdars in the recruitment and maintenance of their soldiers, but they seldom even met their quota of troops, let alone kept up their quality. Invariably they cheated by dressing up pages and servants as soldiers, or borrowed soldiers and horses from each other, to pass muster. Akbar endeavoured to eliminate these irregularities by branding horses and maintaining the descriptive rolls of soldiers, and those practices—certainly the branding of horses—were continued by his successors. Manucci notes that during Aurangzeb's reign, the horses in the emperor's service were branded on the right flank with a special sign, and that those of the mansabdars on the left flank, usually with the first letter of their name.

When the emperor sent a general on a campaign, it was, says Manucci, 'necessary for that officer to appear on the river bank within sight of the palace windows and parade the whole of his cavalry and infantry. Three days after the inspection, he must begin his march.' The rigour of inspection of the mansabdari forces slackened in later times, as evidenced by the fact that though these forces were originally mustered once a year, this became irregular later, and Aurangzeb in the Deccan altogether exempted mansabdars of the rank of 3000 and above from mustering.

In addition to the regular army, the local militia could be called up when necessary. Termed bhumi, the militia consisted mostly of infantry, but had some cavalry too, and sometimes even guns and boats. According to Abul Fazl, the militia in the reign of Akbar had a potential aggregate strength of about 4.7 million men, of whom only some 385,000 were cavalrymen. Mostly peasants on temporary military service, militia infantrymen received no regular pay, and probably served only as camp-followers. The local cavalry, maintained by zemindars, constituted a more regular force. These local levies were not good enough to be used in imperial wars, but they helped to maintain law and order in rural India.

THE CAVALRY WAS the elite wing of the Mughal army, its main battle division, and great care was taken to procure good horses for troopers. More than 100,000 horses were brought into India every year, mainly from Balk, Bukhara and Kabul, and Manucci says that the emperor made good profit from their import: 'At the crossing of the Indus alone a payment of twenty-five per cent on their value is made.' Horses were expensive in India, especially in the Deccan; in Goa a horse cost about 500 pagodas (1000 rupees), while a slave-girl cost only twenty or thirty pagodas (about forty or sixty rupees) in the late sixteenth century. Few Rajputs could afford imported horses, and most of them rode 'little ponies hardly as big as donkeys,' says Monserrate.

In battle, horses and riders were clad in mail, and men were heavily armed, though the Mughals did not have the kind of heavy cavalry in use in Europe at this time. Says Terry: 'I have scene horse-men there, who have carried whole armories about them, thus appointed: at their sides good swords; under them sheves of arrowes; on their shoulders bucklers, and upon their backs guns fastned with belts; at the left side bowes hanging in cases, and lances about two yards and a halfe long (having excellent steele heads), which they carric in their hands.'

The Mughal cavalry charge was an awesome sight, and a cavalier on the gallop a thing of beauty. The horses of amirs, says Careri, had embroidered saddles adorned with precious stones, and tassels of yak tails on the front and back of their saddles as well as on the heads of their horses, 'so that when the Rider spurs on his Horse to a full speed, or if there be any wind, these tassels flying in the Air seem to be so many wings of the Horse, and yield a most pleasant prospect.'

In contrast to the cavalry, the infantry had a low status in the Mughal army, and they received the lowest pay. Even common soldiers disdained to fight on foot. In Akbar's time, porters, postal runners, gladiators, wrestlers, palanquin bearers, water-carriers and other menials were classed as infantry. In numbers, the size of the infantry was immense, but as a fighting force it was nearly worthless—an ill-equipped and ill-disciplined rabble, it was often more a liability than an asset in war.

The common weapons in Mughal India were the sword, the bow and arrow, and the spear. The hand pike was the favourite weapon of Rajputs; 'mounted or on foot, they have no weapon other than a short spear, with shield, sword, and dagger,' says Pelsaert. Indian swords were renowned in the ancient world for their high-quality steel, but in Mughal times they were clumsy and of poor quality. 'Their swords are four fingers broad, very thick, and by consequence heavy; they are crooked a little, and cut only on the convex side,' says Careri. 'The guard is very plain . . . The swords made by the Indian are very brittle; but the English furnish them with good ones brought from England.' European sword-blades were in great demand in India, notes Terry.

Everyone had a dagger a foot long stuck into the girdle, and sometimes a pistol too. Their shields, made of leather, were two feet in diameter, had a great many inch-long nails sticking out from them, and were often 'varnished over with Black,' says Thevenot. In battle, soldiers wore a coat of mail, but emperors seem to have preferred the *jubba*, 'a coat made of very strong quilted silk or cotton, used as armour . . . [which would] turn the sharpest sword, or a spent ball.' Says Tavernier about the weapons of the Golconda soldier: 'They do not wear a sabre like Persians, but a broad sword like the Swiss, with which they both cut and thrust, and they suspend it from a belt . . . Their cavalry carry bows and arrows, a buckler and a battle-axe, a head-piece and a jacket of mail, that hangs down from the head-piece over their shoulders.'

Gunners were classed as infantry in the Mughal army, and had low status and poor equipment. 'Those who carry fire-arms in their army are matchlock-men and people of no rank, known as tufangis,' writes Manrique. 'They carry arquebuses, which being poorly made, are, as it were, awkward arms.' But Tavernier found Indian guns, at least in Golconda, superior to those of Europe. 'The barrels of their muskets are stronger than ours, and much neater; for their iron is better, and not so subject to break,' he says. Bernier too considered Indian guns, though short-barrelled, to be of good quality, especially those of the Mughal royal guards.

Battles in Mughal India were mostly fought with sword and spear in hand, and the deadliest missile was still the arrow. But a change was coming about with the increasing use of muskets and cannons. Gunpowder, invented by the Chinese around the tenth century, was probably first used by the Arabs at the beginning of the fourteenth century to make guns (bamboo tubes reinforced with iron, using arrows as projectiles) and was introduced into India from the Middle East. There are references to the use of firearms in Kashmir, Gujarat and Kerala in the second half of the fifteenth century, though they were then probably little more than curiosities.

It was Babur who first used cannons and muskets effectively in field battle in India. Indians were largely unfamiliar with them. 'The people of Bajaur had never seen matchlocks,' writes Babur, 'and at first were not in the least afraid of them, but, hearing reports of the shots, stood opposite the guns, mocking and playing unseemly antics.' But once a few men were brought down by gunshots, 'the defenders of the fort became so frightened that not a man ventured to show his head for fear of the matchlocks.' The Rajputs had virtually no firearms even at the time of Rana Pratap Singh, and had to hire gunmen from other communities, though the Mughals had by then begun to use guns regularly. Akbar was keen on guns; he introduced several innovations, and a multi-barrelled cannon is said to have been invented by one Hakim Fathullah Shirazi under the emperor's patronage.

The Mughal guns were slow in firing, and their range limited. Sometimes cannons exploded while firing. Babur's cannons could fire a maximum of only sixteen times a day; the range of the great cannon that Ustad Ali-quli made for Babur was a mere 1600 paces, about 1200 metres. Abul Fazl gravely reports that when Akbar attacked Daulatabad, the defenders 'fired a great gun and two men lost their lives at once . . . A wonderful thing was that in that rain of cannon-balls no injury was done to the imperialists.' Says Manucci about cannons in forts: 'Their only use is to make a great noise and smoke on days when a new moon appears, or when it is intended to frighten someone; for to go through any drill with them, or to teach how to aim them in one direction or another, that is an impossible thing.' Lighter field pieces presumably had a greater fire rate and effectiveness. As for the Mughal musketeers, they were 'terribly afraid of burning their beards or bursting their guns' while firing, says Bernier; to fire, they squatted and rested the musket on a 'wooden fork which hangs to them'.

One of the largest deployments of Mughal artillery was in Dara's Kandahar campaign. The prince carried with him 30,000 cannon balls, small and great, 187,000 kilograms of gunpowder, 93,000 kilograms of lead, and 1400 rockets. Among the cannons in his train were two which could fire iron shots of between forty-five and fifty kilograms in weight. Even with all that firepower, the Mughals could not breach the Kandahar fortifications, and had to retreat ignominiously. Cannonading was mostly for atmospherics. Even in field battles, the role of guns was secondary to that of the cavalry. Mughal guns were not effective enough to win battles by themselves. Their main function was to break up the enemy array; battles were still won by the cavalry charge that followed.

The Mughals however attached great importance to artillery, and it was kept directly under the control of the emperor. Europeans were valued as cannoneers and matchlockmen, and were paid highly—Manucci, when he served in Shah Jahan's artillery, was paid eighty rupees a month, which was raised to 150 rupees by Dara; later Aurangzeb fixed the pay of European artillerymen at four rupees a day, and Manucci says that he was as a special case offered five rupees a day, which he declined to accept, saying that he wanted to return to his homeland. The real reason for Manucci's decision was probably that while European gunners were previously required only to aim and fire the guns, Aurangzeb insisted that they should also load them, which they considered beneath their status, and several of them left the Mughal service.

With the growing prominence of artillery, the elephant, which was once the battle tank of India, began to lose its military importance. Elephants 'are naturally timid', says Bernier, 'and have a particular dread of fire, which is the reason why elephants have been used with so very little advantage in armies since the use of fire-arms.' Because of their fear of fire, elephants were inducted into war only after years of training and familiarization with musket fire. Further, to overcome their timidity and to make them ferocious, elephants were, says Monserrate, given 'cat's flesh to eat mixed with their other food'.

For the Mughals, elephants were a new battle experience in India. Ibrahim Lodi had deployed a large number of them at Panipat, and so had Hemu, whose elephants, according to Abul Fazl, were 'capable of disordering a large force. They were especially calculated to confuse the onset of cavalry, as the horses had never seen such terrific forms.' The Mughals themselves later greatly took to elephants. Akbar was an avid collector, and had, according to Abul Fazl, 5,000 elephants grouped in different categories, 100 of which, each having a name, were kept in the royal stables. After the reign of Akbar the use of elephants in war declined, and neither at Dharmat nor at Samogarh do we hear of elephants in action. They were there used mainly as mounts of princes. But at Khajwa, the Bengal elephants of Shuja wrought havoc in Aurangzeb's army.

Elephants were expensive. A good elephant could cost between 4000 and 7000 rupees, a rare elephant as much as 80,000 rupees (which was the value of an elephant Shah Jahan presented to Jahangir) or even 100,000 rupees (which was the estimated value of the elephant presented to Shah Jahan by the sultan of Golconda).

THE MUGHALS WERE attentive to every aspect of land warfare, and spared no expense to do all that was necessary to maintain their military dominance. But they were entirely land creatures—they saw the ocean for the first time in India—and completely neglected the navy. In Asia, only China had a sizable navy in Mughal times. The Cholas in South India were once active in the eastern Indian Ocean, both in trade and war, but that was half a millennium before the coming of the Mughals, and the memory of their overseas adventures had long faded.

There was however a great amount of shipbuilding in India in Mughal times. In the fifteenth century Nicolo Conti and other travellers had noted the presence of large Indian-built vessels in the Arabian sea, used for transporting pilgrims to Mecca. Says Terry of what he saw in Jahangir's India: 'The ship that usually goeth from Surat to Moha (Mokha) is of exceeding great burthen. Some of them I beleeve, at the least fourteene or sixteene hundred tunnes; but ill built, and, though they have good ordnance, cannot well defend themselves. In these ships are yeerly abundance of passengers; for instance, in one ship returning thence, that yeere we left India, came seventeene hundred, the most of which number goe not for profit but out of devotion to visite the sepulchre of Mahomet at Medina.' John Fryer speaks of Aurangzeb's pilgrim ships as 'huge, misshapen things'.

Indian ships were almost entirely for transport, not for battle, and they were easy prey to pirates, so the Mughals often had to seek the help of European warships for the protection of their ports and pilgrim traffic. The nearest thing to a navy that the Mughals had was the Dacca flotilla of 768 armed vessels and boats, mentioned in Todar Mal's 1582 revenue settlement of Bengal. It cost about 29,000 rupees a month to maintain, but was not particularly efficient in deterring pirates. In Bengal, boats were made 'for purposes of war, carriage or swift sailing', says Abul Fazl. 'For attacking a fort, they are so constructed that when run ashore, their prow overtops the fort and facilitates its capture.' Moreland estimates that the aggregate tonnage of 'fighting ships' for all India at the end of Akbar's reign did not exceed 20,000 tuns, including the ships of the Portuguese and the pirates.

Manucci says that Aurangzeb planned to build a naval fleet to combat piracy; he indeed did fit out some ships in Surat in 1682, but nothing much came of the project. Aurangzeb however had a naval auxiliary in Sidi of Janjira, an Abyssinian naval captain who was originally in the employ of Bijapur but was taken into the Mughal service by paying him a subsidy to use his fleet against the Marathas. Sidi was virtually independent, and the English treated him as a separate power. The only other Indian naval forces active in Mughal times were the pirates of Arakan and Malabar, and the Maratha coastal fleet. 'This last yeere the Malabarres vexed the Portugals and tooke or sunke of them at time sixtie saile or more,' says William Finch. 'They are good souldiers and carry in each frigat one hundred souldiers, and in their galots two hundred.'

The Mughals were largely indifferent to what happened on the high seas. Throughout the sixteenth century and the first couple of decades of the seventeenth, the sea around India was dominated by the Portuguese, whose attitude, according to Hawkins, was that 'these seas belong unto the King of Portugall, and none ought to come here without his licence.' The Mughals did not challenge this claim. They saw no need to do that, as they could see no threat to their own power from across the seas. True, European powers fought on the seas—the sultan of Golconda, according to Manucci, in fact believed 'that the Europeans fought nowhere but on the seas'—but they could not see any possible military advantage for themselves in maintaining a navy. Conquest and defence, as they saw, were related only to land. Land could be conquered and occupied, but not the seas.

THE MUGHALS CONSIDERED themselves invincible on land. That indeed was how it was under Akbar. But by the reign of Aurangzeb the situation had changed altogether, and the once awesome Mughal army now cringed at the very approach of the Marathas.

The morale of the Mughal army was dismal at this time. The common soldiers, ill-paid and ill-treated, had no *esprit de corps*; as their commanders looked to their own self-interest, so did the soldiers. Only the soldiers directly employed by the emperor received their salaries with any regularity. They were also the best paid. The Ahadis, the personal guards of the emperor, received, according to Abul Fazl, over 500 rupees a month, a very high salary. Ordinary mounted soldiers in the royal service were paid, excluding the maintenance cost of their horses and equipment, seven or eight rupees a month, but it could go up to thirteen or even fifteen rupees if the trooper had an imported horse, a salary which was comparable to a physician's pay. In the infantry, artillerymen were paid from seven to thirteen rupees, though European officers were paid much higher salaries; matchlockmen got three to six rupees, porters got about three rupees, gladiators and wrestlers got between two and fifteen rupees. Akbar's order of 1595 specified for Rajputs a slightly lower wage structure than that of the Mughal, Afghan and Indian Muslim soldiers—excessive supply had devalued the Rajput soldier.

These scales of pay did not apply to the soldiers maintained by mansabdars, who paid their recruits as they pleased. 'The generals and officers keep to no fixed rules in paying their soldiers,' says Manucci, 'for to some they will give twenty or thirty rupees, to others forty, fifty or a hundred. Usually they make great promises, but not even a half is received . . . The wretched soldiers naturally agree to anything, all the more readily since they have no other means of livelihood . . . The money they get comes in driblets, and when all is said and done it does not come to a great deal. For in respect of one year's service they receive six or eight months' pay. Even that is not all in coin; they are always foisted off as respects two month's pay with clothes and old raiment from the household. Over and above this, there is almost always due to them the pay for two or three years' service.'

To keep going, soldiers had to borrow money from shroffs, who would pay only twenty or twenty-five rupees for a pay order of one hundred rupees, and were often in collusion with the generals with whom they shared the interest. 'If anyone resigns service at his own request, they deduct two months' pay,' notes Manucci. Even in the royal army soldiers were 'harassed and crushed by the oppression of the thievish clerks,' says Shihabuddin Talish. Sometimes soldiers had to resort to mutiny to get their pay. In the reign of Aurangzeb, Mughal artillerymen in the Deccan, who had not received their pay for fourteen months, once pulled out Tarbiyat Khan, the chief of artillery, from his palanquin 'and made him sit down in their midst in rain' for several hours, till they got satisfaction from the emperor, reports Hamiduddin Khan Nimacha.

With such irregular pay as they received, soldiers had no alternative but to sustain themselves by plunder, which in any case was their chief motive for taking to soldiering. Tempted by the prospect of spoils, they sometimes launched into action by themselves, and at such moments even Babur had difficulty in controlling them. On the other hand, when soldiers were loaded with booty, they preferred to avoid battle, for all that they wanted then was to get back home safe to enjoy the loot. Says Inayat Khan of a raid in the Deccan during the reign of Shah Jahan: 'After carrying off almost all the cattle, wealth, and property belonging to the occupants of that town, the Khan (Khan Duran) next moved quickly to Narainpur . . . where likewise he spared no exertions in killing, capturing and plundering the residents. He halted there for the night, as the troops were already heavily laden with spoils.'

Soldiers, more so camp-followers, were totally intractable in the heat of plunder; they plundered everybody, the enemy, the people in their path, and sometimes even the camp of their own masters. After the battle of Deorai, the Rajput escorts specially engaged by Dara to guard his treasure, themselves plundered it. And during Jaswant Singh's desertion at Khajwa, the fleeing Rajputs plundered Aurangzeb's camp. Any abnormal development would set soldiers rampaging—even in moments of victory they sometimes plundered their own camp, as some of Aurangzeb's soldiers did towards the close of the battle of Deorai, because their captain had died in the battle.

Such laxity in discipline was unavoidable in an army as large and as haphazardly organized as that of the Mughals. It was, says Manucci, easy to recruit soldiers in India. 'Whenever the king, or some commander in his name, wants to raise soldiers, infantry or cavalry, it is not necessary to make any great stir,' he writes. 'For a thousand at a time will attend to take service, and of these the best are chosen.'

'The armies of those easterne warres oftentimes consist of incredible multitudes,' says Terry. 'The total amount of troops in Hindoustan is almost incredible,' writes Bernier. The stupendous growth in the size of the Mughal army was a development after the reign of Akbar. The largest army that Akbar ever led was in his Deccan campaign, and it had only 80,000 horsemen. The full strength of his army was of course a great deal more than that, but even then it was very much smaller than the armies of his successors. It is estimated that Shah Jahan's army in 1647 had 440,000 men, made up of 200,000 central cavalry, 8000 mansabdars, 7000 Ahadis, 40,000 musketeers and artillerymen, and 185,000 cavalry maintained by princes and amirs. In addition, there was the militia that could be called up from the districts, so that Shah Jahan was probably not exaggerating when he claimed that he was the master of 900,000 soldiers.

There were about a million paid soldiers in the whole of India in Mughal times, Moreland estimates—more than four per cent of the entire adult male population of the subcontinent. In the mid-seventeenth century, those employed in the Mughal military and quasi-military services, along with their dependents, numbered some twenty-six million people, according to Tapan Raychaudhuri.

The Mughal army swelled to a phenomenal size under Aurangzeb, who had with him in the Deccan alone 170,000 cavalry, with several times as many infantrymen and non-combatants. Bernier says that the cavalry 'commonly about the King's person, including that of the Rajas and Pathans, amount to thirty-five or forty thousand', and with the addition of the cavalry of the princes, his army came to 'a total of more than two hundred thousand horse'. The infantry around the emperor was much smaller, only about 15,000, 'including musketeers, foot artillery, and generally, every person connected with that artillery', but when the emperor was on the march, their size swelled with the addition of servants, traders and other camp-followers, many of whom were loosely reckoned as part of the infantry. It is in this sense that Bernier says that 'the army immediately about the King's. person, particularly when it is known that he intends to absent himself for sometime from his capital, may amount to about two, or even three hundred thousand infantry.'

THE MOST TROUBLING aspect of the Mughal army was that its strength and efficiency declined in direct proportion to its growth in size. The high martial spirit that had once characterized the Mughal army too was gone by the end of Shah Jahan's reign, as Manucci saw in the battle of Samogarh in 1658. 'I saw in this action, as in so many others where I was afterwards present, that the only soldiers who fought were those well to the front. Of those more to the rear, although holding their bared swords in their hands, the Moguls did nothing but shout, *Ba-kush*! *ba-kush*!, and the Indians, *Mar*! *mar*!— Kill! kill! If those in the front advanced, those behind followed the example, and if the former retired the others fled, a custom of Hindustan quite contrary to that of Europe; and if they begin to take flight, by no method is it possible to stop them.'

The quality of men entering the Mughal service had already begun to decline by the reign of Jahangir. Most Mughal soldiers, however well-armed and well-mounted, 'dare not resist a man of courage, though he have for his defence but the worst of those weapons,' says Terry. Tavernier in India during the reign of Shah Jahan believed that 'a hundred Europeans might well beat a thousand Indians.' Careri in the reign of Aurangzeb was even more harsh: 'As for Courage neither Mahometans nor Gentiles have much of it.' A common quip among the English in Mughal India was that one Portuguese could beat three Indians, and one Englishman could beat three Portuguese. Of the 100,000 men in the camp of Aurangzeb's Vizier Asad Khan, there were, says Norris, only '4000 people who pretended to fight, and of those not 500 that dare looke a real enemy in the face.'

These views cannot be dismissed as mere alien prejudice, for they proved to be all too true in fact, with the Marathas and the Persians routing the Mughals, and the Afghans and the British routing the Marathas. Manucci claimed that an army of 30,000 European soldiers could conquer the Mughal empire. He was probably right.

If wars are born in the minds of people, wars are also won in the minds of people. Especially in Mughal times. The martial spirit of the individual soldier was a critical factor in medieval warfare. Antagonists in those days were not abstractions, somewhere high above or far away and out of sight, but were riders bearing down upon each other at a murderous tilt, swinging cutlasses and howling for blood, or on the ground tearing at each other tooth and claw, their breath and sweat and blood upon each other. It took animal ferocity to win medieval wars.

This was what won the Mughals their Indian empire. But basking in the damp heat and promiscuous luxury of India, the Mughal ardour, and the Mughal physique, softened. Manrique in the mid-seventeenth century considered that 'the Mogors were weaklings and luxurious and enervated rather than fighters or warlike soldiers.' The friar was overstating the case, but what he said was a pointer. In India, the Rajputs did a good amount of the fighting for the Mughals. But the Rajputs themselves, for all their valour, needed to shore up their spirit with drugs, and invariably took a double dose of opium when they went into battle. 'It is an interesting sight to see them on the eve of a battle,' says Bernier, 'with the fumes of opium in their heads, embrace and bid adieu to one another, as if certain of death.' Muslim soldiers also took opium before battle; Sikandar Lodi once had to abandon a campaign plan because of the poor poppy harvest that year.

Martial spirit by itself was of course not enough to win battles. Discipline and generalship were essential. In fact, valour without discipline and generalship was a military liability, and was the main failing of the Rajputs. Says Monserrate: 'The Musalmans say that these Rasputi [Rajputs] and Rati know how to die, but not how to fight.' It was discipline and training that melded men into an army, and the early Mughals were strict in these matters. 'Those not at their posts had their noses slit and were led round through the army,' writes Babur. Says Monserrate, 'Zelaldinus (Akbar) vigorously enforced military discipline, and would allow no breaches of it.' Even Jahangir was strict in matters of discipline. Hawkins reports that captains who did not show spirit in battle had their heads and beards shaved and were made to wear women's dress, then were whipped and sent to prison. But standards fell sharply thereafter.

DESPITE THE ENORMOUS size of Indian armies, battles, even great battles deciding the fate of dynasties and empires, were astonishingly short affairs, seldom lasting more than half a day. 'The armies on both sides usually beginne with most furious onsets,' writes Terry; 'but in short time, for want of good discipline, one side is routed and the controversie, not without much slaughter, is decided.' Desertion in the face of the enemy was common. 'As soon as the battle has begun, flight is resorted to on one side or the other,' says Manucci. 'So great is their fear of cavalry, that forty thousand infantry will not stand against two thousand horsemen. As soon as these come in sight, the men on foot begin to run.' Soldiers also fled if their commander fell in the field. 'It is the ordinary custom of this country that on the death of a commander his soldiers forthwith take to flight,' notes Manucci. The men were not fighting for a country or even a king, but only for their pay, and their pay was in jeopardy with the death of their commander. It made no sense to them to stay and fight after their commander fell.

The attitudes of officers were not much worthier than those of the common soldier. There were constant bickerings among the generals, as they worked at cross purposes, hindering each other and frustrating campaigns. Only the presence of a prince or the emperor himself could get the generals to pull together. Shah Jahan, says Inayat Khan, had to appoint young prince Aurangzeb as the commander of the Bundelkhand campaign 'out of fear that the leaders might not act in concert through jealousy of one another, and that their bickerings might produce results fatal to the successful issue of the campaign.' During Aurangzeb's Deccan campaign, Mughal officers at times even took money from the Marathas not to act against them—or gave money to the Marathas, to stop their harassment. Generals commanding armies far away from the emperor tended to dither and not pursue their campaigns assiduously, as they enjoyed great freedom and power as field commanders, says Bernier—it took Mughal general Zulfiqar Khan eight years to take the minor fort of Gingee.

Faith played a major role in medieval wars. Says Babur about his victory at Panipat: 'This success I do not ascribe to my own strength, nor did this good fortune flow from my own efforts, but from the fountain of the favour and mercy of God.' It was religious fervour that won the day for Babur at Khanua. Muslims as well as Hindus performed various rites before battle. Jauhar notes that once, while going into battle against Kamran, 'his Majesty (Humayun), the Prince Akbar, and the general Abul Mauly, perfumed their heads, bathed, and said their Friday prayers, to be prepared for death.' On setting out from Kabul to reconquer Hindustan, Humayun made Akbar bathe, wear new clothes and sit before him, and he read the Koran to the prince, breathing on him at the end of each verse. All Mughal campaigns were launched with a prayer for their success.

Battles were chancy affairs, and could not be won without divine favour—or luck. To be in tune with the cosmic rhythm, the Mughals consulted the stars before setting out on campaigns, and invariably took omens; in India they also added several Hindu practices to their own rich repertoire of superstition.

THE MUGHAL ARMY on the march was like the migration of a whole people, involving several hundred thousand men, women and children, all those connected with the government and the army, along with their families. The army, says Norris, consisted of 'wives, whores, children, eunuchs, shroffs, brokers, merchants & traders.' Significantly, Rajput women seldom moved with the army, as they were rooted in the land, and did not have to wander with the nomadic emperor. In the case of the Marathas, Shivaji strictly forbade women from travelling with the army.

'Armies never march in formed bodies,' says Manucci, 'but always in long files. Almost every soldier has with him in camp his wife and children. Thus a soldier may be seen carrying under his arm an unweaned infant, and on his head a basket of cooking pots and pans. Behind him marches his wife with spears, or else his matchlock, upon her back. In place of a bayonet they stick into the muzzle of the gun a spoon, which, being long, is more conveniently carried there than in the basket borne by the husband upon his head.'

Provisioning the vast horde that made up the Mughal army on the march would have strained the resources of even the best organized commissariat, and the Mughals did not even have a commissariat. Each unit, indeed each man, had to make his own arrangements for food and transport. Soldiers were provisioned by merchants who travelled with the army and set up bazaars at each encampment. The emperor's only responsibility was to ensure that traders moved with the army, and as an inducement for them to do so, they were exempted from the payment of all taxes. The system usually worked well.

Soldiers were normally advanced several months' salary when the army went on a campaign so they could buy provisions on the way. During active military campaigns the army foraged. Provisioning the Indian army was easy, says Bernier, because of 'the temperance . . . and simple nature of their diet.' Only about ten per cent of the soldiers were regular meat eaters, notes Bernier; the rest were satisfied with *kichery*, 'a mess of rice and other vegetables over which, when cooked, they pour boiled butter.'

Sappers went ahead of the army to clear the way, cutting down jungles and building boat bridges. The availability of water was a major consideration in selecting the army's route, but river crossings were hazardous, and were carefully regulated, to prevent crowding and disaster. Monserrate, who accompanied Akbar on his Kabul campaign, reports that as the army advanced beyond the imperial frontiers, scouts were deployed 18 miles in each direction to prevent ambush, and heralds were sent out ahead to warn the local chiefs against hostile action and to reassure them that they themselves had nothing to fear. The emperor usually travelled in easy stages, hunting along the way, though he would career headlong in an emergency. The normal rate of travel of the Mughal army was about 'ten or twelve miles a day,' says Terry.

The emperor and the princes were careful to maintain great magnificence while leading the army. Says Manucci about the splendours of Dara's camp when the prince was on the way to fight the fatal battle against Aurangzeb at Samogarh: 'When placed in the field our army was so well distributed that it looked like a lovely city adorned with beautiful tents, flying innumerable flags of all colours and different shapes, each tent having its own flag and device so that it might be recognized.'

It was a different scene altogether by the end of Aurangzeb's reign. Says Manucci: 'His (Aurangzeb's) army is a filthy, dirty place, more like a scourge sent by God, judging by the daily mortality of men and animals. The common people are dealt with as mere animals after they are dead. Their bodies are searched to see if they have any money, and after the feet have been tied together with rope, they are dragged out of the camp and thrown into the first hole to be found. The same is done to the animals, and both serve as aliment for wolves, dogs and crows.'

THE MUGHAL CAMP might have been filthy, but officers and men dressed their best for going into battle, as if for the last rite of their lives. Khafi Khan says that Raja Ram Singh 'wound a string of costly pearls round his head' when he made the suicidal assault on Prince Murad at Samogarh. There were no uniforms, no dress code of any kind for Mughal soldiers. Each contingent dressed in the fashion of its clan or community, and each individual according to his fancy. This, and the fact that rival armies were made up of men of the same racial types and communities, created problems in distinguishing friend from foe in the thick of battle.

Passwords helped to avoid some of that confusion. 'Passwords are of two kinds,' says Babur. 'In each tribe there is one for use in the tribe, such as *darwana* or *tuqqai* or *lulu*; and there is one for use for the whole army. For a battle, two words are settled on as pass-words so that two men meeting in the fight, one may give one, the other give back the second, in order to distinguish friends from foes, own men from strangers.' In addition, there were war cries—for Muslims, *Allahu Akbar*! and *Ya Muin*!, for the Rajputs, *Ram-Ram*!, for the Marathas, *Har-har Mahadev*!—but such shouts were of little help in identifying the armies, as soldiers on both sides belonged to the same assortment of faiths and sects.

War cries were nevertheless important in medieval battles, for it was on the roll of the whoop that adrenaline surged in the army. The Mughals in particular rode into the battle on a wave of martial frenzy, which struck terror in the enemy—and that was half the battle won. So the Mughals were often deliberately savage in combat. Thus Babur, for all his high culture, did not hesitate to slaughter captured prisoners in cold blood and erect victory towers with their severed heads, to mark his bloody passage through a land. 'Those our men had brought in as prisoners were ordered to be beheaded and a pillar of their heads was set up in our camp,' writes Babur in one of the numerous such accounts in his memoirs. 'I had him flayed alive,' he says of another captive. Cutting off enemy heads was for the Mughals an almost orgasmic act.

Later, as they grew sedate, and their power secure, the Mughals would abandon such gory customs, though terror would still remain an important element in their warfare. Says Inayat Khan about Shah Jahan's Deccan campaign: 'The various forces were to make the territory of Bijapur such a scene of horror and devastation as to force both the rebels and Adil Khan to return to the royal authority.' Often the Mughals wilfully employed brigands—'privileged and recognized thieves' called Bidaris—in their army to ravage the enemy country, says Manucci.

The ferocity of the early Mughals was finely balanced by their intelligent and thorough preparation for every battle. Timur, the founder of the Mughal clan, had a striking ability to innovate winning strategies. Thus when he faced the onslaught of elephants in India, an unfamiliar hazard, he planted spikes and caltrops to obstruct their advance, and drove into their midst camels and buffaloes with piles of straw burning on them, so as to frighten and distract them. Similarly, Babur won at Panipat and Khanua by his superior strategy and careful defensive preparations.

In contrast, Babur's Indian adversaries were set in their military conventions. Says Babur: 'Though the men of Hindustan are often brave swordsmen, yet they are extremely ignorant of the art of war, and of the disposition and conduct of troops . . .' Both Babur and Humayun discussed tactics in war councils, to draw on the experience of their generals, and their discussions were frank, sometimes even heated. Later, smug in their power, believing themselves to be invincible, the Mughals would lose the capacity to innovate, and that would prove fatal in their tussle with the Marathas.

A greater problem was that military technology was changing at this time. The infantry, armed with cannons and muskets, was coming increasingly into prominence, and would eventually displace the cavalry from its dominant role in battle. To use the new technologies effectively, new military discipline, new formations and tactics, were essential, but no Indian state was responsive to such challenges. While the power of the cavalry was in its kinetic energy and impetuosity, the power of the infantry was in its precisely controlled and concerted fire drill, which required a tightness of discipline and training quite unlike the traditional Indian methods. Also, for gun battles it was imperative to array the army in a manner different form the conventional centre-and-wings formation of cavalry battles. A close formation, valuable in man-to-man combat, now became lethal, as the massed, compacted army of a couple of hundred thousand men was more fodder for guns than a fighting force. Yet Indian armies would continue to be organized in this manner for many decades, and that would put them at a great disadvantage in their tussle with European powers. In India, unlike in Europe, says Manucci, 'one division was close to another as trees of a pinewood.'

In conventional Mughal battles, the cavalry charge was decisive. Akbar usually charged the moment the enemy came into sight, but sometimes (as in the case of Humayun's battles with Sher Shah) the opposing forces would lie encamped for weeks, facing each other at close quarters, without engaging. The battle itself began, from the reign of Shah Jahan on, with prolonged artillery barrages, which often did little damage, as the troops stood beyond the range of the cannons. Then came the cavalry onset, which invariably decided the battle in a few hours.

The Rajputs and the Mughals usually disdained to make sneak attacks, for, as Abul Fazl puts it, 'a night attack is the trade of cowards'. But Sher Shah and the Marathas used such tactics with great effect. For the Rajput—and sometimes for the Mughals and Afghans—war was often a sport. Once, when Sher Shah was besieging Raisen, a group of Afghans, provoked by the Rajput claims to superior valour, challenged them to a contest, and the two teams fought on the maidan at the entrance of the fort, while Puran Mal, the Rajput chieftain, 'himself took his seat above the gateway' to watch the bloody sport, says Abbas Khan. The Afghans won the fight—according to Afghan sources.

In spite of that victory, the siege of Raisen dragged on, and eventually Sher Shah had to use a ruse to take the fort. The capture of forts was a slow, tedious exercise in Mughal times, as medieval cannons were not good enough to breach fort walls, and mining them was an arduous procedure which was often foiled by counter-mining by the defenders to remove the explosives. On the other hand, it was extremely risky to attempt to storm a fort, for the defenders, says Abul Fazl, 'discharged confusedly bricks, stones, arrows and bullets and also boiling pitch' on the assaulters; they also fired cannons, threw lighted bombs, blazing sheets steeped in naphtha and bundles of burning grass. It was all rather primitive, but effective. Sieges were usually a stand-off, and often non-military means had to be used to capture forts. Akbar had to resort to stratagem to capture Asirgarh; Shah Jahan failed disgracefully in his three attempts on Kandahar; in the Deccan, Aurangzeb captured forts mostly by bribery, Shivaji mostly by artifice.

THE MODE OF MARATHA warfare was, in the beginning, entirely different from that of the Mughals and Rajputs, and was appropriate for the lay of their land and the genius of their people. The infantry, ideal for hill warfare, was the backbone of Shivaji's army, though cavalry would become prominent in later times, when Maratha power expanded beyond their homeland. The Maratha speciality was guerrilla war, and their success depended on speed of movement, surprise, and quick retreat into their mountain strongholds, where the Mughals could not deploy their massed strength.

'They set off with little provision, no baggage except the blanket on their saddles, and no animals but led horses, with bags prepared for the reception of their plunder,' writes Duff. 'If they halted during a part of the night . . . they slept with their bridles in their hands; if in the day, whilst the horses were fed and refreshed, the men reposed with little or no shelter from the scorching heat, excepting such as might be occasionally found under a bush or a tree; and during that time their swords were laid by their sides, and their spears were generally at their horses' heads struck in the ground; when halted on a plain, groups of four or five might be seen stretched on the bare earth sound asleep, their bodies exposed to the noon-day sun, and their heads in a cluster, under the precarious shade of a black blanket or tattered horse-cloth extended on the point of their spears.'

Organizationally, the Marathas had a great advantage over the

Mughals, in that their army had a well-defined command structure. But what distinguished them more than anything else was their fighting spirit. There could be no greater contrast than that between the Maratha and the Rajput approaches to battle. For the Marathas, victory was all, whatever be the means by which it was achieved; for the Rajput, honour was all. In desperate straits, the Rajput would court honourable death, while the Maratha would run away, to give himself another chance. The Marathas had no custom like jauhar. They saw no merit in death.

The Maratha strength was that they were not romantics pursuing some impossible dream, but were practical men, who did what was necessary and possible. But the rugged pragmatism of the Marathas also had its limitations, in denying them grandness of vision. They looked for gain, not for glory. There would be no Maratha empire.

Chapter Seven

PEARLS
AND PEBBLES

The Razor's Edge

THE SIXTEENTH CENTURY was a period of turmoil in the Muslim world. The first millennium of Islam was drawing to a close, and the faithful everywhere were electric with the expectation, or anxiety, that time itself was coming to an end, and that the day of the Last Judgement was at hand. That set the spiritual ferment in Islam on a high surge. More so in India.

The first Muslims to arrive in India were seafaring Arab traders, who came soon after the founding of Islam and settled peaceably in the port towns on the west coast of India, mainly in Kerala, just as Jews and Christians had done several centuries earlier. Towards the close of the first century of Islam, in 711, an Arab army crossed the Afghan mountains into Sind and established the first Muslim state in India. But that was only a minor eddy in the great sweep of Indian history, barely noticeable. Nearly 500 years would pass before the founding of a dominant Muslim state in India, the Delhi Sultanate, by Muhammad Ghori, a Turk, in the last decade of the twelfth century. By the sixteenth century, when the Mughals arrived in India, Islam, then over 900 years old, had lost much of its youthful proselytizing zeal, and none of the Mughals, not even Aurangzeb, was a rabid religious fanatic.

Islam and Hinduism were in every respect radically opposite religions—Islam had a linear concept of time, beginning with the creation of the world and ending with the Last Judgement, while Hinduism considered time to be cyclic, without beginning or end; Hinduism was pantheistic, but in Islam god was transcendent; Hinduism believed in transmigration, Islam denied it; Islam was monotheistic, Hinduism was polytheistic at one level and monistic at another; Hindus were idolaters, Muslims were iconoclasts; Hindus were cow venerators, Muslims were beef eaters; while Islam was (relatively speaking) a unified religion with one scripture and one set of beliefs, Hinduism was polymorphic, with no one scripture or set of beliefs; Hinduism was passive and exclusive, Islam was aggressively proselytistic; Islam, in theory at least, made no distinction between man and man in society or in the eyes of god, but in Hinduism men were unequal both in society and in the eyes of god. As Albiruni put it in the eleventh century, '[The Hindus] totally differ from us (Muslims) in religion, as we believe in nothing in which they believe, and vice versa.'

Despite such contrarieties, there were hardly any communal clashes in Mughal India. Nor was there any large-scale conversion of Hindus to Islam, even though there were substantial material advantages to be gained by a Hindu on becoming a Muslim. A simple confession of faith and the cutting off of a bit of the foreskin were all that were required for a Hindu to cross over to the ruling class, but amazingly not very many were tempted. There were a few conversions here and there, even a few mass conversions—one of the largest was in the reign of Shah Jahan, when the zemindar of Jogu and 5000 of his men were induced to become Muslims—but none of that amounted to much in the vast mass of Hindu population. There was no Muslim tide in India. Nor did the Muslim state, despite its theocratic nature, make any sustained effort to use coercive power to force conversions.

The two communities, by and large, lived together amicably. More than that, over the centuries, a certain amount of cross-fertilization took place between Islam and Hinduism, with mystics and philosophers finding several affinities between the two religions. Even the rigidly orthodox Firuz Tughluq in the mid-fourteenth century was interested in Hinduism, and had a number of Sanskrit works translated into Persian. Sang Amir Khusrau, the greatest Indian Muslim poet of the age:

> The Hindu, though a non-believer,
> Believes in much that I believe.

Such sentiments, though spurned by orthodox Muslims, were commonly held by the adherents of the Muslim mystical sect of Sufism, who fraternized comfortably with Hindus and even adopted several Hindu religious practices in their worship. Hindu ascetics, especially those of the Vaishnava sect, on their part reciprocated these sentiments and welcomed men of all castes and religions into their fold. At another level, efforts were made to blend Islam and Hinduism philosophically, arguing that the differences between them were superficial and immaterial. That was the thrust of Akbar's religious quest. Typical of the syncretic spirit of the age was a book titled *Allah Upanishad*, written by a courtier of Akbar, which opened with the Hindu mantra Om! and went on to identify Hindu gods with Allah. Dara continued such explorations, translating the Upanishads into Persian, and writing treatises expounding the harmonies between Islam and Hinduism. Elsewhere, a Hindu sage in Bundelkhand wrote a book titled *Mahitariyal*, carrying verses from the Koran and the Vedas side by side to prove that their messages were essentially the same. In Bijapur, Ibrahim Adil Shah II was closely associated with Hindu culture; a votary of Carnatic music and an ardent devotee of Saraswati, the Hindu goddess of the arts, he proudly bore the Hindu title Jagad-guru, universal sage.

Significantly, even in their rapprochement, the two communities revealed their differences. Among Muslims, it was the elite that developed an affinity for Hinduism, while the common folk generally remained aloof, but the reverse was the case with Hindus, indicating that the Muslim response was intellectual while the Hindu response was devotional. Intellectually, Islam was still alive, relatively speaking, but Hinduism was comatose.

On the other hand, Hindus were far more tolerant towards Islam than Muslims towards Hinduism. That was natural. Hinduism with its innumerable gods and goddesses and variegated beliefs and practices could accommodate Islam in its capacious fold without adding much to its load of deities or significantly altering its ethos, but Islam could not take on the immense load of the Hindu pantheon without violating its basic monotheistic principle. Muslims had to go through complex intellectual manoeuvres to harmonize Hinduism with their religion. It was therefore rare for Muslims to join Hindus in worship, but it was not uncommon for Hindus to venerate Muslim saints and visit places of Muslim pilgrimage. Both Shivaji and his father Shahji, for instance, were devoted to Muslim sages, and the Raos, the Hindu kings of Kuchchh, routinely offered worship at temples as well as at mosques.

THE SYNCRETIC AND reformist tendencies of Islam were not uniquely Indian or Mughal developments. In fact, many of the Muslim reform movements that flourished in Mughal India were of Middle Eastern and Central Asian origin, and had entered India before the Mughals, though they thrived best in the liberal environment of the Mughal court. Islam had come under the influence of Greek thought quite early in its history and the Muslim world everywhere has always been alive with philosophical disputations—about whether man had free will or not, whether it was possible for man (the finite) to comprehend god (the infinite); some held an atomist view of the world; Al-Farabi in the tenth century was a Platonist who identified god with absolute good; Avicenna in the eleventh century asserted the primacy of the knowledge of the Being over the knowledge of the physical world. So raged many happy and bitter controversies.

These speculations were not to the liking of orthodox Muslims, who believed that all that was necessary for man to know about the world was in the Koran, so there was no need for him to flog his puny brain for it. The Muslim traditionalist in India had the additional vexation of having to cope with the Hindu influences that seeped into Islam. Barani, a fourteenth-century Indian historian, roundly condemned philosophy as a pernicious vanity, perhaps seeing its effect on his quixotic patron and king, Muhammad bin Tughluq.

Metaphysical speculations were in any case the indulgence of the privileged few. Ordinary Muslims, like ordinary Hindus, lived yoked to custom. But the yoke, in India, was heavier on Muslims than on Hindus. For the Hindu, there was no difficulty in conforming to customary regulations, for his religion and culture were of his land, and their practices suitable to the Indian environment. But Islam came from another land, another setting, which made it awkward at times for Muslims to strictly observe Arab regulations in India.

The straight and narrow path was the razor's edge for the orthodox Muslim, and he had to be watchful of every step he took. 'Know that the key of happiness is in following the Sunna and imitating God's apostle in all his goings out and comings in, in his movements and times of quiescence, even in the manner of his eating, his deportment, his sleep, and his speech . . . ,' wrote Shah Wali-Ullah, an Indian–Muslim scholar of the mid-eighteenth century. 'So you must sit while putting on trousers and stand while putting on a turban; you must begin with the right foot when putting on your sandals, and eat with your right hand; when cutting your nails you must begin with the forefinger of the right hand and finish with its thumb; in the foot you must begin with the little toe of the right foot and finish with the little toe of the left . . . Muhammad b. Aslam used not to eat a melon because the manner in which God's apostle ate it had not been transmitted to him . . . Now it is not fitting to be lax in such matters and say that this is one of the things which pertain to use and wont, so that there is no point in following the Prophet regarding it, because that will lock against you an important gate of happiness.'

From the orthodox point of view, discretionary behaviour, the exercise of free will, was the greatest threat to peace and contentment in life, not to speak of happiness in the life hereafter. A devout Muslim prayed five times a day, at every three hours from sunrise to sunset; he also went on regular pilgrimages, and observed various fasts and austerities—'thus taking more paines to goe to hell then any Christian I know doth to goe to heaven,' as Terry's jaundiced eyes saw it.

Pilgrimage to Mecca was the high point in the religious life of Muslims, and it was often financed by the state—thus Akbar in 1575 ordered that anyone wishing to go on pilgrimage could do so at state expense. Sometimes the emperor sent a troublesome relative or amir on a pilgrimage to Mecca as a polite way of exiling him. In Mughal times pilgrims usually travelled by sea to Arabia, embarking from Surat, after securing from the Portuguese a permit for safe passage. A round trip to Mecca usually took a couple of years, often more.

Like all religions, Islam was a melange of sophistication and naivety. There were a number of great sages and saints in Islam, but there were also many crooks and charlatans who exploited the credulity of ordinary people. Thus when Khusrav, the rebel son of Jahangir died (or was murdered), he was acclaimed as a saint by some, who turned his tomb, as well as the places where his body was kept at night on the way from Burhanpur to Allahabad, into shrines, claiming that 'God had in their sleep ordered them to do so, because Khusrav was an innocent martyr,' reports Pelsaert.

'This devilish folly made such headway in various towns . . . that both Hindus and Moslems in vast numbers went in procession every Thursday with flags, pipes, and drums to his worship,' continues Pelsaert. Mendicants 'on the day of worship used to gather on the road in thousands and swarm like flies, so that no one could walk a yard without molestation', and confectioners 'used to line the whole road in great numbers with stalls of sweet-stuffs, and sold great quantities, together with the hawkers of toys . . . The roads and open places were full, too, of jugglers, dancers, players, and such rabble; the noise was deafening, and the crowd made it even more impossible to see, or find room to move.' Jahangir was not impressed by the popular fervour; he sensibly argued that Khusrav in his lifetime was a sinful and rebellious son, and if indeed he was murdered, 'the guilt attached to the murderer, but did not operate to absolve Khusrav.' The emperor, therefore, ordered the Khusrav shrines to be demolished and the receivers of offerings driven away.

ISLAM HAS TWO basic sects, Shiah and Sunni, each with several sub-sects of its own. The schism between Shiahs and Sunnis arose out of a political rather than a religious dispute—Shiahs wanted the Caliphate to be hereditary through Ali, the Prophet's son-in-law, while the Sunnis wanted it to be elective—but later their religious traditions also diverged. Mughal India was predominantly Sunni, but Shiahs were active in outlying provinces, especially in Kashmir, Sind, Gujarat and the Deccan. Most of the Persians in Mughal service were Shiahs, but they were careful not to let religion interfere with their work, and adjusted so well to the Mughal environment that even Aurangzeb had no difficulty in retaining them in high positions.

Over the centuries, as Islam evolved, it spawned numerous religious movements, mystical, reformist or fundamentalist. The most remarkable of these movements in Mughal India was the Mahdawi cult. It was a belief common among Muslims that at the end of the first millennium of Islam, a saviour. Imam Mahdi, the Lord of the Age, would appear to stamp out crime and vice, and restore the pure shining faith. And on that belief rode many would-be prophets, men of vision as well as those with a sharp eye for the main chance.

In India, during the closing years of the Delhi Sultanate, one Sayyid Muhammad of Jaunpur claimed himself to be the Mahdi and gathered around him a good many followers, but died inopportunely before he could save the world. The flame of the saviour who died too soon was however kept alive by his disciples, and their fervent appeal to rigid puritanism and voluntary poverty attracted the devout among the poor, and even a few nobles. The followers of the sect kept absolutely no worldly possessions. 'Many a one thought it was his duty to empty his cooking vessels at nightfall of the necessities of life, even his salt and flour and water, and let them remain upside down,' says Badauni, 'and they kept nothing in the way of means of existence by them ... saying "Each day brings a new provision."' They spent most of their time in prayers, and once a week made public confessions of their sins.

The Mahdawis, though ascetics, were not hermits, but were active in society, and functioned as a theocratic vigilante group. Says Nizamuddin Ahmad: 'They always carried swords and shields, and all kinds of weapons, and going into cities and bazaars, wherever they saw anything that was contrary to the law of the prophet, at first they forbade these things, with gentleness and courtesy. If this did not succeed, they made people give up the forbidden practices, using force or violence for the purpose.'

During the reign of Islam Shah, the son and successor of Sher Shah, several powerful amirs fell to the temptation of exchanging the fleeting pleasures of the temporal life for the promise of eternal bliss in the life after death, and joined the Mahdawi cult. 'Matters came to such a pass that fathers left their sons, brother left brother, and wife left husband and entered the charmed circle of the Mahdi, voluntarily submitting to poverty and extinction,' says Badauni. Almost every day reports reached the sultan of some Afghan general or other renouncing his office and family and joining the Mahdawis. But the very success of the Mahdawis proved to be their undoing, as they threatened to subvert the established political and religious order. In the end Islam Shah, under pressure from orthodox Muslim leaders, ordered the Mahdawi movement to be suppressed as heresy. The movement then gradually died out in Hindustan, though it continued to have some hold in the Deccan for a while longer.

At the other end of the Muslim religious spectrum from the Mahdawis were the Sufis, an ecstatic, mystical sect. While the Mahdawi movement appealed generally to under-class Muslims, Sufism was an elitist, intellectual movement. The term Sufi was derived from the Arabic word *suf*, meaning wool, which came to be applied to the members of the sect because of the rough woollen garments they originally preferred. Sufis sought to induce religious ecstasy and rouse the latent spiritual powers of man through mystic practices like meditation, religious music and dance, and occasionally self-mortification. Like all mystics, they considered themselves free from social and religious conventions, and did not feel obliged to observe orthodox religious practices of prayers and fasting. 'Demand from thyself whatever thou wishest: for thou art everything,' they advised.

The Sufi movement, which originated in the early years of Islam, first came to India in the wake of Mahmud Ghazni's invasion in the eleventh century. In the course of time the movement branched into several orders, of which the most prominent in India was the Chishtiyya order, which received the patronage of the Mughals. Originally founded in Central Asia, this order was introduced into India early in the thirteenth century by Khwaja Muinuddin, to whom is attributed the typical Sufi saying: 'For years I used to go around the Kaba; now the Kaba goes around me.'

In India, Sufis came under the influence of Hindu mystical sects and adopted the yogic practice of controlled breathing as a means of spiritual elevation. Some Sufis even called themselves *rishis* in the fashion of Hindu sages, and many took to singing Vaishnavite hymns to induce ecstasy. Sufism declined in the late seventeenth century, in consequence of the general decline of intellectual life in India.

Another group of Muslim ascetics, but quite different from Sufis, were Qalandars, wandering dervishes, who did not respect the shariah but had a great reputation as miracle-workers. They shaved off all the hair on their heads and faces, including eyebrows, took marijuana and other psychotropic drugs, and practised terrible austerities—some of them passed iron rods crossways through their genitals to make intercourse impossible.

Sufis and Qalandars, however unorthodox their ways, were movements within Islam, but there were also at this time, especially during the reign of Akbar, quite a few Muslim radicals who openly questioned the authority of the Koran, denied the possibility of an undying, unchanging individual soul, and argued that reward and punishment could operate only through transmigration. These rebels, says Badauni, 'tempted mankind by suggesting the forgery of the Koran, and by going out of the way to show the impossibility of inspiration, and by throwing doubts on the authority of prophets and Imams, and utterly denying the existence of demons and angels, and mysteries and signs and miracles.'

Against these diverse pressures of heresy and reform, the middle ground of Islam was defended by such sages as Sheikh Ahmad Sirhindi of the Naqshbandiyya order. The Sheikh was a contemporary of Akbar, and was appalled by the rationalist and philosophical trends at the imperial court. He wrote several tracts defending orthodox Islam, desired jizya to be reimposed, cow-slaughter resumed, and wanted Muslims to 'avoid infidels as they did dogs'. For his pains, the Sheikh was imprisoned by Jahangir for a while, but he continued to preach strongly against reformist movements, as well as against Shiahs. The movement became so strident in its fundamentalism that even Aurangzeb was obliged to ban its teachings. The order however remained a source of inspiration to Sunni fundamentalists for a long time.

The Ocean of Nectar

THE HINDU WORLD, already dark, darkened further in Mughal times. The only vital element in Hinduism at this time was the Bhakti movement, and even that was nearly a thousand years old, and had begun to wither, its last great exponent being Tulsidas in the reign of Akbar. The movement however continued to have some strong regional expressions, and, despite its great age, it substantially retained its original radical religious spirit, as its devotional path to salvation was, in contrast to the rigidly hierarchic Hindu social organization, open to all, irrespective of caste or sex.

'Your sex or caste does not count' in the pursuit of salvation, maintained Eknath, a Maharashtrian Vaishnavite sage of the 16th century. Eknath found a virtue even in the wickedness of the prevailing Age of Wrath (Kali Yuga), in that it enabled all castes to gain salvation 'just by singing the glory of Hari!' The Bhaktas usually disregarded caste distinctions and venerated such sages as hunter Kanakadas, cobbler Raidas, barber Sena, butcher Sadhana, and even Laldas, who belonged to a robber tribe in Rajasthan. It was thus that Tukaram, an early-seventeenth-century Vaishnavite sage of Maharashtra, could sing exultantly:

> Born a Sudra, free of all pride,
> I hail thee as my father-mother,
> Lord of Pandhari!

The egalitarian thrust of the Bhakti movement was opposed by conservative brahmins, who had a vested interest in preserving the old Hindu order, of which they were the unchallenged and exclusive leaders. Not surprisingly, the only response of orthodox Hinduism to challenges—of reformers from within, and of Islam from outside—was to curl defensively tighter into itself, denying even kshatriyas and vaisyas their status in society, claiming that they had, by neglecting their caste duties, become sudras. That left brahmins as the sole high-caste Hindu community.

Significantly, the brahmins who served at the courts of the few surviving Hindu principalities of the time did not denigrate kshatriyas—indeed

Gaga Bhat, a renowned religious authority of the age, even raised Shivaji, a sudra by birth, to the status of a kshatriya and performed his coronation. For all its orthodoxy, Hinduism had a considerable internal pliability to adjust itself to ground realities.

Such compromises did not mean reform. On the contrary, the compromises were a means to prevent reform, by accommodating and neutralizing potential challengers. Thus Shivaji, his aspirations for kshatriya legitimacy satisfied, became a vigorous champion of orthodoxy. As A.L. Basham points out, Shivaji was more 'a restorer of the old than . . . a builder of the new . . . The Marathas did not encourage reforms in Hindu society, and the India of the eighteenth century was if anything more conservative than it had been in the days of the first Muslim invasions.'

In the end, it was not the reformers but the traditionalists who triumphed in Hindu society. The hatches that some Bhakti sages had opened to let sunshine and fresh air into the musty Hindu society were slammed shut by the brahmin Nibandhakaras, the keepers of tradition, who swore by the Dharmasastras, ancient Hindu law books, and emphasized the need to preserve the ways of the old society. Even some of the Bhakti sages themselves opposed any relaxation of caste rules; Tulsidas, for instance, was rigidly orthodox and scorned lower caste men who took to religious vocations.

The Bhakti movement was in any case primarily escapist in spirit, and sought to transcend rather than combat social inequity. It did not lead to any social revolution. Besides, the socio-economic environment in Mughal India was not conducive to social reform, as it had no powerful group—like the commercial and political classes that favoured the rise of Buddhism in ancient India—to support reform. The only successful revolt against the Hindu social order in Mughal times was of Sikhism, but that movement was confined to Punjab, and had no all-India impact.

INTENSE DEVOTION TO a chosen deity, and hymn singing to induce fervour, were the distinctive characteristics of the Bhakti movement. Sang Eknath in the sixteenth century: 'Even the happiness of *mukti* (salvation) sinks into insignificance before the ecstasy of *kirtana* (hymn singing).'

The stress on devotion to one deity in the Bhakti movement did not negate Hindu polytheism, but merely provided it a particular focus. Every region, indeed every caste and village and every family, had its own special deities and practices in Hinduism, and every devout Hindu had his own favourite deity, which could be any one of the hundreds of gods and goddesses of the Hindu pantheon, or even a deity of his personal conception, after his own heart. All these deities were however in some way or other related to, or derived from, the two primary gods worshipped by Hindus, Vishnu and Shiva, around whom developed the Bhakti cults of Vaishnavism and Shaivism. Of these two, Vaishnavism was in the ascendant in Mughal times.

Shaivism, occult in its practices and militant in its temperament, did not suit the submissive disposition of Hindus under Muslim rule, and it thrived only in the outlying provinces of the Mughal empire or outside its frontiers, mainly in Bengal and South India. The simpler, escapist romanticism of Vaishnavism accorded better with the mood of the times. 'Viznu is the most famous of the Indian false gods,' observes Monserrate.

Vishnu with his many incarnations—Shiva had none—to please very human predilection was closer to the common man, and had a strong nostalgia-tinged appeal, for people to sigh over the golden (though mythical) age when Rama, an incarnation of Vishnu, ruled the fair land. Even more popular than Rama in Mughal times was Krishna, another incarnation of Vishnu, who was cunning and valorous enough to get the better of any situation, apart from being a great lover and the beau ideal of all women. Sang Mirabai, one of the most romantic figures in the religious history of medieval India:

> My beloved dwells in my heart . . .
> Mira's lord is Hari, the indestructible.
> Lord, I've taken refuge in Thee, Thy slave.

Curiously, it was not in Hindustan, the theatre of activity of Rama and Krishna, but in faraway South India that Vaishnavism (as well as Shaivism) arose. The origin of the cult can be traced back to the hymns of Tamil sages of the seventh century, but it remained a localized movement for about 500 years. Then, around the time of the Muslim invasion of Hindustan, began the great surge of Vaishnavism, receiving its stimulus from the teachings of Ramanuja, a twelfth-century Tamil sage. Thereafter the movement spread rapidly through the subcontinent, and in a short time became the dominant Hindu cult.

As the Vaishnava movement spread in North India, it became supercharged with emotion, as a release for Hindus from the frustrations of living under Muslim rule. In the process, the ethos of the cult also changed subtly, with Radha (the first among the innumerable lady-loves of Krishna) gaining prominence as the *hladini sakthi,* the source of infinite bliss. The 'sweet speech of Radha [is] dearer than salvation itself,' professed sage Vithalanatha. But the popularity of Radha and Krishna was transient; Rama would eventually displace them as the leading Hindu deity, largely because of the influence of the Hindi poet Tulsidas, whose rendering of the story of Rama became the pre-eminent religious text of Hindus.

As Vaishnavism advanced, Shaivism retreated, especially its occult Tantric and Sakthi cults, which practised ritual feasting and coitus. In Mughal times, the core area of these cults shifted from north-western to north-eastern India, where cultic human sacrifices continued to be performed. Elsewhere in India, the adherents of these cults were confined to a small number of scattered centres. Around this time there was also an effort to sanitize Tantric practices by reinterpreting its pancha-makara (Five Ms) rite symbolically, to view the drinking of *madya* (wine) as the imbibing of the nectar that flows from the union of Shiva and Sakthi in the head, the eating of *mamsa* (meat) as the annihilation of the animal of karma with the sword of wisdom, the eating of *matsya* (fish) as the control of the flux of the senses, and *maithuna* (coitus) as the experience of the bliss of the union of the male and female principles.

HINDUISM WAS THE most tolerant of religions, but its tolerance was tolerance by exclusion. In a sort of cultural apartheid, orthodox Hindus condemned the intermixing of communities, but maintained that for each caste and each religion its own faith and practices were legitimate. Said a Hindu pundit to Bernier: 'We pretend not that our law is of universal application. God intended it only for us, and this is the reason why we cannot receive a foreigner into our religion. We do not even say that yours is a false religion: it may be adapted to your wants and circumstances, God having no doubt appointed many different ways of going to heaven.'

It was primarily because of this tolerance and adaptability of Hindus that communal harmony generally prevailed in Mughal India. Occasionally, however, there were conflicts between Hindus and Muslims, as well as between sects within these two communities, such as Shiah-Sunni clashes in Islam, and Vaishnavite-Shaivite clashes in Hinduism. According to a late-sixteenth-century Jesuit report, once in Chidambaram, 'the mother Citie of their Superstitions', when a local chieftain, Krishnappa Naik of Gingee, installed a Vaishnavite standard in a Shiva temple, a number of brahmins threw themselves from the temple tower in protest, and 'a woman . . . was so hote in this zealous quarrel that shee cut her owne throat.' Sometimes there was strife between groups within a sect, such as the conflict between Thengalai and Vadagalai Vaishnava brahmins in the Tamil country, with the Thengalais maintaining that a true devotee was equal to a brahmin, and could even impart spiritual knowledge to brahmins, while the Vadgalais asserted the caste superiority of brahmins. The two groups even clashed in the streets of Kanchipuram 'over precedents and rights in Vishnu temples'.

Not much is known about Hindu practices in Mughal times, but there was evidently a general decline in standards. Even rites (most fundamental in the highly ritualistic religion) had become so corrupted and obscure that Shivaji had to engage pundits to investigate and revive authentic Hindu rituals. Earlier, a similar effort was made by Todar Mal in the reign of Akbar, by commissioning the compilation of *Todarananda*, which codified the customs regarding 'fasts, festivals, purificatory ceremonies, gifts, and modes of conduct', and provided information on astronomy and medicine.

Such projects helped to embalm and preserve old customs, but the intellectual elan that had once characterized Hinduism was now altogether missing. Says Bernier: 'They (Hindu pundits) explain themselves so obscurely that I never could really comprehend their opinion.' Ancient Hindu philosophical systems no doubt continued to be studied, but in a perfunctory, mindless fashion. The pundits of Varanasi, concedes Bernier, had complex concepts, which had 'an affinity to the theories of Democritus and Epicurus; but their opinions are expressed in so loose and indeterminate a manner that it is difficult to ascertain their meaning; and considering the extreme ignorance of the Pendets, those even reputed the most learned, it may be fairly doubted whether this vagueness be not rather attributable to the expounders than to the authors of the books.'

Jahangir suspected that brahmins were deliberately obfuscating, to keep religious knowledge to themselves. 'They study religious science themselves but do not teach others,' he writes. This too was the view of Pietro della Valle, an Italian traveller of the mid-seventeenth century, who, while noting the strangeness of Hindu deities and the seeming absurdity of common Hindu beliefs, stated: 'I doubt not that, under the veil of these Fables, their ancient Sages . . . had hid from the vulgar many secrets, either of Natural or Moral Philosophy, and perhaps also of History: and I hold for certain that all these so monstrous figures have secretly some more rational signification, though express'd in this uncouth manner.'

The only fruitful discussions that Bernier had with the pundits were on idol worship and divine incarnations. The incarnations, Bernier was told, had 'a mystic sense' and were 'intended to explain the various attributes of God, but not to be taken literally.' And about idol worship, the pundits said: 'We do not believe that these statues are themselves Brahma or Bechen (Vishnu), but merely their images and representations. We show them deference only for the sake of the deity whom they represent, and when we pray it is not to the statue, but to that deity. Images are admitted in our temples, because we conceive that prayers are offered up with more devotion where there is something before the eyes that fixes the mind; but in fact we acknowledge that God alone is absolute, that He only is the omnipotent Lord.' Pelsaert thought that 'almost all Heathens follow the sect and teaching of Pythagoras,' in their belief in transmigration and the immortality of the soul.

THE MOST DETAILED account of the state of Hinduism in Mughal India is given by Abul Fazl. He examines Hindu philosophical systems and political theories, explains the beliefs of Jainism and Buddhism, describes Hindu deities, places of pilgrimage, ceremonies of death, and social customs. But these are mostly data he had culled from books, not reports on the prevalent practices. As for foreign travellers in Mughal India, they merely report on curiosities. But taken together, the accounts of Abul Fazl and foreign travellers present a picture of Hinduism not much different from what it was in early modern times. European travellers had of course no affinity for Hinduism, the precepts and practices of which were totally alien to their own culture. But their reports are virtually the only descriptions we have of Hindu festivals and rites in Mughal times, and are valuable, though the picture they draw is fragmentary, their judgement warped, and their language offensive.

Bernier, for instance, offers a vivid description of the rituals performed at the Yamuna in Agra during the solar eclipse of 1666. The rich, he notes, pitched their tents on the river bank with screens fixed in the river for the privacy of their women. 'No sooner did these idolaters perceive that the obscuration of the sun was begun than they all raised a loud cry, and plunged the whole body under water several times in quick succession; after which they stood in the river, lifted their eyes and hands toward the sun, muttered and prayed with seeming devotion, filling their hands from time to time with water, which they threw in the direction of the sun, bowing their heads low, and moving and turning their arms and hands, sometimes one way, sometimes another. The deluded people continued to plunge, mutter, pray, and perform their silly tricks until the end of the eclipse. On retiring they threw pieces of silver at a great distance into the Gemna, and gave alms to Brahmens, who failed not to be present at this absurd ceremony. I remarked that every individual on coming out of the water put on new clothes placed on the sand for that purpose, and that several of the most devout left their old garments as presents for the Brahmens.'

Bernier was in Puri during the great car festival of the temple of Jagannath. 'The first day on which this idol is formally exhibited in the temple, the crowd is so immense, and the press so violent, that some of the pilgrims, fatigued and worn out in consequence of their long journey, are squeezed to death: the surrounding throng give them a thousand benedictions, and consider them highly favoured to die on such a holy occasion after travelling so great a distance,' writes Bernier. 'And while the chariot of hellish triumph pursues its solemn march, persons are found . . . so blindly credulous and so full of wild notions as to throw themselves upon the ground in the way of its ponderous wheels, which pass over and crush to atoms the bodies of the wretched fanatics without exciting the horror or surprise of the spectators.'

Tirupati, the most renowned temple in modern India, had an equal repute in Mughal times, and is described by Manucci as the 'famous and ancient temple called Tripiti'. He writes: 'The temple is on a rather high hill, the ascent of which occupies two hours. There are various shelters in which there are many hermits, and hollows occupied by Brahman priests . . . Impelled by their barbarous religion, all the devout go there, and every year there is a festival for fifteen days . . . On this pilgrimage people must shave their heads and faces in order to be cleaned of their sins . . . Many also do penance by climbing the hill on all fours, or on their knees, others at full length, rolling their body over and over. Others carry up water to wash the temple, et cetera . . . I have seen Hindus who, on festival days, through religious fervour, climbed up a mast where there was a wheel bearing two iron hooks, and fixing these into their loins at the back, hung down, and praising the idol, swung around three times, making various gestures with their hands and feet. Such persons are held by Hindus in great esteem . . . Here assemble many people from all parts of India. The shrine is very wealthy from the large and frequent offerings presented, and owing to the large revenue derived from it.' Ovington noticed devotees swinging from hooks being carried about in towns, drawn 'on an Engine with four Wheels'. In Bengal, according to Tavernier, people hung from hooks suspended from trees.

The curious institution of Devadasis (maids of god) predictably caught the attention of foreigners. Parents, Manucci notes, sometimes offered to the temple the virginity of a daughter, as a propitiatory act. 'Many of those dedicated to the idol bear its mark on their arms and head, pricked in by a thorn and filled in with ink, becoming thus set apart, and these must live their whole life along in the service of the temples. The Brahmans profit by the money they earn ... In addition to the above, there are public women, dancers, who are required to appear several times a week to sing and dance before the idol. For this purpose they have some allowance, for which they are under obligation not to be absent.'

'In front of the chariot, and even in the ... temples, public women during festival days dance and throw their bodies into a variety of indecent and preposterous attitudes, which the Brahmens deem quite consistent with the religion of the country,' writes Bernier about the Devadasis of Puri. 'I have known females celebrated for beauty, and who were remarkably reserved in their general deportment, refuse valuable presents from Mahometans, Christians, and even Gentile foreigners, because they considered themselves dedicated to the ministry and to the ministers of the Deura (*devalayam:* temple), to the Brahmens, and to those Fakirs who are commonly seated on ashes all round the temple.'

A peculiar custom that both Manucci and Bernier noted was the Hindu veneration for long-armed men, who were considered as the living replicas of Hanuman, the monkey god. 'In San Thome [near Madras] there was a Portuguese called Joao Carvalho, who had been endowed by Nature with such length of arm that his hands reached below his knees,' says Manucci. 'Owing to this gift of Nature, Hindus when they met him prostrated themselves, worshipping him as they do their idols.' Manucci tells an even more incredible story about another long-armed Portuguese who enjoyed the hospitality of a Hindu temple in Puri for some years—'he led a joyous life, regaling himself with delicate dishes and requisitioning young girls whenever he pleased'—and in the end decamped with the temple jewels.

SUCH CHARLATANS AND crooks abounded in Mughal India, but there were also many genuine Hindu sages and ascetics. The best known of them was Chid Rup who lived in a tiny cave on the outskirts of Ujjain and was revered by Akbar and Jahangir. 'God Almighty has granted him an unusual grace, a lofty understanding, an exalted nature, and sharp intellectual powers, with a God-given knowledge and a heart free from the attachments of the world, so that, putting behind his back the world and all that is in it, he sits content in the corner of solitude without wants,' says Jahangir of Chid Rup. 'He has chosen of worldly goods half a gaz (about half a yard) of old cotton like a woman's veil, and a piece of earthenware from which to drink water, and in winter and summer and the rainy season lives naked and with his head and feet bare. He has a hole in which he can turn round with a hundred difficulties and tortures, with a passage such that a suckling could hardly be put through it.' Chid Rup reminded Jahangir of a Muslim sage who, when people jeered at his tiny dwelling, said, 'Ample for him who has to die.'

'He has thoroughly mastered the science of Vedanta, which is the science of Sufism,' notes Jahangir after visiting the sage in the eleventh year of his reign. 'I conversed with him for six gharis (about two and a half hours); he spoke well, so much so as to make a great impression on me.' Three days later Jahangir went to see the sage again, 'and for six gharis enjoyed myself in his company.' Two years later, on his way to Agra from Gujarat, Jahangir twice called on Chid Rup, and again a couple of times the following year, when Chid Rup shifted from Ujjain to Mathura to live on the banks of the Yamuna. 'As I valued his society, I hastened to wait on him, and for a long time enjoyed his company without the presence of any stranger . . . In truth, his existence is a great gain to me.'

Chid Rup was a hermit, but ordinary Hindu monks lived in society, and lived off it rather well. Bernier describes them as barefooted and bareheaded, well-washed, clean, wearing a piece of cloth around their waist reaching up to their knees, and an upper garment of a white cloth 'which passes under the right arm and goes over the left shoulder in the form of a mantle, but they are without any undergarment.' The monks usually moved about in pairs, and were of 'modest demeanour, holding in one hand a small and fair three-footed earthen pot with two handles.' They did not beg, but were received with ceremony into homes, their visits being considered a blessing. 'Heaven defend him who accuses them of any offence, although everybody knows what takes place between the sanctified visitors and the women of the house: this, however, is considered the custom of the country, and their sanctity is not the less on that account.'

The most exotic of the men of religion in India were the yogis, who, says Bernier, follow 'rules for the binding up of their senses by slow degrees'. The yogi, notes Bernier, would fast for many days upon bread and water, and sitting alone in a sequestered spot, fix his eyes steadily skyward, then 'lower them gradually, and . . . point them both in such a manner that they shall look at one and the same time upon the tip of the nose, both sides of that feature being equally seen; and in this posture the saint must continue firm, the two sides of the nose in even proportions remaining constantly within sight until the bright luminary makes its appearance.'

'No Fury in the infernal regions can be conceived more horrible than the Jauguis,' continues Bernier, 'with their naked and black skin, long hair, spindle arms, long twisted nails . . .' Some stood immobile, covered with ash, holding up one or both hands; some had their 'hair hanging down to the calf of the leg, twisted and tangled into knots, like the coat of our shaggy dogs . . . I have seen them shamelessly walk, stark naked, through a large town, men, women, and girls looking at them without any more emotion than may be created when a hermit passes through our streets. Females would bring them alms with much devotion.' Sometime they went on long pilgrimages, 'not only naked, but laden with heavy iron chains, such as are put about the legs of elephants'.

The yogis were crude, ignorant men, says Bemier. 'Sometime I should have been disposed to consider the Fakirs as remnants, if not as the founders, of the ancient and infamous sect of Cynics, could I have discovered anything in them but brutality and ignorance, and if they had not appeared to me vegetative rather than rational beings . . . How can it be believed that men submit to a life of so much misery for the sake of a second state of existence, as short and uncertain as the first . . . ? I am not to be so easily deceived, said I to them; either you are egregious fools, or you are actuated by some sinister views which you carefully hide from the world.'

Bernier was sceptical about the claims of yogis that they had mystic visions of god 'who appears as a light ineffably white and vivid, and that they experience transports of holy joy', but he surmised that it was 'possible that the imagination, distempered by continued fasts and uninterrupted solitude, may be brought into these illusions.'

Even more bizarre than the yogis were the siddhis, miracle-workers. They could 'tell any person his thoughts, cause the branch of a tree to blossom and to bear fruit within an hour, hatch an egg in their bosom in less than fifteen minutes, producing whatever bird may be demanded, and make it fly about the room, and execute many other prodigies'—so Bernier had been told, but he himself had not seen any such marvels, even though he was willing to pay well for the privilege of being shown some miracle. 'Notwithstanding my diligence to pry into everything, I have never been so fortunate as to witness any marvellous performance . . . it was generally my misfortune to examine and to question until I ascertained that the cause lay in some cheat or sleight of hand.'

In Mughal times there was still a visible presence of Buddhists in India, but 'its adherents are despised and hated, censured as irreligious and atheistical, and lead a life peculiar to themselves,' says Bernier. Nagarkot in the north-west Himalayas, according to Tavernier, was ruled by Buddhist kings who 'believe neither in God nor devil'. In Gujarat, Jains were prominent. 'In Cambia they will kill nothing, nor have any thing killed; in the towne they have hospitals to keepe lame dogs and cats, and for birds,' says Fitch. Visiting one of these hospitals, Pietro della Valle writes, 'The most curious thing I saw in this place were certain little mice, who, being found orphans . . . were put into this hospital, and a venerable old man with a white beard, keeping them in a box amongst cotton, very diligently tended them . . . giving them milk . . . with a bird's feather, because they were so little that as yet they could eat nothing else.'

Sword Is God

IN INDIA, A land of tired old faiths, the only spark of religious vitality in Mughal times was in Sikhism, founded by Guru Nanak at the close of the fifteenth century. Nanak, son of a village accountant, was born in 1469, probably at Talwandi, a village on the Ravi near Lahore. He was of the Khattri caste, the Hindu mercantile community of Punjab to which Todar Mal also belonged. Nanak began his career as a lowly government servant, a store-keeper in the employ of the Lodi governor of Punjab, but he gave up the job, being inclined to mysticism from his childhood, and set out on an extended interreligious pilgrimage through India and the neighbouring countries, which took him as far south as Sri Lanka, eastward into Assam, and westward possibly into Mecca and Baghdad. He travelled on foot, observing, learning and formulating his ideas. His energy was prodigious, his wit scintillating. The story is told that in Mecca, when he was rebuked by a Muslim for sleeping with his feet towards the Kaba, Nanak said, 'Turn my feet in the direction where all-pervading God is not present.'

Such ready and good-natured wit won Nanak friends and admirers wherever he went. Eclectic and non-sectarian, he reached out to both Hindus and Muslims, sang Hindu *bhajans* as well as the praise of Allah, and even adopted for himself a hybrid dress, combining Hindu and Muslim ascetic styles. He thought of god as infinite and formless, beyond time and space, eternally the same, but ineffable. His god did not have a name. Though on occasion Nanak addressed god as Allah, Rama, Hari, and so on, to suit the occasion or his mood, he preferred such gender and creed neutral phrases as Sat Nam (True Name), Sat Kartar (True Creator) or Sat Sri Akal (True Timeless One), and often referred to god by divine attributes, as 'the True, the Immortal, the Self-existent, the Invisible, the Pure.' The name did not matter.

Nanak did not have a name for his religion either, but simply called it Gurumat, guru's wisdom, but his followers called themselves Sikhs, a term derived from the Sanskrit word *sishya*, meaning disciple. The guru occupies the central position in Sikhism, similar to that of prophets in other religions. Total surrender to the guru and strict adherence to his precepts were required of the Sikhs. But the guru was only a divinely inspired guide, not a divine personage; he, like the prophets, was revered but not worshipped.

Though Sikhism was considered a Hindu sect in the seventeenth century, it was really a new religion, in which diverse concepts taken from Hinduism and Islam were synthesized with Nanak's own unique insights. Nanak in fact repudiated the conventional beliefs and rites of Hinduism as useless, and paid no regard to Hindu mythology; he eschewed fasts, pilgrimages and penances, and abhorred idol worship. Nor did Nanak give himself to the seduction of metaphysical speculation, much fancied in Hinduism. He emphasized good deeds, not grand ideas. He sang:

> *Words do not the saint or sinner make,*
> *Action alone is written in the book of fate,*
> *As we sow, so shall we reap . . .*

Sikhism sought to manage life, not escape from it. It was a religion of practical wisdom, which dealt with life in society sensibly, responsibly, even as it strove for the life beyond. Nanak emphasized good conduct, and sought to achieve spiritual liberation through humility, prayer, discipline and devotion to the nameless One God. Unlike Islam and Hinduism, Sikhism had no renunciatory proclivity, and Nanak maintained that the householder was equal to the ascetic in the eyes of god. He felt so strongly about this that he rejected the claims of his son Srichand to succeed him, on the ground that he (Srichand) held the temporal world to be illusory. (Srichand then went on to found a renunciatory sect called Udasis.)

In his social creed, Nanak was entirely egalitarian; he recognized no caste distinctions, made interdining mandatory among his followers, and accorded equal status to women, in society as well as in religion. He denounced sati, scorned purdah. 'How can they (women) be called inferior when they give birth to great men?' he asked. 'Women as well as men share in the grace of God and are equally responsible for their actions to Him.' In all this, Sikhism was like a breath of fresh air in the staid world of old faiths. Unfortunately, Nanak's influence was confined to Punjab. He preached only in Punjabi.

NANAK DIED IN 1539, after nominating his favourite disciple Guru

Angad as his successor. The custom of choosing a successor by merit was followed by Angad also, but his successor, Guru Amar Das, the third guru, appointed his son-in-law, Ram Das, to succeed him, and thereafter the pontificate, like kingship, became hereditary, with even young boys being recognized as the spiritual head, till the office was abolished by the tenth guru, Govind Singh.

Guru Ram Das was succeeded by his youngest son, Arjun. Arjun, who held office from 1581 to 1606, was just eighteen when he took over the leadership of the community, but he was a youth of exceptional leadership qualities, with temporal ambitions to match. He took on the role of a potentate, and introduced the custom of levying a regular tax from Sikhs (in the place of the voluntary offerings to the guru), which was collected by his agents stationed throughout north India, from Kabul to Dacca. He also took to trade in a big way.

Guru Arjun deliberately adopted a lavish lifestyle—in order to emphasize the grandeur of Sikhism, he maintained. He lived in a lofty mansion, wore fine clothes, rode fine horses, even elephants, and surrounded himself with numerous retainers, thus fusing tine temporal and spiritual roles of the guru, a unique feature of the Sikh pontificate. In his spiritual role, Arjun integrated Sikhism into an organized religion, by codifying its precepts and practices, and by compiling the Adi Granth, the sacred book of the Sikhs. With the compilation of the Adi Granth— made up of the hymns and discourses of Nanak and his successors, along with the sayings of several Hindu and Muslim sages—Sikhism assumed the full status of a new religion with its own scripture, not just another Hindu sect. Guru Arjun also built in Amritsar, on land gifted to him by Akbar, a temple (later the Golden Temple) to enshrine the Adi Granth.

The number of converts to Sikhism rose phenomenally under Arjun, but he got into trouble for seeming to support Khusrav's rebellion, and was executed by Jahangir. The Sikh tradition speaks of a dramatic confrontation between Jahangir and Guru Arjun, with the emperor ordering him to pay a fine, and the guru refusing, saying, 'Whatever money I have is for the poor, the friendless and the stranger. If thou ask for money thou mayest take what I have; but if thou ask for it by way of fine, I shall not give thee even a *kauri* (shell), for fine is imposed on wicked, worldly persons, and not on priests and anchorites.' And when he was asked to alter the offensive passages in the Adi Granth, the guru refused, saying that there was nothing in it against either Islam or Hinduism. The guru was then tortured, which he suffered stoically, saying, 'It is all according to God's will; wherefore this torture only affordeth me pleasure,' and eventually died at the hands of his tormentors.

Guru Arjun's martyrdom in June 1606 was a turning point in the history of the Sikhs. Arjun's son and successor Har Govind took the next logical step in asserting the temporal sway of the guru by enlisting an army. 'My *seli* (rosary) shall be a sword-belt and I shall wear my turban with a royal aigrette,' said Har Govind. 'I wear two swords as the emblems of spiritual and temporal authority . . . In the guru's house religion and worldly enjoyment shall be combined.' Har Govind saw no conflict between spiritual and material pursuits. 'Saintliness is within; sovereignty is external,' he maintained.

Har Govind was overreaching himself. For all his proud ambitions, he was hardly in a position to defy the Mughal emperor, and had to suffer the humiliation of being imprisoned by Jahangir for some years, to force him to pay the balance of the fine imposed on his father. On his release, the guru took care to maintain good relations with Jahangir, but he later clashed with Shah Jahan over a trivial matter, by encroaching into the royal hunting ground while Shah Jahan was hawking near Amritsar, and then scrapping with the emperor's servants over a bird. That audacity, and his subsequent victory over a Mughal contingent sent to chastise him, greatly enhanced Har Govind's reputation and won him many followers. But the guru's triumph was short-lived: though he won some engagements against local Mughal officers, he was eventually forced to take refuge in the Kashmir hills, where he died in 1645.

Har Govind was succeeded by his grandson Har Rai, whose pontificate was uneventful. On his death in 1661, his younger son Har Kishan, a boy, was raised as the guru, but he died four years later. There followed a period of turmoil, when twenty-two pretenders staked their claims to guruhood and forcibly collected offerings. Out of this chaos emerged Tegh Bahadur, the youngest son of Har Govind, to assume the leadership of the Sikh community. Initially, Tegh Bahadur was inclined to collaborate with the Mughals, and he even accompanied, as a mercenary commander, the imperial army sent into Assam by Aurangzeb. But later, when Aurangzeb began to tighten the theocratic screws on non-Muslims, he openly defied the emperor, and was consequently arrested, taken to Delhi, tortured for five days, then beheaded. 'Aurangzeb ordered the temples of the Sikhs to be destroyed and the guru's agents for collecting the tithes and presents of the faithful to be expelled from the cities,' says Khafi Khan.

Guru Govind Singh, the tenth and last guru, then took up the sword of vendetta and turned the Sikhs into a military fraternity, declaring that 'he would convert jackals into tigers and sparrows into hawks.' He worshipped the sword, maintaining, 'God subdues enemies, so does the sword; therefore the sword is God, and God is the sword.' He fought

In the name of the Lord of the Sword and the Axe
The Lord of the Arrow, the Spear and the Shield.
In the name of Him who is the God of warriors,
And of horses swift as the wind . . .
. . . to seek redress by truth and sincerity.

Inspired by Hindu myths, Govind Singh saw himself as a saviour of his people, and he gave the Sikhs a unique new identity as the Khalsa, The Pure, by prescribing for them a distinctive dress—they had to wear *kesh* (long hair), *kangha* (comb), *kripan* (sword), *kachha* (underwear) and *kara* (iron bangle)—and by requiring them to be baptized, by drinking water sweetened with sugar stirred in with a dagger. Every Sikh had to bear the community surname, Singh: lion.

Govind Singh's ambition was to overthrow the Mughals and establish a Sikh state. 'I shall make men of all four castes lions and destroy the Mughals,' he proclaimed. He lived like a prince, decked in jewels, guarded by soldiers bearing gold-tipped arrows, and surrounded by sycophants and poets; he travelled with the accompaniment of the kettledrum. But it proved calamitous for him to tangle with the Mughals. Though he made some gains against the petty chieftains in the hills north of Punjab and even defeated some of the Mughal provincial forces sent against him, he was eventually hounded from place to place by the Mughals, lost all his four sons in the fight, and himself barely managed to escape capture.

Govind Singh could breathe easy only on the death of Aurangzeb. Shah Alam, Aurangzeb's successor, conciliated him, and the guru accompanied the emperor to the Deccan in the battle against Kam Bakhsh. There, on the banks of the Godavari River, he was assassinated by an Afghan follower in 1708. And with him ended the line of Sikh gurus, for Govind Singh abolished the pontificate on his deathbed. A period of anarchy followed the death of the guru, as the Sikh community disintegrated into several armed bands indulging in vicious brigandage. But phoenix-like the Sikhs would rise again a few decades later, under the leadership of Ranjit Singh, to build a dominion of their own out of the shattered Mughal empire.

YET ANOTHER RELIGION that was active in India in Mughal times was Christianity. Christianity is said to have been introduced into India soon after the death of Christ, and legend has it that St. Thomas, an apostle of Christ, arrived in Kerala by sea, converted several local families, and was martyred near Madras (now Chennai) in Tamil Nadu. The story is plausible, given India's close contact with the Middle East, but it has no proof. There is however evidence of a flourishing Christian community in Kerala from about the third century, known as Syrian Christians. Presumably made up of migrant Semitic traders and some local converts, they conducted their church services in Syriac, and their women dressed in a distinctive manner, but otherwise became so well integrated into the local society over the centuries that the Portuguese, when they arrived in India in the late fifteenth century, sought to convert these quaint Christians to 'true Christianity'. That led to a schism in the Syrian church, one group accepting the authority of the Pope and the other continuing to acknowledge the patriarch of the Syrian Orthodox Church in Antioch as their head.

The Syrian Christians were not a proselytizing community; they were confined to Kerala, and had no religious impact whatever on the rest of India. Christianity began to penetrate into the interior of India only during Mughal times, through the activities of European missionaries, mainly Jesuits, who established a toe-hold in the Mughal court and even dreamed of converting Akbar to Christianity.

There were several men of outstanding merit among the Christian missionaries in Mughal India, but there were also many cheats and charlatans among them, and Bernier and Manucci, both Catholics, speak in different voices about Catholic missionary activity in India. The Jesuit and Capuchin missionaries, on the whole, seem to have done good work; they were, according to Bernier, good Christians, 'affectionate and charitable'. On the other hand Manucci notes that Goa, the missionary centre of the Portuguese in India, was 'dominated by some disquieting planet, or by demons who throw it into confusion, filling it with murder, disunion, and oppression.' And in San Thome, another Portuguese centre, the priests, says Manucci, lived 'scandalous lives ... they were all licentious ... each one keeping a mistress in his house.'

In a class apart from such 'men of god' was Roberto de Nobili, the most remarkable of the Jesuit missionaries in India in Mughal times. A Florentine aristocrat, he joined the Jesuit order at the age of twenty, and began his mission on the Coromandel coast nine years later, in 1606. A lean, handsome man, with large, pensive eyes, a sweeping brow and aristocratic features, Roberto was an arresting figure. In India he mastered Sanskrit, studied the Hindu scriptures, put on the habit of a brahmin ascetic, and lived in every respect like a brahmin, observing all the taboos of the priestly caste, eating only the food permitted to brahmins, keeping only brahmin servants, and interacting almost exclusively with brahmins. In 1656, after some fifty years of toil in India, Roberto died in Madras (now Chennai), aged nearly eighty.

Early Jesuits like Roberto were highly respected in India, and were called Roman Brahmins. 'They dress like them so exactly that they are taken to be Brahmans, and as such revered by all,' says Manucci. But the syncretic tendencies and the high-caste orientation—which ran counter to the Christian concept that all men are equal in the eyes of god—of these Jesuits angered the Catholic church, which issued a decree in January 1704 prohibiting Indian Christians from adopting names other than those in the Roman martyrology, requiring that the *thali* (wedding pendant) worn by women should have a cross or the image of Christ on it, forbidding the rite of smashing coconuts as a propitiatory act, and even ordering that 'bathing . . . must be confined to physical cleanliness, and such baths taken at times different from the Hindu usage . . .' In egalitarian indignation the church also ordered that 'no one must be excluded from the church or the confessional, not even women when in a state of impurity; no public feast on a girl's arrival at puberty to be tolerated; the pariahs to be treated as on an equality with everyone else—they must be visited during illness, and no differences should be made in the administration of extreme unction.'

Christian missionaries seem to have had some success in South India— 'Of the poor men and Hindus in the kingdom of Tanjor (Thanjavur) alone they have converted about twenty to thirty thousand since they commenced,' says Manucci—but they made hardly any headway in the north, and even the few conversions they made there were of a token nature. 'The truth is they have spilt the water of baptisme upon some faces, working on the necessities of poore men, who for want of means, which they give them, are content to weare crucifixes, but for want of instruction are only in name Christians . . . I also desired to put my hand to this holy worke, but found it difficult,' writes Terry, himself a Christian priest, though not a Catholic. 'I cannot find by good search that there is one Christian really and orderly converted, nor makes the profession, except some few that have been baptized for money,' says Roe.

Withington records that in many cases conversion 'was for money's sake, for the Jesuite give them 3d. a daye. And when the Jesuites . . . were debarred of theire paye from the Kinge, having noe moneye to paye theire newe Christians withall, they dayley came and offered the Jesuits theire beads agayne, tellinge them they had been longe without theire paye and therefore they would bee no longer Christians.' Equally ludicrous were the conversions that Monserrate made in Lahore during a famine in the reign of Akbar—he concentrated on saving the souls of the dying, for the dying offered no resistance to being saved. Manucci too played the farce—'When I became a physician, I baptized in eight years more than fifteen thousand, besides those I found on the roadsides moribund, and whom I baptized,' he says.

Conversion of Muslims to Christianity was even more difficult than that of Hindus. Says Bernier, 'Whatever progress may be made among Gentiles by the instruction and alms of the missionaries, you will be disappointed if you suppose that in ten years one Mahometan will be converted to Christianity.' Three Mughal princes, nephews of Jahangir, were once handed over to the Jesuits by the emperor for conversion to Christianity, but they reverted to Islam after a while. And so did Muqarrab Khan, the Mughal governor of Surat, the only Mughal noble known to have accepted Christianity. The Khan took the name John, sported European dress, and professed Christianity for a while, but only to pester the Jesuits to get him a couple of European maidens. He promised to treat the women honourably, but the Jesuits were not convinced. They found him 'an imperfect Christian'.

Hinduism and Islam being long established and sophisticated religions, it was difficult for Christianity to make any headway against them, and the cynical opinion among missionaries, as expressed by 'the padre Busee' and quoted with approval by Manucci, was that 'the way to preach in Hindustan, whether to Mahomedans or to the Hindus, was with a well-sharpened sword.' So it would be only with the establishment of British political sway over India in the nineteenth century that Christianity would make any significant gain in India.

Cultural Mélange

THE SIXTEENTH AND seventeenth centuries in India were marked by a flurry of cultural activity such as the land had not seen in over a thousand years. Much of this was catalyzed by the elan of the fabulously talented Mughal dynasty, but there were also some very substantial achievements in fields well outside royal patronage, such as in Hindi poetry and Carnatic music. Yet, in a sense, there was no real cultural transformation in Mughal India. The knowledge base of society did not change. The old order endured—the old orders, in fact, for Muslim and Hindu cultures remained fundamentally insulated from each other even after several centuries of coexistence. They did influence each other in some ways, but only superficially.

This cultural imperviousness was in part because of the ruling class/subject class divide between Hindus and Muslims. Centuries of subjection to Muslim rule had reinforced the phlegmatic conservatism of Hindu society, which, instead of creatively responding to the challenge of Islam, passively adjusted itself around it, like a river washing around a hill and flowing on. Muslim society was equally unresponsive, generally treating Hindus with scorn and their culture as unworthy of serious attention. There were some exceptions to all these, but the general mood in both communities was of glum coexistence.

The Muslim prejudice against Hindus was engendered by the arrogance of power, but the dismal state of Hindu civilization in Mughal times could not in any case have evoked admiration in anyone. What Albiruni, the eleventh-century Arab scholar, had said of Hindu civilization was virtually paraphrased by travellers in Mughal India. Said Albiruni: 'The so-called scientific theorems of the Hindus are in a state of utter confusion, devoid of any logical order, and in the last instance always mixed up with silly notions of the crowd . . . a mixture of . . . pearls and dung, or of costly crystals and common pebbles.' A confused, uncomprehending recitation of old formulas passed off as wisdom among Hindus. Says Bernier: 'The Pendets neither comprehend [the concepts] themselves, nor can make [them] intelligible to others.'

The state of Muslim culture in India was not much brighter either, and Muslim scholars were as much sunk in obscurantism as Hindu pundits. The Mughal cultural effervescence was primarily a royal spectacle.

The Mughals came from a lush cultural background, and they valued intellectual, literary and artistic achievements nearly as much as martial exploits. Central Asia, the Mughal homeland, was the cultural cauldron where the three great civilizations of the classical world—of India, China and Greece—intermingled, and even in medieval times cities like Samarkand, Herat, Bukhara and Balkh were fabled centres of wealth and sophistication. In Herat, even wrestlers were aesthetes. 'An unrivalled man was the wrestler Muhammad Bu-said,' notes Babur in his memoirs; 'he was foremost amongst the wrestlers, wrote verse too, composed themes and airs . . . and he was pleasant company.'

The emperors themselves were multi-talented, and some of them had major cultural accomplishments to their credit. Babur was a distinguished author, calligrapher and composer; Humayun a mathematician, astronomer, astrologer, poet, and a compulsive inventor; Humayun's brother Kamran a poet. Akbar was a philosopher, and was also skilled in art, architecture and music; Jahangir was an ardent naturalist and landscaper, and a great authority on painting. Shah Jahan excelled in architecture; besides, he was an authority on gems and jewellery, was devoted to music and dance, and was reputed to have been a proficient vocalist. Dara was an eminent scholar and author. Only in Aurangzeb does the sap dry up, but his daughter Zebunnisa was a zealous patron of learning and culture.

CULTURALLY, THE MOST exciting time in Mughal history was the reign of Akbar, not so much for its achievements, as for the vistas it opened up. Says Badauni: 'Night and day people did nothing but inquire and investigate . . . Profound points of science, the subtleties of revelation, the curiosities of history, the wonders of nature . . . were ever spoken of.' Akbar looked ahead to the challenges of the future, not back into the past for the comfort of tradition. 'No one should be allowed to neglect those things which the present time requires,' he declared.

Typical of the Akbarian spirit was the response of the emperor and his courtier Asad Beg to the imperial physician's objection to the use of tobacco. When the physician contended that tobacco, newly introduced into India, should not be used, because its use was not known in Muslim tradition, Asad Beg asked him: 'How can you, before you have tried a thing and found out all its qualities, pass a judgment on it . . . ? Things must be judged according to their good or bad qualities, and the decision must be according to the facts of the case . . . every custom in the world has been new at one time or other.' Akbar agreed with Asad and said: 'Truly, we must not reject a thing that has been adopted by the wise men of other nations merely because we cannot find it in our books; or how shall we progress.'

That was the royal view. But the very concept of progress would have been incomprehensible to most of Akbar's contemporaries in India, as the pattern of life and civilization had remained largely unchanged in the medieval world. The characteristic attitude of the time was that there was nothing new to learn. Akbar was an exception. He was keenly interested in the technologies and scientific discoveries of Europe, and once sent an amir with several craftsmen to Goa to procure European goods and to learn European crafts. But Indians generally ignored European learning and technology. There was some mimicking of European products, but no absorption of technology. Nor was there any interest in learning European languages. Only one Mughal amir, Mutamad Khan, is recorded as knowing English, though brahmins in Goa and Madras were learning European languages to serve as interpreters for Europeans.

In such an environment it was inevitable that Akbar's efforts at reforming Indian society would yield no enduring result. The same was the fate of his attempt to fuse Hindu and Perso-Islamic cultures. Mughal culture was basically Persian in derivation—even under Akbar, according to Blochmann's calculation, seventy-five per cent of the poets and more than thirty-three per cent of the doctors and musicians in the Mughal court were foreigners—but Akbar gave it a strong Indian orientation. After him, Persian influence grew stronger, and with Shah Jahan, the Mughals settled snug into the Persian cultural mould. By and large the Mughals, for all their power and glory, were the cultural vassals of Persia. Their special achievement was largely in refining the derived model. With Aurangzeb, even that process ceased.

AURANGZEB WAS AN aberration in the Mughal dynasty. His predecessors were all generous patrons of culture, who richly endowed writers, artists, musicians and other professionals by enrolling them as mansabdars, or by giving them tax-free land assignments, or by paying them lavishly for individual works and performances. The nobles emulated the royal practice. But outside the minuscule ruling class there was hardly any patronage for culture in Mughal India—traders were too small in number, and too parsimonious; zemindars were mere rustics, their cultural requirements rudimentary; and the common people of India, like common people everywhere, were too poor and too preoccupied with their physical survival to have the resources or even the energy to spare for refinements. Says Bernier about the general predicament of artists and craftsmen in Mughal India: 'No artist can be expected to give his mind to his calling in the midst of a people who are either wretchedly poor, or who, if rich, assume an appearance of poverty, and who regard not the beauty and excellence, but the cheapness of an article.' Even the nobles, says Bernier, paid for 'a work of art considerably under its value and according to their own caprice'.

Royal patronage gave professionals lifelong financial security, but it was not an unmixed blessing, for it required them to be courtiers, which meant that they had to perform to please the patron rather than to please themselves. The artist therefore tended to become an artisan, the writer a hack. Further, serving an autocratic monarch had its own perils, for if the monarch was in any way displeased, the professional could lose his position, even his life. Sultan Ibrahim of Bijapur, for instance, once beheaded several physicians who failed to cure him of an illness!

The Mughals were not given to such tyranny, but were on the whole tolerant of criticism, even of mockery; it was only rebellion, the threat to their power, that they would not tolerate. Akbar did persecute the mullahs who opposed him, but only because they were inciting rebellion. On the other hand, when historian Badauni openly refused to acknowledge Akbar as his spiritual guide, all that the emperor said to him was, 'Get along then,' though of course Badauni's career slumped thereafter, while his rival and Akbar devotee Abul Fazl thrived.

There was no official censorship of writers in Mughal India. When Badauni's chronicle of Akbar's reign, which he wrote secretly, was made public in the reign of Jahangir, it was not suppressed, even though it was bluntly critical of both Akbar and Jahangir. Similarly, Aurangzeb refused to intervene when a noble appealed to him to punish a satirist who had made fun of nobles and even of the emperor himself. Wrote Aurangzeb on the petition: 'It is not possible to cut out his tongue and sever his neck. We ought to repress our feelings and live in harmony [with others].'

Mughal royal memoirists—Babur, Jahangir and Gulbadan—were quite candid about themselves and their families, open about their failings. Jahangir did not cut out any of the high praise he heaped on Shah Jahan in the first part of his memoirs, though in the latter part he damned him bitterly as a rebel. There was no rewriting of history to suit the emperor's mood. Even in professing modesty, Jahangir was forthright, not coy; he writes: 'As it is not right to write [in praise] about oneself, I must restrain the tongue of my pen from saying more.' There are, of course, several minor discrepancies between the facts presented by the emperors and what are known from other sources, but this was probably because royal memory was as fallible as any one else's, or because they saw events from a different perspective. There does not seem to have been any deliberate attempt to falsify facts.

The candour of Babur and Jahangir is reflected in their literary style, which is simple and direct, without the usual fog of 'extravagant hyperbole' that Bernier found nauseating in courtiers. Most court writers were shameless sycophants trying to cadge their livings. They had little creativity, but were specialists in torturing words and contriving acrostics and other poetic puzzles. Says Badauni (in this case unfairly, because of envy) about Akbar's court poet Faizi: 'He has joined the dry bones together pretty well, but the skeleton has no brains.' The *mushaira*, poetry contest, which turned literature into a competitive sport, was the gladiatorial arena of these contortionists.

The Mughal emperors of the sixteenth and seventeenth centuries were all scholars, who valued books highly and maintained huge libraries. Royal ladies like Salima, Jahanara and Zebunnisa also had their own libraries, and so had many nobles. When Babur captured the fort of Milwat and found some manuscripts there, he treated them as a treasure and took care to share them with his sons, Humayun and Kamran. Along with their other valued possessions, the emperors usually carried their books around with them all the time, even when they went on military campaigns. In the troubled reign of Humayun, one of his major anxieties during battles was to ensure the safety of his books. Once, when Kamran raided his camp in Afghanistan, the only question that Humayun is recorded to have asked is, 'What have they done with my library?' He was delighted to learn that his precious books were safe.

Letters between the princes of the age were elaborate literary compositions, and sometimes even challenges to battle were written in verse and replied to in verse, as in the exchange between Humayun and Bahadur Shah, the sultan of Gujarat. A good part of the letter that Humayun wrote to Shah Tahmasp on entering Persia, says Jauhar, 'was in verse, and replete with compliments'. None of Humayun's writings has survived, but Abul Fazl says that Akbar had in his library a complete anthology written by Humayun, and Jahangir in his memoirs notes that he had in his possession a collection of Humayun's writings 'containing some prayers, an introduction to the science of astronomy, and other marvellous things . . .'

Akbar, though formally illiterate, was a scholar and had a library of 24,000 volumes, valued at nearly 6.5 million rupees. 'Some of the books are kept within, and some without, the harem,' says Abul Fazl. 'Each part of the library is subdivided, according to the value of the books and the estimation in which the sciences are held of which the books treat.' Akbar also maintained a large translation department, which rendered Sanskrit, Greek and Arabic works into Persian. Badauni, for instance, translated, on Akbar's orders, the *Ramayana* and part of the *Mahabharata* into Persian—he did it with unconcealed distaste, moaning, 'Such is my fate!'

Jahangir considered himself to be a poet, and he, like his great-grandfather Babur, wrote his own memoirs, a work of some merit. Nothing is known about Shah Jahan's literary efforts, but he was an admirer of Abul Fazl's florid style, and is known to have been unhappy with the inability of his own court historians to match it. Aurangzeb was a linguist and scholar, and a brilliant though acidic letter writer, but he despised poetry as a hollow vanity, and discouraged even the writing of the chronicle of his reign.

Like the emperors, the Mughal grandees too were usually men of culture and refinement, with wide-ranging intellectual interests, and several of them were reputed as scholars or writers. Even a middle-rung amir like Faizi had, according to Badauni, a library of 4600 volumes. Says Bernier about his patron, Danishmand Khan: 'astronomy, geography and anatomy are his favourite pursuits.' Biram Khan was known as a poet; Todar Mal, apart from being a great general and administrator, was a literary figure of eminence, who translated the *Bhagavatha Purana* into Persian; Abdur-Rahim was a great linguist who was proficient in Persian, Arabic, Turki, Sanskrit and Hindi, and he translated Babur's memoirs from Turki into Persian. Writing history was a favourite pursuit among Mughal amirs, and some of their works are of considerable merit.

A MAJOR CULTURAL development in India during Mughal times was the diffusion of Persian language and literary modes across India, like the pollen of a giant tree over a vast tract. Though Persian had been the language of administration under the Delhi Sultanate, and the greatest Indian poet in Persian, Amir Khusrau, belonged to that period, it had all along remained essentially a language of the ruling elite. Under the Mughals, Persian became the common language of diplomacy and high culture over virtually the entire subcontinent, not only among Mughal allies like the Rajputs, but also among Mughal adversaries like the Marathas. Even rustic zemindars took to patronizing Persian poetry. Only the deep south remained outside the Persian influence.

Persian was of course a foreign language in India. But then, it was a foreign language for the Mughals too. Turki was their mother tongue, and it was in Turki that Babur wrote his memoirs, though he was proficient in Persian. In India, the Mughals lost touch with Turki as a literary language, though it remained their private spoken language till nearly the end of the seventeenth century. Jahangir was the last of the Mughals who was fluent in writing Turki; Shah Jahan as a child refused to learn to read and write Turki, but Aurangzeb acquired a working knowledge of it while serving in Central Asia.

As in much else in Mughal India, Akbar played a decisive role in popularizing Persian, for it was his regulation that revenue records everywhere should be maintained in Persian that made it obligatory for virtually the entire educated class in India to learn the language. The dominance of Persians in government, and the presence of a good number of Persian literary figures at the court also facilitated the spread of the language, though Persians mocked Indian literary efforts in Persian, and considered even Amir Khusrau as a third-rate poet.

Another linguistic development of great importance in Mughal times was the emergence of Urdu (Hindustani) as the common language of India. A hybrid Indo-Persian language, Urdu was originally a pidgin language of the military camps—the term Urdu is derived from the Turki word Ordu, meaning military camp—but it rapidly evolved into a distinct language, using the Persian script, Hindi syntax, and a predominantly Persian-Arabic vocabulary mixed with a few Indian words. From the late seventeenth century, Urdu was the common language spoken in the imperial harem, and it became in a sense the mother tongue of the Mughals, though Persian remained their official language, and Arabic their language of religion. In time, Urdu developed a sophisticated literature of its own, and in the mid-eighteenth century emperor Muhammad Shah, a great-grandson of Aurangzeb, accorded Urdu poetry official recognition at the Mughal court.

Distinct from Urdu, another Indo-Persian dialect, Dakhini, had evolved in the Deccan in the late fifteenth century, a mixture of Persian and local languages, especially Marathi. Unlike Urdu, which arose among the common people from their everyday need to communicate with a numerous

Persian-speaking ruling class, Dakhini arose among a small Persian-speaking ruling class out of their need to communicate with their subjects, and so was largely confined to the Muslims of the region. It had at one time an active literature, and several major works were written in it, including a book on music by Sultan Ibrahim Adil Shah II of Bijapur in the early seventeenth century. Thereafter the language declined, displaced by the newly emergent Urdu, as Mughal power extended into the Deccan.

In the mid-twentieth century, when the Indian subcontinent divided into two independent nations, India and Pakistan, Urdu became the national language of Pakistan, and India came to be organized into a number of linguistic states on the basis of vernacular languages. The genesis of this linguistic provincialism can be traced back to the Mughal period, for it was then that most of the vernaculars came into their own as vibrant literary languages.

The catalyst of this development was the Bhakti movement, which used vernacular languages and the symbolism of erotic poetry to reach out to the common people. The patronage of Muslim rulers—who were generally denied access to the Hindu sacred literature in Sanskrit—also contributed to the growth of regional languages. Akbar patronized Hindi poetry by appointing a Hindi court poet, Kavi Rai, along with the Persian court poet, and the post was retained by Aurangzeb even when he dispensed with the Persian poet.

The Mughal period was exceptionally rich in Hindi poetry. The earliest and one of the most popular of the Hindi poets was Mirabai, a sixteenth-century Rajput princess who, on being widowed in her youth, became a *yogini*, female mendicant. Her Krishna-intoxicated poems were originally composed in the Marwari dialect of Rajasthani, but when rendered into Hindi, and later into other Indian languages, they became celebrated throughout India. Nearly as popular as Mirabai was Surdas, the blind bard of Agra, who was also a devotee of Krishna, and is said to have served under Akbar—Abul Fazl mentions 'Sur Das, son of Babu Ram Das,' as a singer at Akbar's court.

The greatest Hindi poet of the age, indeed of all time, was Tulsidas, considered by many as a reincarnation of the Sanskrit epic poet Valmiki. Vivid imagery and a contemplative tone distinguish his work:

E'en as the tree with golden fruitage blest
Gladly bows down to earth its lofty crest;
Just so, the more enrich'd by fortune kind,
More and more humble grows the noble mind.

Tulsidas was a contemporary of Akbar—and of Shakespeare—but there is no record of the emperor having been aware of his work, though in the reign of Jahangir, Raja Man Singh of Amber and Abdur-Rahim, the Khan-i-khanan, became friends and admirers of Tulsidas. The poet was born around 1532 in eastern Uttar Pradesh. According to popular legend, he was abandoned by his brahmin parents because he was born at an unlucky hour, but was rescued and brought up by a mendicant. Tulsidas lived a quiet life in Varanasi, and died in 1623, aged over ninety. His writing career began rather late in his life, when he was well past forty, but in the next forty odd years he wrote a number of major works, of which his retelling of the story of Rama, *Rama-charita-manasa*, is considered, as Mahatma Gandhi describes it, 'the greatest book in all devotional literature.'

As in Hindi, there was a flowering of literature in other Indian languages at this time—Bengali produced some fine translations from Sanskrit under the stimulus of Vaishnavism; Punjabi, which had no literature before Nanak, flourished under the Sikh gurus; Marathi transformed itself through Sanskritization; Telugu thrived under the patronage of Vijayanagar monarchs; and Malayalam, which had no literature before the thirteenth century, evolved into a distinct literary language, combining Tamil and Sanskrit. But Tamil, which had a literary history far older than that of any other living Indian language, languished in Mughal times, though there were occasional flashes of brilliance in it. Wrote Athiviraraman, a royal poet:

> From a large seed grows
> The sky-labouring palm
> Whose shade none protects;
> From a tiny seed,
> Smaller than a fish egg,
> Grows the mighty banian,
> Sheltering a royal army
> Of elephants and chariots,
> Horses and men.
> The big are not always big,
> Nor the small always small.

The regional languages drew their nourishment from Sanskrit, not Persian, and some of the most important works in them were translations from Sanskrit. Yet, there was also an anti-Sanskrit thrust in them, best articulated by the medieval Marathi writer Ekanatha: 'If Sanskrit was devised by God, was Prakrit born of thieves and knaves? . . . Whether it is Sanskrit or Prakrit, wherever the story of God is told it is essentially holy and must be respected. God is no partisan of tongues. To Him Prakrit and Sanskrit are alike. My language, Marathi, is worthy of expressing the highest sentiments, and is rich-laden with the fruits of divine knowledge.'

A reason for this anti-Sanskrit sentiment was that the advancement of regional languages was opposed by orthodox brahmins, who, according to Sarkar, went so far as to maintain that 'if a person hears the stories of the eighteen Puranas or of the Ramayana recited in Bengali, he will be thrown into . . . hell.' Brahmins had a special interest in keeping the scriptures in Sanskrit, accessible only to themselves. Unfortunately, Sanskrit itself was barely alive at this time, except in South India, where the patronage of Vijayanagar kings, the Nayaks of Thanjavur, and the petty chieftains of Kerala sustained it. But the language was clearly dying. And in dying, Sanskrit passed on its *elan vital* to the vernacular languages.

THE EFFLORESCENCE OF vernacular literature in Mughal times was spectacular, but still it amounted to little more than a few isolated sprays in a vast desert of illiteracy. Books were still handwritten, for India was slow to take to printing—commercial printing in India would begin only two centuries after printing presses were first set up in India by Christian missionaries in the sixteenth century.

Indian rulers, says Ovington, neglected printing because they wanted to protect the interests of copyists. The Mughal aristocrat did not in any case care for printed books, but valued only manuscripts, which were esteemed as much for their beauty as for their contents. Written in elegant calligraphy and profusely illustrated, with elaborate ornamental borders on each page, and richly bound, Mughal books were works of art, which only the privileged few could afford. Among Hindus, the common preference was for the traditional palm-leaf books, though paper was increasingly coming into use. Says Ovington: 'The Paper-Books, in vulgar use among the Inhabitants of India, are long Schrowls of Paper, sometimes Ten Foot in length, and A Foot broad, sowed together at the upper end, as many long Sheets as the occasion of the Writing requires. The Pen they write with is the ancient Calamus, or Reed, about the thickness of a large Goose Quill. And some of their Standishes (ink stands) are made long and square, and an Inch broad, and of sufficient length to contain both Pens, and a place for Ink.'

The Indian indifference to printing was not merely a neglect of new technology, but a neglect of new knowledge, and it would keep India trapped in a lightless medieval world for a long time. Predictably, there was no change in the pattern of education in Mughal India, though Akbar had made an effort to modernize the curriculum. According to Abul Fazl, Akbar recommended that 'every boy ought to read books on morals, arithmetic, the notation peculiar to arithmetic, agriculture, mensuration, geometry, astronomy, physiognomy, household matters, the rules of government, medicine, logic, the *tabi'i* (physical sciences), *riyazi*, (the sciences that treat of quantity, and comprise mathematics, astronomy, music, mechanics) and *ilahi* (theology), sciences, and history . . .'

Not only did the form and content of education remain virtually unchanged in India from what they had been for centuries, but there was not even any significant difference in the educational patterns of Hindus and Muslims, despite their widely different cultures, except that while Hindus taught writing before reading—which Akbar preferred—Muslims did it the other way round. The only change in curriculum in Mughal times was the introduction of accountancy and allied clerical subjects, to cater to the needs of the Mughal bureaucracy.

Muslims, like brahmins, generally attached high value to education. 'Education has a great value for all human beings,' Prophet Muhammad had maintained. 'It is education which enables its possessors to distinguish what is forbidden and what is not. Really it is our friend in the desert, our society in solitude, our companion when bereft of friends, it guides us to happiness, it sustains us in misery.'

There does not seem have been any prejudice against female education among Muslims in Mughal India, though even at home girls were taught separately, by lady teachers. In families where boys were educated, girls were too, and although their formal education ended earlier than that of boys, they were free to pursue studies on their own, and some begums went on to distinguish themselves as writers or scholars.

Among Muslims, education outside the home was imparted at schools called *maktabs* attached to mosques, where students were taught reading and writing and the Koran, while higher education was imparted in *madrasas*. Similarly, Hindus had schools called *tols* attached to major temples, for it was a religious duty of brahmins to impart knowledge, though only to brahmin students. For higher education, Hindus followed the age-old *gurukula* system, in which students attached themselves to a particular guru for several years and learned whatever he could teach. Such education was restricted to brahmins. Affluent Hindus employed pundits to teach their children at home, while the children of traders, artisans and professionals learned their trade or profession from their own elders. But the vast majority of Indians had no education or craft training at all, and were fit only for unskilled manual labour.

The Mughal emperors provided, by medieval standards, generous financial support to education, most of it to Muslim institutions, but some to Hindus as well. Jahangir, for instance, set aside the property of the rich who died intestate for 'the erection and repair of *madrasas*, monasteries, and similar institutions'. Shah Jahan granted a pundit in Varanasi a pension of 2000 rupees per year, a fabulous endowment those days. Even Aurangzeb endowed Hindu scholars and institutions.

Unlike in ancient India, in Mughal India there were no universities as organized centres of learning. And at no stage of education was there any formal examination of students or awarding of degrees. Having studied under a recognized teacher was qualification enough.

Hindu pundits tended to congregate in places of pilgrimage, where they could earn extra income by performing religious rites. The most reputed centre of Hindu pilgrimage and learning in Mughal India was Varanasi. 'It is the Athens of India, wither resort the Brahmens and other devotees; who are the only persons who apply their minds to study,' reports Bernier. 'The town contains no colleges or regular classes, as in our Universities, but resembles rather the schools of the ancients, the masters being dispersed over the different parts of the town in private houses, and principally in the gardens of the suburbs, which the rich merchants permit them to occupy. Some of these masters have four disciples, other six or seven, and the most eminent may have twelve or fifteen, but this is the largest number. It is usual for the pupils to remain ten or twelve years under their respective preceptors, during which time the work of instruction proceeds but slowly; for the generality of them are of an indolent disposition, owing, in a great measure, to their diet and the heat of the country. Feeling no spirit of emulation, and entertaining no hope that honours or emolument may be the reward of extraordinary attainments . . . the scholars pursue the studies slowly, and without much to distract their attention, while eating their *kichery*, a mingled mess of vegetables supplied to them by the care of rich merchants of the place. The first thing taught is the Sanskrit, a language known only to the Pendets . . .'

A fossilized knowledge preserved in a dead language—that was the state of Hindu learning in Mughal India. Though there were distinguished exceptions, the general standard of Hindu scholars was pitiful. As for students, they, says Bernier, 'are of a slow and indolent temper, and stranger to the excitement which the possibility of advancement in an honourable profession produces among the members of European universities.' Hindus learned by rote, almost by physical labour, like acquiring a skill by repetitive practice. Knowledge was not internalized. There was no creativity. Hindu scholarship, says Bernier, consisted of 'long enumeration . . . long, strange, and tedious catalogue, worthy only of an ignorant and low babbler.'

THERE WAS VIRTUALLY no progress in any sphere of learning in Mughal times. Typical was the state of medical knowledge. 'The Gentiles understand nothing of anatomy. They never open the body either of man or beast . . . Yet notwithstanding their profound ignorance of the subject, they affirm that the number of veins in the human body is five thousand, neither more nor less; just as if they had carefully reckoned them,' says Bernier. The practice of dissection insisted on by ancient Indian medical luminaries like Susruta had fallen into disuse in early medieval times.

Quack physicians abounded in Mughal India. Says Fryer: 'Physick here is now as in former days, open to all Pretenders; here being no Bars of Authority, or formal Graduation, Examination or Proof of their Proficiency . . . and those that are most skilled, have it by Tradition, or former Experience descending in their Families . . . Pharmacy is in no better condition, Apothecaries here being no more than Perfumers or Druggists, at best; for he that has the boldness to practice, make up his own medicine.' Common people generally resorted to folk remedies, although both Hindus and Muslims had sophisticated (though stagnant) medical systems, the Auyrveda and the Unani. 'The best remedy [for cholera] is to burn with a red hot iron the middle of heel until the heat is felt, and by this the pain is allayed and the discharge and vomiting stopped,' writes Manucci in all seriousness.

Plastic surgery was widely practised in India, to mend the disfiguring caused by mutilating punishments or war wounds. Manucci has this to say about the method of restoring a nose that has been cut off: 'The surgeons belonging to the country cut the skin of the forehead above the eyebrows, and made it fall down over the wounds of the nose. Then giving it a twist so that the live flesh might meet the other live surface, by healing applications they fashioned for them other imperfect noses. There is left above, between the eyebrows, a small hole, caused by the twist given to the skin to bring the two live surfaces together. In a short time the wounds heal up, some obstacle being placed beneath to allow of respiration. I saw many persons with such noses, and they were not so disfigured as they would have been without any nose at all, but they bore between their eyebrows the mark of the incision.'

Hindu physicians, according to Bernier, believed that 'the sovereign remedy for sickness is abstinence'. They were against patients being bled, which they held should be done only in exceptional cases, but Muslims considered it a panacea, taking as much as eighteen or twenty ounces of blood at a time, 'sometimes even to fainting', says Bernier.

Like all things foreign, European doctors, even quacks like Manucci, were much sought after by Indians. Once a surgeon in the retinue of British ambassador Norris was called on to treat a man dead for several hours—as if he could 'almost raise ye deade', comments Norris. The royal family was however very careful in choosing its physicians. 'It should be understood that before a European can acquire the office of the physician among these princes he must be put to the proof for a long time, for they are extremely distrustful and nice in such matters,' says Manucci.

Curiously, while Indians ran after European physicians, Europeans themselves held Indian physicians in high esteem, and in Goa some of them were allowed to carry ceremonial umbrellas, a signal honour. 'These Heathen phisitions doe not onely cure there owne nations but the Portingales also, for the Viceroy himself, the Archbishop, and the Monkes and Friers doe put more trust in them then in their own countrimen, whereby they get great money, and are much honoured and esteemed,' writes Linschoten.

A Crore for a Song

TO BE A connoisseur, and to be proficient in some art or the other, was an essential refinement in the affluent urbanite in ancient India. The arts, particularly music and dance, were integral to the religious practice of Indians, as of most other ancient civilizations. The Hindu, Buddhist and Jain places of worship and retreats were profusely adorned with sculptures and mural paintings, and so were the palaces of Indian chieftains. These art traditions, especially their secular expressions, had come under Muslim influence during the Sultanate period, and now, under the energetic patronage of the Mughals, the process quickened. Indian art and architecture were transformed in the process, and there were substantial changes in music and dance too, though none at all in sculpture.

Pre-Muslim paintings in India were mostly murals. Miniature painting was also known, as literary evidence and the illustrated manuscripts of the eleventh and twelfth centuries show, but they were on palm leaves, and were constricted in size and style. There was no paper in pre-Muslim India. Paper (and suitable pigments) were introduced into India from Persia in the thirteenth century, and with that, and under Persian influence, gradually the old cramped style of Indian miniature painting gave way to a more open, naturalistic and lively mode, as in the fifteenth century Jain *Kalpasutra* manuscripts of Gujarat. By the time the Mughals arrived, there was a thriving tradition of manuscript illustration in India, especially at centres like Mandu, Ahmadabad and Jaunpur, under the patronage of Muslim rulers. Mandu in the early sixteenth century produced the two most celebrated pre-Mughal illustrated manuscripts of India, *Nimatnama*, a cookery book, and *Miftah-ul-Fuzala*, a dictionary of rare words.

Muslims however had inhibitions about depicting living beings in painting, which the mullahs condemned as parodying god's work. The focus of Islamic art was therefore on abstract design and calligraphy. Painters were generally treated as mere craftsmen in Muslim societies, but calligraphers, many of whom were scholars, enjoyed a high status, because of the sacredness associated with the written word in Islam. Abul Fazl states that eight different styles of calligraphy were in vogue in

India during the reign of Akbar, and that the emperor favoured the Nastaliq school, a fluid style made up entirely of curved strokes, the best-known exponent of which was Muhammad Husain of Kashmir, who bore the title Zarrin-kalam, Gold Pen. Hindus also took to Persian calligraphy, and some of them, like Pundit Lakshmi Ram, Lala Sukh Ram and Munshi Mahbub Rai in the reign of Aurangzeb became renowned for their skill.

DESPITE RELIGIOUS PROHIBITION, figurative painting was patronized by Persians, and by the Mughals in Central Asia under Persian influence. Bihzad, the best-known Muslim artist of the age and called the Raphael of the East, was a contemporary of Babur, and had served at the court of Babur's uncle Sultan Husain Mirza of Herat before migrating to Persia. In India, the Mughals were particularly vigorous in promoting art. Humayun had painters with him even when he was wandering as a fugitive in the deserts of Rajasthan. Jauhar reports that one day in Rajasthan 'a beautiful bird flew into the tent [of Humayun], the doors of which were immediately closed, and the bird caught; his Majesty then took a pair of scissors and cut some of the feathers off the animal; he then sent for a painter, and had a picture made of the bird, and afterwards ordered it to be released.'

Humayun's interest in painting deepened during his exile in Persia. There he came into contact with Mir Sayyid Ali (a pupil of Bihzad) and Mullah Abdus Samad, and persuaded them to join his court in Kabul. Both Humayun and young Akbar took painting lessons from them, and Abdus Samad eventually rose, under Akbar, to hold the rank of the commander of 400, a rank about the same as that of the superintendent of the imperial kitchen, a high and responsible position.

As a child, Akbar loved to draw and practised diligently, and as emperor he employed over a hundred artists in his atelier. Characteristically, he brushed aside the orthodox objections to figurative painting. 'There are many that hate painting; but such men I dislike,' he said. 'It appears to me as if a painter had quite peculiar means of recognizing God; for a painter in sketching anything that has life, and in devising its limbs, one after the other, must come to feel that he cannot bestow individuality on his work, and is thus forced to think of God, the Giver of Life, and will thus increase his knowledge.' Comments Abul Fazl: 'Bigoted followers of the letter of the law are hostile to the art of painting, but their eyes now see the truth.'

Akbar's artists were attached to the imperial library, where their main work was to illustrate manuscripts. Abul Fazl names the prominent eighteen of them, thirteen Hindus and five Muslims. In this eclectic environment, Persian style blended vigorously with Indian skills to produce some of the greatest works of Mughal painting. Among the celebrated artists in Akbar's court was Daswanth, a boy whom Akbar had picked up from the streets of Fatehpur Sikri and turned into a great artist. 'His paintings were not behind those of Bihzad and the painters of China,' says Abul Fazl. One of Daswanth's assignments was to illustrate *Razm-nama*, a Persian translation of the *Mahabharata*.

The largest artistic work produced in Akbar's court (but probably initially commissioned by Humayun) was an illustrated Persian translation of *Hamza-nama*, an Arabic epic. Divided into twelve volumes of 100 folios each, the work took fifteen years to complete, and was the joint effort of some 100 artists working under the supervision of Sayyid Ali and Abdus Samad. Unfortunately, only a few pages of the great work have survived. Among the other important illustrated works of Akbar's artists were *Babur-nama*, *Akbar-nama*, and a translation of the *Ramayana*. They also produced a large number of portrait paintings. 'His Majesty himself sat for his likeness, and also ordered to have the likenesses taken of all the grandees of the realm,' says Abul Fazl. 'An immense album was thus formed; those that have passed away have received a new life, and those who are still alive have immortality promised them.' The interior walls of several buildings in Fatehpur Sikri were also covered with murals, but of them only a few fragments remain.

Mughal painting reached its acme under Jahangir, the most accomplished of the Mughal connoisseurs of art. Jahangir favoured individual paintings over manuscript illustrations, and under him European influences, which had begun to show up in Indian paintings during the reign of Akbar, became more marked, especially in perspective and colouring, and even in subjects and religious motifs, such as angels and cherubs. A number of European paintings, including some of Christian subjects, were copied by Jahangir's artists, and the emperor freely used them as decorative elements in his palace, without any regard for their religious significance. In Agra, notes Finch, 'on the right hand of the King, on the wall behind him is the picture of our Saviour; on the left, of the Virgin'. Significantly, Jahangir did not use Hindu religious motifs for decoration. The reason was probably aesthetic rather than religious, for Jahangir was eclectic in religion and was a votary of Hindu sages. In pictorial motifs, a major contribution of Christian art to Mughal art was the halo—the halo, used first in ancient India to depict the aura of Buddha, thus returned after its peregrinations in Christian lands to crown the Mughal.

At its peak, Mughal painting maintained very high standards. The great Dutch painter Rembrandt, a contemporary of Shah Jahan, was an admirer and collector of Mughal miniatures. Bernier too, despite his general lack of esteem for India, admired Indian paintings. 'I have often admired the beauty, softness, and delicacy of their paintings and miniatures,' writes Bernier, 'and was particularly struck with the exploits of Ekbar painted on a shield by a celebrated artist, who is said to have been seven years in completing the picture.' When Jahangir once got a painting belonging to Roe copied by his artists, the copy was so exact that Roe was unable to tell the original from the copy.

A shortcoming of the Mughal style was its rigid formalism, especially evident in portraits. As Bernier points out, 'Indian painters are chiefly deficient in just proportions, and in the expression of the face.' This was not because of lack of skill, as the spirited line portrait of Akbar and some of the naturalist paintings of the time show. The artist's vision was clear, his hand sure, but conventions crimped him. There was in any case little scope for the medieval artist to show his individuality, as most major works were produced by several artists working together as a team, each contributing his own special skill, one drawing the outline, another filling in the colours, a third refining the features, a fourth adding the background, and so on.

AFTER JAHANGIR, standards in art declined. Shah Jahan had an interest in portraiture and had several of himself painted, and it was during his reign that *Shahjahan-nama*, an acclaimed illustrated folio, was produced. But signs of decadence now began to appear in Mughal painting, in the over-rich use of colour and gilding. Shah Jahan, preoccupied with architecture, also reduced the number of court artists. Under Aurangzeb, there was a further sharp fall in the patronage of art. Though he had some portraits of himself painted, and found a practical use for the painter's art in getting the pictures of his imprisoned son Muhammad Sultan made in order to keep track of his condition, he made a public show of orthodoxy by erasing in Bijapur the paintings that violated Koranic law. According to Manucci, Aurangzeb even ordered the paintings on the main gateway of Akbar's tomb to be covered with whitewash.

Stylistically, Mughal painting was an offshoot of Persian painting, which itself was an offshoot of Chinese painting. In turn, Mughal painting spawned its own regional offspring, as the imperial court moved about the subcontinent and scattered its cultural pollen. Aurangzeb's neglect of the arts also helped the dispersal of artists and the spread of skills. The most prominent of these regional schools was the Rajasthani school, which created the much acclaimed Ragamala (musical modes) and Krishnaleela (frolics of Krishna) paintings. While Mughal artists mainly dealt with subjects of imperial pomp, Rajput artists depicted traditional Hindu religious subjects.

Unlike painting, sculpture did not find favour with the Mughals, possibly because its three-dimensional solidity made it seem more lifelike and therefore more un-Islamic than figurative painting. There are only a couple of major sculptures noted in Mughal chronicles—that of Jaimal and Patta on stone elephants commissioned by Akbar, and of Rana Amar Singh and Prince Karan commissioned by Jahangir. Finch, who was in Agra during the reign of Jahangir reports seeing the 'two Rajaws in stone', and Bernier mentions seeing the statues of Jaimal and Patta in Delhi, apparently shifted there by Shah Jahan. The statues, says Bemier, 'have an air of grandeur, and inspire me with an awe and respect which I cannot describe,' In commissioning the sculptures of the Rajput heroes, Akbar was probably inspired by the elephant statue at the Gwalior fort, of which Finch says: '[there] standeth a mightie elephant of stone very curiously wrought.' A few wooden sculptures are also mentioned in Mughal chronicles. Jahangir refers to 'the two elephants placed on the two sides of the seat of the jharokha, which skillful people had made of wood . . .'

There was not much sculptural activity at this time even among Hindus. Not very many new temples were being built, and even in the few great temples constructed during the reigns of Akbar and Jahangir, sculptural adornment was not as lush as it used to be, because of Muslim influence. Only in the far south, well outside the Mughal empire, did traditional Hindu sculpture thrive.

In stone art, the Mughal preference was for relief-carvings, inlays, marble lattices, and mosaics, and these developed into high art forms under Shah Jahan, as the intricate and delicate marble lattices and fabulous *pietra dura* inlays of the Taj evidence. Akbar favoured low relief sandstone carvings for decoration, especially in Fatehpur Sikri, where it was used most profusely in the building commonly identified as the house of the Turkish Sultana, covering its entire wall surface, inside and outside. The Mughals also used glazed tile mosaic for decoration with great sophistication, notably in Punjab and Sind.

In the related field of jewellery-making too the Mughals made major contributions. 'Among other things, the Indians make . . . such beautiful gold ornaments that it may be doubted if the exquisite workmanship of these articles can be exceeded by any European goldsmith,' says Bernier. Some of the styles attributed to Nurjahan, such as the *karanphool-jhumka* ear ornament, would remain in high fashion well into modern times. The Mughal emperors were connoisseurs of good living, and they turned their goblets, vases, plates, spoons and vessels into jewels, often brilliantly enamelled. The reign of Shah Jahan was an especially good time for jewellers. The emperor himself was a great authority on gems and jewellery, and in the Peacock Throne he created a work that was in the jeweller's art the peer of the Taj in architecture. The throne, says Thevenot, was 'so much talked of in the Indies'. Lapidary work however did not find much favour with the Mughals, as they generally preferred to keep gems uncut, valuing size over brilliance.

'IN HINDUSTAN BOTH Moguls and Hindus are very fond of listening to songs and instrumental music,' writes Manucci. Except Aurangzeb, the Mughal emperors were all keen patrons of music, and there was, as Tavernier noted, always music at the Mughal court. Music was valued not merely as a source of aesthetic pleasure, but also of spiritual rapture. Not surprisingly, the dying wish of sage Sheikh Salim Chishti, according to Jahangir, was to hear Tansen, Akbar's court musician, sing.

Indian rulers were extravagantly generous in the patronage of musicians. Ramchand, the ruler of Batta, 'gave in one day a crore of *zar* (gold pieces or money) to Miyan Tansen Kalawant', says Badauni, illustrating the high regard of Indian rulers for music, though no doubt exaggerating the size of the particular gift. The Mughal emperors were equally open-handed. Jahangir once had Muhammad Nayi, a flautist, weighed against rupees to reward him for an ode he composed in Jahangir's name—he weighed 6300 rupees, and it was given to him along with an elephant. Similarly, Shah Jahan once weighed musician Jagannath against gold and presented the amount to him. On a more modest scale, Akbar on one occasion rewarded Tansen with 200,000 rupees for a performance, and Abdur-Rahim, the Khan-i-Khanan, once gifted 100,000 rupees to musician Ram Das. Abul Hasan, the deposed Sultan of Golconda, while he was a prisoner of Aurangzeb in Daulatabad, one day wished aloud that he had a lakh (100,000) of rupees to give to a musician whom he chanced to hear—and Aurangzeb, coming to hear of it, is said to have sent him, with uncharacteristic generosity, the amount to gratify his wish.

It may be that these flamboyant gestures were intended more for the self-glorification of the patron than for the glorification of the musician, but even then such acts created an environment of generous patronage of music. Musicians could not complain.

Hindu and Muslim musical traditions have been melding and evolving over the centuries, begetting such new musical modes as Qawwali, Thumri, and most importantly, Khayal, which is commonly considered as the highest form of North Indian classical music. The interaction between Indian and West Asian music had begun even before the rise of Islam, perhaps from as early as the fifth century, when a Persian monarch is believed to have established colonies of Indian singers and dancers in his kingdom. Later in India, Sufis took to Indian music as an ideal means for inducing spiritual ecstasy. From the thirteenth century on, it was fairly common for Hindu musicians to serve in Muslim courts, and they often became converts to Islam to secure royal patronage.

Towards the close of the thirteenth century, Amir Khusrau, the greatest poetic and musical genius of the age, made a conscious effort to fuse Hindu and Persian music. Closer to Mughal times, one of the greatest influences on Indian music was the patronage of Raja Man Singh of Gwalior (1450–1528), himself a gifted musician. Under his direction, court musicians investigated the rules governing ragas (melodic formulas), and enunciated them in standard form in a book entitled *Man Kautuhal*. Also around that time, South Indian classical music was systematized by Purandaradasa (1484–1564), the musician saint of Karnataka, who came to be known as the father of Carnatic music.

The patronage of music by the Mughals began with Babur, who was a connoisseur and himself a composer. Nothing much is known about Humayun's involvement with music, but considering his general cultural bias, it is unlikely that he was not an active patron of music. Among the Surs, Adil Shah was a music and dance virtuoso, whom even Tansen and Baz Bahadur acknowledged as their guru.

In the reign of Akbar, Biram Khan set the tone for the promotion of music by taking into his service Ram Das of Lucknow, a gifted musician who had served in the court of Salim Shah, and whom Badauni describes as 'a second Miyan Tansen'. Writes Badauni: 'This man used to be Khan-i-Khanan's companion and intimate associate, and by the beauty of his voice continuously brought tears to his eyes.' Akbar was equally keen on music and was himself a musician; he had, according to Jahangir, mastered Hindi vocalization, and had, says Abul Fazl, 'such a knowledge of the science of music as trained musicians do not possess; and is likewise an excellent hand at performing, especially on the kettle-drum.' Akbar maintained a large troupe of musicians, 'Hindus, Iranis, Turanis, Kashmiris, both men and women', who were 'arranged in seven divisions, one for each day of the week', notes Abul Fazl. Vocalists in Akbar's court were mostly Indians, while instrumentalists came from Iran, Afghanistan and Central Asia.

Among the thirty-six prominent musicians in Akbar's court listed by Abul Fazl was Baz Bahadur, the former ruler of Malwa and now a Mughal mansabdar; he was, says Abul Fazl, 'a singer without rival'. But by far the most gifted musician in Mughal times was Tansen, whose melodies, according to popular legend, could set candles alight or make rain fall. Tansen wrote devotional, panegyrical and descriptive poems, set them to music and sang them himself. 'A singer like him has not been in India for the last thousand years,' says Abul Fazl. Tansen, at the interface of two cultures, was innovative, and he adapted his music to the times he lived in and the people he served. But innovation, even creativity, were anathema to the proponents of pure classicism, so Tansen has been at times criticized by musical purists for supposedly corrupting Indian classical music.

Little is known about Tansen's early career. Muslim tradition has him grow up in the monastery of Muhammad Ghaus in Gwalior, while Hindus claim that he was a disciple of Swami Haridas. He was very likely a native of Gwalior, and probably had his musical training at the school of music founded there by Raja Man Singh—ten out of the thirty-six musicians of Akbar's court listed by Abul Fazl, Hindus as well as Muslims, were from Gwalior. Tansen was originally at the court of the Raja of Rewa, from where, around 1663, Akbar summoned him to Agra. Soon after he entered the Mughal service, Tansen seems to have become a Muslim; his son, also a musician, certainly became a Muslim, like several other Hindu musicians in the Mughal service. Tansen died in 1589, and was buried in a Muslim holy ground, in a corner of the sepulchre of Muhammad Ghaus in Gwalior. His tomb is today a place of pilgrimage for musicians.

Jahangir, like Akbar, was a generous patron of musicians, and had at his court, according to William Finch, many hundreds of singing and dancing girls, who 'attend there day and night, according as their several turnes come every seventh day, that they may bee ready when the King or his women shall please to call any of them to sing or dance in his moholl, he giving to every one of them stipends according to their unworthy worth.' Says Jahangir about one of his musicians: 'Shauqi, the mandolin player, is the wonder of the age. He also sings Hindi and Persian songs in a manner that clears the rust from all hearts.' Shah Jahan was skilled in song and dance, and often performed himself. Aurangzeb, though he was susceptible to the seduction of music, or perhaps because of it, deliberately turned his back on music, and in the latter part of his reign banished music from his court, though he continued to maintain singing and dancing girls for the entertainment of the begums. A number of books on the history and theory of music were written during the Mughal period, but unfortunately much of the music composed at this time has been lost, as the Indian system of musical notation could record only the basic notes of melody, not its ornamentation and variation. Tansen lives on as a legend, but his music has been lost.

Mughal music at first sounded strange and cacophonous to foreigners. Says Bernier of the music played in the band-house in the imperial citadel: 'To the ears of an European recently arrived, this music sounds very strangely, for there are ten or twelve hautboys, and as many cymbals, which play together. One of the hautboys, called *karna*, is a fathom and a half in length, and its lower aperture cannot be less than a foot. The cymbals of brass or iron are some of them at least a fathom in diameter. You may judge, therefore, of the roaring sound which issues from the [band-house] . . . On my first arrival it stunned me so as to be insupportable: but such is the power of habit that this same noise is now heard by me with pleasure; in the night, particularly, when in bed and afar, on my terrace, this music sounds in my ears as solemn, grand and melodious. This is not altogether to be wondered at, since it is played by persons instructed from infancy in the rules of melody, and possessing the skill of modulating and turning the harsh sounds of the hautboy and cymbal so as to produce a symphony far from disagreeable when heard at a certain distance.'

Outside the Mughal empire there were at this time several monarchs who were accomplished musicians—Adil Shah of Bihar, Baz Bahadur of Malwa, and Bahadur Shah of Gujarat. In the Deccan, Ibrahim Adil Shah II of Bijapur was a poet and musician; he composed Dhrupads (Hindu classical music) and wrote a volume of poems—*Kitab-i Nawras*, Book of Nine Moods—to be sung in different ragas. Qutb Shah of Golconda was in the habit of amusing himself in the harem by acting out Krishna's amatory dalliances. Common Hindu themes like *ras-lila* (play of moods) and *vasant* (spring), along with *marsia*, (a Shiah lament) were popular themes of poetry and music in the Muslim courts of the Deccan. And just as the sultans patronized Hindu music, Perso-Arabic music influenced, though to a lesser extent, the court music of the Hindu kingdom of Vijayanagar, as Kallina and Ramamaya, renowned medieval musical authorities of South India, testify.

Dance, like music, was an essential part of Hindu worship and social life. In the temples, the Devadasis sang and danced before the deity, and they were very much a part of the family festivities of the affluent. Some of these customs were adopted by the Mughals. It was customary for dancers to pay their homage to the emperor once a week, and dancers were in constant attendance in the harem. Professional dancers like Kenchens also provided public entertainment. 'Ordinarily the dancing women dance in the principal open places in the city, beginning at six o'clock in the evening and going on till nine, lighted by many torches, and from this dancing they earn a good deal of money,' says Manucci.

The subject of Hindu dance was almost exclusively religious, though dancers performed at temples as well as at courts. But with the decline of Hindu political power since the thirteenth century, and the periodical temple demolitions by Muslim rulers, the patronage of the performing arts by temples declined, and even the depiction of dance images in temple sculpture became rare. Musicians and dancers then moved in droves to the Muslim courts, and in that milieu, Indian and Persian dance idioms combined to evolve Kathak, the north-Indian classical dance. In general, in the visual and performing arts, the adaptation of the traditional Hindu modes to the Mughal environment involved a change of their ethos from religious devotion to secular entertainment.

The Last Spring

THE MARK OF the Mughal is everywhere in India: the fabulous monuments of the emperors and their imitators. The Mughal contribution in architecture was not however in originality, but in refinement. Their buildings, except those of Akbar, were largely Persian in inspiration; they were in fact not even the first to introduce the style in India, for the Delhi Sultans before them had favoured Persian architecture. What was distinctive about the Mughals was that they refined the style to such a degree that their buildings seem to be in a class by themselves. Besides, their passion for the formal garden was unprecedented in India.

The traditional Hindu concept of the garden was quite unlike that of the Mughals. Though Megasthenes, the Greek ambassador to the court of the Mauryas in the fourth century BC, speaks of lovely gardens around the royal palace, and there are many references in Sanskrit literature to public parks and to gardens attached to mansions, these seem to have been groves rather than landscaped gardens. The Turko-Afghans had a more formal approach to gardening, and Firuz Tughluq is said to have laid out over a hundred gardens. But that memory had been long lost, and there was no living tradition of formally laid-out gardens in India at the time of Babur's invasion.

For Babur, a formal garden was an essential requirement of civilized life, and one of his first projects after occupying Agra was to lay out, on the left bank of the Yamuna, a garden he named Gul Afshan, which later came to be known as Aram Bagh. The Mughals—especially Babur and Akbar—were also avid horticulturists, and they introduced several fruit varieties into India from Kabul. 'His Majesty looks upon plants as one of the greatest gifts of the Creator and pays much attention to them,' says Abul Fazl about Akbar. 'Horticulturists of Iran and Turan (Turkey) have therefore settled here, and the cultivation of trees is in a flourishing state.'

With Jahangir too gardening was a passion. He laid out several, including the magnificent Shalimar Garden at the Dal Lake in Srinagar, whose splendour is nearly matched by the nearby Nishat Bagh garden of Asaf Khan, Jahangir's Vizier and brother-in-law. In laying out the

Shalimar, Jahangir redirected streams and sent water gurgling down sloping channels, to cascade in miniature waterfalls or to spray in fountains, and then lulled them to flow gently and lie hushed and still in crystalline pools. There were low-set, low-railed, crib-like seats in the pools, and elegant, domed pavilions in the midst of canals, for the visitor to lose (or find) himself in communion with nature. Flower beds and thick flowering bushes bloomed luxuriantly everywhere. Giant chanar trees sentinelled the pathways.

'Kashmir is a garden of eternal spring . . . a heart-expanding heritage,' says Jahangir. The Mughals groomed and refined the natural enchantment of the valley. 'In former ages, Kashmir contained no fine gardens or houses or fruit,' says Inayat Khan, 'but from the time it was brought under subjection by Emperor Akbar, vast improvements began to be undertaken; such as the construction of mansions and gardens, fountains, and suitable villas, together with the grafting of fruit trees and such like. Under the late Emperor Jahangir's rule, as he had a striking partiality for the place, its splendour rapidly increased. And during the present auspicious reign [of Shah Jahan] . . . it has reached the acme of perfection.' Shah Jahan visited Kashmir several times, but it was in Punjab that he laid out a great garden, the Shalimar Garden of Lahore, on the gateway of which is engraved: 'Sweet is this garden, through envy of which the tulip is spotted.'

The basic grid of the Mughal formal garden was a square or rectangular area divided into quadrants, and so was called *char-bagh*. The four parts were further sectioned into neat geometric parterres—using only straight lines, never any curves—to form an intricate but neat and precisely symmetrical design. The pattern was accentuated by a grid of raised, paved paths diverging from a central square. There was usually a pool at the centre, from which water flowed in broad but shallow canals to the middle of each of the four segments; auxiliary canals and paths further patterned the garden, giving it a classic though somewhat frozen look. Water was an essential element in the Mughal garden, to cool the air and lighten the spirit, and to set a mood of purity and calm reflection or innocent playfulness. The lilt and sparkle of the water courses also somewhat softened the rigidity of the pattern of the *char-bagh*.

The garden was for the Mughals a token of the eternal spring that was paradise, and it was in *char-bagh* gardens that they built their great mausoleums, a tradition derived from pre-Islamic Persian culture. The idea of a monumental tomb, to glorify one who was not god, was not quite in harmony with the spirit of Islam, but when the custom of venerating saints began—in the belief that a holy man's spirit could intercede between man and god—the tombs of saints became shrines and were built as monuments. And as spiritual power was monumentalized, so was temporal power, and the mighty of the land sought to mark their passage through the world with massive piles of brick and stone, though the pious, like Aurangzeb, spurned this vanity.

MUGHAL ARCHITECTURE was radically different from Hindu architecture, in style as well as in spirit, indicating the divergent attitudes of the two cultures towards life and nature. Mughal buildings were open to the environment and had a cheerful, confident appearance, reflecting the lifestyle of a zesty, adventurous people from the salubrious highlands, while Hindu buildings huddled away from the scorching sun and wind of India, and had a diffident, congested look, reflecting the lifestyle of a people curled into themselves. One looked outward, the other looked inward. 'There are no large fruit-trees of any sort [near Mughal mansions], in order not to hinder the delight of an open view,' says Manucci. The Mughals lived in vast, flamboyant buildings open to broad vistas, with sweeping arches and latticed windows that let in the winds to blow, the light to play, while in Hindu buildings, even in the most opulent of them, rooms were small, dark, airless. Hindus revered nature, the Mughals enjoyed nature.

The most impressive Hindu secular structure that the Mughals came across was the Gwalior fort, built by Raja Man Singh, the Rajput chieftain who ruled the region from 1486 to 1516, and was a great patron of culture and learning. Babur, who visited Gwalior in 1528, was ambivalent in his appreciation of the palace complex. 'They are wonderful buildings, entirely of hewn stone, in heavy and unsymmetrical blocks however,' he writes. 'Of all the Rajas' buildings Man Singh's is the best and the loftiest. In parts it is four storeys high; the lower two are very dark; we went through them with candles. On one (or, every) side of this building are five cupolas, having between each two of them a smaller one, square after the fashion of Hindustan. On the larger ones are fastened sheets of gilded copper. On the outside of the walls is painted-tile work, the semblance of plantain-trees being hewn all round with green tiles . . . the sitting rooms are on the second storey, in a hollow even; they are rather airless places although Hindustani pains have been taken with them.'

What the Mughals abhorred about Hindu buildings was their closed, musty environment. Says Jahangir about the great Rajput fort of

Ranthambhor. 'As the buildings inside the fort had been built after the fashion of the Hindus, and the rooms were without air and with little space, they did not please me . . .' For the same reason, Jahangir disliked the architecture of Hindu temples; he writes: 'Although in the time of the late king, the Rajput nobles had built temples after their fashion, and ornamented them highly on the outside, inside them bats and owls had made their abode to such an extent, that on account of the malodours one could not breathe.'

An indispensable requirement of dwellings in India was to provide protection from the summer heat, but the architectural solutions of the Mughals and the Rajputs to this problem were altogether different. Rajput buildings characteristically clustered close together to expose the least surface to the sun, and had few and small windows, which, though they efficiently funnelled out the heat, also kept out fresh air. In contrast, the Mughals created large, high-ceilinged, shady spaces, depending on water channels, pools, fountains and curtains of water to cool the air. They also had underground rooms, built beneath pools and canals, to retreat from extreme heat.

Water was as vital an element in Mughal architecture as it was in Mughal gardens. 'All these palaces are full of gardens with running water, which flows in channels into reservoirs of stone, jasper, and marble,' says Manucci. 'In the rooms and halls of these palaces there are always flowers according to the season . . . [There] are seats and private rooms . . . in the midst of the running water. In the water are many fish for delight.' Says Bernier, 'There is almost no chamber, but it hath at its door a storehouse of running water . . . rivulets, fountains, jets of water . . .' Within the apartments too there were water channels, pools and fountains. Nowhere was the use of water more exuberant than in the Hayat Baksh (Life Giving) Garden in the Delhi citadel, where water sprayed in as many as 281 fountains, so it would have seemed as if it were monsoon there all through the year. Elsewhere rooms were curtained with water falling in silver cascades from the roof. The use of water as an architectural motif turned massive buildings light and shimmering like mirages, opened up space in closed areas.

BABUR, THOUGH HE was in India for only four years and spent most of his time in the battlefield, nevertheless had several building complexes to his credit, and is said to have summoned from Constantinople the disciples of the famous Albanian architect Sinan to work on his buildings. 'Six-hundred men worked daily on my buildings in Agra . . . while 1491 stone-cutters worked daily on my buildings in Agra, Sikri, Biana, Dholpur, Gwalior and Kiul,' Babur notes in his memoirs. But he was not happy with the results. In the Agra fort he had built a large, chambered tank, and near it a mosque, and of that he says, 'The mosque is not well done; it is in the Hindustani fashion.'

Humayun had grand building plans. On a visit to Gwalior, says Khvand Amir, Humayun one night summoned his courtiers and told them of his plan to build a great city in Delhi, and in it 'a magnificent palace of seven storeys . . . surrounded by delightful gardens and orchards, of such elegance and beauty, that its fame might draw people from the remotest corners of the world . . .' The city was to be called Dinpanah, and the area he selected for it was Indarpat, believed to be the site of the epic city of Indraprastha described in the *Mahabharata*. There, after taking 'omens and religious advice', Humayun 'with his holy hand put a brick on the earth' at a time prescribed by astrologers, to mark the beginning of construction. 'On the same date work was also commenced in the King's own palace,' says Khvand Amir. Unfortunately, hardly any trace remains of the construction so auspiciously begun.

Sher Shah, who demolished Humayun's empire, also demolished his city to build his own capital in its place, but did not live to complete the project. Today little more than the shell of Sher Shah's citadel—known as Purana Qila, Old Fort—remains. The fort with it massive ramparts of rubble masonry is, like its builder, sternly practical; only its gateway, built of sandstone ashlar and decorated with white marble inlay and blue glaze, relieves its forbidding severity. The lone noteworthy building in the complex is the royal mosque, Qila-i-Kuhna—Percy Brown, a modern authority of Indian architecture, describes it as 'a gem of architectural design'.

Of greater interest is Sher Shah's tomb at Sasaram, which elaborated and refined the Lodi architectural style, and is described by Percy Brown, with his bias for Sher Shah, as a building of 'surpassing architectural merit'. Built in the middle of a rectangular artificial lake, the octagonal mausoleum is a massive pyramidal pile of three diminishing tiers that rises from a high, square platform, and is crowned by a low, plump dome. Originally the mausoleum had glazed decorations in blue, red and yellow, and the dome was painted white, but time has reduced everything to a sombre gray. The other Sur tombs, like the Lodi tombs on which they were modelled, are little more than masonry piles over corpses, massive without being monumental.

WITH AKBAR BEGAN a new phase in Indian architecture. The very first major structure in his reign, Humayun's mausoleum in Delhi built by his widow, Haji (or Bega) Begum—who had been to Persia with Humayun and is commonly identified with Hamida Banu Begum—introduced a distinctive Persian style into India. It was also India's first garden tomb. The double dome (one to harmonize with the internal layout, the other to match the external contours) of the mausoleum, its great arched alcoves, and the complex of rooms and corridors in its internal arrangement, were all Persian in inspiration, and would serve as the prototype for the Taj. There were, however, a few Indian features in the building, such as the kiosks on its roof. Further, while Persians built with brick and decorated with terracotta and glaze, Humayun's mausoleum was built with red sandstone and decorated with white marble inlay—the Mughals generally built with stone and marble, except in Lahore, where they used bricks and glazed tiles.

Four imposing gateways open into the high-walled, sprawling *char-bagh* garden of Humayun's mausoleum. In the middle of the garden, on an immense, 6.7 metre high, arcaded terrace, the red sandstone tomb rises, a huge, square building, capped by a great marble-encased dome mounted on a high drum and counterpointed by kiosks on slender pillars. The broad flanks of the tomb are relieved by chamfered corners and recessed arches; marble inlays highlight the lines of the building and also open up the plain stone surfaces of the facade. The precise and symmetrical repetitions of architectural motifs and the chiaroscuro of contrasting planes give the mausoleum a graceful, airy aspect, despite its great mass. It is a dignified and tranquil final resting place for a distraught soul.

The highly Persianized style of Humayun's tomb did not suit Akbar. He bypassed the derived idiom and created a vigorously original architectural style of his own, by synthesizing Persian and Indian traditions—Indian in its construction methods, intricacy of ornamentation and overall ambience, but Persian in its openness and expansiveness, it was the self-expression of a blessedly inspired and daring monarch, who, unrestrained by convention, could journey into the unknown with the confidence that time and fortune, wealth and power, abided with him.

Akbar was a compulsive builder, seeking in stone and mortar the permanence that his flesh and bones denied him. His first major building endeavour was in Agra, where he demolished the old Lodi fort and built a new citadel. Akbar, according to Abul Fazl, built in the fort 'five-hundred buildings of masonry, after the beautiful designs of Bengal and Gujarat'. Almost all those buildings are gone, demolished by Akbar's favourite grandson, Shah Jahan; only a small cluster of his buildings in the south-east corner of the fort has survived, the most noteworthy of them being the Jahangiri Mahal.

Akbar built entirely with red sandstone and decorated with marble inlays. Even the Agra fort walls—which are as high as a six-storey building and 2.4 kilometres in circuit—are faced throughout with polished red sandstone. His buildings in Agra have a strong Hindu flavour, and echo the style of the Rajput palaces in Gwalior. Akbar mainly used the beam and bracket Indian construction method; arches, so dominant in Persian architecture, were used only for ornamental purposes. The Jahangiri Mahal, with its elaborately carved stone brackets and struts—mimicking old Indian buildings of wood—has a distinctively Hindu ambience, far removed from the traditional Mughal world. Akbar drew his strength and inspiration from the land and the people he ruled.

Apart from the citadel in Agra, Akbar also built palaces in Lahore, Ajmer and Allahabad, as well as the elegant, ten-span, pavilioned bridge over the Gomati at Jaunpur. But it was in Fatehpur Sikri, his new capital, that Akbar truly expressed his architectural vision. The work on the complex began even before the Agra and Lahore forts were completed. Sikri is believed to have been the domain of the Sikarwar Rajputs before Muslim invasion. Babur had camped at the lakeside there on his way to give battle to Rana Sanga, and after his victory had laid out a garden with a pleasure pavilion in the lake. But what brought Akbar to Sikri was not its historical associations, but personal sentiment—Sikri was the place of residence of Sheikh Salim Chishti, to whose blessing Akbar attributed the birth of his three sons. Akbar, says Jahangir, considered Sikri lucky for him.

Once the decision was made to build the capital there, work proceeded at a scorching pace. Akbar set up camp at Sikri in late 1571, to supervise and speed up the construction. 'Zelaldinus is so devoted to building that he sometimes quarries himself along with other workmen,' says Monserrate. 'Nor does he shrink from watching, and even practicing, for the sake of amusement, the craft of an ordinary artisan.' Most of the principal buildings of the royal complex were ready in a couple of years, and Akbar moved into them, but construction went on at Sikri for many more years, till Akbar abruptly abandoned it in 1585. He would visit Sikri again only once, in 1601, on his way back to Agra from the Deccan.

Built on a rocky ridge of the Aravalli range, Sikri is quintessentially Akbarian in ethos. Robust and sinewy, without the self-conscious aestheticism of Jahangir or the cloying sweetness of Shah Jahan, Sikri throbs with power and vitality. Yet, there is also an unmistakable air of mystery about Sikri. Its layout is complex and confusing, the function of many of its structures unknown, the reason for their curious designs unfathomable. Several different architectural and decorative styles interwove in Sikri, and that too was very much in the character of Akbar. The unity of Sikri is more of character and spirit than of architectural style.

Sikri, like the Agra citadel, was built entirely of red sandstone—Akbar used marble only to adorn, not to build. For decoration he favoured marble inlay, low relief stone carving, and painting on plastered surfaces. He did not use gem inlays, which would under Shah Jahan become the hallmark of Mughal decorative style. There was only one exception to this, the mother-of-pearl and ebony inlay of the canopy of Salim Chishti's tomb, but that was probably a later embellishment.

The buildings in Sikri are predominantly Hindu in character, though the layout is more open, in the Mughal manner. The only major building there in the conventional Islamic style is the Jama Masjid, the first of the great congregational mosques the Mughals would build in India. Standing slightly apart from the palace complex, and occupying the summit of the hill, the mosque dominates the entire town, but is itself dominated by the Buland Darwaza, its lofty gateway, which rises 53.6 metres high—nearly as tall as an eighteen-storey building—from the base of its supporting terrace. A massive, awesome structure, yet elegant, pleasing in its proportions and detail, the gateway is one of the finest edifices of its kind anywhere in the world.

In the courtyard of the great mosque is the tomb of the sage who brought Akbar to Sikri, Sheikh Salim Chishti, who died in 1572, soon after the construction of the city began. Tiny and fragile, the austere white tomb nestles low against the burly red sandstone walls of the mosque, directly opposite the Buland Darwaza. Built of red sandstone, it was originally covered with plaster, but was later faced with a veneer of marble. Early in the reign of Jahangir exquisite marble screens, mosaic flooring, and a marble paved walkway were added to the tomb, giving it a pure, serene appearance.

In contrast, Akbar's own tomb is a turbulent edifice, a building like a forest fire. The construction of the tomb—at Sikandra, eight kilometres west of Agra—was begun during the lifetime of Akbar, but was completed only in 1613, seven years after his death. A fabulous mutant of the Panch Mahal in Sikri, the mausoleum is built in the middle of a vast, square garden, and has as its base a stupendous terrace, over nine metres high and 103.6 metre square. The terrace is built almost solid, except for the central tomb chamber, the arcaded facades, and the porticoes with deeply recessed archways in the middle of each of its four sides. From the centre of the terrace rises a four-storeyed superstructure of successively diminishing girth, the first three of the storeys a thicket of arcades and kiosks built of fire-red sandstone with marble cupolas, which from a distance seem like tongues of flame rising from a great sacrificial hearth.

Only on the top storey, built entirely of cool, white marble, is the seething energy of the building brought to quiescence. The layout here is stark, just a square open court enclosed by arcaded cloisters, with marble lattice outer walls. At the centre of the court, on a low platform, is the cenotaph, open to the sky. Deep below, in a high-domed hall at the ground level that served as the crypt-cum-tomb chamber, is Akbar's sarcophagus, an arrangement which is in itself unusual, for the Muslim custom was to bury the body in a subterranean crypt. A further element of mystery is added by the existence of an inexplicable, low-roofed false tomb on the fourth storey, entered only through a small aperture.

In 1608, when the construction of the mausoleum was in progress, Jahangir visited the site. He did not like what he saw, for he had, he says, 'expected to see an edifice which travellers would pronounce to be unrivalled in the world,' but the architects had gone on 'building after their taste.' So he ordered them 'to build up several parts as I had before directed'. It is not clear what precisely Jahangir's contribution to the tomb is; its design is unmistakably Akbarian, so probably all that Jahangir contributed were the marble embellishments, and maybe the layout of the garden and the plan of the gateways.

The whole mausoleum complex is walled in, with a gate tower on each side, though passage is only through the southern gate. This gate in itself is a monumental structure, distinguished by its fine inlay decorations and slender marble minarets—here the minaret, after a lapse of 400 years since the erection of the Qutb Minar, makes its appearance again in India, later to develop into a major feature of Mughal architecture.

Sikandra was visited by William Finch in 1610. 'Here, within a faire round coffin of gold, lieth the body of this monarch, who sometimes thought the world too little for him. This tombe is much worshipped both by the Moores and Gentiles, holding him for a great saint,' writes Finch, mixing fact and fancy. The tomb, he adds, was 'to be inarched over with the most curious white and speckled marble and to be seeled all within with pure sheet-gold richly inwrought.' Such a plan, if it ever existed, was not carried out. Sikandra, as it is, is the perfect mausoleum for Akbar.

THERE WAS NOT much building activity under Jahangir. Akbar had built enough. Nur Jahan had a greater interest in architecture, and she built one of the finest Mughal monuments, the luminous white marble mausoleum of her father, Itimad-ud-daula. It is a tiny building compared to the great Mughal monuments, only twenty-one metre square, a daughter's loving homage to her father, not a power memorial. But it is exquisitely crafted, and lies like a fabulous, gem-encrusted mother-of-pearl casket in the velvet green of a small walled garden on the left bank of the Yamuna in Agra, diagonally across from the fort.

The first of the Mughal structures built entirely of marble, Itimad-ud-daula's tomb is more like a jewel fashioned by a goldsmith than a monument erected by masons. Its ornamentation is luxuriant, almost baroque in its profusion, covering the entire surface of the tomb, inside and outside, with geometrical patterns, scrolls and floral designs in coloured marble mosaic and *pietra dura* inlay with semi-precious stones like topaz, jasper, carnelian, lapis lazuli and onyx. Though mosaics and coloured stones had been used previously in Sher Shah's mosque in Delhi, in the tomb of Sheikh Salim Chishti in Agra, and in the main gate of Akbar's tomb in Sikandra, in Itimad-ud-daula's tomb the decorative motif was carried to its very limit. Not surprisingly, it took seven years to complete this small building, as craftsmen minutely laboured on it, carving, filling, polishing.

Nurjahan built yet another monument, the mausoleum of Jahangir in Lahore, but this was on an entirely different scale, an emperor's tomb. She was not altogether comfortable with its grand monumentality, and her unease shows in the building, which appears oddly disproportionate, like a miniature enlarged, which in a way it was, its design concept similar to that of Itimad-ud-daula's tomb, but scaled up. The base of the tomb is a 6.7 metre high, 99 metre square, arcaded terrace, from the corners of which rise four tall octagonal minarets, all elaborately decorated with marble inlays, glazed tiles and painted patterns. On the terrace, Nurjahan had built a marble pavilion, probably similar to that of Itimad-ud-daula's tomb, but it was later dismantled and carried away (by the Sikhs in the eighteenth century?) so that the most aesthetic of the Mughal emperors today lies interred in a squat, truncated, misshapen mausoleum.

JAHANGIR'S NEGLECT OF architecture was more than made up for by Shah Jahan, and with him the Mughal style reached its ultimate though icy perfection. Shah Jahan built mostly with marble, preferring its cold, chaste beauty to the earthy warmth of sandstone. In style, he favoured the neatness, geometrical precision and openness of Persian architecture to the clutter and congestion of the Hindu style. So he demolished most of Akbar's buildings in the Agra fort, and in their place built an array of opulent marble edifices. The most enchanting of them was the Shish Mahal, a fairyland pavilion with mimic waterfalls, water-jets and basins, all reflected many times over in the mirrors and innumerable bits of glass set in the gilt and coloured stucco patterns on its walls and ceiling. Of a different ambience, but still marvellous, are the Moti Masjid, the small but peerless royal mosque, and the Diwan-i-khas, the hall of private audience.

But Agra was only a modest prelude to Delhi, where Shah Jahan built a city of his own, Shahjahanabad, and a marble palace complex of unparalleled luxury. He laid the foundations of the city in 1638, and ten years later, when it was completed, shifted his residence there from Agra. Shah Jahan was pleased with his accomplishment, and had a Persian couplet engraved on the arches of the Diwan-i-khas, proclaiming the palace to be the paradise on earth.

The Diwan-i-khas would indeed have seemed paradisiacal to Mughal courtiers. Built of white marble, its pillars and walls were opulently embellished with *pietra dura* inlays, its ceiling an arabesque wrought in gold. Decorated in the same fashion, but even more opulently, were the royal suites, a dozen luxurious marble pavilions on the riverside rampart of the fort, each fronted by a flower garden with watercourses and fountains. Of these, the most charming was the Rang Mahal, Palace of Colours, in the middle of which was a square, shallow, almost flat marble basin, elaborately scrolled and adorned with gem inlays, with a large, stylized, open lotus at the centre, from the pericarp of which water gurgled and sprinkled. Water flowed through the entire palace complex, tapped from the Yamuna some 100 odd kilometres upstream and brought in by a canal, which in the citadel was called the Stream of Paradise.

The gold of the ceilings of the royal pavilions was replaced with silver in a later reign, and that too was afterwards removed ('to supply a pressing need') and replaced with copper, which again was replaced with wood, as the Mughal empire steadily and inexorably ran to seed. Still later, much of the other ornamentation in the palace complex was pried away by vandals or invaders. The water channels and the fountains in the palace ran dry.

Close by to the citadel, to the south-west of it, Shah Jahan built the Jama Masjid, the largest mosque in India, an elegantly proportioned edifice despite its immense size, which loomed over the city in imperious severity. Says Bernier of the mosque: 'Every part appears well contrived, properly executed, and correctly proportioned.'

AROUND THE TIME Shahjahanabad was nearing completion, some 200 kilometres south-east of it, in Agra, the Taj was also nearing completion. The work on the mausoleum had begun in 1632, the year after the death of Mumtaz Mahal, and the main structure was ready in about six years, as the dated inscriptions on the Taj show. But the decorative work took several more years, and now, sixteen years after construction began, the mausoleum was ready, though the work on the forecourt and the ancillaries would go on for another five or six years.

The Taj marked the culmination of the evolution of Mughal architecture, which began with Humayun's tomb, took a detour with Akbar, then returned to its Persian mainstream under Jahangir. The Taj is essentially Persian in temper and style, with some Indian elements, such as the kiosks around the dome and on top of the minarets, and the brackets of the discreet balconies of the minarets. Akbar's vision of cultural synthesis has now been completely abandoned, the spirit of daring adventure he infused in the Mughal dynasty tamed. Between Fatehpur Sikri and the Taj Mahal, the difference is not merely in architectural style but in spirit. Fatehpur is earthy, robust, maybe flawed, but vibrant and inviting; the Taj is narcissistic, absorbed in itself, a solemn and immaculate beauty that would brook no familiarity. The Taj is often considered the most beautiful building of man, the most perfect. That it might be. But it has no animation—frozen in its perfection, the Taj dare not breathe.

The site of the Taj, offering an enchanting view from Shah Jahan's palace in the Agra fort, was itself an admirable artistic choice, the Yamuna pausing in its course to bend sharply to caress the Taj before turning again further downstream. In laying out the Taj, Shah Jahan deliberately deviated from the conventional plan of garden tombs and, instead of erecting the mausoleum at the centre of the garden, placed it at one end, to stand sheer on the riverside, for it to be seen against the horizon and to give depth of perspective to its monumentality. On the river bank, the tomb stands in the middle of a red sandstone platform stretching over the entire width of the garden, with companionable balancing buildings in red sandstone at the far ends of the platform, on the left and the right. The gateway into the garden is at its southern end, an elegant, two-storeyed red sandstone building with a deep, apsed entrance flanked by arched recesses. A broad, shallow canal stretches from the gateway to the mausoleum, punctuated by a square marble pool in the middle, which inverts and ripples the Taj in its wind-ruffled waters.

The river too carries the image of the Taj, its waters lapping the sandstone platform, but never rising above it even in high flood. On the platform, on a high marble terrace of its own, the Taj stands aloof and inviolable. Four lean, tall, stern minarets at the salient and phased corners of the terrace stand solemnly well apart from the tomb, like sentinels. The tomb, like its terrace, is square, but its corners are chamfered to present broad faces to the minarets. The Taj is a massive edifice, yet seems ethereal and dream-like as it stands clear against the azure sky, its immense mass lightened by the wide, deep, soaring recess of its vaulted portal and the double row of arched recesses flanking it. All the four sides of the mausoleum are identical, but the entrance is only from the southern side, facing the gateway.

The crowning glory of the Taj is its immense dome, which is nearly as tall as the rest of the building. The dome bulges slightly as it heaves from its base; a full, firm, alabaster breast, it nipples into a foliated crest, topped by a slender, gold finial. At the chamfered corners of the roof, four small domed kiosks soften the stark nakedness of the great dome, and screen the awkward but unavoidable drum on which it rests.

The interior of the Taj is as elegant as its exterior. Shah Jahan and Mumtaz are buried in an underground crypt, Mumtaz at the centre, directly beneath the crest of the dome, Shah Jahan to her left. Above the crypt is the high vaulted cenotaph chamber. A subdued light, soft but not sombre, douses the chamber. In that half-light, the perforated, jewelled marble screen surrounding the cenotaphs glows faintly. This screen, which took ten years to make, is a peerless work of craftsmanship, its fretted volutes perfect and amazingly intricate, its frame adorned exquisitely with precious and semi-precious stone inlays of flowers and sprays of foliage, each flower and leaf a cameo.

Even more brilliant are the inlays of the cenotaphs, its craftsmanship sure, firm, yet delicate. The tiny flowers and leaves are made of many different pieces of stone to bring out texture and tone, each stone sliced thin, shaped and bedded in sockets cut into marble with surgical precision. In one particular flower there are as many as sixty-four different slivers of stone, and they are laid so exactly that neither eye nor touch can make out the joints.

From a distance, the Taj overwhelms by the sheer perfection of its beauty, but equally dazzling at closer look is the matchless, uncompromising skill of the craftsmen who had laboured half a lifetime adorning it. Everything about the Taj is perfect, from the choice of its site, the layout of its gardens, the deployment of its various architectural elements. Nothing is out of place or out of proportion. Every texture, every colour, every design is exactly as it should be, its symmetry and balance, in colour and form, flawless. The Taj is awesomely intricate, yet breathtakingly simple.

Equally, for all its jewel-like appearance, the Taj is huge, as tall as a twenty-storey building from ground level. It is 56.7 metre square as it stands on its marble terrace, its domed height about equal to its width. The dome by itself, as it rests on its drum, is estimated to weigh over 12,000 metric tons. The Taj is built on a foundation of brick-lined wells sunk deep into the ground at close intervals and filled with rubble and lime, a foundation so strong that there has not been any shift in its original alignment even after three and a half centuries. In building the Taj, subtle artistry combined with superb engineering skills.

The unique perfection of the Taj was recognized even by its earliest visitors. Bernier, who saw it soon after its completion, considered it one of the great wonders of the world: 'I decidedly think that this monument deserves much more to be numbered among the wonders of the world than the pyramids of Egypt, those unshapen masses which when I had seen them twice yielded me no satisfaction.'

The Taj has aged beautifully. Its delicately grained Makrana marble has mellowed, and today, weathered by rain and the sun, the Taj offers a different face to every visitor, to each according to his heart. Its mood and aspect change with every shift in light: it is 'a cold gray at dawn, shimmering white at noon, and suffused with a tender blush rose in the afterglow, with a wide range of half-tones in between,' writes Percy Brown. 'And in the light of the moon another and entirely changed palette is called into requisition . . . a spectacle of supremely moving beauty.'

Shah Jahan had a number of architects and designers helping him with the Taj, but the building is certainly the expression of his own aesthetic taste. The emperor's chief architect was Ustad Ahmad Lahori, known popularly as Ahmad Mimar (Ahmad Architect), who in turn was supervised by Abdul Karim and Makramat Khan, imperial officers. For the construction of the Taj, Shah Jahan summoned to Agra experts from all over the empire and several from abroad: the dome expert probably came from Constantinople, while the pinnacle maker came from Samarkand, calligraphists from Baghdad and Shiraz, a carver from Bukhara, and so on. The master mason was from Agra and the master carpenter from Delhi; the landscape gardener came from Kashmir.

The structural work was carried out by Muslim artisans, with Hindu craftsmen working mainly on inlays and other decorations. In all, some 20,000 workmen laboured for about twenty-two years on the Taj complex, says Tavernier. It is not known what it cost. Inayat Khan mentions five million rupees as the cost, but that probably was only the on-site expenses and did not include the cost of materials; later estimates of the cost vary from eighteen to forty million rupees. One writer puts the cost even at 91.7 million rupees.

AFTER THE PERFECTION of the Taj, there could only be decline in Mughal architecture. Still, the precipitous fall in standards under Aurangzeb is shocking. Aurangzeb was not much interested in architecture, though he had to his credit the small but elegant Pearl Mosque in the Delhi fort. His largest structure was the tomb of his queen Dilras Banu Begum in Aurangabad, a dowdy imitation of the Taj, without the refinement and finesse of the original, style turned into mannerism. The skill of the craftsmen however endured, and is evident in the ornamentation of the brass doors of the tomb. What was lacking was vision.

Outside the Mughal empire, nothing very significant was happening in architecture in India in Mughal times, except perhaps in Bijapur, one of the greatest cities of medieval India. The glory of Bijapur reached its peak in the mid-sixteenth century, during the reign of Muhammad Adil Shah, whose tomb, the Gol Gumbaz, a mountainous structure in a burly style, is considered to be one of the largest domed pavilions built anywhere in the world. The dark-brown local trap used in Bijapur lacked sophistication in tone and texture, and the builders themselves lacked sophistication, paid little attention to aesthetics, so that—except in a few structures, such as the Mihtar Mahal and the Ibrahim Rauza in Bijapur— the general trend in provincial architecture was to substitute size for elegance.

A notable development in Indian architecture at this time was the mutation of the Hindu style under Mughal influence. There were hardly any architecturally significant pre-Mughal Hindu secular buildings in India, but the rajas now built magnificent palaces in Rajasthan and elsewhere in emulation of the emperors, adopting the clean, sweeping lines of the Mughals in place of the usual nervous clutter of Rajput buildings. Mughal influence is evident even in a few Rajput temples of this time, as in the Govind Deo temple at Vrindavan near Mathura and the temples of Orchha. But it was in secular structures that the Mughal influence was most pervasive, and this trend would continue into modern times, giving the urban landscape of India, especially in Hindustan, a distinctive Mughal ambience.

EPILOGUE

The Mughal Legacy

'A WHIRLWIND AROSE, so fierce that it blew down all the tents standing in the encampment, many persons were killed, and also animals, being choked by the dust,' wrote Niccolao Manucci, a long-time Italian resident in Mughal India, about the scene in the Mughal camp at the time of Aurangzeb's death. 'The day became so dark that men ran into each other, being unable to see where they were going; villages were destroyed, and trees were overthrown.'

The storm was a portent of the chaos that would presently engulf the Mughal Empire. 'Of the future there is no hope,' Aurangzeb had written in his farewell letters to his sons a few days before his death. And that indeed was how it came to pass: for him personally, and for the Mughal Empire.

Within a mere decade of Aurangzeb's death, courtiers insolently wrested power from the reigning emperor and turned him into a pawn in their own ruthless power games. Soon the provinces became independent domains. The Marathas bit off large chunks of the empire here and there. And invaders from across the western mountains, Nadir Shah of Persia and Ahmad Shah of Afghanistan, swooped down to ravage the crippled giant. In a few decades the empire disappeared altogether and the authority of the emperor became confined to the city of Delhi alone. Soon he lost even that petty privilege, and became a pensioner, first of the Marathas, then of the British.

He was, however, still called the Mughal Emperor—others might seize his territory, plunder his treasures, deprive him of power, but none could take away his title, or the prestige (however hollow) that went with it. So the Mughal continued to occupy the imperial throne in Delhi for a century and half after the death of Aurangzeb. In 1857 the last Mughal Emperor, Bahadur Shah II—a feeble old man of eighty-one who dabbled in poetry, music and calligraphy—was arrested by the British for his complicity in the great anti-British uprising of that year. Tried, he was found guilty and sentenced to life imprisonment and exile. The emperor was then bundled out of Delhi in a lowly peasant's bullock-cart and deported to Myanmar, where he died in obscurity a few years later.

HOW DID THE great empire come to this whimpering end? Aurangzeb's theocratic policies, contrary to common perception, had little to do with it. By the end of his reign, Muslims had been ruling India for over 500 years, and many of their early rulers had been far harsher than Aurangzeb in their treatment of Hindus. Yet there were no serious religious uprisings against them. Nor were there any against Aurangzeb. His policies certainly gave an edge to the Maratha opposition to the Mughals, but they did not cause that opposition—the primary motive of the Marathas was to gain power, not to defend religion. It is significant that a very large number of Hindus, including several prominent Marathas, continued to serve Aurangzeb despite his theocratic policies; in fact, in the second half of his reign the number of Hindu officers in his service actually increased, and became substantially higher than it had been even under Akbar. And just as there were a number of Marathas in the Mughal service, there were a number of Muslims in the Maratha service. It was all politics as usual.

The main reason for the Mughal collapse was that the empire had grown far too large, beyond the capacity of the emperor to hold it together or to govern it efficiently, especially since most of the later emperors were effete. The administrative problems of the empire were compounded by its financial crisis, because of poor revenue collection on the one hand and the ballooning cost of government on the other. Towards the end of Aurangzeb's reign, the pay of soldiers and officers was usually in arrears, sometimes by as much as three years, which demoralized them, and led to further deterioration of administrative and military efficiency. Moreover, the entire administration had become rotten to the core, shot through with corruption.

'All administration has disappeared,' wrote Bhimsen, a courtier of Aurangzeb. 'There was motion and bustle, without zeal or efficiency: the empire was unwieldy, its system relaxed, and its officers were corrupt beyond all example,' writes the historian Grant Duff. 'It was inwardly decayed, and ready to fall to pieces as much by its own irrecoverable weakness, as by the corroding power of the Marathas.'

OUTWARDLY, THE CENTURY from the accession of Akbar to the accession of Aurangzeb was a glorious period in Indian history. Culture thrived under the keen and knowledgeable patronage of the emperors. Monumental architecture, as the expression of imperial grandeur, was the favoured art form of the Mughals, but they also extended generous patronage to other fields of culture. Akbar and Jahangir were keen patrons of painting, Shah Jahan of music and dance. And all the emperors patronized literature and learning; several of them wrote poetry, and two of them, Babur and Jahangir, wrote absorbing memoirs. And they set the standard in sophisticated lifestyle for the elite everywhere in India.

The Mughals also had major political and economic achievements to their credit—they brought nearly all of India under one rule, standardized currency, weights and measures, and galvanized trade with their insatiable craving for luxuries. Towns prospered under them, a millennium after they had fallen into decay in the post-Gupta period, and urban prosperity in turn stimulated cultural efflorescence.

This was the bright side of the Mughal legacy. But there was a dark side to it, too. The emperor and the nobles lived incredibly luxurious lives—some of the nobles dined on a hundred dishes at every meal, and they and their begums changed their entire wardrobe of expensive clothes every year, giving away the old sets to their servants. As for the emperors, even austere Akbar had a thousand complete sets of clothes made for him every year, while Shah Jahan spent ten million rupees just on materials for his throne.

There was a price to be paid for such profligacy, however. And that price was paid by the common people, who lived in mud hovels, half-naked, half-starved, and 'from whom every drop of sap had been wrung out by their predatory masters, Muslim as well as Hindu . . . At the height of Mughal splendour under Shah Jahan, over a quarter of the gross national product of the empire was appropriated by just 655 individuals, while the bulk of the 120-odd million people of India lived on a dead level of poverty.'*

India was in ruins by the end of Aurangzeb's reign. Incessant wars, the locust sweep of the Mughal and Maratha armies across the subcontinent, had laid waste the country. 'Instead of verdure all is black and barren,' wrote Manucci. 'The country is so entirely desolated and depopulated that neither fire nor light can be found in the course of three or four days' journey.' Famine and pestilence swept the land every few years, scything down hundreds of thousands of lives. Comments the economic historian W.H. Moreland: 'India in the [late] seventeenth century must have been an inferno for the ordinary man.'

---

* *Emperors of the Peacock Throne*, p. 520

THE MUGHAL GOLDEN age was golden only for the elite, and only for the minuscule Mughalized political elite at that. It had no transformative effect on Indian civilization. In this, it differed entirely from the first golden age of India which had flourished a thousand years earlier, under the Guptas. The cultural bloom of the Gupta age was the culmination of many centuries of indigenous evolution, which saw fundamental changes and great progress in nearly every facet of life. The Mughal culture, on the other hand, was an exotic plant introduced into India from another cultural clime—Islamic Persia. The Mughals did refine the derived culture exquisitely, particularly in the field of architecture, and added a few distinctive Indian elements to it, but it remained essentially Persian.

The Persianized Islamic culture had first been introduced into India by the Delhi sultans at the turn of the twelfth century. But even by the eighteenth century, after 500 years of acclimatization, it still remained a hothouse plant which had not sunk its roots into the Indian soil, but looked to Persia for nourishment. So when the Persian culture declined in the late seventeenth century, inevitably the Mughal culture withered too. As for the Hindu culture, it was in a worse state of decadence, having been in decay for many centuries. Neither of the two cultures had the vitality to lift India out of the medieval morass in which it was bogged down.

Perhaps a synthesis of the Hindu and Muslim cultures, along with openness to external cultural influences, could have stimulated the transformation of India. That was the prospect that Akbar's reforms held out. But India was not yet ready to take that path of progress. The cultural ferment that Akbar stimulated did not survive him.

India's prospects at the end of Aurangzeb's reign appeared very bleak indeed. The country was being rapidly sucked into a whirlpool of total anarchy. As Bhimsen put it, 'No man from the sardar down to the ryot ate his bread for a single day in peace; none from the sultan down to the pauper slept for a single night in happiness.'

WHAT SAVED INDIA from terminal chaos was the establishment of British rule. Europe and India had been in direct contact with each other in Graeco-Roman times, but that link broke with the collapse of the Roman Empire in the fifth century. A thousand years would pass before they would meet again. In 1498, twenty-eight years before Babur invaded India, a Portuguese fleet captained by Vasco da Gama circumnavigated Africa and landed in Kerala on the western peninsular coast of India.

Soon other European nations arrived too, mainly the British and the French. Of these, the future belonged to the British. They, like the other Europeans, came as traders, but slowly, without deliberation, almost accidentally, they acquired a few territorial footholds in India, and eventually, three hundred and odd years after Gama's arrival, they established themselves as the dominant power in India, stepping into the power vacuum left by the collapse of the Mughal Empire.

The British, of course, did not conquer India out of altruism, for the benefit of Indians, but to exploit the country for their own gain. Nevertheless, India benefited as much as Britain from the relationship. British rule brought peace to the land by ending the political anarchy and rampant banditry then prevailing in India. It laid the institutional foundations on which a modern economy, society and nation could be built; established a modern judiciary and the rule of law; introduced modern education and democratic practices; and created the infrastructure—roads, railways, telegraph—essential for the political and economic integration of the country.

The primary motive of the British in doing all this was to consolidate their power and exploit India's resources more efficiently. But they also, incidentally, provided the lifeline for India to pull itself out of the vortex into which it had been sinking. And by and large the British ruled the country justly, especially in contrast to the notoriously corrupt, arbitrary and whimsical rule of the decadent rajas and sultans. Furthermore, the reformist zeal of the Benthamite radicals in England led to the introduction of many social reforms in India, curbing evils like sati, infanticide, the inhuman treatment of the outcastes and so on.

More than anything else, the British provided this ancient civilization with the external stimulus it needed in order to catalyse its evolution into a modern nation.

Incidental Data

Chapter 1

- Bernier: Indians are 'tenderhearted towards animals of every description, man only excepted.' Indians, says Ovington, are 'profligate of their own lives', though caring towards animals.

- In the deep south, except in Kerala, there were very few Muslims in Mughal times. Mughal chronicler Muhammad Sharif Hanafi, a contemporary of Shah Jahan, writes about Madura: 'There is not a single Musulman there. Occasionally a Musulman may visit the country, deputed by Nizam Shah, Adil Shah or Qutb Shah, but the natives are all infidels.'

- Jats were probably descendants of the ancient nomadic Getae; their habitat was the extensive region from the Punjab eastward to Agra. They were a turbulent people. As the common saying in Mughal times had it, 'The Jat, like a wound, is better when bound.'

- A census of 1837, when Delhi was in a state of decline, showed a population of 130,000 in 28,000 households, excluding the residents of the palace and the suburbs, which would have added about 50,000 people, giving a total of about 180,000.

- It was out of the medieval serais that the dak bungalow of later times evolved, as the halting places for both the dak (post carrier) and the traveller.

Chapter 2

- Mirza Haidar Dughlat, a cousin of Babur, speaks in his memoirs about acquiring, as a prince in Central Asia, 'many accomplishments and much learning . . . In the arts of calligraphy, reading, making verses, epistolary style, painting and illuminating I became not only distinguished, but a past-master. Likewise in such crafts as seal-engraving, jeweller's and goldsmith's work, saddlery and armour making; also in the construction of arrows, spear-heads and knives, gilding and many other things which it would take too long to enumerate: in all these, the masters of each could teach me no more . . . Then again in the affairs of the state, in important transactions, in planning campaigns and forays, in archery, in hunting, in the training of falcons and in everything that is useful in the government of a kingdom . . .'

• When ambassador Norris was presented with a *sarapa* by Aurangzeb, he retired from the durbar hall to another room to be invested in the dress, and after the audience rode back to his camp wearing the Mughal dress over his European dress and the turban over his hat.

• To keep track of the emperor's age, a string was kept in the harem, to which a knot was added for each year.

• Once a lovelorn blacksmith named Kalyan, who was infatuated with a widow who spurned him, sought Jahangir's intercession on his behalf. 'Having summoned both of them into my presence, I cross-examined them, and however much I advised her to unite herself to him, she did not agree,' says Jahangir. 'At this time the blacksmith said that if he could make sure that I would give her to him, he would throw himself down from the Shah-burj (the royal tower) of the fort. I said by way of jest: "Never mind the Shah-burj; if your love be genuine, fling yourself from the roof of this house, and I'll make her submit herself to you." I had not ended before he ran like lightning and threw himself down. When he fell, blood began to flow from his eyes and mouth. I repented myself greatly of that jest, and was grieved in my mind, and had Asaf Khan take him to his house and look after him. As the cup of his life was brimming over, he died from the injury.'

• In Vijayanagar, there were contests of women wrestlers.

Chapter 3

• Emperors often conferred extravagant gifts on amirs. Thus Babur once gifted to Tardi Beg the town of Sirsawah, which he had captured on the way to Panipat. 'His Majesty listened to these praises [of the town by Tardi Beg] and said: "It is yours, take it," and immediately afterwards the revenue and management of that place were granted as inam to Amir Tardi Beg, and were so entered in the records of government.'

• Murder in the open court was the ultimate revenge. An aggrieved mother once said to her son: 'If you do not kill this shameless wretch in the Court, I shall not give you a quittance for my milk.'

Jahangir on the people of Kashmir: 'Men and women wear a woolen tunic, and call it pattu. If they do not put on a tunic, they believe that the air affects them, and even that it is impossible to digest their food without it . . . the common women do not wear clean, washed clothes. They use a tunic of pattu for three or four years; they bring it unwashed from the house of the weaver, and sew it into a tunic, and it does not reach the water till it falls to pieces. It is considered wrong to wear drawers; they wear the tunic long and ample . . . Although most of the houses are on the river-bank not a drop of water touches their bodies. In short, they are as dirty outside as inside, without any cleanliness.'

• The common ailments in Mughal India, according to Terry: 'Bloodie fluxes, hot fevers and calentures; in all which they prescribe fasting as the principall remedie. That filthy disease, the consequence of incontinencie, is common amongst them.' Smallpox too was common, afflicting even princes: Shah Jahan had suffered from it, and so had Murad. Plague struck periodically, and one of Aurangzeb's wives died of it.

• According to Nuniz, the chief minister of Vijayanagar had lands which fetched him about two million rupees annually, out of which he had to maintain a large force, but which still left him, according to Moreland's calculation, a surplus of 200,000 or 300,000 rupees, about the same as the personal income of the Mughal mansabdar of 5000 in the reign of Akbar.

Chapter 4

• Itibar Khan, a high-ranking officer of Aurangzeb, when he was visited by his parents who had sold him as a child to be eunuchized, reproached them, according to Manucci: 'How have ye the great temerity to come into my presence after you have consumed the price of my body, and having been the cause, by emasculating me, of depriving me of the greatest pleasures attainable in this world? Of what use are riches to me, having no sons to whom I could leave them?'

• Very fair women were not preferred by Indians, for that was the colour of lepers, says Terry.

• There are no first-hand accounts of the Mughal harem in the days of the Great Mughals, but we have a description of the harem as it was in the nineteenth century, given by Meer Hassan Ali, a lady of high rank.

There were, she writes, residences on three sides of the courtyard, with kitchen, offices and lumber-room on the fourth side. The apartments had no windows on the sides and at the back, but the front portion was open. There were curtains for privacy. The apartment consisted of a long hall with small rooms with doors at the back for valuable items to be stored. There were bedsteads of gold and silver.

• Nur Jahan is said to have loved to dance.

• Zebunnisa, Aurangzeb's daughter, was keen on *mushairah* (poetry contest), and when suitors were brought to her, she questioned them, but none satisfied her.

• Before the Muslim invasion, Indians had only metal mirrors, but Muslims introduced *aaina-i-billour*, glass mirror.

• The mode divining whether a child to be born would be a boy or girl: 'Two pieces of paper are inscribed, one with a boy's name and one with a girl's, and enwrapped in clay and set in water. The first name disclosed, as the clay open out in the moisture, reveals the secret,' says Gulbadan.

• Women of the defeated were seldom molested in India, 'according to a custom most scrupulously observed amongst Eastern despots', says Bernier. But they could be enslaved and sold.

Chapter 5

• Hartal by the Hindu merchants of Surat in 1669, as reported in a letter from the English factors in Surat to England, dated 26 November 1669: When the overzealous kazi of Surat 'forcibly circumcised [a Baniya merchant] for no other reason but that five years past he had eaten part of a watermelon which the Cozzy [kazi] had eaten of . . . The poor Bannian, as 'tis said, killed himself for greife'.

In protest, 8000 Baniya merchants of Surat ('all the heads of the Bannian families, of what condition so ever') left the city and moved to Bharuch, leaving their families 'under the charge of their brothers and next of kin'. The kazi sought to prevent the exodus, but the Mughal governor refused to stop them on the ground that 'the king's subjects . . . may travel in his country where they please'. The kazi then threatened to circumcise all the principal Baniyas and destroy their temples, but the merchants, 'grown hardy by often sufferings' threatened to take the matter to the emperor.

Meanwhile trade in Surat came to a standstill. 'Ever since the flight of the Bannians the trade of Surat hath suffered great obstruction, and it is the opinion of many wise men that it will prove of fatal consequence, to the utter ruine of it, in case the King doth not take some effectual healing order for the making up of this breach. For most of the sheroffs and moneyed men doe thinke of calling in their stocks and (according to the custome of this country) burying the greatest part under ground; the bulke of trade, which is maintained and carryed on chiefly on credit, must necessarily fall.'

The hartal lasted a couple of months. The merchants returned to Surat and resumed trade only after Aurangzeb issued 'letters of favour'.

• The habit of burying wealth continued in India into the twentieth century. In 1886–87, in the palace of Scindia, 31,837,783 silver coins buried in pits and wells were dug up; in 1889 it was estimated that there was in India buried gold bullion worth not less than 270 million pounds, and that it was increasing at the rate of three millions annually.

• Doctor's fees were sometimes paid in kind. An Uzbeg once paid Manucci with nine melons and a quantity of dried fruit.

• Asian goods sold in Europe at four times its Asian price. But nearly half the goods were lost in transit.

• Gold from the Americas brought to Europe found its way to Turkey, from where it trickled to the Persian Gulf and the Red Sea ports—'which gold and silver is exported to Hindustan by the vessels that arrive every year, in the mausem, or the season of the winds,' reports Bernier. Further, 'all the Indian vessels, whether they belong to the Indians themselves, or to the Dutch, or English, or Portuguese, which every year carry cargoes of merchandise from Hindustan to [other countries] . . . bring back to Hindustan from those countries a large quantity of precious metals . . . And in regard to the gold and silver which the Dutch draw from Japan, where there are mines, a part is, sooner or later, introduced into Hindustan; and whatever is brought directly by sea, either from Portugal or from France, seldom leaves the country, returns being made in merchandise.'

• Karl Marx read Bernier in 1853; his concept of the Oriental Mode of Production was based on the information in Bernier.

• In the nineteenth regnal year of Shah Jahan, because of the high price of food, people sold their children in Punjab. The emperor ordered the price money of children to be paid from the treasury and the children restored to the parents.

- Tavernier on Banjaras: Each group of Banjaras specialized in a particular commodity—those who carried rice, carried only rice; those who carried salt, only salt, and so on—and they had distinguishing marks on their foreheads to indicate their speciality. Thus those who carried wheat marked their foreheads 'with red gum, about the breadth of a crown; and then they draw a streak all the length of their nose, sticking grains of wheat upon it, sometimes ten, and sometimes twelve.' Similarly, rice carriers had a yellow streak with rice stuck on it; millet carriers wore a gray streak and millet grains; and those who sold salt had a bag of salt hanging from their neck.

All the Banjaras had around their neck a little silver box, like a relic-box, 'wherein they enclose a little superstitious writing which their priests give them . . . they tie them also about their oxen and other cattle . . . for which they have particular affection, and love them as tenderly as children . . . The women wear only a piece of Calicut, white or painted, some six or five times doubled from their waists downward. From their waist upward they cut their flesh into several forms of flowers, as they do that apply cupping glasses, which they paint in various colours with the juice of grapes, that their skin seems to be all made of flowers.'

The Banjaras lived a nomadic life, travelling with their families, priests, and even their shrines. 'Every morning, when the men load their beasts, and women fold up the tents,' the priests set up 'a certain idol in the form of a serpent in wreaths, upon a . . . [stand] six or seven foot high; to which they come all in files to worship, the women going three times about.' After the ceremony, the priest loaded the idol on a specially designated ox.

- The process of tracing the counterfeiter in Mughal India, as described by Tavernier: the man who was caught with a bag of counterfeit coins was asked to give it to the man from whom he got it, and this man in rum had to give it to the one from whom he got it, and so on all the way back to the counterfeiter.

- There was a great amount of shipbuilding in Mughal India, using the plentiful timber along the west coast of the peninsula. Shipbuilding techniques had improved at this time under European influence, and the bulk of the ships plying in the Indian seas, under whichever flag they sailed, were built in India, both coasting (40–50 tuns) as well as sea-going ships. Some of the ships built in India were very large, as large as 1000 tuns. Even carracks of 1500 to 2000 tuns are mentioned in contemporary writings.

Chapter 6

• In Mughal towns, sweepers called Halakhors went around with donkeys to remove garbage.

• Akbar's rules regarding interest to be charged on the loans given to amirs from the treasury: If the amir returned the money within a year, no interest was charged, but in the second year he had to pay 6.25 per cent over the loan amount; in the third year the additional amount he had to pay was doubled to 12.5 per cent of the loan; for the fourth year it was doubled again to twenty-five per cent, and again doubled to fifty per cent for the fifth to the seventh year; from the eight to the tenth, he had to pay seventy-five per cent more, and from the tenth year on 100 per cent more.

• The marriage tax imposed by Akbar: under it, a mansabdar had to pay up to ten gold coins (*muhrs*), a middle-class man had to pay one rupee and the common people one dam; the tax had to be paid by both parties. Such taxes were collected in Vijayanagar as well as by the Marathas, and was called lagnapatti.

• In Hindu tradition, the prescribed tax rate was between one-twelfth and one-sixth of the gross produce of the land, though in emergencies one-fourth was allowed to be taken. Under the Delhi Sultans, the rate varied from reign to reign, but hovered at around one-fifth of the gross produce, though it was as high as one-half under Alauddin Khilji.

• Akbar on sycophants: 'Flattery should not be liked as very often many works remain unfulfilled on account of the flatterers. And all of sudden one should not be harsh towards them because it is necessary for a servant to indulge in flattery.'

• Aurangzeb's instructions on confirming an officer: 'Firstly, he must every year increase the revenue of [his] district; secondly, he must not practise oppression upon the Ahadis and must not ruin any village; thirdly, he must make free of robbers the boundaries of his own faujdari and make them full of safety, so that travellers, wayfarers, merchants . . . [may] travel without any anxiety.'

• Defeated Mughals showed their submission by presenting themselves 'with swords round their necks and shrouds in their hands'. Afghans, says Babur, surrendered 'with grass between their teeth . . . [implying] "I'm your cow."' Turks surrendered with turbans in hand.

- 'Flight from overwhelming odds is one of the traditions of the Prophet,' says Badauni.

- 'The Christians are not bold in the use of the sword,' says Khafi Khan.

- Roe on the presents that could be given to the royal family: 'Fine needle woorke toyes, fayre bone lace, cutt-worke, and some handsome wrought wastcote, sweetbagges or Cabinetts, wilbe most Convenient . . . I would add any fair China bedsteeds, or cabinets or truncks of Japan are here rich presentes.'

Chapter 7

- Jats pillaged the Agra fort in 1764, removing the *pietra dura* inlay and carrying away marble tanks and reservoirs. Later, the citadel was pillaged by the British, who sent baths as present to the Prince Regent, and built barracks and PWD buildings in the citadel. Governor Bentinck auctioned off a lot of decorative marble pieces. There was even a proposal to sell the Taj as scrap.

- Lord Curzon on vandalism at the Taj: 'It is not uncommon thing for the revellers to arm themselves with hammer and chisel, with which they whiled away the afternoon by chipping out fragments of agate and carnelian from the cenotaphs of the Emperor and his lamented Queen.'

- Jadunam Sarkar on the medieval Maratha culture: 'To the over-polished descendants of the Mughal capitals, the warriors from the south appeared as a race of upstarts, insolent in prosperity, and lacking in grace, refinement, and even good manners. They had no taste for the fine arts, no elegance of address, not aptitude for the amenities of social life. Even their horsemanship was awkward and graceless, though eminently practical. The period of Maratha ascendancy has not left India richer by a single grand building, or a beautiful picture, or a finely written manuscript. Even the palaces of the Peshwas are low, mean-looking, flimsy structures, with small rooms and narrow staircases, relieved from their utter insignificance only by their richly carved wooden facade . . .

'Their poetry consisted of short jingles and apopthegms or monotonous metrical couplets.' There was no prose in Marathi literature till the eighteenth century. 'The prose that was created by the official class in their letters and chronicles was a barbarous jargon composed nearly three-fourths of Persian words and grotesque literal translations of Persian idioms.

The highly Sanskritized, elegant and varied prose that is now used, is a creation the British period . . . Not only was their literature poor, but their popular spoken tongue was a rough, practical speech, incapable of expressing ceremonious courtesy, indirectness, and delicate shades of meaning of the highly developed Urdu language.'

• Bernier on the Hindu knowledge of geography: 'In geography they are equally uninstructed. They believe that world is flat and triangular; that it is composed of seven distinct habitations, differing in beauty, perfection, and inhabitants, and that each is surrounded by its peculiar sea; that one sea is of milk; another of sugar; a third of butter; a fourth of wine; and so on; so that sea and land occur alternately until you arrive at the seventh stage from the foot of the Someire mountain, which is in the centre.'

Notes

Dates in the book generally conform to those in the *Cambridge History of India,* Vol. IV.

The sources of all quotations are given in the text. All quotations, except a few comments by modern historians, are from works of the Mughal period. In about half a dozen instances, the wording of the English translations of Persian sources has been slightly altered, or sentences from different translations integrated, for the sake of clarity. Where sources differ in minor detail, I have chosen the version that seemed plausible to me, or have combined bits from different sources to tell a consistent and credible story—for instance, in the description of Prince Murad's arrest by Aurangzeb.

For everyday life in Mughal India, the only sources are the writings of foreign travellers, and I have used them extensively. Though marred by prejudices and fanciful frills, the essential truthfulness of the picture drawn by travellers is validated by the congruence of the views of different writers, though they came from different countries and were in India at different times; and by the fact that their statements generally agree with the data in other sources, wherever such data are available. Besides, their portrait of Mughal India generally matches the conditions in early modern India. Modern research has validated the reports of Bernier and Manucci which were previously dismissed as prejudiced views or as bazaar gossip.

In my assessment of the Mughal economy, I have in broad terms favoured the analysis of Bernier (mid-seventeenth century) and Moreland (early twentieth century). Indian nationalist historians usually disagree with their views, but this has more to do with sentiment than facts.

It is tricky to calculate the value of Mughal coins in modern currency, and I have generally avoided doing so. But in a couple of places I have given the value in the currency of the mid-1990s. The method used for this conversion is simple: according to *The Cambridge Economic History of India,* Volume I, one rupee of 1600 could be converted to twelve rupees of 1970. Between 1970 and 1995, the wholesale price index went up by over six times. So I have taken that one Mughal rupee would be equal to about seventy rupees in 1995.

Bibliography

Medieval Sources

Abbas Khan Sarwani (an Afghan noble in Akbar's service): *Tuzuk-i Sher Shahi* in H. M. Elliot and John Dowson (E&D): *The History of India as Told by Its Own Historians*, London, 1867–1877 / Delhi, 1990, vol. iv, pp. 301–434.

Abdulla (a contemporary of Jahangir): *Tarikh-i Daudi*, E&D iv, pp. 434–513.

Abul Fazl (courtier of Akbar): *Akbar-nama*. 3 vols., Tr: H. Beveridge, (Calcutta, 1907–1929 / Delhi, 1989.

—— *Ain-i-Akbari*, 3 vols., Tr: H. Blochmann and H.S. Jarrett, Calcutta, 1873–94 / Delhi, 1977.

Asad Beg (courtier of Akbar): *Wikaya-i Asad Beg*, E&D vi, pp. 150–74.

Aurangzeb (Mogul emperor): *Ruka'at-i-Alamgiri or Letters of Aurangzeb*, Tr: Jamshid H. Bilimoria, London, 1908 / New Delhi, 1972.

Babur (Mogul emperor): *Babur-nama*,(Tr: Annette Beveridge, London, 1922 / Delhi, 1979.

Badauni (courtier of Akbar): *Muntakhab-ut-Tawarikh*, 3 vols., Tr: Ranking, Lowe and Haig, Calcutta, 1884–1925 / Delhi, 1980.

Bakhtawar Khan (courtier of Aurangzeb): *Mirat-i-Alam*, E&D vii, pp. 145–65.

Bernier, Francois (a French physician in mid-seventeenth century India): *Travels in the Mughal Empire*, Tr: Archibald Constable, Westminster, 1891 / Delhi, 1968.

Bhara Mal (courtier of Shah Jahan and Aurangzeb): *Lubbu-t Taiwarikh-i-Hind*, E&D vii, pp. 168–73.

Careri, J.F.G. (an Italian in India at the close of the seventeenth century): His account in *Indian Travels of Thevenot and Careri*, Ed: Surendranath Sen, New Delhi, 1949.

Coryat, Thomas (an Englishman in India in the second decade of the seventeenth-century): His letters in William Foster: *Early Travels in India*, London, 1921 / Delhi, 1989, pp. 234–87.

De Laet, Joannes (a mid-seventeenth century Dutch compiler of Mogul history from Humayun to Jahangir, based on contemporary European sources): *The Empire of the Great Mogol*, Tr: J.S. Hoyland, Bombay, 1928 / Delhi, 1975.

Du Jarric, Fr. Pierre (an early-seventeenth-century French compiler of Mogul history, based on Jesuit sources): *Akbar and the Jesuits*, Tr: C.H. Payne, Oxford, 1926.

Ferishta (contemporary of Jahangir): *Tarikh-i-Ferishta,* 4 vols, Tr: John Briggs, London, 1829 / Delhi, 1989.

Finch, William (An Englishman in India in the first decade of the seventeenth-century): His journal in Foster: pp. 122–87, London, 1921 / Delhi, 1985.

Fitch, Ralph (an English trader in India in late sixteenth-century): His journal in Foster: pp. 1–47.

Foster, William: *Early Travels in India,* 1583–1619, Oxford, 1921 / Delhi, 1985.

Fryer, John (an Englishman in India in late seventeenth-century): *A New Account of East India and Persia*, 1672–1681, Hakluyt Society, London, MDCCCCXV.

Guerreiro, Fr. Feranao (an early-seveneteenth-century Portuguese historian, who based his account on the reports of Jesuits): *Jahangir and the Jesuits*, Tr. C.H. Payne from the Relations of Fr. Guerreiro, London, 1931.

Gulbadan Begum (sister of Emperor Humayun): *Humayun-nama*, Tr: Annette Beveridge, 1902 / Delhi, 1972.

Haidar, Mirza, Muhammad (cousin of Emperor Babur): *Tarikh-i-Rashidi*, Tr: N. Elias and E. Denison Ross, London, 1895 / Delhi, 1986.

Hamid-ud-din Khan Nimcha (courtier of Aurangzeb): *Ahkam-i-Alamgiri*, Tr. J. Sarkar as *Anecdotes of Aurangzeb*, Calcutta 1928 / 1988.

Hanafi, Muhammad Sharif (a contemporary of Shah Jahan): *Majalisu-s Salatin,* E&D vii, pp. 134–40.

Hawkins, William (East India Company's trade representative at Jahangir's court): his account in Foster pp. 60–121.

Inayatu-lla (a courtier of Akbar): *Takmila-i Akbar-nama*, E&D vi, pp. 103–15.

Inayat Khan (Shah Jahan's courtier): *Shahjahan-nama*, Tr: W.E. Begley and Z.A. Desai, Oxford: Delhi, 1990.

Ishwardas Nagar (courtier of Aurangzeb): *Futuhat-i Alamgiri*, Tr: Tasneem Ahmad, Delhi, 1978.

Jahangir (Mughal emperor): *Tuzuk-i-Jahangiri*, 2 vols., Tr: Alexander Rogers, London, 1909–14 / New Delhi, 1989.

Jauhar (a personal servant of Emperor Humayun): *Tazkirat-ul- Waqiat*, Tr: Charles Stewart, London, 1832 / Delhi, 1972.

Khafi Khan (courtier of Aurangzeb): *Muntakhabu-l Lubab*, E&D vii, pp. 207–533.

Khvand Amir (Khondamir) (courtier of Humayun): *Humayun-nama*, E&D v, pp. 116–26.

Lahori, Abdul Hamid (courtier of Shah Jahan): *Badshah-nama*, E&D vii, pp. 3–72.

Linschoten, John Huighen Van (a Dutch trader in India in late sixteenth-century): *The Voyage of John Huighen Van Linschoten to the East Indies* in *Purchas*, vol. X, Hakluyt Society, 1884, pp. 222–318.

Manrique, Sebastien (an Augustinian friar in India in mid-seventeenth-century): *Travels*, 2 vols., Tr: C.E. Luard, Hakluyt Society, 1926–27.

Manucci, Niccolao (Italitan adventurer in India in the second half of the seventeenth-century): *Storia do Mogor*, 4 vols., Tr: William Irvine, London, 1907–08 / Delhi, 1989.

Maulana Ahmad and others (courtiers of Akbar): *Tarikh-i-Alfi*, E&D v, pp. 150–76.

Mildenhall, John (an English merchant at Akbar's court): his account in Foster, pp. 48–59.

Monserrate, Fr. Anthony (a Jesuit at Akbar's court): *Journey to the Court of Akbar*, Tr: J.S. Hoyland, London, 1922.

Mufazzal Khan (contemporary of Aurangzeb): *Tarikh-i Mufazzali*, E&D vii, pp. 141–44.

Muhammad Amin (a contemporary of Jahangir): *Anfau-l Akhbar*, E&D vi, pp. 244–50.

Muhammad Hadi (courtier of Jahangir): *Tatimma-i Wakiat-i Jahangiri*, E&D vi, pp. 392–99.

Muhammad Kazim (a courtier of Aurangzeb): *Alamgir-nama,* E&D vii, pp. 174–80.

Muhammad Salih Kambu (courtier of Shah Jahan): *Amal-i Salih,* E&D vii, pp. 123–33.

Mundy, Peter (an English traveller in Shah Jahan's India: *Travels in Europe and Asia,* vol. ii, Ed: R. C. Temple, Hakluyt Society, 1914.

Mustaid Khan, Muhammad Saqi (a late contemporary of Aurangzeb): *Maasir-i- Alamgiri,* Tr: J. Sarkar, Calcutta, 1947.

Mushtaqui, Shaikh Raiq Ullah (a late contemporary of Shah Jahan): *Waqi'at-e-Mushtaqui,* Tr: I.H. Siddiqui, Delhi, 1993.

Mutamid Khan (Jahangir's courtier): *Ikbal-nama-i Jahangiri,* E&D vi, pp. 400–38.

Niamatu-ila (courtier of Jahangir): *Tarikh-i Khan-Jahan Lodi,* E&D v, pp. 67–115.

Nizamuddin Ahmad (courtier of Akbar): *Tabaqat-i-Akbari,* Tr: B. De, Calcutta, 1936.

Norris, William (British ambassador in the court of Aurangzeb): *Journals* in Harihar Das: *The Norris Embassy to Aurangzeb,* Calcutta, 1959.

Nurul Hakk (courtier of Jahangir): *Zubdatu-t Tawarikh,* E&D vi, pp. 182–94.

Ovington, J. (an Englishman in India in late seventeenth-century): *A Voyage to Surat in the year 1689,* Ed: H.G. Rawlinson, Oxford, 1929.

Pelsaert, Francis (a Dutch trader in India in the second decade of the seventeenth-century): *Remonstrantie,* Tr. W.H. Moreland as *Jahangir's India,* Cambridge, 1925 / Delhi, 1972.

Qandahari, Muhammad Arif (courtier of Akbar): Tarikh-i-Akbari, Tr: Tasneem Ahmad, Delhi, 1993.

Roe, Sir Thomas (British ambassador at Jahangir's court): *Observations Collected out of the Journal of Sir Thomas Roe* in *Purchas His Pilgrims,* vol iv, Glasgow, MCMV, pp. 310–469.

Sirhindi, Faizi (a contemporary of Akbar): *Akbar-nama,* E&D vi, pp. 116–46.

Stevens, Thomas (an English Jesuit in India in the last quarter of the sixteenth-century: his letter in *The Principal Voyages, Traffiques &*

Discoveries of the English Nation by Richard Hakluyt, vol. iv, London, MCMXXVII.

Tavernier, Jean-Baptiste (a French jewel merchant in India in mid-seventeenth-century): *Travels in India,* 2 vols., Tr: V. Ball, Calcutta, 1905.

Terry, Edward (an English clergyman at Jahangir's court): his account in Foster, pp. 288–332.

Thevenot, M. de (a Frenchman in India in mid-seventeenth-century): his account in *Indian Travels of Thevenot and Careri,* Ed: Surendranath Sen, New Delhi, 1949.

Tirmzi, S.A.I.: *Edicts from the Harem,* Idarah-i Adabiyat-i-Delhi, 1979.

Varthema, Ludovico di: (an Italian traveller in India in the first decade of the sixteenth-century): *The Itinerary of Ludovico di Varthema of Bologna from 1502-1508,* Tr: J.W. Jones, London, 1928.

Waris, Muhammad (courtier of Shah Jahan): *Badshah-nama,* E&D vii, pp. 121–122.

Withington, Nicholas (English traveller in India in the second decade of the seventeenth-century): his account in Foster, pp. 188–233.

Yadgar, Ahmad (a late contemporary of Humayun): *Tarikh-i Salatin-i Afaghana,* E&D v, pp. 1–66.

Zain Khan, Shaikh (courtier of Babur): *Tabaqat-i Baburi,* Tr: Sayed Hasan Askari, Delhi, 1982.

Later Works

Abul Khadir Muhammad Farooque: *Roads and Communication in Mughal India,* Delhi, 1977.

Ali, Athar: *Mogul Nobility Under Aurangzeb,* Bombay, 1970.

Ali, Meer Hasan: *Observations on the Mussalmauns of India,* Oxford, 1832 / 1917.

Altekar, A.S.: *The Position of Women in Indian Civilization,* Delhi, 1938 / 1959.

Amini, Iradj: *Koh-i-noor,* New Delhi, 1994.

Ansari, Muhammad Azhar: *Social Life of the Mughal Emperors,* New Delhi, 1983.

Asher, Catherine B.: *Architecture of Mughal India*, Cambridge, 1992.

Basham, A.L.: *The Wonder That Was India,* vol i, New York, 1954.
Beach, M.C: *Mughal and Rajput Painting*, Cambridge, 1992.
Beagley, Raymonds (Ed): *Voyages & Travels:* 2 vols., Westminster, 1903.
Begley, W.E. and Desai, Z.A.: *Taj Mahal,* Harvard, 1989.
Bharatiya Vidya Bhavan: *History and Culture of the Indian People:* vol. vii: *The Mughal Empire,* Bombay, 1984.
Binyon, Laurence: *Akbar*, Edinburgh, 1932.
Brown, Percy: *Indian Architecture*, 1942 / Bombay, 1956.
—— *Indian Painting Under the Mughals*, Oxford, 1924.

Cambridge Economic History of India, vol. i, Ed: Tapan Raychaudhuri and Irfan Habib, Orient Longman, 1982 / 1991.
Cambridge History of India: vol. iv: *The Mughal Period,* Ed: Wolseley Haig and Richard Burn, Delhi, 1937 / 1987.
Chandra, Satish: *Mughal Religious Policies, The Rajputs & The Deccan*, Delhi, 1993.
Chopra, P.N.: *Some Aspects of Social Life During the Mughal Age*, Jaipur, 1963.
Cole, Owen W. and Piara Singh Sambhi: *The Sikhs*, Delhi, 1989.
Cunningham, J.D.: *History of the Sikhs*, Delhi 1849/ 1990.

Dabisttan: The Religion of Sufis, London, 1979.
de Bary (Ed): *Sources of Indian Tradition*, Columbia, 1958.
Duff, James Grant: *History of The Mahrattas,* 3 vols., 1863 / Delhi 1990.

Embree, Ainslie T (Ed.): *Sources of Indian Tradition*, Penguin, 1991.
Erskine, William: *A History of India Under the First Two Sovereigns of the House of Timur, Babur and Humayun,* 2 vols., Oxford, 1854 / 1974.
Edwards S.M and Garrett H.L.O.: *Mughal Rule in India*, Delhi, 1974.

Findly, Ellison Banks: *Nurjahan*, Oxford, 1993.

Gascoigne, Bamber: *The Great Moghuls,* London, 1971.
Godden, Rumer: *Gulbadan*, New York, 1980.
Gordon, Stewart: *The Marathas —1600–1818*, Cambridge, 1993.
Gupta, I.P.: *Agra*, Delhi, 1986.

Habib, Irfan (Ed): *Medieval India 1*, Oxford, Delhi, 1992.
—— *Agrarian System of Mughal India*, Bombay, 1963.
Hasrat, Bikrama Jit: *Dara Shikuh,* Visvabharati, 1953.
Hutchinson, Lester: *European Freebooters in India*, Bombay, 1964.

Ikram, S.M. (Ed): *The Cultural Heritage of Pakistan*, Oxford, Karachi, 1955.

Kaul, H.K. (Ed): *Historic Delhi*, Delhi, 1985.
—— *Traveller's India*, Delhi, 1979.
Kulke, Hermann and Rothermund, Dietmar: *A History of India*, Delhi, 1991.

Lall, John and Dubey, D.N.: *Taj Mahal,* Delhi, 1982.
Lane-Poole, Stanley: *Babur*, Delhi, 1964.
—— *Aurangzeb*, Delhi, 1971.

Maclagan, Edward: *Jesuits and the Great Mogul*, London, 1922.
Moosvi, Shireen: *The Economy of The Mughal Empire*, Oxford, 1987.
Moreland, W.H.: *From Akbar to Aurangzeb*, London, 1923.
—— *India at the Death of Akbar*, Delhi, 1990 / 1920.
—— *The Agrarian System of Moslem India*, Delhi, 1990 / 1929.

Nizami, Khaliq Ahmad: *State and Culture in Medieval India*, New Delhi, 1985.
—— *Akbar and Religion*, New Delhi, 1989.

Prasad, Beni: *History of Jahangir,* Allahabad, 1930.

Qanungo, K: *Sher Shah*, Calcutta, 1921.

Randhawa, M.S.: *A History of Agriculture in India*, vol. ii, New Delhi, 1982.
Richards, John F: *The Mughal Empire*, Cambridge, 1993.
Rizvi, S.A.A.: *The Wonder That was India*, vol ii, London: 1987.
Ruby Maloni (Ed): *European Merchant Capital and the Indian Economy*, New Delhi, 1993.

Saksena, Banarsi Prasad: *History of Shah Jahan of Delhi*, Allahabad, 1932 / 1969.

Sarkar, Jadunath: *History of Aurangzeb,* 5 vols., Calcutta, 1912–24 / Longman, 1973–74.

—— *Historical Essays,* Calcutta, 1912.

—— House *of Shivaji,* Calcutta, 1940 / 1978.

—— *Shivaji and His Times,* Calcutta, 1920.

—— *Mughal Administration,* Calcutta, 1924.

—— *Military History of India,* Orient Longman, 1960.

Sarkar, Jagadish N: *Studies in Economic Life in Mughal India,* Calcutta, 1975.

Sharar, A.H.: *Lucknow: The Last Phase of an Oriental Culture,* Colorado, 1975.

Singh, Dhananajaya: *The House of Marwar,* New Delhi, 1994.

Singh, Khushwant: *History of the Sikhs,* Oxford, 1963.

Smith, V.S.: *Akbar the Great Mogul,* Oxford, 1917 / Delhi, 1966.

Spear, Percival: *Delhi, a Historical Survey,* Oxford, 1937.

—— *India,* Michigan, 1961.

—— *A History of India,* vol. ii, Penguin, 1965.

Srivastava, M.P.: *Society and Culture in Medieval India,* Allahabad, 1975.

—— *Socio-Economic Culture in Medieval India,* Allahabad, 1993.

Thapar, Romila: *History of India,* vol. i, Penguin, 1966.

Tod, James: *Annals of Mewar* (part of Tod's *Annals and Antiquities of Rajasthan* published between 1829 and 1832), Ed: C.H. Payne, Delhi, no date.

Veluthat, Kesavan: *The Political Structure of Early Medieval South India,* Orient Longman, 1993.

Williams, Rushbrook: *An Empire Builder of the 16th Century,* (1918 / Delhi, no date.

Yasin, Mohammad: *A Social History of Islamic India,* Lucknow, 1958.

Zinat Kausar: *Muslim Women in Medieval India,* Patna, 1992.

Index